PRAISE FOR OTHER
BY STEPHEN HARROL

Sacred Plant Medicine: Explorations in the Practice of Indigenous Herbalism

[*Sacred Plant Medicine*] offers the doorway into the heart of the green world that so many people have been waiting for.

—Rosemary Gladstar, author and herbalist

This is a fascinating book on the sacred use of plants that heal. It is useful as a reference book and inspires the reader to look again at the plant world as a source of life and healing.

—Joan Halifax, author of *Shamanic Voices* and *The Fruitful Darkness*

Sacred Plant Medicine beautifully makes it clear that one does not have to be of a certain color or ethnic background to seek and find a way of being in harmony with the North American land . . .

—Brooke Medicine Eagle, author of *Buffalo Woman Comes Singing*

This is the first in-depth analysis of the processes used by Native Americans to communicate with the plant world for the purposes of healing human illness. It is a work long overdue . . .

—William S. Lyon, co-author of *Black Elk: The Sacred Ways of a Lakota*

One Spirit Many Peoples: A Manifesto for Earth Spirituality

This may be the best book yet by a non-Indian [on] the contemporary issues facing Native American religious practice and the non-native spiritual seeker.

—Joseph Bruchac, Native American author

As an outspoken advocate of restoring an indigenous mind for all people who love the earth, Buhner has gathered an impressive array of arguments to support his position.

—*NAPRA Review*

A dog is used to pull the still sleeping mandrake from the earth. (Illustration from Tacuinum sanitatis, *in* Medicina sanitatis, Codex Vindobonensis.*)*

SACRED
and # HERBAL
HEALING
BEERS

The Secrets of Ancient Fermentation

STEPHEN
HARROD
BUHNER

An Imprint of Brewers Publications
A Division of the Brewers Association
Boulder, Colorado

Siris Books, an imprint of Brewers Publications
A Division of the Brewers Association
PO Box 1679, Boulder, CO 80306-1679
(303) 447-0816; Fax (303) 447-2825
www.BrewersAssociation.org

Printed in the United States of America

10

ISBN-13: 978-0-937381-66-3
ISBN-10: 0-937381-66-7

Siris Books. Who is Siris? She was the daughter of Ninkasi, the Sumerian goddess of
beer. Anthropologists personify Siris as the beer itself.

Please direct all inquiries to the above address.

Disclaimer. Many of the formulas (recipes) for beers (fermented beverages) in this
book were commonly consumed in historic times, and traditionally included the use
of poisonous plants. In such cases the recipes and instructions for these beers are for
historical and educational purposes only. The Publisher and the Author do not recommend the making or use of these beers by the reader. The Author and Publisher
shall be held blameless for any injury to the reader that may occur from the ingestion
of any of these beers.

Library of Congress Cataloging-in-Publication Data
Buhner, Stephen Harrod.
    Sacred and herbal healing beers : the secrets of ancient fermentation / Stephen H. Buhner.
      p. cm.
    Includes bibliographical references and index.
    ISBN 0-937381-66-7 (alk. paper)
    1. Beer. 2. Brewing. I. Title.
TP577.B84 1998   98-17064
641.2'3—dc21   CIP

It is impossible to dedicate

a book to "Nobody."

This one then is for Maria.

CONTENTS

ACKNOWLEDGMENTS ix

AUTHOR'S NOTE ON THE TEXT xi

PROLOGUE xiii

PREFACE xv

CHAPTER ONE: *The Well of Remembrance* 1

CHAPTER TWO: *The Mead of Inspiration: Mead, Honey, and Heather* 19

CHAPTER THREE: *Yeast: A Magical and Medicinal Plant* 61

CHAPTER FOUR: *Sacred Indigenous Beers* 79

CHAPTER FIVE: *Alcohol: Aqua Vitae, the Water of Life* 135

CHAPTER SIX: *The Fermentation and Sacredness of Grains* 145

CHAPTER SEVEN: *Psychotropic and Highly Inebriating Beers* 165

CHAPTER EIGHT: *Beers and Ales from Sacred and Medicinal Trees* 223

CHAPTER NINE: *Beers and Ales from Sacred and Medicinal Plants* 265

EPILOGUE 425

The Appendices 427

APPENDIX ONE: *The Ancient Magic of Making Beer* 429

APPENDIX TWO: *Some Meads of the Middle Ages* 441

APPENDIX THREE: *Herbs Used in Meads of the Middle Ages: A Brief Compendium* ... 469

APPENDIX FOUR: *Sources of Supply and Useful Books* 479

CHAPTER REFERENCES 483

INDEX 513

COLOR PLATES FOLLOWING PAGE 246

Sacred Plants and Trees Used in Recipes for Beers, Ales, and Meads

Agave	Dock	Molasses
Avens	Elderberry	Mugwort
Banana	Elderflower	Myrica
Barley	Elecampane	Nettle
Betony	Eyebright	Oak bark
Birch	Fir	Palm
Borage	Gentian	Pennyroyal
Bracken fern	Ginger	Peppermint
Broom	Grains of paradise	Pine
Buckbean	Ground ivy	Rice
(or bogbean)	Heather	Rosemary
Burnet	Henbane	Rue
Calendula	Honey	Saffron
Caraway	Hop	Sage
Cardamom seed	Horehound	Saguaro
Carrot seed, wild	Hyssop	Sarsaparilla, wild
Chamomile	Irish moss	Sassafras
China root	Juniper	Scurvy grass
Clary sage	Lemon balm	Serviceberry
Coriander	Lettuce, wild	Spruce
Corn	Licorice	St.-John's-wort
Cornstalk	Mandrake	Sweet flag
Costmary	Manioc	Tansy
Cow parsnip	Maple	Wintergreen
Cowslip	Meadowsweet	Wormwood
Dandelion	Millet	Yarrow
Darnel	Mint	

(See the index for page numbers.)

ACKNOWLEDGMENTS

This book would not have been possible without: my editor, Toni Knapp, who bugged me for a year to write it (all the blame goes to her); Alan Eames, who opened his extensive library for my research, his home to my presence, and his phenomenal knowledge of beer and brewing to my endless questions; Dale Pendell, whose remarkable *Pharmako/poeia* helped me to find the heart of this book; and Mikal Aasved, his tremendous 1,380-page doctoral dissertation *Alcohol, Drinking, and Intoxication in Preindustrial Society: Theoretical, Nutritional, and Religious Considerations*, his insight, depth of respect, encyclopedic research, and willingness to challenge Western beliefs about what alcohol is and is not. Thanks to all.

*The Lord hath created medicines out of the earth,
and he that is wise will not abhorre them.*

—ECCLES. 38.4

---

*As they fell from heaven, the plants said, "Whichever living soul we pervade,
that man will suffer no harm."*

—RIG-VEDA

Rise up, become abundant with thine own greatness, O barley.

—ATHARVA VEDA

From man's sweat and God's love, beer came into the world.

—ARNOLDUS

AUTHOR'S NOTE ON THE TEXT

I have structured this book, perhaps, in an odd manner. Information on how to make beers is in here, but this is not a simple manual. Probably the closest thing to a step-by-step instruction to making beer is contained in appendix one. This book is primarily intended to share the poetry and beauty of ancient fermentation and only secondarily to share recipes, some more than 2,000 years old, for making ancient sacred and healing beers. Any recipe in this book that calls for malted barley can be altered by the use of canned (unhopped) malt extract or a combination of brown sugar and molasses (see appendix one for the details). And since so many people keep asking: No, I haven't made all these beers, but I have made more than one.

PROLOGUE

The ancient legends tell how the goddess took pity on the miserable plight of humanity and so loved her daughters that she bestowed the gift of beer to their sole keeping. It is almost a universal human belief that beer did come into the world so that the sons and daughters of men might celebrate possessed by the spirit of the earth mother and forget the sorrows of death with the barley cup of forgetfulness that gladdens hearts in song and rejoicing.

All human cultures, however separated by time and geographical distance, tell much the same tales or myths in explanation of how things in our world came to be. Virtually every culture, for example, has some variation of the story of Pandora's box. For the ancient Greeks, Pandora was charged with guarding the box of the gods having been warned to never open the casket. Her basic curiosity succumbed, unleashing forever disease, famine, death, and all the other horrors and sorrows upon humanity. The end of this tale is that Pandora found one item left in the box . . . a gift to mankind. At the bottom of Pandora's box remained hope. And hope was all that was left to a suffering species. In the folktales of tribal Africa, a black Pandora repeats her Greek sister's rash act except the African makes a different discovery remaining in the casket. Not hope . . . but rather, a gourd of beer.

Long before the bearded patriarchal male gods, there was the goddess—feminine spirit of birth and fertility. The earth mother. *Twenty thousand years ago, it was a goddess who gave life and abundance and it was the goddess who, out of a mother's love and pity for her fallen children, gave the gift of brew to the women of mankind. The cup of bliss, the gourd of temporary forgetfulness was filled with beer. . . .*

In all ancient societies, in the religious mythologies of all ancient cultures, beer was a gift to women from a goddess, never a male god, and women remained bonded in complex religious relationships with feminine deities who blessed the brew vessels.

—Alan Eames, 1995[1]

All the great villainies of history, from the murder of Abel onward, have been perpetrated by sober men, and chiefly by teetotallers. But all the charming and beautiful things, from the Song of Songs to bouillabaisse, and from the nine Beethoven symphonies to the Martini cocktail, have been given to humanity by men who, when the hour came, turned from tap water to something with color to it, and more in it than mere oxygen and hydrogen.

—H. L. Mencken[2]

The drunken consciousness is one bit of the mystic consciousness, and our total opinion of it must find its place in our opinion of that larger whole.

—William James
The Varieties of Religious Experience, 1902[3]

P R E F A C E

When I began research on this book I had little idea that I would be encountering the kinds of problems I was destined to find. To be sure, the usual research problems arose: difficulty in tracking down source material (no definitive archive of the history of brewing—at least a 10,000-year human endeavor—exists in the United States), horrible book indexing (try finding three paragraphs about an obscure juniper beer in a 500-page book when it is not indexed and you will know what I mean), bad computer databases (the University of Colorado, for instance, has almost nothing on the history of beer listed in their computer system), the assumptions by writers of 300, 400, and 500 years ago that their readers would understand things commonly known then, but which are now long forgotten (I still don't know what "make it B.M." means). But more problematic and of greater difficulty was encountering unsuspected truths about our relationship with fermented beverages, and knowing how badly those truths will fit with the current spasm of Puritanism sweeping the United States. For I found in my research that alcohol enhances many physical and mental functions; that most beers were traditionally made with herbs that were medicinal, aphrodisiacal, highly inebriating, or psychotropic; and that these plants and the fermentations made from them seemed to play a crucial role in our development as a species.

That human consciousness is not limited to a narrow spectrum of socially acceptable choices is resisted mightily in our country. Throughout history human beings have experienced a wide range of mental states—many spontaneous, some of them from the ingestion of alcohol, and others from the ingestion of various plant species. As I was to find while working on this book, though many plants were used for their medicinal, spiritual, and ceremonial properties, a not inconsiderable number produced significant alterations in human consciousness when used in fermented beverages. What becomes clear, in any deep exploration of the use of fermented beverages in human history, is that the time in which we live is an aberration in that same history. The normal range of human consciousness and the behavior that derives from it has never been so narrowly defined as in our time. This narrowing process (an attempt to provide a safety not inherent in life itself) is becoming ever more extreme. This can be seen in the drive for increasing restrictions over the use of alcohol and tobacco and in the early movements toward testing babies at birth to determine if they have genetic predispositions toward alcoholism, drug use, depression, anger, or rebellious behavior. Some political figures and social workers have advocated that those babies with predispositions toward such behaviors should be medicated from birth.

Such behaviors are an irremovable aspect of human life and its interaction with fermentation. And our ancestors seemed to understand this, to understand that it is impossible to sand all the rough corners off life. They knew that what is crucial is not that bad things happen to us but what we do with those things after they occur. And it is this struggle to survive the burdens of our weaknesses and integrate tragedy into the fabric of our lives that defines our character, that teaches us our lessons, that allows us to develop as human beings. To eliminate the dark will not leave only the light but will result in a uniform grayness that knows neither triumph nor failure.

I do not believe that the drive to eliminate the darkness, the mistaken belief that it *can* be eliminated, is good for us as a species. Therefore, this book is written from the perspective that fermentation and plant use—as medicine, as psychotropics, as teachers, as companions on our life path—are an inescapable part of our exploration of what it means to be human; that, in fact, our humanness (as we now understand it) could not have occurred without the gift of fermentation or plants. Thus, this book conflicts with a number of popular beliefs about alcohol, plants, and the primary assumptions our culture holds about the nature of material reality. It is, therefore, *not* politically correct.

Vision Mountain
July 1998

ONE

The Well of Remembrance

Oh, sweet spontaneous earth . . . how often has the naughty thumb of science prodded thy beauty?

—e e cummings

Soon we realized that these men . . . they were mad. They wanted the land; they wanted to carry away the wood; they were also searching for stones. We explained that the jungle is not something to be tossed over your shoulder and transported like a dead bird, but they did not want to hear our arguments.

—Isabel Allende, _The Stories of Eva Luna_

*A*FTER HOURS IN a tiny bone-rattling, fume-filled bush plane the pilot yells over the roar of the engine and points down. Alan Eames, the beer anthropologist, peers through the insect-spattered windshield. In the midst of the dense jungle of the Amazon interior, near the muddy river snaking its way to the horizon, there is a clearing. Tiny figures can be seen scurrying among the simple shelters and fields of manioc. "That's it," the pilot says. Alan nods and the plane banks, heading for the nearest landing, a field that lies many miles to the south.

It takes days of travel to retrace the journey from the ground. First a long trek by foot to the river, then miles of paddling upriver by canoe. The heat and humidity penetrate everything. The air is filled with the raucous sounds of birds and the penetrating smells of river and jungle vegetation. Eventually, the guide signals toward the bank; the paddles dip rapidly into the swirling water and urge the canoe to the shore. The men step out into the shallows and draw the canoe up onto the bank. There is a sense of stillness and great age to the jungle; like the air, it penetrates everything. The packs are quickly slung over shoulders, and the men follow the thin forest trail until they glimpse the outlying edge of the village. Here they wait. They have not passed unnoticed. Soon a small group of villagers appears.

"What do you want?" they ask.

Alan puts it very simply. "I have heard of your beer, even in America. And I have come to ask if I might taste what you have made."

The villagers are shy but obviously pleased that their fame has spread so far. "Yes, yes, it's true," they admit. "We do make good beer. Please, come into our village."

They introduce him to the most famous brewer of their village. She is tiny, shrunken with time, incredibly wrinkled. But her eyes sparkle and she looks deep, seeming to understand Alan even before his guide finishes interpreting. Her hut is simple and quite dirty by

American standards. Her brewing utensils are clay pots, woven baskets, long stick stirrers. Her recipe for the beer she makes is 10,000 years old. They give her the gifts they have brought. She smiles. It is good when strangers also come to give.

The beer, when it is ready, is a beer unlike any in North America. It is a beer made with prayer to the plants from which it is made, to the ancestors who went before, and to the spirits of those who taught them in the long-ago times how to ferment beer. A beer that equals the finest Belgian *lambic* beer.

Alan drinks deep and smiles. The villagers are pleased.

"We told you," they say, "we make good beer."

Not far away by plane the rainforest is burning. Some of the thinnest top-soil on earth is being exposed for the first time in millennia to the sun and rain. The air is filled with the mechanical scream of chainsaws and bulldozers and the penetrating smells of machine oil and burning vegetation. The machinery and huge fires eat at the rainforest like dogs at the belly of a wounded animal they have brought down. The men work hard, and sometimes they pause, as men do, to wipe the sweat from their faces, to share a joke, or drink something for their thirst. As the logging trucks disappear up the long, muddy track to civilization, the men drink thin, bottled, commercial beers or soda made by multinational corporations. The empty bottles and cans litter the ground and are soon crushed into the thin soil by the heavy tread of logging trucks and bulldozers.

The contrast between these stories is painful but inescapable. It is not only the rainforest that is being chewed up in the industrial machine, but also human cultures 30,000 years old, ways of thinking radically different from Western approaches, plants that may never be seen again, and things that many of us will never know we lost. One of those is that beer Alan Eames traveled so far to find. It may seem a small thing, for beer is rather pedestrian. It summons up images of sweaty guys in T-shirts knocking back some brewskies before the ball game. But there are many things in this world that are much more than they seem. Beer is one of them.

The ancient beers, created independently around the world between 10,000 and 30,000 years ago, were quite different from what we know as beer today. There were hundreds if not thousands of them, using some 20 different kinds of yeast, perhaps 15 different sugar sources, and more than 200 different plant adjuncts.

Many were sacred beers, scores were highly inebriating or psychotropic, and hundreds contained medicinal herbs. They were made for sacred ceremony, for attaining nonordinary states of reality, for communicating with the ancestors, as potent nutrient foods, and for healing. Such beers were the expression of an entirely different way of seeing the world. They came out of a worldview in which the sacred is ever present with us, where all things possess a soul, the rocks are alive, and in which rabid destruction of the rainforest is inconceivable. The ancient beers come from cultures that, on every continent on Earth, say human beings did not discover fermentation at all. They say it was given to humankind through the intercession of sacred beings, and they insist that these ancient beers contain within themselves some of the essence of the sacred source from which they come. So when we look beneath the surface of "beer," a world entirely different from our own begins to be revealed.

The Tarahumara Indians, when making pulque, a fermented agave cactus beer, place the sweet water-and-sap mixture in special clay jars. They call fermentation "boiling," and once a jar "learns to boil," it is placed near other jars (filled with unfermented pulque) that have not learned how to boil so that they might be taught to do so. The tribal highlanders of New Guinea say that the rainforest wildlife is not only good to eat but also "good to think." And native holy people throughout the Americas insist that if a person treats the spirits of plants like they treat other human beings, then the plants will talk and teach their use as medicines.

The belief that fermenting jars can teach one another to boil, that it is good to think forests, that plants can talk to people, or that rocks are living beings pervades the indigenous world, but these are strange concepts in our modern technological world. For most of us are taught from childhood that the universe is composed of inanimate matter, that the life-forms with which we share this world are "lower," that we alone of all life on Earth (except maybe dolphins) have intelligent awareness. This way of thinking is inconceivable to ancient and indigenous peoples. Indeed, if you enter the indigenous mind-set, you will find that in that world, the livingness of rocks is not an *idea* at all but a real, everyday experience. It is no wonder, then, that it has been so hard for indigenous peoples and technological peoples to communicate with each other. They live in different worlds in which the basic assumptions are very dissimilar. Each perspective is to the other somewhat insane.

For those of us in the West, there are certain assumptions about the nature of reality that makes it nearly impossible to understand the Indigenous Mind. And if we cannot, then we certainly cannot understand indigenous people's use of plant medicines nor the world in which their beers were created. It is important to understand that older, ancient world and why it has become so foreign to us now.

Though it might seem going rather far afield, in many respects the point in time when we in the West began to move out of that older perspective begins with Galileo. Remembered mostly for his struggles with the Catholic Church, his trial, and his loss in court to the petrified thinking of Catholic politicians, his contribution is somewhat more involved. He was the first to put forward the idea that the universe is a great machine, put into motion by God, but nevertheless still a machine. It is this concept that leads to the inability of us in the West to understand the Indigenous Mind.

First and foremost, the acceptance of Galileo's premise means that there is no inherent depth in the material universe—no soul, no feeling. The universe operates by set (physical) rules and actions that can be discovered and known by human beings. Those rules and actions, indeed the universe itself, are all morally free. There are only various forms of matter interacting by specific rules that, though not completely understood, can be discovered. This reduction of the universe to material interactions conflicts with essential aspects of ancient and indigenous assumptions.

For instance, within *all* indigenous cultures, plants are considered to possess intelligence, awareness, and a soul. They are experienced as being able to speak with human beings and convey information about how they may be used as medicine. This concept strikes at the heart of the universe-as-machine perspective, and no one in America can take it seriously without beginning to "twitch nervously," as the herbalist Michael Moore observes.

Second, the idea of the universe as a great machine gives rise, inevitably, to Darwin's theory of evolution. That is, it is hypothesized that humans evolved over a very long time in a complex interaction of environmental survival pressures and species adaptation and selection. Human life is simply one random expression of the workings of the great machine.

There is an embedded assumption in evolutionary theory that the human race came from some prehuman source and through natural selection is heading someplace incredible, some peak of evolution that is our ultimate destination. This belief naturally engenders the perspective that the human achievements of the past were all right for our ancestors, but in the here-and-now are obviously primitive and hopelessly old-fashioned. Too, where we are now is better, though not as good as where we are going. There is thus an inescapable disrespect for the cultures of the past, an inherent though subtle denigration of our present state, and a desire to get where we are going so we can finally be of worth, finally be evolved, that affects nearly all Western perspectives. This Western acceptance of the truth of evolutionary theory inevitably leads to its application in the human cultural realm. At its most basic it means a simple denigration of older or nonindustrial cultures. At its worst it becomes culturally sanctioned ethnocentrism or racism. As a result, any knowledge of the universe gleaned by our forefathers that comes from systems of information-gathering other than the universe-as-machine model is routinely ascribed to our ancestors' lack of evolution and summarily dismissed and discredited.

ALL THOSE PRIMITIVE PEOPLES

Western scholars argue that primitive tribes are the earliest form of humankind in society, and within this perspective our ancestors' perceptions of the *sacred* are viewed as fantasies or projections generated to explain what they could not understand. We, civilized man, evolved from these early beginnings. Indeed, humankind's sophisticated religious forms themselves evolved from these early forms of projection on the universe. And as modern man, scientific man, evolves, he has less and less need for projections on the universe. Primitive man needed a lot, modern man needs less; eventually, when our growth as a species goes far enough, we will not need any.

This perspective is prevalent in many Western writings on religion and nonindustrial cultures. An example is to be found in Peter Farb's *Man's Rise to Civilization (As Shown by the Indians of North America from Primeval Times to the Coming of the Industrial State)* (New York: E. P. Dutton, 1968). Farb's book quickly became a best-seller and a Book-of-the-Month-Club selection. The following quotes from the book give a fairly succinct overview of Western academic perspectives of historical, nonindustrial cultures.

> Eskimo belief is among the simplest known, and it incorporates the two common denominators of all religions everywhere: spirits and magic. It completely lacks all the other ideas of religion found in advanced societies: revelation, a redeemer, a priesthood, orthodox rituals, articles of faith, and so on. Probably the Eskimo spiritual beliefs do not differ much from man's earliest gropings toward religion, but that will never be known for sure.

The debate as to where "magic" ends, and "religion" begins is an old one that seemed settled some decades back when scholars concluded that there was no discernable boundary between them. As a result, the two were often lumped together as "magico-religious," in much the same way that the compromise word "sociocultural" originated. . . .

Eskimo magic differs from Christianity, Judaism, Mohammedanism, and Buddhism in that it does not attempt to regulate behavior in the society as a whole or to propagate a code of conduct and belief. It is not interested in the totality of the invisible world, but is instead limited to the individual's relationship with his food supply and to his physical environment. The Eskimo's magic operates through an elaborate system of hundreds of taboos that constrain his every action. A wise Iglulik Eskimo once told Knud Rasmussen: "What do we believe? We don't believe; we only fear." This sums up the attitude of Eskimos as well as of other peoples in simple societies. They live in a world of anxiety, frustration, inadequacy, and vulnerability, in which the spirits control everything that cannot be explained rationally. The modern American, of course, does not suffer the same kind of anxiety, since he has exerted technological control over many of the things that make the Eskimo fearful. In place of science, the Eskimo has only magic to bridge the gap between what he can understand and what is not known. Without magic, his life would be one long panic.[1]

To avoid that condition, Farb comments, people in many nonindustrial cultures seek after magic or power in the spirit world. One manner to obtain such magic or power has been through experiences of nonordinary reality. These are generally produced, according to his perspective, through self-torture. He comments that this was especially common among the Plains tribes:

> [An Indian] did this by isolating himself, fasting and thirsting, and practicing self-torture, at the same time imploring the spirits to take pity on his suffering.
>
> The spirit might at last take pity on the youth— actually it was dehydration, pain, and delirium taking their effects—and give him supernatural guidance. . . . A particularly lucky youth might also receive his own songs, which when sung served as a call to supernatural aid; that they sounded like gibberish to everyone else only reinforced the belief that he had received a unique vision.
>
> . . . Finally, in retelling his vision, he unconsciously reconstructed it and filled in gaps, adapting it to the norms of behavior of his culture—much as we do when reporting an incoherent dream, no matter how sincerely we believe we are not distorting it. . . .
>
> The various responses of different cultures toward visions partly explain why some Indians took enthusiastically to the White man's alcohol and others did not. The use of firewater was particularly intense among Plains, as well as nearby forest Indians, who were the ancestors of many Plains Indians. Alcohol was promptly recognized by the Plains Indians as a short-cut method of producing derangement of the senses and hallucinations.[2]

FEARFUL ANXIETY?

This picture, a common one among many Western academics, is that our ancestors lived in one long state of fearful anxiety until the rise of civilization, at which point technology saved them. What most academics do, of course, is to project *themselves* (in their imagination) into a living situation analogous to that of the Eskimo or a Plains tribe. What *they* feel in response to their projection is "anxiety, frustration, inadequacy, and vulnerability." Such feelings, for them, are inescapable. They are not trained to live in such circumstances, and the instinctive response to their projection is a feeling of fear and a gratitude that their life is not lived so primitively. This kind of modern projection has also been applied to the discovery and use of fermented beverages (inevitably) and is called (naturally) "anxiety theory."

The scholar Donald Horton, the father of anxiety theory, maintained that "the primary function of alcoholic beverages in all societies is the reduction of anxiety."[3] Approximately 50 years ago he developed his theories concerning the uses of alcohol among human cultures, and they have held dominance almost since their inception. Like Farb, he argued that the members of nonindustrial cultures live in a constant state of anxiety and that alcohol allows them brief periods of time in which to escape that state. His perspectives fit nicely with dominant Euro-centric, Christian, and Protestant temperance beliefs as well—indeed, they are an extension, a reflection, of them. As a result, more accurate, culturally neutral perspectives have long been ignored. Horton, and others who echo his perspectives, insist they are "objective." However, as Mikal Aasved comments in his seminal exploration of the sacred use of fermented beverages by nonindustrial cultures:

> In reality, such objectivity is rare. Many trained observers merely pay lip-service to the possibility that

cultural factors may influence drinking, and then proceed to fit their observations into the anxiety model of
their choice. Objectivity is even more infrequent among
untrained observers. From the examples already given, it
is evident that many descriptions of native drinking are
strongly ethnocentric, emotionally moralistic, and even
blatantly racist in tone. Thus alcohol, the perfect scape-
goat, has been held responsible for the collapse of entire
cultures ranging from small tribal units to the Roman
Empire itself.[4]

Any in-depth reading of accounts by Western scholars and scientists about historical fermentation and its uses in indigenous cultures
invariably echoes the perspectives and projected beliefs of Farb and
Horton. But when the members of indigenous cultures are asked directly
about plants and fermentation, or when oral histories are explored, quite
a different picture emerges. Anxiety theory fails to explain either the
experiences of the indigenous people themselves or the remarkable similarity of description between cultures that are geographically and tempo-
rally distinct and separate.

Many members of indigenous cultures deny that a state of fearful anxiety is at the root of their lives. Quite the contrary. When one is immersed
in such a culture from birth, the world looks much different than Western
academics would have us believe. Indigenous cultures live more immediately with death than late twentieth-century industrial cultures, but any
comprehensive reading of interviews with members of indigenous cultures
from the sixteenth to the twentieth centuries reveals a much different picture than that developed by Farb. They neither saw nor see anything
wrong in such a lifestyle, nor is extreme terror its most basic component.
In fact, many preferred it to what they were forced to adopt after European
dominance. As Oku'te, an Oglala Sioux, noted in the early 1900s:

An animal depends a great deal on the natural conditions around it. If the buffalo were here today, I think they would be different from the buffalo of the old days because all the natural conditions have changed. They would not find the same food nor the same surroundings. We see the change in our ponies. In the old days they could stand great hardship and travel long distances without water. They lived on certain kinds of food and drank pure water. Now our horses require a mixture of food; they have less endurance and must have constant care. It is the same with the Indians; they have less freedom and they fall an easy prey to disease. In the old days they were rugged and healthy, drinking pure water and eating the meat of the buffalo, which had a wide range, not being shut up like the cattle of the present day. The water of the Missouri River is not pure, as it used to be, and many of the creeks are no longer good for us to drink. A man ought to desire that which is genuine instead of that which is artificial.[5]

Many indigenous peoples say that living in harmony with the genuine comes from a recognition of the sacred, meaning-imbued world that lies under all things. But Western academics insist that the inherent *meaning* in the world that indigenous cultures describe is merely projection, and that their assertions that they can interact with that meaning and affect outcomes in the human sphere are only a kind of "magical thinking." Inevitably this magical thinking is attacked in the scholarly work of Western academics. As Ken Wilber comments about the beliefs of ancient cultures, "Mind and world are not clearly differentiated."[6]

In-depth examination of hunter-gatherer societies has, however, conclusively shown that their lives have been empirically based, more efficient, less terror-ridden, less stressful, and less concerned with food production than our own. As the anthropologist Mikal Aasved observes, "The ethnographic record speaks for itself in refuting the myths and outmoded ideas concerning the life of early man." [7] Aasved goes on to note that the anthropologist Richard Lee, in the mid-1960s, engaged in the first controlled study of subsistence living among hunter-gatherers with the ¡Kung Bushmen of Africa's Kalahari Desert. The region in which the ¡Kung people live is among the harshest on Earth. Lee, through the use of detailed diaries, kept a complete record of food production and intake during his stay. He noted that the ¡Kung consumed an average daily diet containing 2,140 calories and 93.1 grams of protein, figures that, Mikal Aasved notes, are "high even by American standards." [8] Lee determined that the average daily intake of food consistently exceeded the ¡Kung tribespeople's metabolic requirements, that they did "not lead a substandard existence on the edge of starvation as has been commonly reported," [9] that anxiety levels were low, that only 60 percent of the population (those aged 20–60) engaged in food gathering, and that the total amount of time they spent procuring sufficient food was only 12 to 19 hours per week. The rest of their time was spent in what might be called leisure pursuits. [10] It is important in reading this to understand that the region inhabited by the ¡Kung is extremely marginal, some of the most inhospitable on Earth, and that Lee's study occurred during one of the worst droughts on record. Lee observes that cultures living in lusher climes would spend even less time on food production than the ¡Kung. His findings have subsequently been corroborated by other researchers studying other historical and contemporary hunter-gatherer cultures. The anxiety theory that has been such a mainstay of Western scholars is completely without merit.

Wilber, Farb, Horton, and most Western academics miss a crucial point: our forefathers were anything but fools. They survived for a very, very long time using something other than what Farb and Wilber call science. Such lack of differentiation between world and self as described by both Farb and Wilber would result in nonsustainable and nonfunctional societies. Indigenous cultures, contrary to Western scholars' assertions, are extremely observant of the natural world. In fact, the members of such societies observe the actions of the ecosystem more exactly than Western observers. But more than this, they are working with systems of information gathering that are completely different from ours, systems based on different predicates, in language as specific as that used by science.

Many contemporary writers are beginning to recognize this. Some have begun to suspect that in throwing out all the ancient perspectives in favor of a scientific approach, we might have lost something intrinsic to who we are as a species. Perhaps no one has stated this so well as Vaclav Havel, the president of the Czech Republic, when he noted:

> [T]he relationship to the world that modern science fostered and shaped now appears to have exhausted its potential. It is increasingly clear that, strangely, the relationship is missing something. It fails to connect with the most intrinsic nature of reality, and with natural human experience. It is now more of a source of disintegration and doubt than a source of integration and meaning. It produces what amounts to a state of schizophrenia. Man as observer is becoming alienated from himself as a being. Classical modern science described only the surface of things, a single dimension of reality. And the more dogmatically science treated it as the only dimension, as the very essence of reality, the more misleading it became. Today, for instance, we may know immeasurably more about the universe than our ancestors did, and yet, it increasingly seems they knew something more essential about it than we do, something that escapes us. The same is true of nature and ourselves. The more thoroughly all our organs and their functions, their internal structure and the biochemical reactions that take place within them are

described, the more we seem to fail to grasp the spirit,
purpose and meaning of the system that they create
together and that we experience as our unique self. [11]

Many of us who have been raised in a universe-as-machine perspective have sensed this truth that Havel has made plain. Many of us
suspect that the "essential" thing that our ancestors knew about the universe is that there is more to it than simple matter. That it is in some
way alive. That sense, covered over by 500 years of "rationality," points
toward the ancient mind-set that I call the Indigenous Mind. And many
of us try in our own way to find the way back. Such a journey is a difficult one. But it can be made. It involves, as Ralph Metzner, one of the
pioneers in the study of nonordinary states of reality, describes it, drinking from the Well of Remembrance. But dipping into such waters
always involves a price.

The ancient Nordic saga, the *Elder Edda*, says that the Well of
Remembrance is located at the foot of Yggdrasill, the world tree. It

confers on anyone who drinks
from its waters the ability to
see in new ways and to tap into
the ancient knowledge and
wisdom of Earth and mankind.
As the saga relates, Odin, hearing of this well, desired to
drink from it, and he
approached the well's guardian,
Mimir, (from whose name the
word memory comes) to ask
for permission. After question-
ing Odin, Mimir agreed, but
first told Odin that there
would be a price—it would

cost him one of his eyes. Odin agreed and gained what he desired, but forever after he saw this world through only one eye.

It has often been said that the wisdom in this is that to gain knowledge and vision of the ancient worlds, one must give up how one has been seeing. For those of us raised in perhaps the most materialistic era the Earth has ever seen, drinking from the Well of Remembrance allows us to see as our ancestors did thousands of years ago. But in return we must sacrifice some of the worldview that we have been taught *is* reality.

Among us in the West, perhaps those who remember this the most are the artists and poets. They see into other worlds and bring back to us other ways of seeing that are encoded in the poetry they write. Perhaps that is why poets in the ancient world were known as the "bearers of the mead of Odin." One such poet, who has brought back knowledge of the Indigenous Mind and encoded it in his poems, is the writer Norbert Mayer. In this poem he writes of the livingness of stones.

Just now
A rock took fright
When it saw me.
It escaped
By playing dead. [12]

Mayer captures something that many of us intuitively know to be true—that there is more to our world than inanimate matter and human beings, that there is a livingness in nature. His poem shifts the focus of the reader's mind, causing the world to be seen in an entirely new way. In this instance, to perceive the rocks we pass by without notice each day as alive and aware. And, by extension, to wonder if perhaps everything else might also be alive. Such writers as D. H. Lawrence, e e cummings, Henry Thoreau, Wendell Berry, Barry Lopez, and Edward Abbey have written eloquently and passionately of the livingness of the world. Walt Whitman in *Leaves of Grass* is equally eloquent.

I believe a leaf of grass is no less
        than the journeywork of the stars,
And the pismre is equally perfect, and a grain of sand,
        and the egg of the wren,
And the tree-toad is a chef-d'oeuvre for the highest,
And the running blackberry would adorn
        the parlors of heaven,
And the narrowest hinge in my hand
        puts to scorn all machinery,
And the cow crunching with depressed head
        surpasses any statue,
And a mouse is miracle enough to stagger
        sextillions of infidels. [13]

The truth found by Whitman and set down in his timeless classic is also a truth long recognized in both indigenous and ancient cultures. *They* live in that world, they are raised in it. But it remains part of the birthright of all human beings. John Seed, the Australian rainforest activist, describes a meditation he teaches so that people imbued with a Western mind-set can begin to enter the indigenous worldview:

We have a practice where we approach a leaf as though approaching our revered Zen master. We breathe to this leaf the oxidized carbon of our body. We do so with the gratitude and the generosity that is the signature, the clue to the Nature of which we are a fragment. As we add consciousness to the ancient processes of sharing respiration, we savour the leaf in our imagination. Now we must notice and then lay aside our prejudice that we are the only one capable of consciousness in this transaction, this holy communion that accompanies our every breath. We consciously nourish a leaf and invite the leaf to nourish us not just with the oxygen it creates, but with further communications. The most "primitive" peoples naturally do this. They live deeply embedded in their "environment" and all practice ceremonies and rituals that affirm and nourish this interconnectedness, this interbeing of the human tribe with the rest of the Earth family.

It is not really possible to touch the deeper levels of fermentation unless one is able to approach a leaf like a "revered Zen master," and, casting aside convention, journey into that older world and understand the Indigenous Mind. Thus we drink from the Well of Remembrance and see once again the world with luminous eyes and feel its wonder with luminous heart.

TWO

The Mead of Inspiration
Mead, Honey, and Heather

It is so ancient a beverage that the linguistic root for mead, "medhu", is the same in all Indo-European languages where it encompasses an entire range of meanings, which include "honey," "sweet," "intoxicating," "drunk," and "drunkenness." For this reason it has been suggested that fermented honey may be the oldest form of alcohol known to man.
—Mikal Aasved, 1988[1]

[Mead is] the ancient liquor of gods and men, the giver of knowledge and poetry, the healer of wounds, and the bestower of immortality.
—Robert Gayre, 1948[2]

*H*ONEY IS CERTAINLY the oldest easily accessible natural sugar in the world. Long before human beings learned to make wine from the grape, to free the sugars in grains by malting barley, to process corn and sugar cane, to tap trees such as maple and palm for their sweet juice, there was honey. It is not then so surprising that the most ancient of fermented drinks is made from honey. Called mead throughout the oral traditions, and now encoded in mythology, it is known as the drink of both gods and men. Honey, mead, and the bee all hold special places in our ancestors' descriptions of humankind's relationship with the sacred.

Bees are the messengers of the gods, bringing the sacred to human beings, with a kinship to the soul essence that all people possess. As Robert Gayre, the historian of mead, comments, "It was closely associated with the Great Mother Goddess, and it was figured in the mouth of the lion, in the religion of Mithra, and thereby was intended to represent the Word of God. In Chaldee, the actual word 'bee' is the same as 'the Word.'" [3] Interestingly, the bee appeared on Earth shortly before those hominids that scientists identify as our earliest ancestors. Thus, the human species and the bee have been companions from the beginning, and some writers speculate that the bee played an integral part in the development of our species. Many of our most ancient legends insist that poetry, sacred language, "the Word," came out of humankind's relationship with the bee and its creation—honey. Honey itself has long been viewed as originating in sacred realms in the form of dew on flowers that is then collected and stored by bees. Mead is the fermentation of honey, producing a liquor that allows human beings, for a time, to experience sacred states of mind. And more, all three things—bees, honey, and mead—confer on humankind some of the immortality of the gods, giving them long life, health, and a deepening of consciousness and awareness. The following story—retold from the *Edda*—captures exquisitely the sacredness and poetics of mead. It is Nordic and extremely ancient.

⊷

Gathering Herbs
*from the title page
of the* Grete
Herball, *London,
Peter Treveris,* 1526

Thus it was that in the beginning the gods warred amongst themselves. The older gods, the Vanir, strove mightily with the Aesir, the young gods who sought to supplant them, but neither could gain advantage. Then tiring of the ceaseless battle did they agree to meet and make peace among themselves. And in this way did they decide to heal the rift between them: a large earthen vessel was brought, and each leaned and spit within, the fluids of all being mingled, until it was full to overflowing. Then, unwilling to let this mark of their peace perish, they spoke together, and deciding, reached out with their power and shaped that which they had given into a man whom they called Kvaser, the all-knowing—one so wise that there was no question that he could not answer. And when he spoke all were touched by the power of his voice, wherein lay the power and sacredness of the gods.

For long did Kvaser walk the heavens, the symbol of the peace of gods. But there came a time when, straying far, he was taken and bound by the dwarves who loved him not. By them he was slain, and taking three jars, they ran his blood into them, mixing it with honey. Thus was made mead, and such was its power that any who drank of it became skald and sage. And the dwarves kept it jealously, sharing it only among themselves. But news of the mead came to the giant, Suttung, and in him great desire was born to have the mead for his own. After long planning and coming in stealth, he stole the three vessels of dwarven mead and hid them in the place called Hnitbjorg. And calling on his daughter, Gundlad, he spoke to her, telling her to guard it well and let no one come near.

But the leader of the young gods, Odin, hearing what had occurred, set out to find the mead, and many adventures befell him before he came at last to Hnitbjorg and the giantess, Gundlad. Using his power, Odin disguised his countenance so that she knew him not, and in sweet voice he spoke to her, and her heart went to him, for she had been long alone. Taking him by the hand, she led him to her couch, and there they lay for three days and nights, where he satisfied her greatly. And being most wondrously happy, she offered him, to slake his thirst, three draughts from the vessels that Suttung had bade her watch. Taking her leave to drink once from each, Odin put his lips to the mead in the first, then the second, and then the third. And he commented to her that it was most wonderful. But at that moment so did Suttung come. Looking into the vessels, he found them empty, for Odin, desiring to take the mead to Asgard, had consumed it all.

Seeing Suttung's rage and taking on the guise of an eagle, Odin fled. And seeing this, Suttung too took up the guise of an eagle and flew after him. Long they flew, Suttung ever close behind, until at last they came to Asgard. And the gods, seeing Odin come, made haste to gather vessels and place them outside. And coming close, Odin spewed the mead out of him and into the jars. But so hasty he was with Suttung close behind that three drops fell to earth. And men, wandering upon the Earth, came upon them. Wondering to themselves what this might be, they put their hands to it, and lifting it to their lips, tasted of the mead made from Kvaser's blood and the honey of the bee.

Thus this is called "the share of the poetasters" and from it doth all poetry and song come. Hence, songship is called Odin's prey, Odin's find, Odin's drink, Odin's gift, the drink of the Aesir, and poets are known as the bearers of the mead of Odin.[4]

The deep and important connection between humankind and the Mead of Inspiration, between poetry (and great literature) and fermentation, between becoming wise and the ingestion of honey or mead, and between sacredness and inebriation has long been understood by human beings. Recorded memories, embedded in mythological legend, are pervasive throughout the world. For instance, in the Rig-Vedas, the holy books of the Hindus, Vishnu and Indra are called *Madhava*, the honey-born ones, and their symbol is the bee. And the ancient Celtic legend about the grain goddess, Cerridwen, and Gwion Bach (recounted in chapter 6) bears many similarities to the story of the origin of the Mead of Inspiration.

Throughout recorded history, poets and writers have remarked on the connection between poetry (art in language) and fermentation, affirming the wisdom embedded in Odin's tale. Horace long ago wrote that "No poems can please long or live that are written by water-drinkers." And in the ancient poem, the *Runahal*, it is said that

> *A drink I took of the magic mead,*
> *Taken out of Othrorir.*
> *Then I began to know and to be wise,*
> *To grow and to weave poems.*[5]

And Ralph Waldo Emerson observed that

> [The poet speaks] not with intellect alone but with the intellect inebriated by nectar. As the traveller who has lost his way throws the reins on his horse's neck and trusts to the instinct of the animal to find his road, so must we do with the divine animal who carries us through the world. For if in any manner we can stimulate this instinct,

new passages are opened into nature. . . . This is the reason why bards love wine, mead, narcotics, coffee, tea,
opium, the fumes of sandalwood and tobacco, or whatever other procurers of animal exhilaration.[6]

But of all these substances, the oldest is mead. Throughout human
history, oral tradition, and legend, it is connected to a change in consciousness of humankind—a change that brought with it the beginnings
of a peculiar form of art encoded in language and called poetry. Like all
myth, that of Odin's search for the mead of Kvaser has been changed and
altered as it traveled to us orally through time. But there is much wisdom
in it for those who look deep.

MEAD

*Metheglin [a type of mead] keeps a humming in the brain, which
made one say that he loved not metheglin because he was used to
speak too much of the house he came from, meaning the hive.*
—John Howell, ca. 1650[7]

Mead is made wherever honey can be found, and many indigenous cultures still make meads throughout Central and South America and Africa
as their ancestors did thousands of years ago. There are many ancient references to mead, and they occur in such a manner as to show that mead
long predated wine and beer. Plato writes that "Plenty [was] drunk with
nectar [i.e., mead], for wine was not yet invented." In the Orphic myth it
is noted that Kronos was made drunk by Zeus with honey, "for wine was
not." (And one of Zeus's names is *Melissaios*, meaning "one belonging to
the bees.") Many of the ancient European writers comment that although
certain religious offerings are to be made with wine, such was not always
the case—before wine, mead was all that was used.[8]

Honey, thought not to be indigenous to North America, was, in fact, common in Florida and the southern parts of the United States and Mexico, and was historically used in fermented beverages among the cultures that lived there. And mead was made by all the cultural groups of Europe, Africa, India, and Asia.[9] The dwarves referred to in the *Eddas* are almost certainly the Picts, who were a short, dwarflike people, one of the original indigenous tribes of Britain. And their mead, made from heather honey and heather, has long been thought to be the original Mead of Inspiration.

Heather was used first in mead; then, as beers and ales became more common, in them as well.

HEATHER MEAD AND ALE

In the wide-striding Vishnu's highest foostep,
There is a spring of mead.

—Rig-Veda

There may also an excellent Drink be made from the Tops and
Flowers of Heath, *seasonably gathered and dryed, and brewed as*
you have occasion for it.

—Dr. W. P. Worth, 1692[10]

Heather mead, for millennia, was considered to be a unique fermentation that produced remarkable effects in those who drank it. Though common for at least 4,000 years in the area known as Scotland, it, like many kinds of indigenous, sacred, and herbal beers, nearly died out in the late nineteenth to early twentieth century. Heather mead and ale has also been traditionally brewed in other parts of the United Kingdom. Dr. Plot, writing in 1686, observed that throughout Staffordshire (an area of England) "they frequently used *Erica vulgaris*, heath, or *ling*, instead of hops to preserve their beer, which gave it no ill taste."[11] And in Westphalia (now a part of Germany), it is noted that in the fifteenth century there was "a beer . . . called Koit from the old Welsh and Breton *coit*, a heather beer." [12] In Denmark and Norway, brewing with heather was also common. One nineteenth-century writer commented that "It is a tradition prevalent in the north of Ireland that the Danes, when in possession of the country in the ninth century, brewed beer from heath."[13] And one local Scandinavian brewer, commenting on their traditional beers, noted, "If one wanted ale with a special taste, or ale of a different kind, one could mix into it a kind of heather, or *sisselroot* (common polypody), or yarrow."[14] In fact, though heather meads and ales have been traditionally ascribed to *only* the historical area of Scotland, it appears that they were in common production throughout Europe, the Scandinavian countries, and all of the United Kingdom. And in every place it has been brewed, heather mead and ale was thought to possess remarkable properties.

Making a heather mead or ale is fairly straightforward. The following are two modern recipes.

Heather Mead

Ingredients

> 6 pounds heather honey
>
> 10 cups lightly pressed (unwashed) flowering heather tops
>
> 4 gallons water
>
> yeast

> Heat water to 170 degrees F, add 6 cups heather flowers, and allow to stand covered overnight. Strain liquid and boil, remove from heat and add honey. Stir until dissolved. Run hot wort through a sieve filled with 2 cups of heather tips into the fermenting vessel. Allow to cool, add 5 grams dry Windsor brewing (Danstar) yeast, and ferment until fermentation slows down. Then remove 1/2

gallon of ale, add 2 cups of heather flowers, and warm to 158 degrees F. Cover and steep for 15 minutes, then return to fermenter. When fermentation is complete, prime bottles (if carbonated mead is desired), fill, and cap. Store from two weeks to two years for aging.

Recently, heather ale, using barley instead of honey for the fermentable sugar, has been rediscovered and is now being brewed commercially in Scotland by its strongest advocate, Bruce Williams. What follows is his recipe for a homebrewed heather ale.

Heather Ale

Ingredients

> 6 pounds U.S. two-row malted barley
> 10 1/2 ounces amber malt
> 12 2/3 cups lightly pressed flowering heather tops
> 3/10 ounce Irish moss
> 5 gallons water
> yeast and nutrient

Mash the malt at 153 degrees F for 90 minutes. Sparge to collect 5 gallons. Add about one-half gallon of lightly pressed heather tips and boil vigorously for 90 minutes.

Run hot wort through a sieve filled with 2 cups of heather tips into the fermenting vessel. Allow to cool and ferment at 61 degrees F for 7 to 10 days. When the gravity reaches 1.015, usually the fifth day, remove 1/2 gallon of ale, add two cups of heather flowers and warm to 158 degrees F. Cover and steep for 15 minutes, then strain and return to fermenter. When fermentation is complete, prime bottles, fill, and cap.[15]

Bruce Williams's heather ale is available in the United States if you make a concerted effort to find it, though it does take an unshakable intention. Its flavor is truly remarkable. There is a slight bitter taste that balances well with the richness of the barley malt. It has a firm, oily body that rolls smoothly off the tongue and a light flowery bouquet that dances on the taste buds and infuses the senses. It is the most remarkable ale I have ever tasted.

ABOUT HEATHER

Erica spp.

> *Wormus speaks of the drinking of heather-beer, as one of the pleasures which the souls of departed heroes enjoyed in the society of the gods.*
> —W. T. Marchant, 1888[16]

There is considerable evidence that fermented heather was one of the sacred beverages of the Picts and Celts and an integral part of Druidic sacred life and ceremonies. Its use is ancient in fermentation. Williams notes that "An archeological dig on the Scottish Isle of Rhum discovered a Neolithic shard, circa 2000 B.C., in which were found traces of a fermented beverage containing heather."[17] Considered to be the first fermented beverage in the British Isles, it has enjoyed wide historical use throughout ancient Druid lands, its production (in small homestead brewing) continuing until the early twentieth century. Both the Greeks and Romans commented on Pictish production of a remarkable fermented beverage brewed from heather and coveted it highly. Those among the Picts who brewed the heather ale for ceremonial use were highly revered in Pictish society (some asserting that only the chiefs among them were allowed to make it).

A powerful indigenous culture who made extensive use of tattooing and body painting, the Picts are the origin of our English word *picture*.

They occupied Britain and the Scottish highlands for millennia and were a very short people renowned as fighters with tremendous endurance. The legends of dwarves who live under the mountains, embodied so well in J. R. R. Tolkien's *Lord of the Rings*, are the Picts moved by time and oral tradition into legend. They fought off invasions from Europeans, Anglo-Saxons, the Irish, and even stopped the Romans in their attempts to conquer Britain. The Picts were eventually defeated and assimilated by the Scots in A.D. 846.

There is a story, retold in so many places and times that it makes sense to assume there is some truth in it, about the Picts' loss of the knowledge of brewing heather ale during the final battles and their defeat by the Scots. Robert Louis Stevenson, growing up with the traditional tale, retold it in perhaps its most famous version.

From the bonny bells of heather
They brewed a drink longsyne,
Was sweeter far than honey,

Was stronger far than wine.
They brewed it and they drank it,
And lay in a blessed swound
For days and days together
In their dwelling underground.

There rose a king in Scotland,
A fell man to his foes,
He smote the Picts in battle,
He hunted them like roes.
Over miles of the red mountain
He hunted them as they fled,
And strewed the dwarfish bodies
Of the dying and the dead.

Summer came in the country,
Red was the heather bell;
But the manner of the brewing
Was none alive to tell.
In graves that were like children's
The brewsters of the Heather
Lay numbered with the dead.

The king in the red moorland
Rode on a summer's day;
And the bees hummed,
        and the curlews
Cried beside the way.
The king rode, and was angry,
Black was his brow and pale,
To rule in a land of heather
And lack the Heather Ale.

It fortuned that his vassals,
Riding free on the heath,
Came on a stone that was fallen
And vermin hid beneath.
Rudely plucked from their hiding,
Never a word they spoke:
A son and his aged father—
Last of the dwarfish folk.

The king sat high on his charger,
He looked on the little men;
And the dwarfish and the
        swarthy couple
Looked at the king again.
Down by the shore he had them;
And there on the giddy brink—
"I will give you life, ye vermin,
For the secret of the drink."

There stood the son and father
And they looked high and low;
The heather was red around them,
The sea rumbled below,
And up and spake the father,
Shrill was his voice to hear:
"I have a word in private,
A word for the royal ear."

"Life is dear to the aged,
And honour a little thing;
I would gladly sell the secret,"
Quoth the Pict to the king.

His voice was as small as a sparrow's,
And shrill and wonderful clear:
"I would gladly sell my secret,
Only my son I fear.

"For life is a little matter,
And death is naught to the young;
And I dare not sell my honour
Under the eye of my son.
Take HIM, O king, and bind him,
and cast him far in the deep:
And it's I will tell the secret
That I have sworn to keep."

They took the son and bound him,
Neck and heels in a thong,
And a lad took and swung him,
And flung him far and strong,
And the sea swallowed his body,
Like that of a child of ten;
And there on the cliff stood
        the father,
Last of the dwarfish men.

"True was the word I told you;
Only my son I feared;
For I doubt the sapling courage
That goes without the beard.
But now in vain is the torture,
Fire shall never avail:
Here dies in my bosom
The secret of Heather Ale."[18]

But in spite of the brutal decimation of the Pictish people some knowledge of heather brewing did survive, and heather ale was still made by rural folk well into the twentieth century.

The heather plant, itself, assumes primary importance wherever it grows. It has traditionally been used for thatching, bedding, broom making, firewood, basket weaving, and food production—especially the production of honey and ale. In its broad range of uses to indigenous peoples, it was the plant equivalent of the buffalo to the Plains Indians of the United States. Even today the national consciousness of many parts of the British Isles is intimately related to the presence of heather. It has been a part of the psyche, the poems, stories, and identity of the people since their origins on that part of the Earth. Many country people still use heather in the ways it has been used for the past 4,000 years.

Heather belongs to the *Ericaceae* family. Interestingly, many of the plants in this family have been traditionally used in ales, and a number of them are known for their psychotropic or highly inebriating effects. Some of the more notable are yellow rosebay (*Rhododendron chrysanthemum*), a Russian intoxicant and antirheumatic; American rosebay (*Rhododendron maximum*), a plant with narcotic properties; the fruit of strawberry tree (*Arbutus Unedo*), also said to be narcotic; marsh or wild rosemary (*Ledum palustre*), considered to be highly intoxicating when added to a fermenting beverage; Labrador tea (also *Ledum*); and whortleberries (*Vaccinium ulignosum*), these last two considered by some to possess narcotic properties.[19] Heather, too, is reputed to be narcotic. The legendary nature of ale made from heather, and the many attributes given to drinking it, all point to not only the sacred power of the plant, but to the deeper properties inherent in the plant itself.

Recently, before beginning commercial production of heather ale, Bruce Williams sent samples of heather tops for analysis to a botanist and brewing chemist, Keith Thomas, in England. His findings are interesting. People harvesting heather tops for ale production had noted a fine white powder that covered their clothes and hands during harvest. This white powder is produced by a moss (locally called *fogg*) that grows on the woody stems of the plant and is disturbed during harvesting. After analysis, Thomas noted that the white powder possessed narcotic and mildly hallucinogenic properties and should be washed off prior to making any beer from the heather tops. (Rumor has it that the college students who were harvesting the plant enjoyed many a late-night tea made from heather tops during their stay in the field.) The heather beer now being produced in Scotland is made from vigorously rinsed heather tops to avoid the problem.[20] Remarkably, the moss, or fogg, also contains a wild yeast that has been traditionally used to ferment the heather ale. The Scottish dictionary notes, "The Picts brewed some awful grand drink they ca't heather ale out of heather and some unknown kind of fogg."[21]

Apart from the properties of the moss, heather possesses mild narcotic and sedative properties in its own right. It has been traditionally used in herbal medicine as a mild sedative and also for urinary and kidney problems and to relieve rheumatic and arthritic pains.

Honey produced from heather is famous throughout its range, and it, too, is sublimely interesting. It has a singular taste with a pronounced flavor, delicious to the palate. Its aroma is pungent and penetrating, filling any room with its smell, even when kept in a closed cupboard. Honey from heather has unique properties possessed by only two other honeys, one from New Zealand and the other from India. Both, like heather honey, are from specific plants. They all display a property known as thixotropy. That is, in its undisturbed state, the honey is extremely thick and gelatinous—much like Jell-O. The Jell-O-like property of heather honey decreases when it is vigorously stirred, eventually attaining a consistency much like that of ordinary honey. After sitting for three days to a week, its gelatinous nature reasserts itself and it is once again like Jell-O. These two states of heather honey may account for the confusion between the honey/mead-drink/food that the Greeks called both nectar and ambrosia. These sacred substances, food and drink of the gods, were sometimes considered a food, sometimes a drink—sometimes being a liquid and drunk, sometimes a solid and eaten.

Unlike other honeys that contain only a trace of protein, heather honey contains a great deal. It is composed of from 1/2 to 2 percent protein, which is responsible for its Jell-O-like consistency.[22] This unique property means that the extraction of heather honey from the honeycomb is extremely difficult. Historically, it was almost impossible to extract the honey unless the entire comb was removed from the hive and boiled. In the making of mead from heather honey, this would mean that the entire contents of the hive would be boiled together: angry bees, propolis, pollen, royal jelly, honey, and wax. Further, the mead so produced would be extremely high in protein content. Not only would the heather honey supply an inordinate amount of protein for a honey, the fermenting yeast would also add its own protein enhancement (which is considerable), making the combination a formidable food source. This may account, in part, for the ancient assertion by the Scots that "mead-drinkers have as much strength as meat-eaters," and the German saying, *Bienen kommen eben so weit als Bare*—"mead is as strengthening as meat."[23]

The moss, or fogg, from the heather plant would also likely be a component of mead, not only from its unavoidable presence in the hive but also from the additional heather tops used in mead production. The result would be a remarkable fermented beverage possessing tremendous food properties as well as medicinal and narcotic aspects—truly a mead of inspiration. Extremely ancient accounts indicate that the Picts and Celts brewed a fermented beverage from heather *only*, without any barley at all. It is likely that this was a combination heather/heather honey mead. The fact that fermented heather beverages are considered to be the first "beers" brewed in the British Isles, that their brewing can be traced back some 4,000 years, and that they were brewed by a wandering indigenous culture (the Picts) indicates that barley probably wasn't a part of the original heather "beers," that in fact it was produced from heather honey. Some sources note that as early as A.D. 100 the Celts made a heather and heather honey mead that was known to be highly intoxicating.[24]

The main species of heather in the British Isles (and that from which heather honey is made) is ling or broom heather (*Erica vulgaris*—also denoted as *Calluna vulgaris*). The flower is generally a purplish pink and literally covers hundreds of square miles of land throughout the British Isles and Europe. It is a low, fernlike shrub, about 15 inches in height, with sharp, needle-like leaves. It grows well on sandy or acid soils and covers the vast areas of waste or sterile lands in Europe and the British Isles called moors. This species does also produce, rarely, white flowers, which are considered to possess special properties by the local people.

There are also three other species that are somewhat common in Europe and the British Isles, all being used for heather ale and heather honey: bell or Scotch heather (*Erica cinera*), Cornish heather (*Erica vagans*), and cross-leaved heather (*Erica tetralix*). All four species are naturalized in the northeastern United States. Ling heather is only common in western New England, though it is grown as an ornamental shrub throughout the United States. It possesses pink, blue, or white flowers. There are six species fairly common in the western United States—mountain heather (*Cassiope mertensiana*), firemoss cassiope (*Cassiope tetragona*), starry cassiope (*Cassiope sterreriana*), pink mountain heather (*Phyllodoce empetriformis*), brewer mountain heather (*Phyllodoce breweri*), and cream mountain heather (*Phyllodoce glandulifera*). All are members of the heath or *Ericaceae* family. All the species are smallish to woody, matted shrubs, with a fondness for acidic soils. Mountain heather is found from Alaska and Canada south to central California, northern Nevada, and western Montana. Its flowers are small white bells that grow in clusters. They hang from the tips of slender red stalks that sprout from the axils near the ends of the branches. Firemoss cassiope grows near the Canadian border, and starry cassiope grows in bogs from Mount Rainier in Washington State northward. Pink mountain heather is a low, matted shrub with pinkish to red flowers that also hang in clusters. They possess a long stamen protruding from the center of the hanging bell-like flower. Its range is Alaska to northern California, and Idaho and Colorado. Brewer mountain heather grows primarily in the

California mountains, and cream mountain heather ranges in the Oregon and Wyoming mountains northward.

The two main species being used in brewing are ling heather (*Erica vulgaris*) and bell heather (*Erica tetralix*). The species flower from July to October in the United States and somewhat earlier in Scotland—April to June for bell heather, August to September for ling heather. (It would be interesting to find out if the other species in the United States would produce the same wonderful taste in ales and if they also possess the moss or fogg found on the European varieties.) The top two to three inches of the flowering stalks are collected and should be used within 36 hours of picking or else refrigerated. They lose their aroma if kept longer.

ABOUT HONEY, BEE POLLEN, PROPOLIS, ROYAL JELLY, AND BEE VENOM

[Eat thee of honey] wherein is healing for mankind.
                                            —the Koran

Among the Finns . . . there existed the belief that high in the sky was the storehouse of the Almighty, containing the heavenly honey, which had the power to heal all wounds.
                                            —Robert Gayre, 1948[25]

Many health-enhancing attributes have long been associated with mead. As the historian of mead, Robert Gayre observes, "From the earliest times men have recognized that honey, and particularly mead, have strong revitalizing qualities, as well as healing virtues. As a consequence of this it was believed to be an elixir to prolong life, and this, no doubt, is why the magic mead of heaven was believed to confer immortality upon the mortals who partook of it."[26] Regular consumption of mead, it was claimed, would restore youthfulness, increase sexual drive, prevent illness, and cure diseases such as arthritis, stomach ulceration, bronchitis, impotency, general weakness and debility, heart disease, and cancer, as well as many others.

Modern writers have generally assumed that these claims are merely fantasy. However, all fermentations, whether beer, ale, mead, or wine, possess the medicinal actions of whatever ingredients they contain or are made from. If the medicinal effects of the ingredients of mead are examined, it is interesting to note that they are identical with many of the ancient claims made about mead. In spite of modern dismissals of the healthy effects of drinking mead, no studies have ever been conducted to see if any of these ancient claims have any foundation in fact. It is important to remember, however, that mead was originally made from the entire hive. That means that everything went into the pot: wax, honey, propolis, bee pollen, royal jelly, and angry bees. It makes sense, then, to look at the medicinal actions of these separate parts of the hive and see if their medicinal actions in any way match the claims made by our ancestors for mead. It could very well be that the medicinal effects of every ingredient in mead combine to produce the healthful effects long attributed to mead. That is, the actions and properties of honey, bee pollen, propolis, royal jelly, bee venom, yeast, and alcohol from the fermentation act together to create highly beneficial effects on human helath.

HONEY

Honey is the nectar of the flowers of plants, gathered by the bee and stored in its stomach for transport to the hive. Nectar begins with glucose being produced by the plant. The plant makes glucose by combining carbon dioxide gas and water in its leaves through the use of chlorophyll and sunlight (photosynthesis). Then part of the glucose is converted into fructose, and all of it together is combined into sucrose. This is circulated throughout the plant to produce energy for growth. Some of this sucrose (along with other compounds) is diverted to the plants' flowers to coax nectar gatherers into cross-pollinating them.

Ignoring the other plant compounds, nectar is primarily sucrose, a disaccharide—that is, it is a double-molecule sugar, made from one fructose molecule and one glucose molecule linked together. The bee's stomach enzymes take the sucrose molecule and break it apart into glucose and fructose. Glucose is slightly less sweet than sucrose (white sugar), and fructose is sweeter. Because fructose is so much sweeter than glucose, it takes fewer calories of fructose to achieve the same level of sweetening produced by the other sugars. In the hive, the bee regurgitates the nectar into the wax cells of the comb (which brings up images of Odin and the Mead of Inspiration). The nectar is moved from cell to cell to facilitate drying. Eventually large numbers of bees band together, and by fanning their wings, perform the final evaporation to thicken the nectar into what we call honey, which is about 80 percent solids and 20 percent liquid. Unlike sucrose, fructose and glucose in combination and at such a concentration are very stable. The fructose is the most stable, being nearly impossible to crystallize. When honey does crystallize, it is the glucose you see—the remaining liquid is fructose. Fructose helps keep the honey liquid for extended periods of time.

Ancient honeys were from a profusion of wildflowers, whatever grew locally. It was exceedingly uncommon for honey to be gathered from a single species of plant, such as the alfalfa or clover honeys of today, unless that plant species existed in great abundance (as heather does). As such, the honeys of antiquity generally possessed the essence of a multitude of wild plants—all of them medicinal. Honeybees find a great attraction to many strongly medicinal plants—vitex, jojoba, elder, toadflax, balsam root, echinacea, valerian, dandelion, wild geranium—in fact, almost any flowering medicinal herb, as well as the more commonly known alfalfas and clovers. The nectar from a multitude of medicinal plants is present in any wildflower honey mix. That some of the power of the plant from which it is collected remains in the honey can be seen from the fact that honeys made from poisonous plants will poison people who eat them. Charles Millspaugh in 1892 commented that the honey of

Trebisond, produced from the Persian *Rhododendron ponticum*, is poisonous, as is honey produced from *Azalea pontica*.

Ancient records have attributed at least one defeat of Roman soldiers
to eating poisonous honey the night before a battle. Even today, beekeepers are warned to avoid allowing their bees to collect nectar from
plants known to produce poisonous honey. It is amazing that it has not
been recognized that the concentrated nectar of medicinal plants also
holds within it the concentrated medicinal power of the plants from
which it is collected. But this concentration of medicinal essence explains,
in part, the healing power long attributed to honey and mead. However,
in addition to the plants' own medicinal qualities, the plant nectars are
subtly altered, in ways that modern science has been unable to explain, by
their brief transport in the bees' digestive system. Before regurgitation,
the nectars combine in unique ways with the bees' digestive enzymes to
produce new compounds.

Honey, often insisted to be just another simple carbohydrate (like
white sugar), actually contains, among other things, "a complex collection
of enzymes, plant pigments, organic acids, esters, antibiotic agents, and
trace minerals."[27] Honey, in fact, contains more than 75 different compounds. Besides those already listed, it contains proteins, carbohydrates,
hormones, and antimicrobial compounds. One pound of (nonheather)
honey contains 1,333 calories (compared to white sugar at 1,748 calories), 1.4 grams of protein, 23 milligrams of calcium, 73 milligrams of
phosphorus, 4.1 milligrams of iron, 1 milligram of niacin, and 16 milligrams of vitamin C.[28] The content of each of these substances varies
considerably depending on which type of plants the honey is gathered
from. Some honey may contain as much as 300 milligrams of vitamin C
per 100 grams of honey.[29] It also contains vitamin A, beta-carotene, the
complete complex of B vitamins, vitamin D, vitamin E, vitamin K, magnesium, sulphur, chlorine, potassium, iodine, sodium, copper, manganese, and a rich supply of live enzymes.[30] Honey also contains relatively
high concentrations of hydrogen peroxide and formic acid,[31] and

many of the remaining substances in honey are so complex that they have yet to be identified.

Honey has been found to possess antibiotic, antiviral, anti-inflammatory, anticarcinogenic, expectorant, antiallergenic, laxative, antianemic, and tonic properties.[32] It is also antifungal and an immune stimulant.[33] Because honey increases calcium absorption in the body, it is also recommended during menopause to help prevent osteoporosis.

It has been found to be highly effective for treatment of stomach ulceration; all seven strains of the *Helicobacter pylori* bacteria that cause stomach ulceration are completely inhibited with a 5 percent solution of honey.[34] In comparison tests, honey was found to be more effective than a number of other, more commonly used, antimicrobial agents in the treatment of *H. pylori* ulceration.[35]

The British Journal of Plastic Surgery reported that clinical trials found honey to provide faster wound healing than traditional pharmaceuticals.[36] Other studies have found that recovery from Caesarean delivery and gangrene infection by honey-treated patients was far superior to patients treated with antibiotics and pharmaceutical wound dressings.[37] These studies have been echoed by a number of other researchers, all finding that honey's antibacterial action and wound-healing properties are exceptionally effective on all types of wounds.[38] A number of people have insisted that this antimicrobial activity comes from the high sugar concentration of honey—an activity also found in high concentrations of white sugar. However, even a diluted honey solution of .25 percent has been found to be highly antibacterial, inhibiting *Staphylococcus aureus* bacteria.[39] Numerous other studies have shown that, though the high sugar concentration is antimicrobial, honey itself possesses active compounds that are, in themselves, antibacterial.

Some of the wounds that clinicians have seen healed with honey are bed sores, varying in size from the width of a finger to a fist that extended to the bone. Such ulcerations, healed with the use of honey, left no indentation and no muscle loss.[40] Even wounds that were so infected they would not respond to *any* antibiotic therapy have responded to honey.[41] Dilute honey solutions have been successfully used to preserve corneas, bones, and blood vessels intended for surgical transplantation.[42] And Chinese researchers have found honey to be an effective treatment in first, second, and third-degree burns, preventing scarring, inhibiting infection, and in many instances alleviating the need for skin grafts.

Honey is also exceptionally effective in respiratory ailments. A Bulgarian study of 17,862 patients found that honey was effective in improving chronic bronchitis, asthmatic bronchitis, bronchial asthma, chronic and allergic rhinitis, and sinusitis.[43] It is effective in the treatment of colds, flu, and respiratory infections, and general depressed immune-system problems.[44]

Generally, raw, unprocessed, and unpasteurized wildflower honey should be used in the production of mead and as food and medicine. For wounds and burns it is generally placed, liberally, on the affected area and covered with a sterile bandage, the dressing changed daily. For infectious diseases, it is used liberally in food and as a supplement, either undiluted, in tea, or as mead—one tablespoon 8 to 12 times daily.

Honey as food is different from white sugar, though many dieticians will tell you otherwise. Honey is composed of (approximately) 38 to 40 percent fructose, 31 to 34 percent glucose, 1 to 2 percent sucrose, 17 to 20 percent water, 2 to 4 percent identified plant and mineral compounds, and 4 to 7 percent unidentified plant and other compounds. The two primary sugars of honey, glucose and fructose, are monosaccharides (simple sugars) and, as a result, do not require additional processing by the body to be digested. White sugar (a disaccharide) does need to be additionally processed.[45] Honey is, in health food terms, a live food, and as such, is easier to digest and better for the body. Fruits and vegetables, though high in vitamins, tend to lose them over time. Spinach, for example, will lose 50 percent of its vitamin C content within 24 hours after picking. Honey, on the other hand, stores its vitamins indefinitely. Wildflower honeys generally have the largest overall concentration of vitamins.

Single-species honeys tend to increase concentrations of one vitamin to the detriment of others. For example, orange honey is relatively high in thiamin (8.2 micrograms per 100 grams) but low in nicotinic acid (.16 milligrams per 100 grams), while fireweed honey is low in thiamin (2.2 micrograms) and high in nicotinic acid (.86 milligrams).

Though the levels may seem small, honey as a consistent addition to food has shown remarkable results in medical trials. In an Austrian study prior to World War II, of one group of 58 boys, 29 were given two table-spoons of honey each day (one A.M. and one P.M.); the other 29 boys were given none. All received the same diet, exercise, and rest. All were the same age and in the same general health. The group receiving honey (after one year) showed an 8 1/2 percent increase in hemoglobin and an overall increase in vitality, energy, and general appearance.[46] Other stud-ies in Switzerland and the United States echo these results. A number of modern researchers, in order to test the nutritional value of honey, have subsisted on diets of honey and milk for up to three months. In all cases they maintained their normal body weight and state of health.[47]

One drawback of honey, in terms of mead production, is that fruc-tose is harder for yeast to consume. As a result, fermentation of mead is a longer process than for beers made from other sugars. Initially, the yeast in a fermenting mead will form a vigorous frothy head, which then sub-sides. In any other type of beer, this would mean that fermentation is complete. However, with mead making, it only means that the glucose in the honey has been consumed. The yeasts are now working on con-suming the remaining fructose sugars. This fermentation will be much slower and can easily take several weeks. The only way (besides experi-ence) to tell if fermentation is actually complete is to taste the mead. If it is still sweet, fermentation is not complete. The drawback to this is that every time you expose the mead to air to taste it, you risk infection of the wort. But bottling too early will result in a highly carbonated beer that will either explode the bottles or foam vigorously when opened. Done correctly, mead will taste, depending on the type of honey used, like a fine, dry champagne or wine. And like wine, it benefits from lengthy aging in the bottle. It may be served uncarbonated, like wine, or carbonated like champagne.

BEE POLLEN

Bee pollen has been recognized as a powerful food and medicinal substance for millennia: The ancient Egyptians recognized its importance in a number of their surviving writings, and the Greeks and Romans also used it extensively. Roman legions were issued the dried, pressed cakes of bee pollen as standard issue trail food while in the field. Written accounts of its use exist among the ancient Chinese and Hindu cultures.

Pollen is a fine, powderlike substance, produced by plants as the male contribution—the semen—of plant reproduction. Plants utilize two types of pollination, one accomplished by the wind and the other by insects. Bee pollen, though often containing small amounts of the pollen from wind-pollinated plants, is primarily composed of pollen from insect-pollinated plants. Pollen grains are remarkably varied in color: yellow, buff, orange, purple, dark red, green, chocolate, and black. (Most of the darker colors are rejected by beekeepers who sell pollen. What you get when you buy pollen is usually limited to the yellow, buff, and orange colors.) Bees don't accidentally gather pollen—it is intentionally harvested for the hive's use. The bees carry the pollen from flower to flower during nectar collection, at each stop gathering more. A small number of the pollen grains are distributed to new flower heads during nectar collection, thus performing cross-pollination. But the vast majority are taken to the hive and stored as food for the bees. The bees carry the pollen in what most beekeepers call "baskets" on the bees' legs. The "basket" is actually a hollow or concave part of one joint on the bees' hind legs. When the bees collect the pollen, they mix it with a little nectar and some digestive juices into a soft mass and place it in the basket on their legs. Long elastic lances, like thick hairs, curve inward around

POLLEN, LIKE HONEY, contains a number of unidentified plant compounds and other organics. The moisture content is about 25 percent, the rest being proteins, carbohydrates, fats, vitamins and minerals, and unidentified compounds.[48] The protein in pollen varies from 8 percent to 40 percent depending on the plant source, and it is exceptionally high in water soluble vitamins. It contains vitamins A, C, D, E, B_1, B_2, B_6, niacin (200 mg per 1,000 mg of pollen), biotin, inositol, and folic acid. Pollen also contains minerals such as calcium, phosphorus, potassium (600 mg per 1,000 mg of pollen), magnesium, iron, manganese, silicon, sulphur, chlorine, copper, and zinc. It also contains up to some 27 trace elements,[49] 17 percent of rutin (vitamin P),[50] and a number of ether oils, plant waxes and resins, flavonoids, and carotinoids.[51] In one of the few studies on the difference between pollen before and after being gathered by bees, researchers found that the pre-bee pollen varies in caloric content from 5.56 to 5.97 calories per gram of weight (C/G). However, after the bee gathers the pollen, the caloric content increases to the range of 6.23 to 6.60 C/G.[52] Bee pollen also contains a number of amino acids: arginine (4.7 parts per hundred—pph), histidine (1.5 pph), isoleucine (4.7 pph), leucine (5.6 pph), methionine (1.7 pph), phenylalanine (3.5 pph), threonine (4.6 pph), tryptophan (1.6 pph), valine (6.0 pph), and glutamic acid (9.1 pph). It also contains gonadotropic and estrogenic hormones and Human Growth Hormone Factor (HGH).[53]

the basket to hold the pollen in place. These spears, or lances, penetrate the pollen mass and keep it from dislodging. The majority of the pollen is carried back to the hive in this manner and stored in the comb as a food source, along with honey, for the bees and their young.

Honey provides a highly charged energy source that enables the bees to perform their work and also serves them as a winter food source. Bee pollen, sometimes called bee food, is also a major food source and contains many nutrients, most especially protein, not available in sufficient quantities in honey to meet the bees' needs. The freshly collected pollen varies a great deal in composition, depending on the plant species from which it comes and the weather.

Little really is known about the medicinal effects of *plant pollens* as opposed to *bee pollen*. Like the plant nectar that is altered to form honey, pollen is subtly changed in its interaction with the bees during transport to the hive. To my knowledge, no research has been conducted comparing the medicinal and nutritional effects of any pollen to the plant from which it comes. Such a highly concentrated part of medicinal plant species will inevitably possess medicinal actions, just as the leaves, seeds, and roots do. What little is known about pollen, its medicinal actions, and properties comes from the study of plant pollens after they have been transported and stored by the bees in their hive.

Rita Elkins's exceptional book on pollen and hive products (*Bee Pollen, Royal Jelly, Propolis, and Honey* [Woodland Publishing, 1996]) has some of the best information on the clinical uses and studies of pollen.

Pollen is perhaps the best single source of rutin and protein (assuming you have a high-protein bee pollen). Rutin strengthens capillaries, minimizes bleeding, and encourages coagulation, making it useful for those who bruise easily. The high protein content and other components in pollen have been found to enhance energy and endurance in people who consume it regularly. One British athletic coach, who participated in a clinical trial, noted:

In October 1973, I was asked to test the efficacy of a bee pollen product. I was initially skeptical of the results likely to be obtained by the use of this product. However, I asked five athletes training under me to take bee pollen in accordance with the manufacturer's directions; that is, one to three pills a day. Within a period of 12 months, the athletic performance of all of the five athletes had substantially improved.[54]

Bee pollen has been found to be antibiotic, antiviral, astringent, relaxant, tonic, and nutritive. It has been found effective in treatment of allergies, bacterial infections, asthma, capillary weakness, chronic fatigue, immune depression, menopausal symptoms, nutritional disorders, prostate problems, chronic cystitis, and urinary tract infections.

The primary use of bee pollen as medicine has traditionally been nutritive. Chicken embryo heart growth was found to accelerate when treated with pollen extracts, and gastrointestinal damage in test animals was reversed with a significant increase in weight after taking bee pollen extracts, and two studies on hospitalized children showed significant weight gain and increased serum protein levels when bee pollen was added to their diets.[55] Pollen is so good as a nutritive medicinal that researchers at the Royal Society of Naturalists in Belgium and France noted, "The nutritional tests supervised by the station at Bures on hundreds of mice have demonstrated that pollen is a complete food, that it is possible to let several generations be born and live without the least sign of distress while nourishing them exclusively on pollen."[56] A number of clinicians have commented that it is so effective as a nutritive food that human beings could live on nothing more than a diet of pollen and water.

In countries from Japan to Brazil researchers have used bee pollen in treating a number of prostate problems: prostata-hypertrophy, chronic prostatitis, and prostata vesiculitis. "The experimental-clinical results point to the fact that pollen extracts can be very valuable as specific drugs in the therapy of [prostate illness]."[57] In one Japanese clinical trial on the effects of bee pollen on urination disorders caused by prostatic hyperplasia, researchers noted that "sense of residual urine improved 92%, retardation improved in 86%, night frequency improved in 85%, strain in urination improved in 56%, protraction improved in 53% and the force of the urinary stream improved in 53%."[58] Numerous other studies showed similar results. Even more studies have shown its beneficial effects on prostatitis. One-third to one-half of the patients in clinical trials reported a complete cessation of symptoms; 75 percent noticed significant improvement. No side effects have been noted in any patients. As one report noted, "*In vitro* studies suggest that [bee pollen] is a potent cyclo-oxygenase and lipogenase inhibitor and a smooth muscle relaxant."[59]

A number of researchers have noted "unambiguously good" results from use of pollen extracts in treatment of chronic cystitis and urinary tract infections. One component in pollen, B-sitosterin, was identified as strongly anti-inflammatory and of especial use in cystitis. Researchers commented, however, that there were obvious synergistic actions in pollen that they did not yet understand, noting that the isolated B-sitosterin was not as effective as the bee pollen itself when used for the same conditions.[60]

Though the flavonoids in pollen are not as high as in propolis, another hive product, "these very widespread floral compounds also play a determining role in the medicinal effects" of pollen.[61] Flavonoids provide antiviral action through their ability to stop viral cells from breaking open and infecting the viral host (i.e., us). This antiviral activity combines well with its antibacterial action. Pollen has been found to be effective against *Escherichia coli, Proteus,* salmonella, and some other strains of colibacillus.[62] It has been found in clinical trial that people who consume bee pollen regularly have significantly fewer upper respiratory infections.[63]

Bee pollen was also found to significantly reduce the side effects from radiotherapy. In one trial, women being treated for inoperable uterine cancer experienced less nausea, stronger immune system response, an increase in red and white blood cell count, good appetite, and less weakness and sleep disruption.[64]

Many people with hay fever, allergies, and asthma have experienced good results from the use of bee pollen in alleviating or improving symptoms. The HGH hormones in pollen seem to play a significant role in increased body weight and healthier growth in both clinical trials and empirical studies. In studies in Turkey, bee pollen has been found to be effective in the treatment of male impotency, low sperm count and motility, and male sexual drive.[65] Researchers are presuming the gonadotropic hormones in bee pollen play a role in these results. Conversely, the presence of estrogenic hormones seem to help explain the effectiveness of bee pollen in alleviating the symptoms of menopause in women.

Many of the properties of pollen are in the ether oils and plant resins that are not easily water soluble. Ingesting either the bee pollen itself or an alcohol and water extract, or else including it in fermentation is best. Unlike propolis and honey, bee pollen does not keep well; the fresher the better. The medicinal activity of pollen over one to one and a half years decreases sharply.

PROPOLIS

> *There is a balm in Gilead that makes the wounded whole;*
> *There is a balm in Gilead that heals the sin-sick soul.*
>
> —From an old Christian hymn

Propolis, called Balm of Gilead in the Bible, is a gummy, resinous substance gathered by bees from the leaves and bark of trees. It is gathered from such trees as aspen, poplar, birch, elm, alder, horse chestnut, willow, pine, and fir. The Balm of Gilead—known to the Muslims as balsam Mecca—was gathered from the Middle Eastern evergreen *Commiphora opobalsamum* and the tree from which myrrh comes, *Commiphora absynnica*.[66] However, bees who have hives where there is insufficient tree growth will resort to other substances, such as paint, rubber compounds, and asphalt—not the kind of propolis to take for health.[67] In gathering the resin, the honeybee bites into the sticky substance and transfers it to the pollen basket on its hind legs. It is taken back to the hive, where another bee unloads it for use.

The tree resin is combined by the bees with nectar, pollen, wax, and their own enzymes to make the final propolis mixture. It is then applied to cracks and holes as a sealant in the hive, and it lines the entrance to the hive. Propolis protects the hive from contaminants and sterilizes return-ing bees as they enter the hive. It is a stabilizer, cement, insulator, filler, varnish for the comb, and antiseptic.

Propolis varies in color from light yellowish-green to a dark brown, depending on the plants from which it is gathered and its age. When warm, it is sticky and pliable (as you might expect in a resin), but when cold, it is hard and brittle.

Though rarely used in medicine in the United States, propolis has a long traditional and contemporary use in Western and Eastern Europe. It was widely prescribed by Hippocrates, and in the first century A.D., Pliny the Elder noted that "current physicians use Propolis as a medicine because it extracts stings and all substances embedded in the flesh, reduces swelling, softens indurations, soothes pain of the sinews, and heals sores when it appears hopeless for them to mend." It was used throughout the Middle Ages and even recommended by Culpepper for inflammations and fever.[68]

Propolis has more bioflavonoids than oranges—a major bioflavonoid source—and contains all the known vitamins except vitamin K and all the minerals needed by the body except sulphur. It is composed of 50 percent tree resins, 30 percent wax, 10 percent bee pollen, and 10 percent essen-tial oils. As with honey and pollen, not all the compounds in propolis have been identified.[69]

Propolis has been found effective as an antibacterial, vulnerary, antivi-ral, antibiotic, antifungal, anti-inflammatory, antioxidant, antiallergenic, immune system enhancer, and antiseptic. It retains these qualities, when stored under proper conditions, for many years.

Propolis has been used in Soviet medicine to effectively treat tuberculosis (TB), gastric and duododenal ulcers, eczema, puritis, and septic wound infections. Standard Russian clinical practice for TB recommends 15 to 30 grams of propolis two to three times per day or 15 to 35 drops of an alcohol extract for from one to three months. Ulcers are treated with 12 drops of the extract three times a day for 30 to 35 days. Use has alleviated the heartburn, pain, nausea, and vomiting concomitant with ulceration. Soviet physicians have effectively used propolis in the treatment of juvenile ulcerous stomatitis. The propolis is tinctured one to four in 95 percent grain alcohol and, after tincturing, an equal volume of water is added to the tincture. Dosage is as above.[70] Research has shown that propolis is inhibitory to *Helicobacter pylori*, the bacterium that causes ulcers.[71] The propolis solution described above, 60 drops in a glass of water, used as a gargle, has been found effective in sore throats from colds and flu.

Skin diseases and infected wounds are treated topically,[72] and propolis has been found to be highly effective in the treatment of herpes zoster. Use of a 5 percent propolis solution in 20 cases of herpes completely reduced pain within 48 hours and significantly advanced sore-healing time.[73] Romanian clinicians have used propolis in the treatment of severe acne, prostate inflammation, mouth infections and dental cavities, and burns. Acne and prostate inflammation have been treated with propolis in capsule form. Mouth infections and burns have been treated topically.[74] Propolis has been used with success in filling cavities, preventing further decay, and killing the invading bacteria.

In antiviral studies, a number of compounds in propolis have been found to highly inhibit the replication of various virus types. In combination, these compounds show a highly synergistic activity, producing inhibition beyond their individual activity.[75] Propolis apparently strengthens the virus's protein coat, keeping it isolated from any organism it enters by inhibiting the enzyme that allows the virus to break out of its shell. Propolis also has been found to stimulate phagocytosis and speed detoxification.[76] As such, it has been found to be effective in the treatment of colds and flu. In addition, it seems to obviate fatigue when taken as a daily supplement.

Both alone and in combination with honey, propolis has been found highly effective in the treatment of serious burns. Russian physicians note that it curbs inflammation, disinfects, and stimulates new skin growth.[77] Additional controlled trials were performed in the Netherlands: patients with serious bone necrosis and infection that would normally require amputation and in which standard medical protocols were ineffective were effectively treated with a honey and propolis combination.[78] And Polish studies using propolis found it to inhibit antibiotic-resistant strains of *Staphylococcus aureus*.[79]

Researchers at Columbia University found propolis effective against cancer, inhibiting abnormal cells without affecting normal ones. The Columbia researchers commented that "caffeic acid esters, present in the Propolis of honeybee hives, are potent inhibitors of human colon tumor cell growth."[80]

Traditionally, propolis was difficult to remove from the hives, though modern beekeepers have developed methods to make removal easier. Historically, when mead was made from honey, as noted earlier, the greater portion of the comb, including large amounts of propolis, was taken and boiled to produce the wort from which mead was made. The propolis content of such a historical mead would have been high.

ROYAL JELLY

Royal jelly is a truly unique creation of honeybees. It is synthesized by "nurse" bees—young worker bees between 5 and 15 days of age. The royal jelly is synthesized by the nurse bees' hypopharyngeal glands from a diet of bee pollen and honey. It is a thick, creamy, milky-white substance upon which the queen bee feeds. Royal jelly has remarkable effects upon the queen bee. Born no different from other bees, her life is extended from the usual six weeks that most bees enjoy to five years. She grows to 17 millimeters in length and attains a weight of 200 milligrams, as compared to the normal bees' length of 12 millimeters and weight of 125 milligrams. The queen lays approximately 2,200 eggs each day (200 times her body weight), more than 2,000,000 in her lifetime—a feat no other creature on Earth equals.[81] The eggs laid by the queen that are destined to become queen bees are identical in every respect to eggs that become workers—the only difference is the exclusive diet of royal jelly that makes a bee a queen. Worker bees, during the larval stage, are given royal jelly for a period of about three days. Royal jelly is even more complex than the other hive products. Like those, scientists have been unable to identify all the compounds of royal jelly. Synthetic royal jelly has been made and marketed, but used on young bees it fails to produce queens, and it does not produce the same effects in clinical trials on people as those produced by bee-produced royal jelly. Whereas honey, propolis, and bee pollen all differ from location to location and country to country, no differences have been found in the royal jelly produced by bees throughout the world. Moisture content is about 66 percent, protein 12 1/2 percent, fat 5 1/2 percent, carbohydrates 12 1/2 percent, and 3 1/2 percent of the content of royal jelly has not been identified. Due to the high moisture and nutritive content of royal jelly, it should be an excellent medium for bacterial growth, but it is not—neither in the hive nor out. One compound of royal jelly that might explain this is 10-hydroxy-2-decenoic acid, which possesses strong antibacterial and antifungal activity and makes up 2 to 3 percent of royal jelly.[82] Royal jelly is rich in bee pheromones; natural hormones; amino acids (including all eight essential amino acids), particularly cystine, lysine, and arginine; B vitamins, especially pantothenic acid (B_5); nucleic acids (including DNA and RNA); sugars, sterols, fatty acids, phosphorus compounds, and acetylcholine.[83]

Pantothenic acid helps arm the human body against infection, helps process nutrients, and has shown antiaging effects in clinical trials. Studies have shown consistent and significant increases in the life spans of lab mice fed a pantothenic acid–enhanced diet.[84] Dr. Albert Saenz, in his report "Biology, Biochemistry, and the Therapeutic Effects of Royal Jelly in Human Pathology" (1984) remarking on trials held by the Pasteur Institute of Paris, noted that royal jelly showed remarkable effects in a number of areas. Patients with high blood-serum cholesterol levels who were given royal jelly showed a normalization of readings, patients with Buerger's disease (thromboangiitis obliterans—another arterial disorder) showed significant improvement of symptoms, and elderly patients with mental disturbances and senility also showed significant improvement—probably due in part to the high acetylcholine levels of royal jelly. Acetylcholine plays a crucial role in the transmission of impulses from one nerve fiber to another across synaptic junctions, making it highly useful in the treatment of Alzheimer's disease, Parkinson's disease, and multiple sclerosis. Trials have shown that the trembling associated with Parkinson's disease is markedly reduced in patients taking royal jelly. Saenz also reported that royal jelly showed significant positive effects in treating "deficiency states, referring to malnutrition, slow convalescence after illness or operation, physical or mental exhaustion, loss of appetite, and abnormal loss of weight caused by anorexia nervosa."[85] Researchers in Greece have shown that royal jelly produces significant effects in the treatment of arthritis. And trials in Argentina have documented the high levels of gamma globulin and a precursor to collagen in royal jelly. Use of royal jelly by those researchers in clinical trials produced significant antiaging effects in patient populations, not only slowing tissue degeneration but, in some cases, reversing it completely.[86] Clinical trials at the University of Sarajevo showed that royal jelly possesses strong antiviral activity. When combined with propolis and honey (10 percent royal jelly) and diluted 1 to 10, significant antiviral activity was detected in the patient population. Only 6 percent of the trial subjects receiving the dilute solution suffered viral infections; 40 percent of the placebo group became ill.[87] Canadian researchers in trials on nearly 1,000 lab mice found significant antitumor activity in royal jelly. A mixture of active tumor cells and royal jelly were injected into one group of mice, active tumor cells alone into another. All the mice receiving royal jelly survived with no incidence of tumor growth; the non–royal jelly mice all died within 12 days.

Royal jelly is considered antibacterial, antiviral, antibiotic, antitumor, tonic, nutritive, antiaging, euphoric, alterative, adaptogenic, a hormonal normalizer, and antidepressant. It targets nearly all the systems of the body: immune, cardiovascular, endocrine, integumentary, nervous, reproductive, cellular, skeletal, hepatic, and respiratory. Dr. H. W. Schmidt, in a lecture before the German Medical Association in October 1956 remarked:

> The effects of the active substances and nutrients contained in royal jelly take place throughout the entire body [and it] regulates all [its] functions. From all the investigations and observations that have been made with royal jelly, it is apparent that this substance is a powerful agent composed of hormones, nutrients, enzymes, and biocatalysts. Royal jelly revives and stimulates the functions of cells and the secretions of glands. It also steps up the metabolism, and stimulates the circulatory system. To summarize, . . . [it] works to preserve life and strength in the organism, . . . delays the aging process and helps the organism retain for as long as possible the physical freshness of the body, elasticity of the mind, and psychic buoyancy of youth.[88]

Although clinical trials have not been conducted on reviving sexual function, royal jelly has a long history (some 4,000 years) of normalizing or revitalizing exhausted sexual function. Royal jelly also produces a natural "high" or euphoria when consumed that has occasioned comments by a number of researchers. The use of royal jelly is extremely ancient, especially in China, where it is used in a great array of products from skin care to medicines. Interestingly, the Chinese have made a royal jelly wine for many thousands of years.

The scientific evidence for the efficacy of royal jelly is strongly supportive of the claims that have been traditionally made for the use of meads and honey in diet—that they produce remarkable effects on health, mental functioning, sexual activity, and life span.

BEE VENOM

It may seem odd to also include bee venom in this chapter on meads, but it does have its place. Angry bees were often an inadvertent ingredient of mead making. A hive was located, dug out of its hiding place, and the whole thing placed in a kettle to cook off the wax. The bees were anything but passive in this process. Bees, bee larvae, and the queen were often still present in the hive, and angry worker bees ferociously assaulted the hive stealers, following the hive as it was moved. These might seem to our modern sensibilities somewhat unsavory additives to the brew, but are quite important in their own right. At their most basic, the bees and larvae are significant protein sources, but they also include the other thing that the bee is best known for besides honey—its sting.

Bee venom was widely used in nineteenth-century medicine and is enjoying a strong resurgence today in many parts of the world. Today it is often used clinically through the stinging of live bees, but formerly it was used as Apis extract. *King's American Dispensatory*, authored by John Uri Lloyd and Harvey Felter in 1895, described its production for use by physicians. It involved taking a swarm of live honeybees, placing them in a large jar, and shaking it vigorously to "excite their anger." Alcohol was then added to the jar, the mixture left for a month, and the resulting solution then strained for use. Apis was specific for urinary tract and bladder infections, sore throats, hives and skin inflammations, coughs and colds, and neuromuscular disorders. It was considered diuretic, diaphoretic, anti-inflammatory, and alterative. *King's American Dispensatory* (Cincinnati: Eclectic Publications, 1895) notes:

> We have known of well authenticated cases, where individuals suffering from rheumatism have been cured of that complaint after having been severely stung by the hivebee. We do not recommend this form of hypodermic injection, but prescribe [Apis] for rheumatic conditions with blanched puffiness and the peculiar stinging pain.[89]

Research and clinical practice in the latter part of this century have shown bee venom to produce significant positive results in the treatment of rheumatoid arthritis, gout, multiple sclerosis, lupus, neuralgia, and shingles.[90] Russian research has shown that bee venom blocks the transmission of stimuli to the peripheral and central synapses, strongly influencing the nervous system. It raises the functional activity of the hypophysial-adrenal system, prevents development of convulsive states, is hypotensive, anticoagulant, and expands blood vessels in the brain. Russian clinicians have successfully used bee venom to eliminate prethrombosis states in patients suffering from atherosclerosis and thrombophlebitis.[91] A number of bee venom advocates have insisted that live bee venom (that is, an actual sting) is more efficacious than Apis or other forms of gathered bee venom. However, research by a number of clinicians over a five-year period of time failed to find any significant difference in outcomes in treatment of arthritic patients between live venom and collected venom. No toxicity has been reported in arthritic patients who use bee venom therapy.[92] Sixty-five to 75 percent of the patients with arthritis who used bee venom therapy in clinical trials

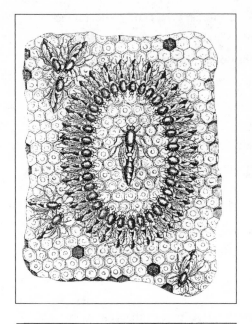

A bee hive.

experienced success with the treatment. Bee venom has been shown to be one of the most potent anti-inflammatories known. One of its components, mast cell degranulating peptide—peptide 401—has been shown to be 400 times as powerful as cortisone. However, hip joints are one of the few areas of the body that do not respond to bee venom.[93] Bee venom is no longer collected in the manner John Uri Lloyd described in 1895; today, electric shock stimulates the bees to sting and the resultant venom is collected. Venom consists of a large number of peptides, enzymes, and amines—the exact makeup and action are not understood.[94] Interestingly, many of the compounds in bee venom also exist in stinging nettles. And nettles have shown positive activity in many of the same conditions for which bee venom is used, such as multiple sclerosis, arthritis, gout, urinary tract inflammation, and hives.[95]

The original meads, made with angry bees included, certainly appear similar to the process of making Apis. It seems quite likely that bee venom was an active component of the ancient healing meads.

HIVE PRODUCTS AND HEALTH

The long-lived of antiquity who ate a diet primarily composed of bee products is impressive: Pythagoras, the Greek philosopher and mathematician, lived to the age of 90. His disciple, Apollonius, lived to 113.

Anacreon, another Greek of antiquity, lived to 115. The Greek Democritus, perhaps one of the world's greatest physicists, lived to 109.

Pliny the Elder researched the ages of people living exclusively on honey and hive product diets late in the first century A.D. He found that in the region of the Apennine mountains, there were an analomous number of people more than 100 years of age. Fifty-four were 100, 57 were between 100 and 110, 2 were 125 years old, and 7 were 135 years of age or older. In Parma, he located 5 who were more than 125, and nearby another 11 more than 100.

Piast, the King of Poland in A.D. 825, was a beekeeper who subsisted primarily on honey and other hive products. He lived to be 120 years of age. One Hebrew tribe, the Essenes, were noted beekeepers and were renowned for their great age—many passing 100 years. Plutarch (A.D. 46–A.D.120) observed that the Britons, who subsisted on great amounts of honey, "only begin to grow old at one hundred and twenty years of age."[96] The original Bardic name of the British Isles was "the Honey Isle of Beli"—beekeeping was a major industry and honey one of its principle commodities. When Pliny the Elder visited the British Isles, he commented that "These islanders consume great quantities of honey brew."[97] A pre–World War II investigation of tombstones in Britain noted that there were many long-lived Britishers who ate a great deal of honey from the comb. A few: Sir Owen of Scotland died at 124 years of age, his last son was born when he was 98, and he walked 74 miles in six days in the last year of his life. Peter Garden, a Scot, died at the age of 131, keeping the appearance of a young man until the very end. William Ellis—130; Mr. Eccleston, Irish—143; Colonel Thomas Winsloe, Irish—146; Francis Consist—150; John Mount, Scot—136; Thomas Parr—152. And throughout the world beekeepers and mead drinkers have been reputed to enjoy extremely long life and good health.[98] Sir Kenelm Digby (see appendix 2) remarked on this when he commented about one of his mead recipes that

> This Meath is singularly good for a consumption, stone, gravel, weak-sight, and many more things. A chief Burgomaster of Antwerpe, used for many years to drink no other drink but this; at Meals and at all times, even for the pledging of healths. And though he were an old man, he was of an extraordinary vigor every way, and had every year a Child, had always a great appetite, and good digestion; and yet was not fat.[99]

Perhaps the most interesting example of remarkable health from modern day is that of Noel Johnson, who at the age of 70 and in poor health began eating a diet consisting largely of honey and hive products. At the age of 90 (1993) he was title holder of the World's Senior Boxing Championship and a seasoned marathoner competing in events on every continent on Earth. He looks to be about 55 years of age.

Too, consumption of mead and honey have long been reputed to enhance sexual prowess and fertility in all cultures that make extensive use of honey. In part, this reflects the procreative supporting properties of royal jelly and bee pollen. Hindus have long eaten honey to increase virility and our own term *honeymoon* comes from the ancient European practice of newlyweds eating nothing but honey for the first 30 days after marriage (a practice that was instituted to increase fertility of the couple and enhance the possibility of an immediate pregnancy).

Though these reports are anecdotal, science is beginning to bear them out in many areas of research. There is good reason to believe that the remarkable properties of heather and honey together produce all the effects attributed to the ancient Mead of Inspiration.

A Complete Hive Mead

Ingredients

> 6 pounds wildflower honey
>
> 1 ounce propolis

1 ounce bee pollen

1 ounce royal jelly

3 gallons water

yeast

Boil honey and water for 30 minutes and skim off foam. During cooling, add propolis, bee pollen, royal jelly— do not strain. Cool to 70 degrees F. Pour into fermenting vessel, making sure the undissolved solids from the propolis, jelly, and pollen go into the fermentation vessel also. Add yeast. Let ferment until complete—16 to 26 days. Add 2/3 teaspoon honey to each bottle (if carbonated mead is desired), fill bottles, and cap. Ready to drink in two weeks to a year, depending on how long you wish to store it—the longer the better.

Please note: I have found that honey beers, meads, sometimes ferment so slowly that it seems as if the fermentation is complete. Then when you bottle them, thinking it finished, the mead continues to ferment, creating tremendous pressure in the bottle. This has sometimes caused the bottle to explode, with can be quite dangerous. To avoid this I now let the meads ferment up to a year in the fermenter or else use a hydrometer to make sure that the fermentation is complete.

THREE

Yeast
A Magical and Medicinal Plant

We cannot draw the wort until the bryggjemann *(brewing man)*
comes. We know he is here when air bubbles start bursting around
the rim of the filter-vat.

— Norwegian village brewer, ca. 1950[1]

Yeasts are so ubiquitous that other plants have to hide their sugars,
whether by skin, by bark and cellulose, or by molecular structure
(by storing the sugar as starch). Yeast has its own allies, however:
enzymes. And at the right temperature the enzyme ally can convert
starch to sugar.

— Dale Pendell, 1995[2]

God made yeast, as well as dough, and loves fermentation just as he
loves vegetation.

— Ralph Waldo Emerson[3]

*T*HE WORLD IS FILLED with those tiny, invisible plant organisms called yeasts. They pervade all parts of the Earth's ecosystem. There are many different kinds, but one in particular has a special relationship with humankind—it is used in fermentation and in baking bread. Called *Saccharomyces*, it is always seeking out sugar; sugar is its food. Unlike the green plants that created the atmosphere and allowed our species to live on this planet, the *Saccharomyces* do something quite different.

Green plants use the chlorophyll in their bodies in interaction with sunlight to create glucose from carbon dioxide and water. Half the glucose they make is changed by them into fructose, and the two molecules hook together to form a two-molecule sugar, sucrose. Sucrose is their energy material; it flows throughout the plant. A little of it is put into the flowers to entice the bees to cross-pollinate them.

Saccharomyces are named from the Greek for sugar or sweet, *saccharo*, and fungus, *mycete*. They are the fungi that eat or like sugar. What they do is different from green plants. They eat sugar and turn it into carbon dioxide and ethyl alcohol, reversing, in part, the process the green plants began. The carbon dioxide is used again by the green plants to make more sucrose that can be eaten again by the yeasts.

To save sugars from the wandering appetite of the yeasts, living beings store or protect the sugars in their bodies in many ways. We protect the sugars in our bodies with our skin and by conversion into glycogen. Plants use bark and skin, too, and they also use a conversion process, turning sugar into starch so the yeasts can't get at it. (And when *we* need those plant sugars for food that have been transformed into starch, an enzyme in our saliva coaxes it out of where it has been so carefully hidden.)

Yeasts are everywhere; their conquest of the world is complete. Dale Pendell comments:

[They] travel on dust, in the air. In cold climates [they]
can winter over, if need be, in the ground, and then take
to the air again in the spring, traveling on anything that
flies. . . . One variety of wild yeast colonizes the wax
bloom right on the skins of grapes. Kind of like a message from God.[4]

Yeasts have had a relationship with humankind since our emergence
on this planet. We love their excrement, the waste products they give off
as they eat sugar—alcohol and carbon dioxide. In baking we want the
carbon dioxide to make the dough rise. In brewing, we want the alcohol
to do the same thing to our spirits. (And isn't it odd that carbon dioxide in
beer promotes alcohol absorption into the bloodstream through the walls
of the stomach at a much faster rate?) In both we want the yeast bodies.
The yeasts themselves have formed an integral part of the human diet for
millennia. We love the alcohol and the carbon dioxide; but beverages
were considered not only drink but a drink/food. And they formed an
important part of the diet of our ancestors.

Like plants, many yeasts have been domesticated. They have been
used by brewers and bakers for a very long time—as humans measure
time. But like medicinal plants, the wild species are more potent, less
liable to weaken. If you compare the power of a wolf—look into its
eyes—with a dog, you can see the difference between the wild and the
domesticated. This distinction is evident in the domesticated plants as
well. They are not as potent, not as strong as wild plants. Nor are they as
strong in resisting disease.

In ancient times, wild yeasts were all that were used. The sugars
were freed from grain by malting, or used directly through the use of
honey or the sap of trees, or converted by saliva or molds, and set out in a
water solution, an offering for the magic yeast. And the yeast would
come. Once ensconced safely in its new food, the yeast would take steps

to protect it. A thick head of foam would form on the surface of the sugar/liquid and the feeding yeast would give off clouds of carbon dioxide gas. Both prevent other yeasts from settling in the food and feeding.

In the Middle Ages but even more today, such wildness is frowned upon, and we avoid wild yeasts whenever possible. Wild yeasts were not always predictable—unwanted yeasts could spoil the brew. So our ancestors developed highly complex ceremonies to prevent such a thing.

Ancient peoples did not have microscopes, but they knew that there was a unique, special substance that came through the air, or sometimes on things, that caused the sugar water (the wort) to become ale. Ancient Norwegian terms for yeast are suggestive of how it was thought of, its *meaning*.

Norway, like much of the world, was mostly composed of isolated settlements; people didn't get around much. As such, each area of Norway, like much of the world, had its own terms for things. The different regions of Norway named the thing that brings the ale into being *gjar*—"working," *gjester*—"foaming," *berm*—"boiling," *kveik*—"a brood that renews a race," *nore*—"to kindle a fire," *fro*—"seed," and one whose exact meaning is unknown—*gong*. But when the wort begins to work in that region, the brewer says that "*Gong* had come into the ale."[5] All the words are suggestive: there is a boiling, a fire being kindled, a new race being born. The commonness of terms associated with burning, boiling, and kindling a fire, for instance, are interesting. Yeast works through a rapid oxidation of the sugar, a kind of burning. And when it is at its most active, the brew—the wort—actually bubbles energetically. This association is clearly a part of older terms for yeast. A term meaning "boiling" is used throughout the world. It is common in many indigenous cultures. Too, when preserved yeast is added to new batches of beer, it is a brood renewing a race that has been dormant (and it is interesting that kveik comes from the same root word as *kvaser*—the being from whom the Mead of Inspiration was made). This concept of livingness and activity is present in all cultures that brew. All old European cultures and indigenous cultures viewed the moment when the wort began to work as one when life had entered it, when the fire had been rekindled.

Once the gong or *bryggjemann* or kveik had come, the brewers and their culture had a special relationship with them.[6] In many cultures, indigenous and otherwise, the wild yeast that came into the wort would be kept and nurtured as a part of the family. Like sourdough starters, some wild yeasts were used for many hundreds of years—no new wild yeasts being coaxed out of the heavens. All regions and clans, even brewers within families, used many differing methods to make the bryggjemann a home until it was time to feed him again. Inside South American and Egyptian clay brewing pots, when they were being made, lines, almost like language, were inscribed in which the yeast could live, in hibernation, until the next brewing. In the southwestern United States, the Papago would sometimes keep a little of the fermented *tiswin* in a special pot until the next year's ceremonial brewing, or else the baskets into whose weave the yeast insinuated itself were saved and used again for only this purpose. In Norway they often used a log or juniper branch.

Juniper branches would be placed in the barrel with the fermenting wort. As the yeast ate and produced offspring, a thick layer of yeast built up in the bottom of the barrel or fermenter, covering the juniper branches. After the beer was drawn off and the barrel was emptied, the yeast-covered juniper branches were taken out and hung up to dry. At the next brewing, a branch was taken down and put into the bottom of the barrel with new juniper branches. The wort was added, and the yeasts awakened from their hibernation and ate, making new beer once again. If a yeast log was used, a section of a birch tree was cut. Sometimes it was shaped and carved, sometimes simply placed in the wort. The yeast covered the log, and at the end, it, too, was hung up to dry. At the next brewing it was placed in the bottom of the fermenter, new wort was added, and fermentation began once again. Interestingly, birch has an extremely sweet sap, somewhat like maple, though weaker. The sap from the freshly cut tree draws the yeast deep within it as they search out its sugar. Then, during drying, the wood of the log cracks, forming deep crevices that allow the yeast to penetrate deep inside during the next brewing. Yeast can easily live a year in such a manner, and if tended to with devotion, will always produce good ale.

At the marriage of children, when a new household was setting up and had no yeast of its own, sometimes the couple would get some from a neighbor, a juniper branch or a scraping from a log. Other times they would begin by trying to get a good ale yeast to come and live at their house, allowing a wild fermentation. This new, wild yeast would then become the kveik that was specific to the new household, and throughout the life of the family it would be the special bryggjemann that came to make ale for the family.

Yeast likes a temperature of around 70 degrees F (like most people). As the temperature drops, the yeast begins to slow down, and when it hits 41 degrees F it goes into hibernation. As the temperature rises, the yeast gets more active. Though yeast will ferment at higher temperatures (100 to 120 degrees F) many think the yeast degraded and the beer produced inferior.* No thermometers were used (or are used now by any rural or indigenous culture); brewers learned the temperature the yeast liked best. The tradition of some Norwegian brewers is quite beautiful. They reach in and touch the back of the hand, gently, to the wort. This might not seem that special until you understand that no one in Norway caresses lovers, family, or children with the palm of the hand; only the back, or "tender" side, is used. The palm is not "nice enough" for showing love.

When the wort was the right temperature, "just a little warmer than the lips," the yeast log was added. Soon, they would say, the kveik or bryggjemann would wake up and come into the wort.

---

* In the seventeeth century, legislation, sponsored by do-gooders of the time, was passed prohibiting hot wort ale brewing in Norway, which was thought to make a more highly intoxicating beverage. One activist remarked, "I trust that if the latest praiseworthy regulation is obeyed, such a harmful habit will be abolished. It is a pity the size of the area makes it difficult for the authorities to get news of every crime."[6]

All parts of the brewing process were attendant with a religious earnestness in every ancient culture. Two aspects of this are of especial importance regarding the yeast. First, cultures seemed to take one of two approaches to yeast—one noisy, the other quiet and solemn. In one approach, it is felt that excited, sometimes even angry, strong energy helped the yeast to work more effectively. The Papago, in making the fermented tiswin, dance and sing noisily alongside the building where tiswin is made to encourage the yeast to wake up and act strongly. Some Norwegian brewers, when making extra-strong ale, would stamp around and act angry. "The angrier he was the stronger the ale."[7] Alternatively, it is felt that the wort must be protected from anything that could "startle" the yeast and stop the fermentation. This attitude of respect and reverence is the more pervasive of the two throughout the brewing world. It is felt that the bryggjemann, or the spirit of the yeast, should be left alone to work in peace. The disrespect of stomping about, of looking in the fermenter as it worked, might scare the yeast and thus produce a bad ale. The bryggjemann would be upset and not do his work well.

It is easy for scientists to ridicule such beliefs, though it is unlikely they would ridicule such Western actions as praying before a meal—at least not in public. But this kind of reverence pervades indigenous and older societies. Each life-form, whether a cactus, stone, or yeast, is viewed as an expression of the sacred, with its own intelligence, awareness, and sacred nature. Human disrespect of other life-forms and of the sacred, it is felt in all cultures except the technological ones, can lead only to a bad outcome.

The second common element of reverence related to yeast is the initial ceremony just before the yeast is added. This is common in many cultures. The Papago have one when they make tiswin and many older Norwegian brewers do also. For instance, one very old Norwegian brewer commented that she always took a little of the sweet wort before adding the yeast, went to the four corners of the brewing house, and poured a little in each corner "for the corner crones." Another commented that "The brewer [always gives] the spirit some of the first and best of the wort from the filter-vat. It [is] poured into the four corners of the hearth, and the gift [is] repeated when the copper start[s] to boil."[8] This offering to the four directions, for instance, with tiswin, is common throughout the indigenous world, and in many respects is similar to the offering of a "spirit plate." Spirit plates, used often in Native American ceremonies, are filled with a selection of each of the foods at any ceremonial meal and left outside as an offering of respect. This is done in those cultures for much the same reasons it has been done in Norway. If there is no reverence for the sacred, if the proper ceremonies are not followed, the least that can be expected is that the ale will not ferment. In the worst case, if spirit is not "fed," given nourishment, it disappears from human life. And human life, then, becomes empty. Neglecting to give proper reverence to spirit is an arrogance, a belief that human beings can rely only on themselves, an assertion that all successful things come from themselves alone. Within indigenous cultures, to do such a thing causes, as Black Elk, the Lakota holy man, once observed, everything that a human does to become foolish.

But when the sacred is recognized and nourished, it helps human beings in their endeavors. Odd Nordland shares one story from a Norwegian brewer.

> [Tone Lund] was used to seeing the ale "dressed" in foam in the course of an hour, but this [new] ale did not react at all.
>
> While she was resting for a moment on the bed in despair, a woman entered. Tone thought she knew her, though she could not quite place her. But she [the woman] was lively and good natured.
>
> "I can't get the ale to start working," said Tone. "I don't know why," she said.
>
> "Don't you know?" said the woman. "You have forgotten to give something to the spirit of the hearth," she said.

When reminded, [Tone] gave the spirit his share at
once, and the ale "dressed" immediately. It started working so violently that it ran over the edge of the tub.[9]

The success of the fermentation is of great importance in all older
cultures, and because it was held to be a religious event, not a secular one,
its every element was imbued with sacred meaning. One of the difficulties
of viewing a sacred activity from a secular perspective is that within a secular orientation, all things are viewed as without meaning—as just events.
From value-free judgments, observers of non-Western, meaning-imbued
cultures have too often moved into valueless observations. To cultures
that have felt the life force of plants or of brewing, who have felt themselves make a deep connection with that life force, brewing is not a science—it is an art filled with the actions of the sacred. If they fail to show
proper reverence in their actions, if their mind wanders, if they aren't
properly attentive to the life force in each part of brewing, they and their
community pay for it by the failure of the ale. In some instances, the ceremonial brewing is of such importance, as with the Papago, that failure is
filled with tremendous danger to the continuance of the community.

The activity of yeast, and what it offers to human beings, has been
an integral part of human success since the dawn of time. Its presence was
integral to most of the food production and to the ceremonies around
which food production occurred.

In some cultures, such as the ancient Egyptian, brewers harvested
excess yeast from brewing. They sold or gave it to the bakers, who made
bread. And in many cultures, especially the Egyptians', bread was made
into beer and ale that made more yeast that made more bread. Yeast can
be gathered from off the top of the fermenting beer, from the thick fluff
that forms to protect the sugar water, or gathered from the bottom of the
fermentation after the beer is drawn off.

The terms *ale*, *beer*, *wine*, and *mead* can be somewhat confusing. In
reality, all of them are simply natural fermentations, very much the same

thing. All natural fermentations can be thought of as wines. Indeed, fermented barley was thought of by the Romans as a barley wine, not a beer. Fermented beverages from birch or palm saps are sometimes called a wine, sometimes a beer. Originally, however, ale was any fermentation made from grain, usually barley. Beer was *only* an ale with hops added during brewing. Mead was fermented honey, and wine was fermented fruits, usually grapes. Now natural fermentations are generally called either beer or wine, and the old distinctions between beer and ale have fallen away. But if a distinction is still to be made between ale and beer, it is that a certain kind of *Saccharomyces* likes to feed on the bottom of the fermenter at cooler temperatures. This bottom feeding—*Saccharomyces uvarum* or (originally) *Saccharomyces carlbergensis*—yeast is what is used to make beer. *Saccharomyces cerevisiae* like to eat on the top and prefer it warmer. They make ale, and are members of the same family, but with different table manners.

The *Saccharomyces* yeasts are not the only ones that eat sugar and excrete carbon dioxide and alcohol, they are just the commonest that are used, the ones we like the taste of best. There are many others. Some commercial brewers in Belgium still use only wild yeasts in their fermentation of lambic. More than 30 different wild yeasts ferment their beers, the main ones being *Brettanomyces lambicus* and *Brettanomyces bruxellensis*. Indigenous beers contain scores more. Numerous species of *Pseudomonas*, *Lactobacillus*, *Leuconostoc*, *Schizosaccharomyces*, *Endomycopsis*, *Hansenula*, and *Saccharomyces* have all been identified. Every type of yeast conveys its own special properties and flavors during fermentation. All of the yeasts have specific nutritional and medicinal qualities.

Apart from any medicinal or nutritional qualities contributed by hops or other plants used in making traditional beers, the act of fermentation itself creates a powerful medicinal and nutritional beverage. For instance, consider only a few of the changes that occur in Indonesian *tape*, a primitive rice wine or beer, during fermentation: lysine is increased 15 percent, thiamine increases 300 percent, and protein content is doubled.

This is common in all grains, sugars, and plants that are fermented. Yeasts synthesize B-complex vitamins to foster fermentation. Through fermenting, they produce the primary source of B-complex vitamins in many indigenous diets. Brewer's yeasts contain essential trace minerals: selenium, chromium, and copper, in amounts comparable to fresh fruits and vegetables. The yeast plant itself is also high in protein. The longer a beverage is fermented, the greater the number of yeasts produced. Thus, in the fermentation of beers, a protein source is created where none or little existed before. For example, natural cassava root protein is about 1 1/2 percent. Fermented cassava, on the other hand, is about 8 percent protein.* This "biological ennoblement" of plants and sugars through fermentation produced a primary dietary source for our ancestors.[10]

Brewer's yeasts also contain the highest glucose tolerance factor (GTF) found in *any* food. GTF acts with insulin to promote glucose utilization by the body. Thus, it helps the body utilize glucose more efficiently. Brewer's yeast, because of its high GTF levels, can reduce the insulin requirements for diabetics. It additionally has been shown to reduce serum cholesterol and triglyceride levels in elderly patients. Yeast, too, has long been used in the effective treatment of beriberi (caused by vitamin B_1 deficiency) and pellagra (from niacin deficiency).

Saccharomyces yeasts were used in standard practice herbal medicine in the nineteenth and early twentieth centuries and were considered stimulant, tonic, nutritive, antiseptic, and laxative. They maintained normal bowel movement in those with tendencies toward constipation, built up those suffering from nutritive wasting or from a long illness, and showed remarkable antiseptic properties. Brewer's yeast was used as a poultice, along with slippery elm bark, on sloughing ulcers, festering wounds with

---

* The temperance movements, primarily Protestant groups (now with the addition of social workers), have traditionally had a serious effect on indigenous health. When colonial governments were motivated to prohibit traditional fermentations, the native cultures began to suffer from diseases their traditional beverages had specifically prevented. Zealously insisting that they were *promoting* native health, temperance movements have had quite the opposite effect.

a tendency to gangrene, boils, and carbuncles. And it was used regularly in the treatment of diabetes. Contemporary medicine uses it in treatment of pellagra, beriberi, as a nutritional additive, for diabetes, and for lowering serum cholesterol levels.[11]

That indigenous cultures knew the importance of fermentation to their diets cannot be doubted. Most of the world subsists, in the main, on vegetarian diets. Vegetarians tend to lack sufficient vitamin B_{12} for health (a vitamin that fermenting yeasts make in profusion). Rice diets, in addition, lack riboflavin and thiamine (leading to beriberi), which yeasts make in profusion. Maize diets are low in niacin (leading to pellagra), which yeasts also make in profusion. And many diets are low in vitamin C (leading to scurvy), especially during winter, which most fermented beverages contain in profusion.[12]

African diets that consist primarily of maize are low in niacin, but those who drink substantial quantities of Kaffir beer never get the disease. In spite of a lack of fresh vegetables and fruits, the Otomi Indians of Mexico rarely get scurvy, because their traditional pulque, an agave cactus beer, contains so much vitamin C. Otomi who don't drink pulque get cheilosis (a riboflavin and B-complex deficiency disease), but the disease is rare among the pulque drinkers. And no Otomi who drink pulque ever get thiamine deficiency diseases.[13] However, it must be pointed out that indigenous cultures and rural European drinkers, such as the Norwegians, tend to drink beer that is not as clarified as the type we drink in the United States. All traditional beers were unclarified by today's standards. The yeast remained in the brew and was drunk along with it. So, if you are making your own, let the yeast that settles in the bottom of the bottles flow into your glass—it's good for you.

But, these practicalities aside, in all cases where oral accounts still exist, the knowledge of fermentation was a gift of the gods, of the sacred, to humankind. Indigenous cultures and older European brewers recognized that *all* the stages that led to successful brewing were sacred and should be attended with mindfulness and ceremony. Of all the steps, however, it was the moment when fermentation was ready to begin that was most important. It was at this time that "evil influences" could intervene and spoil the beer. Even thinking of this from our Western perspective, we can agree with that older perspective. It is at this moment that another kind of yeast, a yeast that will produce bad beer or wine, can get into the wort and produce an undrinkable fermentation. So once the wort has been prepared, great steps are always taken to protect the wort and usher in only the one spirit, the yeast, that will produce good beer.

The Charoti of South America view the time of fermentation as "the birth of the good spirit"[14] in the wort. And they take steps to make sure that no "bad spirit" gains entry first. There is a religious reverence attending this stage of brewing and a great mindfulness. The Charoti believe that brewing must take place at night (a belief also common to many Norwegian brewers). However, it is at night that many evil spirits are abroad, making the process much more difficult. The Charoti say that there are many bad spirits that will try to "prevent the birth of the good spirit."[15] So they sing and play musical instruments throughout the first night while waiting for fermentation to begin. Once the good spirit enters the wort, it is powerful enough to stop any bad spirits from getting into the beer. Throughout the ceremony of encouraging the good spirit to enter and begin fermentation, the Charoti singers keep their attention focused on the essence of the good spirit, calling its intelligence into awakening, urging it to hear their call, exhorting it to come to them and settle into the home they have prepared for it.

Hearing the description of this process without prejudice and comparing it to the description of Western brewers, it is not so very different. We wish only one yeast, the good one, to come and ferment our beer. And we take steps to prevent the bad ones from getting there first. We know, too, that once the good yeast is in the wort, it is very difficult for a bad one to gain entry. We place our emphasis on sterility and personally introducing a yeast that we buy. But those cultures who depend on wild yeasts use prayer to influence its appearance. Though to our Western way of thinking this is superstition, modern science is continuing to show that human perception and intention, prayer, can affect outcomes. (See, for instance, Larry Dossey's *Healing Words* [New York: Harper Collins, 1993.]) Further, Western science is beginning to understand the Earth's ecosystem as one living entity, Gaia, a claim that indigenous peoples have made for thousands of years. Indigenous cultures go further, however. They insist that Gaia has intelligence and awareness and that human beings can communicate with her. They also insist that it is possible for human beings to communicate with individual elements of the ecosystem, such as plants. Studies, such as those discussed in *The Secret Life of Plants* (New York: Harper Collins, 1989), show that plants grow better when people talk to them, when music is played, when they are, as one medicine man observed, treated like human beings.

Interestingly, as regards medicinal plants, cultures widely disconnected have found not only the same medicinal uses for plants, but also the same spiritual uses. It is suggestive that almost all indigenous cultures have similar beliefs and ceremonials about yeasts and the beginning of fermentation. How could cultures in South America and North American and Siberia and Africa, which have never had contact with each other, have the same kinds of ceremonies and beliefs about the moment when yeasts enter the fermentation vessel? By our way of thinking, they cannot. Yet, they do. The members of indigenous cultures insist that they are not making this all up but that they *know* the good spirit that enters the wort. It has a certain feeling to it, a certain essence, an intelligence that they can feel. And their descriptions of the process are very much like our own. Some cultures, like the Norwegian and the Papago, often keep the spirit of the yeast, the "good spirit," in hibernation until needed again. Others rely on a new wild one each time they brew. But they do recognize what happens even if they describe it differently than we do.

The Charoti are not alone in how they think. The Tarahumara of northern Mexico are similar. They, like the Otomi, brew a beer called pulque from the sweet sap of the agave cactus. And they, too, pray to usher in the spirit of fermentation. They do not dance, being of the "quiet" school. They believe that they have to be particularly mindful when the moment of fermentation comes, because if they are not, if they do not hold the "space" for the spirit to enter the agave wort, the liquid will not ferment. The Tarahumara, like some Norwegians, call it "boiling" when fermentation begins. They use special fermentation jars that are considered sacred and are never washed. Once a jar "learns to boil," it is

Medieval cooks.

placed near other jars (filled with unfermented pulque) that have not learned how to boil, so that they might be taught to do so. (The yeast in the jar that has learned how to boil then enters the unfermented pulque and begins fermentation, thus "teaching" the new jar.) Once a jar learns how to boil, it is sacred and kept only for making pulque. Never washed, it has residues of yeasts in it and initiates fermentation whenever new, unfermented pulque is added to it. Interestingly, the Tarahumara (and some other cultures) place wormwood, an *Artemisia* species (see "About Wormwood" in chapter 7), on top of the covered jars once they start fermenting to "frighten away the evil spirits who might want to spoil the liquor."[16] *Artemisia* is strongly antibacterial, antiseptic, and antifungal—it can be used in the treatment of yeast infections.

The Ainu, the indigenous tribal culture of Japan, see fermentation in much the same way as the Tarahumara. When the wort is ready, they circle around it and make prayers and offerings to Kamui Fuchi, the hearth goddess and guardian spirit. They call on her to protect the wort from the intrusion of "bad spirits" that can infect the wort and help bring the good spirit to awaken their rice or millet beer into potency. In return they offer her the first drink of beer, poured onto the hearth. While it is fermenting, they chew quantities of mugwort, an *Artemisia* species (see "About Mugwort" in chapter 9), and place it, along with other things, around the brewing vessel to protect it from infection.[17]

And the Ifuagao headhunters of the Philippines dance. Like the Papago, the Charoti, and many others, they dance and call on the spirit to come and infuse the wort, to "increase and improve the brew"[18] and to ask help in preventing bad influences from infecting the fermentation. Then, later, they perform the *tungale* rite to, again, increase the rice beer's potency and its quantity. They call their rice beer "the wine of the children."

> We do the *tungale* rite for the wine of the children so
> that it will increase miraculously, so that it [will] be like
> a slow whirlpool, so that it [will] be like the stars, so
> that it [will] be like the bamboo of the Downstream
> Region which does not become watermarked and is
> impregnable [i.e., will not become infected], so that it
> will overcome the kindred [i.e., other, less benevolent
> spirits] on both sides.[19]

Yeasts, like more complex plants, respond to being "treated like a human being." The scores of recipes for beer I offer in this book suggest the use of a domesticated, store-bought yeast. But if you can bring your-self to experiment, you might try making some of them with wild yeast. When the wort is ready, you might leave it out, uncovered, in a container with a wide opening. Then sit near it and begin to talk with the spirit of the yeast—to call on the bryggjemann or kveik to come—and see what it is like. To do so means reconnecting to the ancient tradition of fermenta-tion—to connect to the thousands of wise women and wise men standing over their brewing vessels in small villages around the world calling on the spirits of fermentation to come to the wort and kindle the fire in it. Once you have brought a wild yeast to live at your home, place a carved stick in the fermenter and allow the yeast to fall deeply within its carvings. When the beer is finished, take the stick out and hang it up to dry somewhere out of the way. At your next fermentation, take it down and place it in the fermenter and call on it once again to awaken to life.

If you do risk calling on a wild yeast and the wort turns out badly, what will you do then? you might ask. The wise ones might answer, "Perhaps you will have to dance harder the next time."

Some little things I planted in my field
Crawling on hands and knees
With my weed hoe.
Nothing could I raise
That would ferment.

Only my child knew the plants
That were around us.
Repeatedly did he go picking them,
And in the palm of my hand he placed them.
With water I mixed them;
Crouching before the jar I sat,
Desiring that speedily it would ferment.
After two mornings it felt kindly toward me
And gloriously it fermented.

—Part of the Papago Mockingbird Speech
at the making of tiswin[20]

FOUR

Sacred Indigenous Beers

Just as the life force of an animal is contained in its blood, so are fermented beverages infused with the life force of the plants from which they are made. Those plants that are more important to the survival of man, or which have stimulating psychological effects upon him, are, in tribal and early Western societies, thought to incorporate a particularly powerful force. Thus, throughout the ancient Mediterranean regions, alcoholic beverages "assumed a mythologic and sacred character, being, as it were, the very life essence of the cereal god." When the spirits of these plants are personified by a patron deity, the beverage then becomes the "blood" or "milk" of that god or goddess which embodies all the life-giving, stimulating, and other supernatural and magical virtues of these most sacred of substances.

—Mikal Aasved, 1988[1]

*S*ACRED INDIGENOUS BEERS are central to the culture in which they are used. All of them center around their sacred origins and purposes, the one to three plants that are used to make the fermented beverage, the moment of fermentation, and the consumption of the beverage itself. All of them are considered essential to the ability of the culture to successfully continue, and all of them are known by the culture to be a gift of the sacred to humankind.

Because the vast majority of indigenous cultures have a sacred fermentation, there are literally scores of such fermentations throughout the world. The only areas that do not appear to have developed fermentation as an essential part of their culture are Australia and a few areas of North America. Plant fermentations exist throughout Africa and South America, all of them, primarily, still indigenous or tribal in nature. Indigenous European brews are almost extinct, having been transformed into large commercial processes over the past 500, and especially the last 75 years. Shadows of the original indigenous beers of Europe, remarkably similar to those in Africa and South America, still do exist in a few, small cultural islands that have not yet completely succumbed to industrialization. These are most often found in Scandinavia and Eastern Europe. Asian fermentations are an interesting mix, as is almost everything in that amazing continent. In the highly industrialized centers, fermentation is heavily commercialized and not so different from that in the United States. But Asian cultures have not really discovered the idea of suburbia; there is a remarkably sharp differentiation between city and country life. Few in the West know that there is still an indigenous tribal culture in Japan, the Ainu, who live much as their ancestors did. And they still have a sacred fermentation of their own, though it is now prohibited by the Japanese government. Even in the heavily commercialized brewing of Asia, however, it is still possible to discern the roots of traditional fermentation. And many rural peoples still use, essentially, the same basic processes that have been followed for thousands of years.

One recurring problem with the discussion of indigenous beers is that the word "beer" is never used within the indigenous cultures themselves. Each sacred fermented beverage has its own, unique name. And anthropologists can't seem to make up their minds about indigenous fermentations. Some call them "beer"; others call the very same drink "wine" and there seems to be little logic in the decision process. Fermented maple sap is usually called a beer, fermented birch sap may be called either a beer or a wine, fermented palm sap usually a wine but sometimes a beer, and fermented agave cactus sap is usually called just pulque and rarely referred to as either a beer or a wine. I am not sure I have the capacity to solve this linguistic tangle. I think of them all as fermentations and, for the purposes of this book, as beers.

It would be possible to focus an entire work on the indigenous beers of the world, but many of them use essentially the same grains, fruits, or trees. The legends, too, are remarkably similar about the appearance of those plants and the process of fermentation. Here are some of them.

TISWIN

THE SACRED SAGUARO BEER/WINE OF THE PAPAGOS

Saguaros . . . they are Indians too. You don't ever throw anything at them. If you hit them in the head with rocks you could kill them. . . . You don't do anything to hurt them.

—Frank Crosswhite, 1980[2]

Dizziness is following me!
Close it is following me.
Ah, but I like it.

Yonder far, far
On the flat land it is taking me.

Dizziness I see.
High up there I see it.
Truly I like it.
Yonder they lead me.
And dizziness they give me to drink.

'Tis at the foot of little Gray Mountain
I am sitting and getting drunk.
Beautiful songs I shall unfold.

—Traditional Papago song after drinking saguaro wine[3]

The saguaro, the largest cactus in the world, is, in many respects, the sacred tree of the Papago, and from its fruits they make a sacred fermentation called tiswin or, sometimes, *nawai*. Like many indigenous fermentations, anthropologists sometimes call it a wine, sometimes a beer, a source of great confusion to the reader.

The Papago Indians are an agricultural tribal people who live in the Sonoran Desert of northern Mexico and southern Arizona; they call themselves *Tohono O'odham*, "the Desert People." Unlike surrounding tribes, they have no major rivers or canals available for irrigation. The annual rainfall is scant, and the Papago have developed an agriculture centered around three plants: the saguaro, the tepary bean, and corn. Their skill in desert "water harvesting" agriculture is one of the most sophisticated in the world.

Saguaros often stand to 20 feet in height, and their fruits are harvested with a specially constructed, extremely long pole. The Papago make no fewer than 12 products from saguaro fruit, all of which play a major role in the cultural life of the tribe. Among them is a sweet concentrated fruit syrup, somewhat like molasses. This is made by taking two parts fruit pulp to one part water and cooking it slowly, one to two hours, to reduce the liquid. The syrup is then strained to remove the foreign matter and returned to the pot for another hour or so of gentle boiling. It is stored in clean jars for future use. For fermentation, the syrup is mixed with water to thin it. Various concentrations of syrup to water have been used: 1 to 1, 1 to 2, 1 to 4, or even 1 to 16.

Tiswin

> *Ready, friend!*
> *Are we not here drinking*
> *The shaman's drink,*
> *The magician's drink!*
> *We mix it with our drunken tears and drink.*
>
> —A portion of the Papago ritual of the tiswin ceremony[4]

Ingredients

  8 quarts cleaned saguaro cactus fruit pulp (though it is not identical, fruit from the prickly pear can be substituted and is available in many Mexican food markets—it has been used by other tribes to make a similar drink)

  4 quarts water

  wine yeast

Slowly cook the fruit pulp and water for one to two hours after it begins to boil. Let cool enough to handle; strain and return the syrup to the fire for another hour, boiling slowly. Remove from heat and cool to 70 degrees F. Pour into fermenter and add wine yeast. Seal with air lock and allow to ferment four days (if you want to taste a traditional tiswin) and drink. Or wait until fermentation is complete, bottle, and store.

ABOUT SAGUARO
Carnegia gigantea

> *In that [mist] for you the red liquor*
> *I dipped and poured;*
> *I, having drunk, gave to you;*
> *I drew you forward and set you in the circle.*
> *You swallowed and were gloriously drunk,*
> *Then I was not ungenerous with beautiful speech*
> *And with beautiful singing.*
> *Thus, vying together, we made an end.*
>
> —A portion of the Papago ritual of the tiswin ceremony[5]

It is said that in the long ago times, at the time of the first people, there was a sacred infant who was left unattended by his mother. I'itoi, Elder Brother, saw this and his tears fell to Earth and upon the child, whereupon they both sank into the ground. The first people, when they found the child gone, began to search, but they could not find him until Crow began flying over their heads, calling out to them. Hearing this, they began to follow, and Crow landed on top of a 30-foot-tall saguaro cactus, a plant they had never seen before. Here, Crow ate some of the saguaro fruit and regurgitated it into a basket, saying to it, "you know what to do." Whereupon the fruit began to ferment. When it was finished fermenting, the wine began to sing the Rain Song.

> *Here I stand,*
> *The Wind is Coming Toward me,*
> *Shaking.*

> *Here I stand,*
> *A Cloud is coming toward me,*
> *Shaking.*[6]

The people all gathered there together and drank the fermented fruit wine. They were so intoxicated that they became afraid and decided to get rid of the saguaro. They called upon Badger, giving him all the seeds of the plant, which he was instructed to throw into the ocean. On the way he met Coyote, who tricked him into throwing the seeds up in the air, where the wind took them and spread them. Soon saguaro began coming up everywhere.

When the people saw this, they gathered at a saguaro to decide what to do. As they were standing there, the child for whom they had been searching rose out of the top of the saguaro. Patiently, the boy showed them how to make the sacred saguaro wine. The people were told, "Now you must do something in return for this gift." One of the young men asked, "What must we do?" In response, the child began to sing the first of more than a hundred rain songs that the Papago must remember and sing each year. The first was "I Draw the Rain."

Here I am sitting
and with my power I draw the south wind toward me.
After the wind I draw the clouds,
and after the clouds I draw the rain
that makes the wild flowers grow on our home ground
and look so beautiful.[7]

The people were told that they must always remember the songs and ceremonies and do them each year, for if they stopped, there would be no more rain. I'itoi then came and gave the women the cactus poles for gathering the ripe fruits, agave-fiber head rings for balancing the collecting baskets on their heads, told them the injunctions that governed the use of the saguaro, and showed the people the ceremonies they were to follow in preparing the wine. "I'itoi [then] told the people to drink the saguaro juice just as the earth drinks rain, and that will help the rain come."[8] And this they have done ever since.[9]

‹Ꙩ›

Of the Papago's primary agricultural crops, the saguaro is a wild plant; the other two, tepary bean and corn, are domesticated. The tepary bean is unique, having an astonishingly rapid life cycle, perfectly adapted to the desert and its summer thunderstorm pattern. The Papago species of corn, unlike other indigenous corns, has an extremely low sugar content (which probably explains, in part, why they never ferment it) and only needs the scant rainfall of their region in order to grow.

The seasonal thunderstorms are crucial to the Papago, and tribal life centers around their arrival. The fruits of the saguaro cactus ripen at the time of greatest food scarcity for the tribe, just before the arrival of the annual rains. The fruits ripen at the end of the past year's seasonal cycle and the beginning of the new. The last month of the Papago calendar (May) is called *Kai Chukalig Mashad*, the month when the saguaro "seeds are turning black." The first month of the new year is called *Hashani Mashad*, "Saguaro [harvesting] month." The tiswin ceremony is then the major ceremony of the Papago year. It is a time of purification for the past year and an opening up to the potential of the new. It readies the land, the people, and the crops for new growth and calls the rains to come.

Each part of the harvesting of saguaro fruit and the making of tiswin is filled with sacred meaning. Even as they approach the saguaro, the Papago honor it and offer prayers, and they call out to each other, saying, "See, the liquor is growing." The fruits are experienced as beginning their fermentation at the moment they are picked. Once harvested, they are taken back to camp, and the pulp is separated from the seeds and cooked down into syrup. To each jar of syrup the medicine man then comes, and with his breath and tobacco smoke he purifies it. It is then mixed with water. Young men, using only their hands, slowly mix the liquid for up to four hours, saying as they begin, "I am now mixing you up. Do me the favor to bring good wind and clouds and rain, and to keep the people from bad behavior after they have drunk the wine."[10] The elders of the tribe taste the mixture, and when they feel it is ready, it is taken into a "round house" called *yahki*—which means "the rain house"—where it is poured into four containers (fermentation *ollas*) of five to six gallons each, one at each of the cardinal directions. Each is settled into a shallow depression in the ground lined with straw. A fire of mesquite or ironwood is kept burning in the round house to keep the temperature constant. The wine is fermented by using a "starter" from the previous year, by wild yeasts, or by the yeast residues in the containers from the previous year. The fermentation is fairly rapid and is allowed to continue for four days. During this time the Papago dance and sing outside the round house to "help the beer along." The fermenting beer is closely watched during its fermentation. If it ferments too fast, more water is added; if too slow, more syrup is poured in.

The fermenting beer is watched over by an elder and four assistants, who watch round the clock in two shifts. This is to make sure "that it should never be alone and subject to evil influences."[11] And they constantly sing the songs they were taught in the original time—the songs always being sung four times or a number of times divisible by four. Lumholtz (1912) noted the enthusiasm and passion of their singing. "In their enthusiasm they seemed to be trying to wring the rain from the gods. . . . Every time a new stanza came around, they intoned as is their custom, the first words with all the power of their lungs, giving [the] singing a triumphant expression."[12]

The moment when fermentation begins is the most important and also the most fraught with peril. To prevent any possible problem, the old men sit with the fermenting vessels "to sing, lest any magic influence it, and outside, the people must sing it into fermentation."[13] Such singing, as I note in *Sacred Plant Medicine* (Boulder, CO: Roberts Rinehart Publishers, 1996), is an integral part of the sacred knowledge of plant medicine in the Americas. Plant song is, as Kathleen Harrison has so ably observed, "part of an encyclopedia on the sonic level of the same thing that seeds are on another level."[14] Such songs are an integral aspect of the gathering of sacred plant knowledge from sacred realms. They are a mnemonic device that re-creates the sacred states in which the sacred dimension of plants were first encountered. Such songs are never "made." They are given in vision states when knowledge of the sacred plant itself is conveyed to mankind. The anthropologist Ruth Underhill observed that these songs also hold within them powerful magic,

> [a] magic which called upon the powers of Nature and constrained them to man's will. People sang in trouble, in danger, to cure the sick, to confound their enemies, and to make crops grow . . . song became not only the practical basis of Papago life, but also the most precious possession of the people. . . . The describing of a desired event in the magic of beautiful speech was to them the means by which to make that event take place. All their songs describe such desired events. . . . Magic will be worked if the description is vivid and if the singing or the recitation is done, as it should be, at the right time and with the right behavior, on behalf of all the people.[15]

For the songs to re-create the requisite sacred states, the singers must hold within themselves the experiential knowledge of the state of being and the sacred territory from which the song is manifested. Thus, the song is an expression of that sacredness and re-creates, renews in the world the particular sacredness out of which it originally came. This reinvigoration of the secular world with the sacred through song, in the particular instance of the Papago, manifests the necessary sacred movements toward rain that are integral to the survival of the Papago and that are intimately connected to the powers of the saguaro.

The focus of mind of the participants must never waver, or the sacredness they are re-creating, and, subsequently, the return of the rain they are calling, might fail. Therefore, an "atmosphere of order, sincerity, and devotion" pervades the entire process of making tiswin.[16] When the fermentation is complete, the people gather, and the stories of the gift of the beer to the people are retold, as are the injunctions for proper behavior that I'itoi laid upon them. A first bit of the wine is given to each of the four directions and to I'itoi and Mother Earth. Then the people begin to drink. They do not stop until it has all been consumed.

Unfortunately, like many deeply religious indigenous ceremonies, for a long time, the saguaro beer ceremony was forbidden by both American and Mexican authorities. A major impetus for these legal restrictions by secular government came from religious groups, especially women's religious temperance groups such as the Ladies' Union Mission School Association, who, in 1895, mounted a strong campaign against the making of tiswin. Spanish Catholic priests and Protestant ministers alike condemned the beer ceremonies, and a 1925 legal challenge to the law, arguing that the ban violated the First Amendment, was defeated in the Arizona courts. Many tribal members were subsequently converted to Christianity and abandoned their traditional ceremonies, and in the last 50 years the practice and understanding of the ceremony has deteriorated badly. However, there is now a general return to traditional Earth ceremonies among many indigenous peoples, and a number of groups (including those that at one time helped pass bans) are supporting the reemergence of the saguaro wine ceremony among the Papago.

Besides being a nutrient and the source of a sacred beverage, the saguaro and its products have a number of medicinal properties. Saguaro fruit and wine, in sufficient quantities, act as an emetic. Smaller quantities of the mashed fruit pulp have traditionally been used as a gruel to stimulate lactation after childbirth.[17] Slices of the fresh stem are used by the Seri Indians as a cure for rheumatism and aching joints.[18] The seeds are very nutritious, with a high fat content. ("One 4-H boy produced prodigious growth in his poultry flock with these seeds."[19])

The alcohol content of saguaro wine is about 5 percent. Some, sampled in 1871 after being stored in the Smithsonian for three years, was described as being "in every respect superior to much of the wine on sale [in the United States]."[20] It reputedly tastes similar to strawberry wine, though other Anglo tasters thought it had "the taste and smell of sour beer."[21]

PULQUE

The Aztecs regarded their sacred pulque, the fermented juice of the agave cactus, as the "milk of the Mother," a divine gift from the goddess Mayahuel—a gift which must not be abused.

—Mikal Aasved, 1988[22]

Pulque is (like birch, maple, and palm beer) made from the sweet sap of a plant. In this case, the agave cactus. For the Tarahumara Indians of the northern Sierra Nevada, the agave cactus was the first plant that Onoruame—the great father—created. And like all things, it has its own soul, "otherwise [it] would not be able to live and grow."[23] To the Tarahumara, the soul of the agave is extremely sensitive and must be treated with great respect so that it will continue to be willing to help humankind. The making of pulque was taught to the first humans by Mayahuel, the Earth Mother, so the intelligence or soul that the Tarahumara believe resides in the heart would be able to travel to sacred realms. In memory of this gift, the Tarahumara (like their Aztec ancestors before them) call pulque "the Milk of the Mother."

About every 8 to 10 years, the agave cactus puts up a thick floral stem from its center. When they want to make pulque, the Tarahumara approach the plant and make prayers and offerings to its spirit. The thick floral stem is then cut off in such a way that a cup-shaped cavity is left in the center of the plant. Each day, the sweet sap, called *aguamiel*—meaning "honey water"—that accumulates in the cavity is scraped out to stop the cavity from sealing over and to maintain the flow. It is placed in a gourd, mixed with saliva or water, and placed in a special container, where it ferments for 8 to 12 days. When it is ready to drink, the first dippers of beer are taken from the pot and offered to Onoruame and then to each of the four cardinal directions.

The sweet sap is also present in the root and leaves of the plant, and a number of tribes gather it from those parts to make pulque. When the sap is fermented, it becomes a thick, white liquid, usually about 5 percent alcohol.

Pulque

Ingredients

> 1 gallon agave sap
> enough water to thin it to slightly thicker than a barley beer wort
> yeast

> Find several wild agave cacti that are flowering. After appropriate prayers, cut off the flowering stalk, leaving a cup-shaped depression. Allow the sweet sap to accumulate. Scrape it out of the depression regularly until 1 gallon of sap is collected. Thin the sap with water until slightly thicker than an ordinary beer wort. Pour into fermenter, add yeast. Allow to ferment until complete, one to two weeks. Drink when ready or siphon into bottles and cap.

ABOUT AGAVE

Agave spp.

> *The neighboring Tepehuane Indians believe that the spirit of the agave is so sensitive to vital forces that "if one passes a jar in which it is being boiled the liquid will not ferment."*
>
> —Mikal Aasved, 1988[24]

The Tarahumara, or *Raramuri*, as they call themselves, believe that people have many souls of differing sizes within their bodies. Each part of the body that moves has a unique and specific soul. The joints of the fingers, for instance, have very tiny souls; the mind and the heart have very large souls. The terms *ariwi* and *iwiba*, which the Tarahumara use to denote these souls, mean, when translated, "breath." Like many indigenous cultures, for example the Seminole, who call the Creator Breathmaker, the Tarahumara associate the sacred Creator with breath, the essence of life itself. And the breath of the Creator is within each soul in a person's body.

For the Tarahumara, the larger souls are more capable of intelligence, thought, and action. The largest is located within the heart, the next largest within the head. From time to time the heart and mind souls need to travel outside the body. It is during these times that the person becomes drowsy and sleeps, and later remembers these travels, if at all, as dreams. During these times the heart and head souls journey to spirit realms to gain knowledge and help for the individual they are a part of. Usually they encounter no difficulty in returning, but occasionally they are waylaid and unable to return; without them, the body begins to fall ill. As any of the body souls can become ill, an in-depth knowledge of the structure and action of each soul and their relationship to each other is learned by Tarahumara medicine men during their training.

The drinking of pulque frees the heart soul from the body; the more pulque consumed, the farther the heart soul travels. When a great deal of pulque is consumed, the mind soul also leaves, causing the person to fall asleep. During this pulque-induced travel outside the body, the heart soul again encounters spirit realms and gains knowledge that may be used to help in both personal and cultural life.[25]

This Tarahumara perspective of aggregate souls and their relationship to the body and health bears remarkable similarities to both transactional analysis and traditional Chinese medicine. Both identify nonmaterial "centers" that exist within the body that may fall out of balance and create illness. Both suggest approaches to help the individual and aggregate "centers," and thus heal illness. Pulque, as a primary catalyst for activity in the two large souls, is important as both a sacred and healing beverage.

The main agave species, also known as maguey or century plants, grow throughout the western United States in higher desert and rough terrain—on mesa sides, limestone slopes, and rocky mountainsides. There is one eastern species, *Agave virginica*, that grows eastward into the Ozark and Appalachian Mountains.

Agave looks, to some extent, like yucca, but its leaves are much thicker and wider and are graced with sharp thorns along their edges. The agave can grow quite large, the thick, succulent, spiny leaves reaching 6 feet in height, the thick, flowering stalk 20 to 40 feet. When cut, the plant exudes a liquid something like, though not as thick as, that of aloe, another, smaller, plant that resembles agave. The sweet sap is sometimes evaporated to make a thick syrup for use as a food, pulque can be distilled into the liquor mescal, and the fibers of the leaves are a traditional source of thread and cordage.

Agave has a long tradition as a medicinal plant. It is diuretic, carminative, antispasmodic, antirheumatic, stomachic, and laxative. Both the tincture of leaves and root and the fermented pulque relieve arthritis and rheumatic pains and inflammation, cramping in the stomach and intestines, gas, and act as stomach and gastrointestinal tract tonics. The fresh root, high in saponins, is a traditional shampoo and soap. The fresh sap is useful, like aloe, on burns, cuts, and skin abrasions. I am unaware of any clinical studies on agave, but those on aloe have shown the sap to cause wound healing acceleration and to possess antiviral activity, anti-inflammatory action, and antiulcer action, in vivo and in vitro.[26]

CHICHA AND CORN BEER

For thousands of years, indigenous peoples of the Americas have formally recognized corn as a teacher of wisdom, the spirit inseparable from the grain. Through corn's natural ways of growing and being, the spirit sings of strength, respect, balance, harmony. Of adaptability, cooperation, unity in diversity. Songs of survival.

—Marilou Awiakta, 1993[27]

Corn has long been used not only as food and medicine, but for fermentation. It was the most important fermentation in the Aztec Empire and central to their economy and most of their ceremonies. Their architecture, road systems, town construction, and irrigation were all oriented, in part, around the making of corn beer. Tribal cultures in North America, contrary to common belief about their historical access to alcohol, also fermented corn (and other) beers. These beers were ubiquitous not only in Texas and New Mexico but throughout the southeastern regions of the continent—another form of the Corn Mother's gift to humankind.[28]

Chicha, one form of corn beer, is one of the oldest of indigenous fermentations. It refers, generally, to beers made from corn, sorghum, millet, plantain, and manioc, but in the main almost always refers, now, to those made from corn. Traditional chicha is made through saliva conversion of cornstarch to sugar. However, a number of cultures also use germination to produce starch conversion. The word itself is derived from the Spanish *chichal*, meaning "saliva" or "to spit," and comes from the common indigenous method of converting starch in corn to sugars by using the enzyme ptyalin in human saliva (see chapter 6).

TRADITIONAL CHICHA OF THE QUECHA INDIANS

The Quecha of Bolivia make chicha in the traditional manner throughout the country. They use a dozen maize varieties, two being *culli*, a cherry-red to almost black maize (that produces a burgundy-colored chicha) and *huilcaparu*, a bluish-brown corn with a silvery sheen that makes a darker, brownish chicha.

The dried maize kernels are coarsely ground by hand between a traditional half-moon-shaped stone rocker and a flat stone. The maize flour is slightly moistened with water, rolled into a small ball, and placed in the mouth. It is thoroughly worked with the tongue until it is completely saturated with saliva. As it becomes saturated, it begins to take on a sweetness as the ptyalin converts the cornstarch to sugar. It is then pressed by the tongue against the roof of the mouth to form a single mass, popped loose, and taken out to dry in the sun. This saliva-malted maize is called *muko*. To make the beer, two-thirds muko is combined with one-third unmalted corn (there is enough extra ptyalin enzyme available to convert this unmalted corn) and (sometimes) pulp from a local squash (*Curcurbita ficifolia*) and (sometimes) the fruits of the prickly pear cactus.

Hot water is added and the mixture is stirred for an hour, then allowed to cool and settle undisturbed. It separates into three layers: a liquid on top (*upi*), an almost jellylike layer in the middle (*misqui kketa*), and the ground grain on the bottom (*hanchi*). The liquid, upi, is scooped out with a gourd spoon and placed in another container. The misqui kketa is placed in a shallow pan and slowly cooked until it takes on a caramel color and flavor. The hanchi is pressed and the remaining liquid thus extracted is added to the upi. This upi mixture is boiled for three hours, then removed from the fire, and the misqui kketa is added and all of it well mixed. It is allowed to naturally ferment until fermentation ceases (about six days), and it is then drunk.[29]

The fermentation takes place in porous clay pots that usually contain yeast residues from prior batches of chicha. Thus, new fermentations usually begin from the old yeast held in the porous clay. Like all indigenous beers, the making of chicha is highly ceremonial.

Chicha

Ingredients

> 3 pounds coarsely ground cornmeal
>
> 1 pound squash pulp (any will do, from pumpkin to winter squash)
>
> 1 pound prickly pear cactus fruits
>
> 3 gallons water
>
> yeast

> Make muko from 2 pounds of the cornmeal. Making muko is best as a family event as it is in Mexico and

South America. The family gathers around and shares stories and companionship until it is done—two to three hours. When the muko is dry, combine with the rest of the cornmeal, the squash pulp, and the prickly pear fruit pulp removed from the pods. Add the 3 gallons of water heated to 150 degrees F and allow to stand until cool. Ladle out the top layer and set aside. Scoop out the middle, jellylike layer and cook in a stainless steel pot on the stove until it attains a caramel-like color. While this is cooking, press the grain, squash pulp, and cactus fruit pulp. Add this liquid to the initial liquid you drew off. Boil the two for one hour. When the cooking jellylike middle layer is ready, add it to the boiled liquid. Cool to 70 degrees F, pour into the fermenter, and add yeast. Allow to ferment until complete, siphon into bottles, prime, and cap. Ready in about a week.

TESGUINO

THE TRADITIONAL CHICHA OF THE TARAHUMARA INDIANS OF MEXICO

Because the Sun and Moon often fall ill, the Tarahumara continue to "cure" them with tesguino. Every ceremony begins with a libation to these heavenly bodies but they sometimes require ceremonies held especially for them, and particularly for the Moon.

—Mikal Aasved, 1988[30]

Some traditional chicha beers are also made from germinated or malted maize instead of saliva converted corn. A number of cultures in South America make beers from malted maize, and there are several such beers in North America. The Mescalero Apache make *tulpai;* another is the *tesguino* of the Tarahumara tribe in Northern Mexico. As with all the indigenous cultures of the Americas, maize is sacred to the Tarahumara. Onoruame, the Great Father, gave maize or corn beer to the Tarahumara to help them in their work as human beings, to ease their spirits, and to bring them joy.

They make tesguino by germinating the maize in large pots that can contain up to 75 pounds of grain. The maize is covered with water and soaked in a pot that is kept warm for two or three days. After that time it is drained, and while still moist is placed in a prepared shallow trench. The trench is a foot to a foot and a half deep, dug in a sunny location, and lined with pine needles and grass. It is then covered with more pine needles and grass and small stones and left alone to germinate. When it has germinated, it is dried and coarsely ground. Sometimes lichens, mosses, other plants, or wild oats are added for flavor and additional properties. The fermentation is started, unusually, by brome grass that contains a naturally occurring yeast. The tesguino is allowed to ferment for three or four days and then drunk. After the beer is fermented, and before any is drunk, it is first dedicated to Onoruame. "A little beer is dipped three times from a larger gourd and tossed in each of the four directions."[31]

After the corn harvest, the remaining cornstalks are also used to make a corn beer, *paticili*. The stalks and leaves are pounded on rocks, then squeezed in a net to extract the juice from the plants. The juice is strained and boiled and a number of local roots and herbs are added. When it cools, it is fermented, usually with a starter from tesguino.[32]

Corn is generally considered more difficult to germinate than other grains; the first European settlers in North America found it so difficult they relied almost exclusively on birch and maple sap to make their beers—at least until they began growing barley. In South America, germinated corn, called *jora*, can be bought quite easily. Some South American grocery stores in the United States carry it, but you may have to make your own.

Authors and homebrewers Wendy Aaronson and Bill Ridgely have experimented perhaps more than anyone else in making traditional chicha from home-germinated corn. The following process is theirs. If you wish to make a more "indigenous" chicha, you can take the time to search out American Southwest blue or red corn or simply buy "Indian" corn and remove the kernels from the cob yourself. Do not use seed corn unless you are sure it has not been treated with pesticides. Feed corn, available in 25- or 50-pound bags, is a yellow sweet corn and is fairly easy to find.

To germinate corn, soak two pounds in cold water for 24 hours. Place the corn in a colander for germination. Spray cold water on the corn twice a day and turn it once a day. This prevents drying of the seed head and prevents its molding. Germination should start after two days, and the sprouts should reach two inches after five days. (Aaronson and Ridgely suggest expecting no more than 50 percent germination.) The germinating corn usually develops a sweet-sour aroma that some find unpleasant. After the sprouts reach two inches in length, take them from the colander and spread on a plastic sheet to dry in the sun, or dry them in the oven at the lowest setting. What follows is Aaronson and Ridgely's recipe for chicha.

Chicha from Germinated Corn

Ingredients for 1 gallon

    8 quarts water
    1 pound germinated corn (jora)
    2 cups brown sugar
    8 whole allspice or cloves
    ale yeast

> Crush *jora* rather coarsely and place in the brewpot with 8 quarts cold water. Stir and let sit one hour. Bring to a boil, add the sugar, then lower the heat and simmer three hours (stirring regularly). Add spices at end of boil. Remove and let sit undisturbed one hour. Then strain the liquid portion into a fermenter using a colander or wire basket lined with cheesecloth. When cool,

pitch yeast. Ferment at room temperature (60 to 75 degrees F) for five days. Rack to secondary and ferment one or two more weeks until clarified. Bottle using 1 teaspoon corn sugar per bottle for priming. Allow two more weeks of bottle-conditioning before drinking.[33]

FRUTILLADA

Frutillada is chicha with strawberries or other fruit added. I suspect the more ancient chichas exclusively used prickly pear or other indigenous fruits rather than strawberries. To make frutillada, use two to three pounds crushed strawberries per gallon of chicha. Add the fruit to the secondary fermenter after primary fermentation is complete, then rack the chicha onto the strawberries. It will ferment strongly from the additional sugars in the fruit. When this is complete strain and bottle as above.

CORN PLANT ALE

Many cultures, like the Tarahumara, have also made corn beers from the corn plant itself. The corn plant is extremely sweet, much like sugarcane, and is even sold in some parts of the world to be eaten like sugarcane. The sweetest plants are either the young plants before they put out ears of corn or the larger mature plants from which the budding corn has been removed before attaining maturity. The sweetest corn varieties, of course, produce the most sugar in the plant. Early in the American colonies and throughout the indigenous world, many peoples used the corn, then cut the stalks and used them to produce sugar or a ferment.

Corn was not native to New England. It did not make the long journey to that part of the world until about A.D. 1000. The Indians of that region had a tradition that firmly connected corn to the southwestern United States. Roger Williams, writing in 1643, noted that the Indian legend of the gift of corn to the Northeast held that "the crow brought them at first an Indian Grain of Corn in one Eare, and an Indian Beane in another, from the great God *Kautantouwits'* field in the Southwest."[34] The Indians passed their knowledge of corn on to the American colonists, who used it as a primary food staple. The sugar extraction process the colonists used to make beer from cornstalks is remarkably similar to that used by the Tarahumara Indians of Mexico. Landon Carter, writing in 1775, describes it:

> The stalks, green as they were, as soon as pulled up, were carried to a convenient trough, then chopped and pounded so much, that, by boiling, all the juice could be extracted out of them: which juice almost every planter knows is of as saccharine a quality almost as any thing can be, and that any thing of a luxuriant corn stalk is very full of it. . . . After this pounding, the stalks and all were put into a large copper, there lowered down in its sweetness with water, to an equality with common observations in malt wort, and then boiled, till the liquor in the glass is seen to break, as the brewers term it; after that it is strained, and boiled again with hops.[35]

The sugar obtained from the cornstalks was boiled to about half its volume before being used to make beer, being then about the same sweetness as malt wort.

Cornstalk Beer

Ingredients

    1 1/2 gallons water
    6 six-foot green cornstalks, cut in 2-inch sections
    yeast
    herbs, fruit, or spices as desired

Pound the sections of cornstalk with a wooden mallet until reduced to a pulp. Add pulped cornstalks and any liquid to 1 1/2 gallons of water. Boil for one hour and let cool. Pour off the liquid and squeeze the cornstalks in a cloth until they are as dry as you can get them, collecting this squeezed liquid in the same pot that holds the original liquid. Place the liquid back on the fire and reduce to 1 gallon total volume. Cool to 70 degrees F, pour into fermenter, add yeast. Ferment until complete, then siphon into primed bottles, cap, and store. It is ready in one week. For extra flavor, since corn sugar is somewhat bland, you might add herbs, fruit, or spices of your choice. Corn in general makes a mild, sparkling beer, somewhat cidery in taste and appearance.[36]

CHIACOAR

THE TRADITIONAL CORN BEER OF THE SURINAME INDIANS OF SOUTH AMERICA

Chiacoar is a fermented beverage made by the Suriname Indians of South America from maize. The maize is ground, baked into bread after which is it crumbled and macerated in water and allowed to ferment. . . . Another method of making chiacoar [is one] in which the meal is wrapped in banana leaves. The Indians boil the packages in water and then hang them in huts for 15 or 20 days. They become covered with a mold of yellow in the high altitudes, but with one of green in the lowlands. They are then taken down and the contents dissolved in water and sweetened with unrefined sugar. The product is strained and placed in a wooden vessel to ferment: and sometimes kereli is added. In three days it is ready for drinking.

—Ernest Cherrington, 1925[37]

This traditional beer of the Suriname Indians is included because one form of it is unusual, using a type of fermentation most commonly found with rice—that of a mold to convert the starches to sugar in order for fermentation to occur. I haven't found any other reference to it than that cited above, but it suggests that mold fermentation is more common than usually supposed (see "Chang" in this chapter). Additionally, though I have not gone into this in any detail, many cultures made beer by another, entirely different, method. That is, they would take regular grain, grind it, make it into bread (though cooked only half the time usually used for bread), and then crumble the bread, as above, into the fermenter for brewing. The type of pots, strainers, and stance used in South America are identical to those used in ancient Egypt. Again, this leads credence to the emerging speculation that there was an ongoing transatlantic trade with Egypt for thousands of years (see chapter 6).

ABOUT CORN
Zea Mays

> *The Law is in the Corn*
> *the people of the southwest say this . . .*
> *to be there with the morning sun in that sacred time . . .*
> *to talk to the corn, to hear it talk in the wind*
> *in the language of movement . . . what to do.*
> *Out here at the Eastern Door, we say it is*
> *the Original Instructions . . .*
> *This is called Democracy.*
> *It is in the land, it is in the seed.*
>
> —Alex Jacobs, *Karoniaktatie*[38]

Corn is, perhaps, *the* sacred plant for many of the indigenous cultures of the Americas. The story of the coming of the Corn Mother (which is much longer and richer than what I will share here) has long been an important teaching story for indigenous peoples (as it is, indeed, for all people), and it contains much wisdom. Selu, the Corn Mother, was sent as a companion to the first man to comfort his loneliness and help him remember the sweetness of his heart; in so doing, she became his wife and the mother of all humankind. Her body, besides giving life to the first children, was also an essential nourishment for the bodies of humankind. I see the following stories as both being about Selu. One as Maiden when she first came, and the other as Grandmother, later when her children had children. There are numerous stories of the origin of corn, its sacredness, and how it came to human beings. Perhaps the best book about the sacredness of corn is Marilou Awiakta's *Selu: Seeking the Corn Mother's Wisdom* (Golden, CO: Fulcrum Publishing, 1993).

It is said that in the beginning Creator made the first man, who was named Kanati, father of all the human beings. Kanati, for a long time, enjoyed being on the Earth. He had been created a great hunter, and as time went on, it was all he thought about, all that he did. And, in time, he did it too much. The animals, upset at how many of them were being killed, went to Creator and complained, saying: "Kanati is killing too many of us. If it keeps on like this, soon there won't be any of us left."

Creator, not having noticed because he was busy with other things, thanked the animals, and thought long about what to do to help them. After awhile Creator realized that Kanati needed a companion. So Creator sought out Kanati, found him sleeping in the sun, and caused a corn plant to grow up beside his heart. The plant grew up tall and straight, and from the top of the cornstalk Selu—the Corn Mother— came, strong, tender, and singing.

Kanati, hearing the song, woke up and looked around, wondering what was happening. And then he saw Selu. Immediately, he was taken by her, and the sweetness in his own heart was kindled to overflowing. He reached up his hand and asked Selu to come down to him. She smiled and told him to wait, and then she reached up and took an ear of corn to

"Of Lovely,
Sweet Scents,"
*woodcut by
Weiditz from
Petrarch's* Von
der Artzney
Bayder Glück,
*Augsburg, H.
Steiner, 1532*

bring with her, knowing that, as for all human beings, your heritage must be taken with you. Then, giving Kanati her hand, she stepped down, the first woman, companion to the first man.

Together they went to Kanati's home. Selu went into the kitchen, and soon a wonderful smell came from the kettle bubbling on the stove. And breathing it, Kanati felt in harmony with all life.

It is also said that much later there was an old woman with two grandsons. They were good hunters and there was always enough to eat. One day when they were readying their weapons for hunting, their grandmother came to them and said, "I see you are going hunting today."

And they replied, "Yes, we are."

"Well," she said, "when you get home I will have something wonderful for you to eat. Corn."

While they were hunting, though, they were wondering about that strange word their grandmother had used—corn.

They killed a deer and took it home. The kettle was on the fire, bubbling, and a wonderful smell came from it. "What is in the pot?" they asked their grandmother.

"It's the corn I told you about." They sat down to dinner, and it was the most wonderful food they had ever eaten.

Each day this happened. They went hunting, and when they came home she had cooked more corn, and each time they felt it was the most wonderful food they had ever tasted. One day, though, they began to wonder where this corn came from. One said to the other, "I will hide today and see where that corn comes from." And the other brother agreed.

So, hurrying off, the younger brother hid and watched. After awhile he saw his grandmother coming with the kettle from the stove. She put it down, and then leaning over she began to strike her sides. Each time she hit her side, corn fell from her body into the pot until it was quite full. Then she carried the kettle back to the fire and began cooking.

The young man, filled with this knowledge, hurried off and told his brother what he had learned. "It comes from her body," he said, "that is what we have really been eating."

And the other brother, horrified, said, "Well, we can't eat any more of that. It is not a good thing."

So the brothers agreed that they would not eat any more of the corn.

When they arrived home from hunting, the corn was cooked and waiting for them. But this time neither brother would eat what she had made.

"What's wrong?" asked the grandmother.

"Nothing," they said. "We're just not hungry."

But the grandmother looked keenly into their faces and replied, "What is wrong? Don't you like me? Or did you find out something that makes you not want to eat?"

The boys would not meet her eyes and did not answer. And as she sat there, the grandmother began to become ill. She then knew they had found out where that corn had come from. She struggled up from the table and went to her bed. As she lay down she turned to them and said, "Now that I am in bed, I am going to die. And you must listen to what I tell you."

Her grandsons came close.

"When I am dead, you must bury me outside in the ground and put a fence around my grave. In time a plant will grow up from where I am buried. When it gets big it will have large ears of corn growing on it and a brown tassel coming out. That is how you will know when it is time to pick the corn. After you pick it, you must save some of the kernels, and in the spring, plant them. Thus more corn will grow. And so I will be the Corn Mother," she said. "Don't ever forget where I am buried."

And these things her grandsons did.[39]

When humankind began to look too deeply into Selu's secrets, to sneak around without respect, something wonderful was lost to mankind forever. Vaclav Havel (referenced in chapter 1) touches on this dynamic:

> Today, for instance, we may know immeasurably more about the universe than our ancestors did, and yet, it increasingly seems they knew something more essential about it than we do, something that escapes us. The same is true of nature and ourselves. The more thoroughly all our organs and their functions, their internal structure and the biochemical reactions that take place within them are described, the more we seem to fail to grasp the spirit, purpose and meaning of the system that they create together and that we experience as our unique self.

In seeing only the physical, humankind has long been forgetting the nonmaterial and spiritual aspects of our world and human life. We have become so far removed that, in fact, it is not uncommon now to have Western scholars seriously conclude that there is *no* nonmaterial aspect to life at all. Many now think that the assertion is sensible even if overly simplistic. But the wisdom of the Corn Mother reminds us, in its own way, that there is more to life than the material. Some of the most brilliant scientists are beginning to hear her.

Corn has long been a plant studied by geneticists, not only for the enhancement of food production, but to better understand genetics itself. In the latter part of this century, in 1983, a corn researcher, Barbara McClintock, was awarded the Nobel Prize for her work on corn. What she discovered is truly remarkable.

McClintock, a cytologist specializing in genetic research, spent more than 60 years studying corn. Her findings challenged many of the most basic findings in genetics and evolution. Organisms, she found, when under stress, engage in genetic changes not predictable from their genetic makeup, a process now known as "jumping genes." And these "jumps"—gene crossings and genetic changes—are under the intentional control of the organism and the environment it lives in (the land). In other words, organisms intentionally respond to environmental stress by combining genes in unpredictable ways that allow the organism to better survive. McClintock's biographer, Evelyn Keller, comments: "Where do the instructions [for gene rearrangement] come from? McClintock's answer—that they come from the entire cell, the organism, perhaps even from the environment—is profoundly disturbing to orthodox genetics."[40] She continues, noting that there is "a degree of fluidity of the chromosomal complement (or genome) of organisms and thus our genetic structure" now needs to be thought of as a dynamic structure, rather than a static linear message inscribed in the sequence of DNA."[41] McClintock's findings undercut significant components of Darwin's theory of evolution (survival of the fittest over slow eons of time) and also open up new directions in the exploration of the intelligent actions of the Earth, Gaia. Like many people who truly embrace the essence of science, McClintock was in touch with greater truths than those understood by less well endowed researchers.

McClintock commented that science often misses the crucial understanding of the whole because its practitioners too often focus on the isolated parts. She observed that one must have "a feeling for the organism" and insisted that the corn itself "guided and directed her work" and "spoke to her" throughout the long process of her studies.

I still remember her standing bemused in front of the scores of journalists and television reporters who had traveled to her remote laboratory to question her after she was awarded the Nobel Prize. When they asked her what she was going to do with the money, she replied, "They give you money for that?"[42]

McClintock's findings have the same wide-ranging implications for the nature of human reality and humanity's relationship with universe that Godel's incompleteness theorem, Einstein's theory of relativity, and Heisenberg's uncertainty principle do. Marilou Awiakta, whom I mentioned earlier, is one of the few writers that I know of who has seen the importance of the general applicability of McClintock's work to the human condition. The difference between McClintock's work and that of other researchers is that the corn itself revealed what it wanted her to know. McClintock did not "spy" on the corn without permission. And isn't it interesting that it was a woman who brought this knowledge of the wisdom of corn to mankind?

Like beers made from honey, beers made from corn possess both the medicinal and nutritive properties of the substance from which they are made. Researchers such as Clifford Gastanieu in his *Fermented Food Beverages in Nutrition* (New York: Academy Press, 1979) have shown that corn beers are a powerful part of indigenous dietary regimens and that they effectively prevent or cure many diseases. Still, like most fermented beverages, little, if any, research has been done on the medicinal effects of corn beers. However, many early observers commented that the corn beers of indigenous cultures acted to prevent many diseases.

The Spanish writer Garcilaso de la Vega (1539–1616) commented that he was highly impressed

> with the remarkable curative properties of corn, which is
> not only the principle article of food in America, but is
> also of benefit in the treatment of the kidney and blad-
> der, among which are calculus and retention of urine.
> And the best proof I can give of this is that the Indians,

whose usual drink is made of corn, are afflicted with none of these diseases.[43]

Corn is anodyne (soothes pain), diuretic, demulcent, anti-inflammatory, and tonic. It is used throughout the world in the treatment of kidney stones (calculi, gravel, and strangury), cystitis, acute and chronic inflammations of the bladder, urethritis, and prostatitis. Its coating and soothing qualities in combination with its pain relieving properties and anti-inflammatory and diuretic actions make it a primary herb to use for any urinary tract infection. In contemporary herbal practice, the corn silk is usually used. Cornmeal has long been used as a poultice in the external treatment of ulcers, wounds, swellings, and rheumatic pains. The mush has long been used for those with debilitated digestion or recovering from long illness, and for allaying nausea and vomiting.

In some instances corn will become infected with a particular fungus, *Ustilago segetum*, that also has a long tradition of medicinal use. *Ustilago*, in its effects on human beings, is considered to be a cross between rye ergot and large doses of nutmeg, both hallucinogenic in their effects. *Ustilago* is also a cerebral stimulant, with attendant narcotic and hallucinogenic effects on the human organism. Medicinally, it has been used in minute doses as a uterine contractant to help during labor and as a cerebral stimulant. It also possesses powerful abortifacient activity and is a strong astringent useful in postpartum hemorrhage and hemorrhages from the lungs and bowels. Overdoses are quite serious in their effects—the loss of all body hair, spontaneous abortion, convulsions, and eventually, death, if the dose is large enough.[44]

MASATO OR MANIOC BEER

Manioc, a major source of beer, is one of the most important garden crops of all South American horticulturalists.

—Mikal Aasved, 1988[45]

Manioc, sometimes called cassava or yucca (*not* the same yucca that grows in North America), is an indigenous plant of South America that grows very fast and produces a root that may weigh up to 30 pounds. The roots develop in about three months, are a foot or two long, and two to six inches in diameter. Manioc has been used for food and fermentation for at least 4,000 years.

Generally known as *masato*, manioc beer is also known under a variety of names according to the tribe or region in which it is made. Masato comes in a rainbow of colors depending on the techniques or ingredients used by individual brewers: milky-white, amber, brown, bluish-white, or even yellow. Usually about 4 percent alcohol by volume, some masato is stored for years underground and attains a powerful 14 percent alcohol strength. The best of it, in spite of the simple and unhygienic conditions in which it is brewed, is reputed to taste much like the best Belgian lambics.

The Jivaro of South America brew two kinds of manioc beer— *nihamanchi*, the most common, and *sangucha shiki*, their powerful ceremonial beer. Essential to this process, like many indigenous beers, is the use of human saliva to convert starch to sugar.

Probably the oldest written account of the making of fermented manioc beer, made similarly to nihamanchi, is the account of the Huguenot minister Jean de Lery. In 1556, he traveled to Brazil, a young member of the first Protestant mission to the New World. In 1578, de Lery published the accounts of his travels and observations in his *History of a Voyage to the Land of Brazil, Otherwise Called America*. His stories of the making of *caouin*, the traditional fermented manioc beverage of the Tupinamba Indians, provide the earliest written account of how it is made. (Manioc roots contain cyanide, which must be removed before consumption. Cyanide is water soluble and, also, is destroyed by heat.)

> After the women have cut up the roots as fine as we
> cut turnips for stewing, they let the pieces boil in
> water in great earthen vessels; when they see them

getting tender and soft, they remove the pots from the fire and let them cool a little. When that is done, several of the women, crouched around these great vessels, take from them these little round pieces of softened root. First they chew them and twist them around in their mouths, without swallowing them; then they take the pieces in their hands, one after the other, and put them into other earthen vessels which are already on the fire and in which they boil the pieces again. They constantly stir this concoction with a stick until they see that it is done, and then removing it from the fire a second time, without straining it, they pour it all into other bigger earthen jars, each having the capacity of about an eleven-gallon Burgundy wine-measure. After it has clarified and fermented, they cover the vessels and leave the beverage until people want to drink it.[46]

The Jivaro process is essentially the same, except only half of the cooked manioc roots are chewed and mixed with human saliva. The rest, mashed into a paste, are mixed with the chewed manioc, into the consistency of mashed potatoes. Water is added, and this is then fermented from one to three days.

Manioc Ale

If you cannot find manioc, and you probably cannot, you can use tapioca. Tapioca is usually made from manioc roots, though some brands are made from potatoes. Try to find the real thing. If you are lucky, you may be able to find manioc at a South American market in the United States or from someone in Florida. In which case, you can try a traditional recipe in which you boil the root first (see "About Manioc").

Ingredients

> 2 pounds tapioca
> 2 gallons water
> yeast

Roughly grind 1 pound of the tapioca (which comes in small round pellets). Get the largest pellets available. You don't want a fine powder, so make sure you grind it coarsely. After grinding, moisten it slightly so that it can be rolled into small balls from 1/2 to 3/4 of an inch in diameter. Follow much the same method as for chicha beer. Pop a ball into your mouth and thoroughly work it with your tongue until it is completely mixed with saliva. Keep your mouth closed, as the heat in your mouth makes the process more effective. It is done when it will stick to the roof of your mouth. Push it forward with your tongue and remove and let dry. When dry, take the malted tapioca and add it and the rest of the tapioca, also roughly ground, to a fermenting pot. Add 2 gallons water at 150 degrees F. Let it cool naturally until it is 70 degrees F. Add yeast, cover, and ferment until complete. Siphon into bottles, prime, and cap. Ready in approximately one week.

ABOUT MANIOC
Manihot esculenta

The origin tales of manioc are remarkably similar across South America and also bear great similarities to those of corn, rice, and barley.

It is said that in the long ago times there was the daughter of a great chief. One night, while she was sleeping, the spirit of the Earth Mother came to her and said that she was with child, a child that was bringing to all the people a sacred gift of the Creator. And so it was that the daughter became pregnant, but as yet she told no one. However, as the year went by and her pregnancy became obvious, her father became quite angry, thinking she had been sleeping with the young men of the village. But the daughter insisted that she had been with no man and then recounted to him her dream. And this, in turn, was told to the people of the village.

As she came closer to her time, all the people awaited with wonder for the birth of the sacred child she carried within her. And finally, after nine months she gave birth to a beautiful baby girl whom she named Mani. The baby was of so wondrous an appearance that people came from "all the tribes of the region to see and wonder at 'this creature of a new and unknown race.'"[47] Her presence was so powerful and wondrous that all who saw her were affected by it. She grew quickly and was strong and healthy, but after a year, for a reason none could understand, she died. Mani, the divine child, was buried with all the ceremony and custom of the tribe, and her tomb was well tended and watered. Soon afterward, a plant that none knew began growing on her grave. The people tended it until it finally flowered and grew fruit. It was then that representatives of all the birds of the forest came to the plant and began to eat of the fruit; all became intoxicated, the first time that human beings knew of such a thing. Soon thereafter the plant died, and the people dug it up, finding a large and wondrous root. They learned to make food from it and a sacred drink that also brought intoxication to them so that their spirits flew like the birds. They named the plant *mani oca*, "the house of transformation of Mani."[48]

Other versions of the gift of manioc to the people are similar throughout South America. Among the Jivaro it is said a woman was walking in the forest and she came upon Nungui, the Earth Mother. With Nungui was her small baby, Manioc, who was helping her tend the plants of the Earth. The woman asked for something to help her people, because they were hungry, and Nungui gave her the baby, Manioc. Manioc taught the people how to grow manioc (of which she was the spirit essence) and how to make it into beer.

The Jivaro, also, believe that all things come from the sacred and that all things thus possess *wakani*, a soul. To them, like the indigenous cultures in North America and throughout the world, the plants are living beings who can talk and who will, if treated "like a human being," help humankind. The Jivaro, like many indigenous cultures, also experience plants as predominantly either male or female. And thus how one works with them is shaped by their sex. As Mikal Aasved observes:

> The Jivaro also believe it is essential that the plants be tended by those of a kindred spirit who are thought to be better able to exercise a greater supernatural control over them to promote their growth. Therefore, garden plants which have a woman's soul must be tended by women while those with a man's soul must be tended by men. Because the earth deity is a woman, however, women are thought to have a far greater ability "to exert a special, mysterious influence upon the growth of the crops." They exercise this power by singing and chanting not only to the ancestral *wakani* or spirit residing within a plant, but also to Nangui, the Earth Mother, who lives in the soil and whose spirit permeates all plants growing there.[49]

Since manioc is female, only the women grow it in their gardens, and only the women make it into beer. For as the Jivaro say, "only a woman can properly influence it for the purpose of bringing it to fermentation."[50] The making of *sangucha shiki*, a powerful manioc ceremonial wine or beer, is done somewhat differently than the process described earlier for caouin or nihamanchi and bears remarkable similarities to Norwegian brewers' traditional juniper beer (see chapter 8).

Sangucha shiki is made for only the most ceremonial occasions among the Jivaro, one of which is the *tsantsa*, or men's Victory Celebration feast, held for the slayer after the killing of an enemy.

The manioc for the beer must be gathered in an especially sacred manner. The slayer's wife, her hands held by an *ohaha* priestess, offers prayers to the manioc, and then uproots the first plant and carefully lays it in her basket. All of the women of the village then carefully and with attentive mind harvest the rest of the plants to be used in brewing.

Half of the plants are prepared in the normal manner by the women, boiling the roots and chewing them into a paste. The other half are taken whole by the men and roasted over a fire. Each step of their preparation is attended with a great deal of ceremony and respectful prayer. When enough roasted manioc to fill three baskets has been prepared, the baskets are taken inside, where the women have been preparing the boiled manioc roots. The roasted roots are cut open, and some salt, manioc bark, saliva, and mold from earlier fermented manioc roots are inserted inside them. They are put in pots with some previously chewed and fermented manioc paste to inoculate the roots, and then they are hung in the rafters and allowed to ferment for three days. They are then taken down and chewed by the women, just as is usually done in the preparation of everyday manioc beer. Once it all has been masticated, the ceremonial preparation continues.

Before the slayer, his family, and the officiating shaman, or *whuea*, is a large jar. Beside them are two large banana leaves, one containing wooden pins from the *shuya* tree, the other leaves from the *apai* tree. Mikal Aasved describes this part of the ceremony:

> The shaman holds the slayer's hands as he reverently takes one of the pins and slowly places it into the jar. Then his wife and daughter, with their hands also held by the shaman, repeat this gesture. The rest of the wooden pins, which will cover the bottom of the jar [in

a flat layer], are placed by a third man who completes the task with no further ceremony. After all the pins have been put into the jar, the slayer, aided by the shaman, picks up an *apai* leaf and "cautiously" lays it over the pins. Again, his wife and daughter repeat this act. More leaves are added until the wooden pins are completely covered. The leaf layer is then punctured many times with another wooden pin so that it will act as a sieve when the roasted manioc substance is placed over it.[51]

The jar is then filled with the roasted manioc root, the top covered with large leaves and tied with vines. Over two days and nights the "essence" of the manioc beer collects in the bottom of the fermenter. When it is ready, it is treated with great reverence, and the liquid is drained off. It is consumed the next morning in a special and highly sacred ceremony.

Manioc beers, like all indigenous beers, perform two important functions. First, they are an integral part of the daily diet, adding crucial proteins, vitamins, nutrients, and the medicinal properties derived from the manioc plant itself. Second, for the people of South America, making and then drinking manioc beer is a re-creation of the sacred giving of the beer to humankind. When they take the beer into their bodies, they also take into themselves the "house of transformation of Mani" and thus partake of her essence directly. Mani, to these indigenous cultures, is not a myth or legend, but a living being, present and active in all human affairs and cultural life. It is through the ongoing and complex cultural interrelationship and dependence on manioc and manioc beer that Mani herself is communicated with and involves herself in human affairs. It is at the moment of fermentation that the greatest power of Mani manifests itself, and thus, as with all indigenous fermentations, the moment at which they come to know her most intimately.

The ceremonies of making manioc beers bear remarkable similarities among all the tribes that do so. The normal alcoholic content is from 1 1/2 to 3 percent, though the longer-fermented beers are stronger.

Manioc grows throughout South America and even in some areas of Florida. It is almost always a cultivated plant. As mentioned earlier, manioc roots contain cyanide in varying amounts; some types contain a great deal. The cyanide is removed from the roots, when used for fermentation, by boiling, and manioc poisoning is extremely uncommon. Manioc contains more calories per acre of growth than any other food crop in the world, including rice, corn, and potatoes. Unlike other starchy tubers, the starch obtained from manioc is almost completely pure. Manioc is more than 80 percent starch, while potatoes, for instance, are only 20 percent. Its protein content, at about 2 percent, is relatively low. However, the high starch content means that there is a large quantity of fermentable sugars. Once fermentation takes place, the vitamin content of manioc is significantly enhanced, and the protein level rises to 8 percent.

The manioc itself seems to possess antimalarial activity; researchers have observed that the consumption of manioc appears to play a part in protecting against incidence of the disease.[52] In traditional Western herbal medicine, the only part of manioc to be used is the starch, called tapioca, which was considered to have nutritive and demulcent properties. For babies, the sick, and the convalescent, it was considered to be an important easily digestible food, used much like barley. Because it is demulcent, it coats and soothes inflamed mucous membranes, making it good for use in severe dysentery. It is easily digested, making it good first solid food for babies, and useful for those with digestive ailments and those recovering from severe sickness.[53]

The natives of Brazil distinguish between two varieties (though botanists now insist there is only one—they used to agree with the natives), a less toxic sweet variety called *aipim* (*Manihot Aipi*) that is much smaller, weighing about six ounces at most, and the larger, more bitter

Manihot esculenta. Because of its larger size, the bitter variety is the most commonly used. Manioc is prepared in many ways. Fried it tastes like french fries, made into flour it is used to make bread and pancakes, and cooked and mashed it resembles mashed potatoes.[54]

CHANG

Chang (or chung) is one of several names given to these regional beers. The Indians call the beer pachwai *and brew it mostly from rice. In Nepal, chang is brewed from rice, millet, barley and occasionally corn. Tibetan chang is brewed almost exclusively from barley, although buckwheat and millet are occasionally used at lower elevations.*

—Wendy Aaronson and Bill Ridgely, 1994[55]

Though there are many fermented beverages made from millet, rice, and barley, chang is distinguished primarily by the use of yeast cakes for the conversion of starch to sugar.

Yeast cakes are a unique way of producing fermentation and probably came from regions where rice was the staple crop. Rice, after it is processed, does not possess the embryo that other grains do, and thus germination cannot work to begin the conversion of starch to sugar. Yeast cakes contain a number of different fungi. Some ferment the available sugars to alcohol, but others work first by converting the starches in the grain to sugars that can be fermented.

The yeast cakes are made from crushed and dried gingerroot and rice or barley flour. Moistened, they are combined into small cakes (dime to half-dollar size), covered with a moist cloth, and allowed to ferment. The natural fungi in the gingerroot multiply and grow, providing the *Aspergillus* fungi that converts starch to sugar, and then wild *Saccharomyces* come to eat the sugar. The wide use of ginger in beer is perhaps because of its natural starch-converting fungi that help in converting all available starches to sugars. Other fungi, such as *Hansenula, Mucor,* and *Rhizopus,* also form and help in the later fermentation of chang. When the smell of fermentation is strong and spore growth is visible, the cakes are uncovered and allowed to dry in the sun. These dried cakes are then used to make traditional chang and are also used in making sake.

Yeast cakes are sometimes available from Asian markets, and a good substitute is said to be possible from a combination of commercial-grade *koji* (steamed rice on which *Aspergillus oryzae* has been grown) and a liberal amount of commercially available dried ale or beer yeast.

Wendy Aaronson and Bill Ridgely understand, perhaps better than anyone, the intricacies of making chang, which they describe in their article "Adventures in Chicha and Chang: Indigenous Beers of the East and West."[56] The following is their recipe for a generic chang that I have shortened and condensed. Specifics for indigenous millet and rice chang follow.

Chang

Ingredients

> 2 pounds whole unmalted hulled grain (millet, barley, wheat, or rice)
> 1 gallon water
> 1/2 cup flour (rice, barley, wheat, or millet)
> 1 yeast cake

> Boil grains until soft, drain and cool, then spread them out on a tray or tabletop covered with a cut-open plastic trash bag. Crush the yeast cake (one cake will generally ferment two pounds of grain) and mix it with a little flour. Work the mass thoroughly together. After mixing, place the *lum* (the mixture) into a clean plastic, glass, or stainless steel fermenter or pot with a tight lid. Leave no more than one inch of air space but do leave some. Keep

the fermenter warm, at least 60 degrees F. When fermentation becomes evident slowly pour one gallon of water over the lum. Let the liquid sit for about an hour, then draw it off using a ladle or siphon hose. Strain if desired. Refrigerate immediately and consume within one week. Additional water can be added and drawn off over a period of two or three weeks.

Young chang is milky white in color and has a rather refreshing, tart, somewhat sweet and citric flavor reminiscent of hard cider. In older chang, the aroma and flavor of alcohol also are evident, along with the characteristic sourness.[57]

MILLET BEERS

Millet, *Panicum miliaceum* or *Eleusine coracana*, is a grass/grain that has small, edible seeds. It is grown throughout the world for food, though it is used in the United States almost exclusively as a forage crop. The grain can sometimes be bought and used for both bread making and fermentation. A wild yeast, excellent for initiating fermentation, is found on many species and is the primary yeast used in African "Kaffir" or millet beers.

Millet beers are made throughout Africa, South America, and Asia and have been made for thousands of years. Some are made as chicha is—through salivation—some through malting, and some as chang is—with the use of a yeast cake. The Tupinamba of South America made millet beers as a form of chicha. Jean de Lery, in 1556, noted that millet beer was one of the two traditional beers they made, the other being from manioc. It was prepared in the same manner as manioc. "Our American women likewise boil and then chew the coarse millet they call *avati*, and make a brew like that made from the roots I have mentioned. . . . [And] since these roots and the coarse millet that I have spoken of grow in their country the year round, they make this beverage in all seasons."58

But like all plants used as food and in fermentation, millet and the beer made from it is considered to be sacred. Thus, among the Lepcha of the Himalayas (as Mikal Aasved comments):

> *Chi*, the sacred millet beverage, originated in heaven and is itself considered a deity which is personified in Don-Dyo-chi-log who is accorded the same status as Tashe-Thing, the Supreme Deity. *Chi* [is] the drink of divine immortality.59

And among the indigenous Ainu of Japan:

> The traditional millet beverage of the Ainu, now outlawed by the Japanese government, [is] called Inau-korashkoro, which translates literally as "our sacred fermented liquor.". . . "It is sacred . . . because it [is—like millet itself—] a *kamui* in its own right. . . . Under its inspiration the Ainu felt at one with their gods."60

To the Ainu, *kamui* are the spirits or souls that exist in all physical reality. Both millet and inau-korashkoro were given to the Ainu by Aeonia, the Great Teacher, or Creator. Like many similar ceremonies, the Ainu rituals wherein they drink inau-korashkoro consist, in part, of offerings to the spirits of the hearth, called, among the Ainu, *Kamui Fuchi*.

Throughout Africa, millet is one of the primary grains used in fermentation. And, as among the Lepcha and the Ainu, it is both a sacred grain and the source of a sacred fermentation. African tribes primarily use a malting process to make millet beer. Himalayan cultures usually use a yeast cake fermentation.

The following recipe is from Bertrand Remi, who lived in Nepal for many years. His method for a millet chang is somewhat different from that outlined by Aaronson and Ridgely and calls for either a yeast cake or any kind of powdered yeast.

Traditional Himalayan Chang
Ingredients

>2 quarts millet
>
>1 gallon water
>
>small amount of flour
>
>1 slice bread
>
>yeast [or yeast cake]

>Boil millet until soft. Drain and discard the water. [Crumble the yeast cake and] Sprinkle yeast mixed with flour onto the damp grain. Stir well, place one slice of bread at bottom of pot, cover with millet, and then cover the pot and keep warm, approximately 80 degrees F. Let ferment three days then add one gallon lukewarm water. Let stand until cold. The beer may now be either sucked up through a tube with a strainer at the bottom to keep out the solids or may be strained into a glass and drunk. Both methods are used in Nepal.[61]

Traditional African "Kaffir" Beer
Ingredients

>4 pounds millet
>
>1 gallon water
>
>yeast

>Traditional Kaffir beer is made from malted or germi-nated millet. To germinate the millet, soak 4 pounds in

cold water for 24 hours. Place the millet in a large colander or on a plastic tray with a like number of holes poked in the bottom for germination. Spray cold water on the millet twice a day and turn it once a day. This prevents it from drying out, and the turning prevents molding. Germination should start after two days; let it germinate for five days after germination begins. Take it from the colander and spread it on a plastic sheet and dry completely in the sun (or place it on trays in the oven at lowest setting and dry). After it is dried, grind it coarsely (too fine a grind makes a beer paste). Add the hot water at 170 degrees F. For a real Kaffir beer, keep the mixture at this temperature for 15 hours until it begins to slightly sour. This marks the presence of *Lactobacillus* organisms and gives Kaffir beer its unique taste; it also adds important nutritional components. Then cool it to 70 degrees F and add yeast. Ferment three days and then drink without bottling. A more conventional American version would be to hold it at heat for two hours, strain the liquid into the fermenter, and add yeast. Ferment until complete, siphon into primed bottles, and cap.

RICE BEER

A rice-beer is made by the women of Formosa who boil the rice until it is quite soft, when they pound it into a paste. They then chew rice-flour and put it aside until they have enough to use as a ferment, which they mix with the rice paste working the two together like dough. The compound is then covered with water and allowed to ferment for two months or more.

—Ernest Cherrington, 1925[62]

Rice is one of the most important and sacred grains of Asia. As mentioned earlier, unlike other grains, it cannot be germinated to convert starch to sugar. But, most Asian cultures, like a few South American cultures, discovered that some molds will convert starch to sugar. The mold they use naturally occurs in and on gingerroot and is generally one of the main ingredients used in preparing yeast cakes. Most rice beers and wines are made with such yeast cakes.

Both rice and rice beer are attributed to sacred origins by the Gonds, a tribal people of India. They note that the Creator gave them the knowledge of rice beer "for no other purpose than to cheer them up."[63] When they were told by missionaries to stop their drinking, they replied, "Liquor comes from heaven, and who could resist so gracious a blessing."[64]

The stories of the sacred origins of rice are very similar throughout Asia. The one recounted in chapter 6 from the Himalayan region is very similar to this one from Indonesia, which in turn has many similarities to the tales told about the origins of manioc.

Patoto'e (the unknowable sacred center of all things—"he who fixes destinies"), sent his son, Batara Guru, who created all the things of the Earth. Batara Guru built a heavenly palace on Earth where he lived with many people whom he taught the ways of the Earth. His first daughter, Sangiang Serri, died after only seven days. She was buried, and from her body came the rice to humankind.

Rice is, perhaps, the most important plant in Asia, both for food and ceremony. To all Buddhists and Hindus it is considered sacred, one of the nine sacred plants—the *navapatrika*—created by Bramha for humankind. Rice was the final, or ninth, plant created. Navapatrika are the embodiment of Durga, the Earth Mother, who is also called *Sakambhari*, meaning "the herb-bearing or herb-nourishing one."

Like all fermented beverages, rice wine and beer are an integral part of ceremonies throughout their range. The fermented beer or wine is offered to the ancestors, to sacred beings, to the gods, and to the spirits of plants and the land.

A traditional rice chang can be made following the recipe under "Chang." Here is another, Bertrand Remi's recipe for a rice beer using a standard beer or ale yeast. The best kind of rice to use is an aromatic variety such as basmati, though any kind will work.

Rice Beer
Ingredients

  1 quart cooked rice
  1 gallon water
  12 ounces white sugar
  yeast

> Dissolve 12 ounces sugar in 1 gallon water. Add 1 quart cooked rice and yeast. Let ferment until complete, then strain into secondary fermenter with airlock. Let stand until sediment falls. Prime bottles, fill, and cap. Ready to drink in seven days.[65]

ABOUT RICE
Oryza sativa

> *Rice wine has so much supernatural power that spirits are drawn to it like flies to honey.*
> —Mikal Aasved, 1988[66]

Rice is rarely used as medicine. Primarily it is nutritive. It finds its best usage as medicine for those in the West who have long relied on an improper diet with high levels of sugar, fat, and meat. Heavy reliance on such a diet over time produces inordinate amounts of body fat, with all the problems that go along with that condition. Rice is extremely low in fats and is, like manioc, more than 80 percent starch. As a result, it is one of the best food grains in the world. One of the first results of switching to rice as a primary component of a regular diet is the reduction of high levels of body fat. This, in and of itself, can help alleviate many diet-related conditions. Medicinally, rice has been used in nutritionally debilitated states, for those with debilitated digestive systems, for diarrhea, febrile diseases, and inflammations of the internal organs. Rice water, a decoction of rice, is listed in the *Pharmacopoeia of India* as a demulcent and refrigerant for use in dysuria and in febrile and inflammatory diseases. Rice and rice flour have been used as poultices for erysipelas, burns, and scalds.[67]

BANANA BEER

As well as being considered a healthful dietary supplement and medicine prescribed for certain ailments and fevers, nwenge [banana beer] is a customary sacrament in numerous traditional rituals and ceremonies. Libations of nwenge are used to consecrate new home and garden sites, houses, and canoes. It is also a requisite offering to placate and propitiate ancestral ghosts, spirits, and gods.

Nwenge also plays a significant customary role in ceremonies such as birth and naming, twin ceremonies, marriages, lineage and clan succession ceremonies, funerals, and public celebrations.

—M. Robbins, 1977[68]

This is a traditional fermentation called *pombe* of the Wachagga tribe who live near Mt. Kilimanjaro in Africa. It is very similar to *nwenge*.

Banana Beer

Ingredients

> 2 quarts very ripe bananas
>
> yeast
>
> 5 quarts water
>
> 3 quarts malted millet or barley

> Mash the bananas and cook without water. When cool add the yeast and let ferment 4 days in a wooden pot. On the fifth day add 5 quarts water. [Traditionally, the Wachagga use malted millet for the next step. It is not easily found, and you can substitute malted barley instead. To malt millet, follow the instructions under "Tesquino" and "Millet Beers," for malting grains. When the millet is malted, dry it, and grind coarse.] On the sixth day take the coarsely ground millet or barley and pour on enough boiling water to make a dough. Strain the banana water and mix it very gradually and thoroughly with the malted millet or barley dough. Let it stand, covered, twenty four hours. Then drink. Like all traditional fermented beverages this banana beer is not strained. It is considered a food/drink and the whole is consumed.[69]

ABOUT BANANA

Musa acuminata

> *Broad and big are the fronds or leaves of the [banana] and they are used for their purity and for their antiseptic property as plates on sacred occasions for taking meals, particularly in the prominent feasts of the Hindus.*
>
> —Majupuria and Joshi, 1989[70]

Throughout Africa, Asia, and South America, banana (or plantain) is used in fermentation, as medicine, for sacred ceremonies, and for food. In all places that it grows, its leaf is an essential part of sacred ceremonies. The rituals of Hindus in Asia and tribespeople in South America and Africa all use banana leaves in much the same manner. The leaves are laid out and everything to be used in the coming ceremonies are laid thereon, each taken up in its time.

Though banana fruit is known everywhere, its use as a medicinal herb is little recognized outside traditional communities. The fresh juice of the stem is powerfully diuretic, the root strongly astringent and hemostatic. Used for excessive bleeding in childbirth, the fresh root is grated, the pulp is squeezed through a cloth, and a tablespoon (maximum three) is given every five minutes. The fruit itself is a reliable medicinal. Long used in its well-ripened form as a tonic and nutritive food for babies and invalids, it possesses a number of other important medicinal properties. The fruit is a reliable, though mild, antibacterial. It has been found to possess antituberculosis and antiulcer activity and to be effective against *Bacillus coagulans, Bacillus stereothermophilus,* and *Clostridium sporogenes* in in vitro studies. In general, the riper the better.[71]

Ashes from the burned plant or the dried leaves are traditionally used in India and Nepal for scurvy, ulcers, heartburn, and intestinal worms. As in South America, both the Nepalese and Indians use the juice of the root or plant for checking bleeding. As an external poultice, the green or slightly ripened banana is strongly astringent (remember how it dries out your mouth?) and mildly antibacterial, making it useful for bleeding wounds. The juice of the flower is used for dysmenorrhoea and menorrhagia. The fruit is considered antiscorbutic, antibacterial, laxative, diuretic, and nutritive.[72]

PALM WINE AND BEER

Preparation of the [palm beer] is surrounded with religious beliefs and takes place as part of a religious ceremony, but among the

> *Gonds, as in other tribes, the magic of fermentation begins even before the harvest. Prior to tapping any tree for the first time, for example, offerings must be made to the seven heavenly maidens.*
>
> —Mikal Aasved, 1988[73]

Like maple trees, the palm is tapped for its sweet sap, which is made into beer and wine. Its use extends to all cultures on all continents where the palm grows: North, South, and Central America, Africa, and Asia. And among all the cultures that use it, the palm is considered to be sacred and to have come from a sacred source. In India and Nepal the palm is considered to possess a living spirit that must be honored. Offering life and nourishment to people, it is thought of as a mother to human beings, and killing one is considered the same as matricide. This feeling for the palm is evident in many other cultures. Among the Warao of South America, it is called the "Tree of Life." And Siamese monks revere the soul of the palm so deeply that they will not cut or damage any part of the tree. The fermented sap is also considered sacred, a gift to the people to help them communicate with the nonmaterial world and to uplift their spirits. There are many origin stories of both the palm and fermented palm sap. One origin tale is recounted in chapter 6; here is another from the Gond tribe who live in India.

It is said among the Gond that the palm that is tapped for beer and wine, which they call *salphi*, came from Tallur Muttai, the Mother Earth. It is said that seven salphi maidens were born to the Earth Mother, but there was but one placenta among them. After Tallur Muttai cut the cord and was burying the placenta, the seven maidens ran away and hid where they could never be found. When she discovered her loss, Tallur Muttai went to where she had buried the placenta and, in sorrow, let the milk from her breasts fall upon the Earth. Soon a wonderful tree grew from the placenta, the sago palm, the tree born from milk that always gives milk, the milk of the Earth Mother.[74]

⌇

Among all tribal cultures, the first knowledge of fermentation was a momentous event. Among African tribes who ferment palm sap, perhaps the greatest number live in Ghana. There are many origin stories of the time they received the knowledge of fermentation. Here is one from the Fante tribe; similar variations exist among many other tribes of Ghana.

Throughout all the long history of the Fante, there was never a greater hunter than Ansa. It is told that one time, as he was preparing for the hunt, he approached the holy man of the tribe and asked for rituals to prepare him for the hunt. Making offerings and prayers, the holy one told Ansa that this time on the hunt he would find something of great importance to the Fante, something other than the animal he sought. But, the holy one continued, it would entail a great sacrifice by Ansa. Not deterred, Ansa accepted the blessings of the holy one and, taking his best dog, set out on the hunt. He was not gone long before he felt the powers of the Earth leading him to a certain place. There, in a clearing in the forest, he found a tree, pushed down by an elephant. In the center of the trunk was a great depression made by the elephant's foot. Leaving his weapons, Ansa approached and found the depression to be filled with a milky-white liquid. He wished to taste it, but remembering what the holy one had said, he called his dog and offered it to him. The dog sniffed at it, then began to greedily drink it. Ansa waited, and the next morning, seeing no harm had come to his dog, he drank also. Soon he was filled with an experience he had never known, and he knew that this was the thing he was to bring back to the Fante. Taking his water container, Ansa filled it with the fermented palm sap. Retrieving his weapons, he traveled back to his village and told the king of his find. Interested, the king drank what Ansa had brought, and he liked it so much that he drank all that remained, falling into a deep slumber. The people, seeing their king dead (so they thought), killed Ansa and his dog in revenge. But as they were mourning, the king awoke, and asking after his hunter, was told what had happened. The king, angry and saddened, decreed that the gift that Ansa had brought would be known forever as *ansa*, though over time the name has been shortened and is now called *nsa*.[75]

Among African tribes, the ancestors hold an especially important place in spiritual devotion. In their religious cosmology, the Creator—Onyame—is higher than all other things; next are the gods—*abosom*, and finally the ancestors—*nsamanfo*. The elders of the tribes communicate with the ancestors (who are more accessible), who then communicate with the gods and the Creator. Through both drinking the beer and through ritual offerings of beer to the ancestors (who also like to drink it), communication with the ancestors is achieved and their help is obtained for the tribe.[76]

The Twi, for example, understand that Onyame created a universe impregnated with his own power. And the universe thus created contained numerous participants: spirits, ancestors, human beings, animals, and plants—each of which possesses a potent, and nonmaterial, life force called *sasa*. Tribal spirituality is concerned with understanding and learning to affect the nonmaterial world, for it is recognized that material reality alone cannot explain the totality of human life. To affect the unseen, nonmaterial world, power must be accumulated. Gaining such power therefore involves an understanding of cosmology, the forces that affect outcomes in the material world, and a knowledge of how to affect them. Alcohol enables the elders to temporarily access the spirit realm and communicate with the ancestors, who in turn speak to the gods and Onyame on their behalf. Because of their nonmaterial existence, the ancestors know the world of the gods and the Creator more intimately and can intercede for human beings more effectively.

Alcohol "dethrones" reason and allows other human faculties to become enhanced, allowing communication with spirit realms. Palm beer bridges the gap between the material and nonmaterial world and enables communication, leading to a harmonious balance between the two, a necessary state for the continuance of human life. One tribal elder remarked,

"Nsa [palm beer] is a definite link between man and his ancestor because it is spiritual. The ancestors are spiritual, and this [nsa] is a spirit."[77]

This orientation is also seen among other Ghana tribal cultures, such as the Akan. To the Akan, the Creator is the Eternal One (named *Odomankoma*) or the Creator of All Things (in their language *Bore-bore*). Human beings are created of three things: blood from the mother (*mogya*), spirit-personality from the father (*ntoro*), and soul from the Creator (*kra*). There is kra in all things, and a bit of the Creator lives in every person's body. Thus, knowledge of the Creator is innate in all things and all people. The Twi people say, therefore: *obi nkyere abofra Onyame*—"No one shows a child the Supreme Being." And the Akan believe that all people have direct access to the Creator, and therefore, *obi kwan nsi obi kwan mu*—"No man's path crosses another's." Hunters, because they are immersed more than other tribal members in the wildness of the world, are more directly connected to the kra in material things. Thus, they are a human, and cultural, connection between the human and supernatural worlds. It is fitting, therefore, that it was a hunter that found the first fermented palm sap and brought it back to the tribe.[78]

Palm Beer

Ingredients

> 1 gallon fresh palm sap
>
> yeast

> Tap one or more palms until 1 gallon of sap is obtained. Add yeast and palm sap to fermenter. Ferment until complete. Siphon into bottles, prime with 1 teaspoon of sugar if carbonated beer is desired, and cap. Ready to drink in one to two weeks.

ABOUT PALM

Cocus nucifera, Phoenix sylvestris, et al.

Numerous palm types can be tapped for sap. The most common are the moriche, sago, coconut, palmyra, and date palm. Palm sap is a clear, colorless liquid with a sugar content of about 10 to 12 percent. It is very sweet to the taste. The trees are tapped by cutting the trunk, much as indigenous peoples once tapped sugar maples, or by cutting the unopened flower spathes. Each tree will produce 1 1/2 to 3 liters per day of sap. Usually, the sap is naturally fermented from airborne wild yeasts. However, the same pots that collect palm sap are used over and over again, and they are not cleaned between uses. Each pot contains residues of old palm beer and yeasts, which begin fermentation when they are refilled with palm sap. The pots that are used to collect sap are called, among the South Africa Thonga tribe, *gandielos*, meaning "altars."

Palm sap, when fermented, can attain 10 percent alcohol, is milky-white in color, and tastes somewhat like a sweet, dry champagne. Like all indigenous fermented drinks, it is high in nutrients, vitamins, and protein. Nigerians, for instance, drink up to a liter of palm wine per day.[79]

While little Western research has been done on the medicinal aspects of palm species, they are used throughout the world for medicine. In India and Nepal, the coconut palm is used for medicine in many ways. There is a soft substance on the lower parts of the leaves that is used as a hemostatic and for application to stubborn ulcers. The bark is used for treatment of toothache and earache. The root is considered a powerful diuretic and has been used for uterine toning, bronchitis, liver complaints, and for treatment of high fevers. The young roots and flowers are strongly astringent and have been used for dysentery, gum toning, and gargling for sore throats. The fresh sap is considered diuretic and refrigerant and is used, with a little rice flour, as a poultice for ulcers and carbuncles. The fermented sap is slightly laxative. The fruit and its milk have numerous medicinal uses as astringents, for urinary tract disorders, purifying blood, checking vomiting, dysentery, and cholera. Coconut oil has shown inhibition of tuberculosis in vivo. An extract of the dried shell has shown in vitro activity against a number of bacteria. For medicinal purposes, the coconut palm is used in much the same manner wherever it grows.[80] The date palm is used in very similar ways, though in its case, the emphasis is on the fruit and sap. These are considered nutritive, analgesic, antiarthritic, anthelmintic, aphrodisiac, brain sedative, cardiac tonic, carminative, dentifrice, diuretic, emollient, expectorant, and nerve tonic. They have been used for brain and heart weakness, colds, coughs, fainting and dizziness, seminal weakness, toothache, and worms.[81] Interestingly, many of the origin stories of the palm assert that one of its reasons for being created was as an aphrodisiac and sexual stimulant to help one of the gods procreate. It was found by humans after its creation, and they continued to use it for this purpose. Palm sap is still used as an aphrodisiac and in medicinal treatment for sexual debility, infertility, and lack of desire.[82]

FIVE

Alcohol
Aqua Vitae, the Water of Life

For art to exist, for any sort of aesthetic activity to exist, a certain physiological precondition is indispensable: intoxication.
—Frederic Nietzsche[1]

If every man is to forego his freedom of action because many make licentious use of it, I know not what is the value of any freedom.
—J. Risdon Bennet, M.D., ca. 1890[2]

The little playful women,
The little playful women,
Whence they got the dizziness?
Therewith they made my heart drunk.
The little playful women,

When they are dizzy
Surely they will take me.

Dizzy women
Are seizing my heart.
Westward they are leading me.
I like it.
One on each side,
They are leading me.

—Papago tiswin song[3]

The notion that a beverage which contains any amount of alcohol can have a nutritional value beyond that of ordinary table wine, or any medicinal value at all, runs counter to what most Westerners "know" to be true about them.

—Mikal Aasved, 1988[4]

*A*LCOHOL. How strange it is that for millennia women were the makers of beer and wine, that the gift of fermentation was given to them to hold for all human beings, and that the major force to outlaw alcohol has also come from women (in the temperance movement). Was it because in the Middle Ages the men took from them the power over fermentation? Was the goddess who brought fermentation speaking with anger through her daughters, mankind's gatherers of the sacred beverage, alcohol?

It is now accepted as an axiom among us that alcohol is a bad thing but that it is impossible to get rid of—people are going to use it anyway. The battle thus turns to narrowing those times and places where it may be used, to making sure that those who use it know of their flaws of character, that its sublime qualities and our relationship with it as human beings are safely forgotten. Who among us now can celebrate its nature, can sing its praises, can honor its gifts without a nervous glance over the shoulder? Who among us can applaud its use to travel to other realms, to free the chained voice of poetry, to comfort us in our mortality, to celebrate life and feel no fear of rebuke or condemnation? Who can print a book that advocates its use, that exhorts its teachings, that sings unashamed of its nature without hurried consultation with attorneys, disclaimers in the text, fingers nervously crossed? Have we forgotten so soon what it has given us and what it still can?

All vertebrates sometimes enjoy alcohol. Elephants will knock down wine palms, step on the tree to make a depression in the trunk, wait while the sweet sap fills the hole and ferments, then drink what they have made. Birds get drunk on fermenting berries, and even bees, nonvertebrates that they are, have been observed to become intoxicated. But it is humankind who has had the longest and most involved relationship with alcohol.

That ancient relationship is now viewed from sociological, psychological, or commercial orientations alone. But until the past 150 years, it was viewed from other, more sacred, perspectives that were remarkably similar throughout the world. These spiritual views about the purpose of alcohol can be found in the myths of our ancient tribal forebears and the oral traditions of living indigenous peoples. To put it most clearly: Alcohol was given to the first people, our ancient ancestors, by a direct action of the sacred in order to help us as human beings. In particular, alcohol helps us by giving the gift of travel in sacred domains; conferring on human beings the capacity to create—specifically, art—even more specifically, poetry; and, finally, to help with one particular and unique suffering we experience as human beings—the knowledge of our own mortality.

Alcohol's activity as a euphoric and mood- or consciousness-altering substance is well known. Generally, this is now thought of as something we would be better off without—that only the weak among us would need or want such a thing. And alcohol's connection to art (how many writers were/are heavy drinkers?) is also well known. These are both important contributions of alcohol, but it is its last purpose, to help us bear our knowledge of mortality, that is most fundamental and pervasive in myth and oral tradition.

Many legends of the origin of fermentation connect it to human mortality. Many cultures say that the knowledge of fermentation was given to us to help us deal with the impact of knowing our own mortality. And nowhere is this so beautifully articulated as in the ancient Sumerian epic, *Gilgamesh*. (And it is to be remembered that some believe that Sumer is the ancient birthplace of beer.)

The epic story of Gilgamesh is very long, but the essential portion of it that applies here is contained in "Gilgamesh and the Huluppu-Tree." Gilgamesh is a divine-human hero—one of those progenitors of the human race from whom human knowledge of life and behavior has come. His inseparable friend was Enkidu. Enkidu and Gilgamesh fought and defeated the monster Humbaba and then killed the miraculous Bull of Heaven that was sent by the goddess Ishtar to kill them. The goddess cursed them for the killing, and in outrage Enkidu threw the bull's right thigh in her face and insulted her. In response, the gods decreed that

Enkidu would die. (Insulting the gods always turns out badly.) For Gilgamesh, the death of his friend was devastating; knowing the inevitability of death for the first time, Gilgamesh could not stop thinking about it, and no action, no part of life, seemed worth living. His heart went out to all human beings who must suffer mortality. By this he was precipitated into a mythic journey in search of a way that the human race could escape death. Deciding, eventually, to go to the source of human mortality, he sought out the gods who gave death to humankind. After long trial and many journeys, he found them in a great cedar forest and confronted them about why human beings must die. No more beautiful response to this conflict exists anywhere in human literature than in their reply to Gilgamesh.

> *Gilgamesh, whither rovest thou?*
> *The Life thou pursuest thou shalt not find.*
> *When the gods created mankind,*
> *Death for mankind they set aside,*
> *Life in their own hands retaining.*
> *Thou Gilgamesh, let full be thy belly,*
> *Make thou merry by day and by night.*
> *On each day make thou a feast of rejoicing,*
> *Day and night dance thou and play!*
> *Let thy garments be sparkling fresh,*
> *Thy head be washed; bathe thou in water.*
> *Pay heed to the little one that holds on to thy hand,*
> *Let thy spouse delight in thy bosom!*
> *For this is the task of mankind!*[5]

And to help humankind with this task, the gods, in pity, gave to us the gift of fermentation. The gift of beer throughout myth and oral tradition is firmly connected to both a divine origin and an easing of human pain in the face of mortality. Though the many origin stories of fermentation and the plants associated with it vary from culture to culture, this common thread can be found. What is so remarkable about this is that *all* cultures throughout history assert some origin of fermentation that connects the sacred, an action of sacred beings, and human knowledge or experience of mortality.

What is even more remarkable (to me) is that when confronted by such unanimity of expression, modern researchers instead assume that our ancestors were unable to make a distinction between things they made up and deep experiences of the sacred. Culture after culture, few having temporal or geographic connection to the others, say, for instance, that the knowledge of this plant medicine came to them from an experience of the sacred, or the plant told them. In the case of fermentation, the sacred beings gave it to them because they wept for the human condition and wished to bring human beings joy. What if ancient and indigenous cultures were not engaging in highly inventive storytelling but were actually articulating a real experience in their oral tradition? Intelligent, perceptive human beings throughout history, even today, assert there is something beyond the merely human. They give this something many names in order to define it, but it represents some *sacred* order of reality.

Human beings have the capacity to perceive extremely subtle states of mind and spirit. They have insisted that there is a realm of reality that they call (in whatever language they use) *sacred*. And, they insist, they have the capacity to experience it. There are powers greater than we, but, we, as human beings, can make contact with them, learn about them, and in so doing learn about and transform ourselves. Many people in indigenous and ancient cultures spent a great deal of time developing their capacity to perceive and understand that order of reality that we call the sacred.[6]

It is extremely difficult to understand the importance and meaning of fermentation to indigenous and ancient human beings and their cultures without understanding that their primary frame of reference was a sacred one and was concerned with transcendent realities. Though growing further and further removed from such transcendent realities, we in the West are not strangers to them—aspects of transcendent reality are still part of our culture. Our culture was founded on transcendent principles such as dignity, freedom, and the pursuit of happiness. These intangibles have shaped our American culture and they come in turn, at least as far as Thomas Jefferson was concerned, from a divine source.

It is irritating to anyone who believes in universe-as-machine to accept that the initiating factors that generated human civilization may have come from the sacred and not human action alone. But it is impossible to grasp the nature of our ancestors' relationship with plants and fermentation without understanding that they believed actions of the sacred were at the heart of their world. And so, as Solomon Katz and many other researchers have begun to assert, it may in fact be true that the genesis of human civilization is the appearance of fermentation—that it was not a later development of humankind but the first.

What seems clear is that human knowledge of fermentation arose independently throughout human cultures, that each culture attributed its appearance to divine intervention, and that its use is intimately bound up with our development as a species. Frederich Nietzsche touches on this truth when he remarks that "Man is no longer an artist, he has become a work of art: the artistic power of all nature here reveals itself in the tremors of drunkenness to the highest gratification of the Primordial Unity."[7]

That fermentation holds within it some magical substance, a spirit, that can awaken in human beings capacities that lay dormant has long been known. The search for that substance, the spirit of alcohol, was accomplished by the Islamic alchemists through distillation (though some researchers insist that the Aztecs also independently discovered distillation) when they isolated the pure spirit of alcohol, aqua vitae, the water of life, the water that burns like fire. The French term *eau de vie*, the Scandinavian *aquavit*, and the Gaelic *usquebaugh* (from which comes the word *whiskey*) all mean water of life. From the time of its first use, alcohol has been experienced by human beings as possessing life-enhancing properties—the "spirit" in alcohol was believed to "preserve youth, prolong life, and prevent senility."[8] And in every culture in which it exists, alcohol has been used for healing, in ceremonies and rituals, to personally take on attributes of the sacred, and as a source of song and poetry.

Conventional medicine is based in part on finding the "active constituent" in plants (or any healing substance), isolating it, making it into a drug, and using it medicinally. Most clinicians have noted that these "active constituents" produce side effects out of proportion to their use in the whole plant. Plants, complex beings that they are, contain scores of substances, many of which function to either enhance the activity of "active constituents" or to ameliorate their side effects. The isolation of alcohol came out of the same thinking process that led to the isolation of other active constituents in plants. And like all "pure" substances isolated from plants, alcohol is more toxic and the side effects are more pronounced when it is separated from its fermented plant context. This toxicity, new to the human species, plays a crucial part in the efforts of the temperance movement to limit alcohol use.

The power of the temperance movement is directly related to three things: the degree to which women no longer participate in fermentation, the Protestant Reformation, and the separation of alcohol from is original context—the isolation of the "pure" substance from its plant matrix. But alcohol embedded in its original context is much different in its actions from those of the isolated "spirit" obtained from distillation.

Without distillation, fermentation will produce a beer or wine that contains from 1.5 percent to 14 percent alcohol. Generally, the range is from 3.5 percent to 12 percent in almost all fermentations. And in this original, most ancient of contexts, alcohol is mildly anesthetic, mildly antiseptic, a general tonic, and a moderate stimulant. It relaxes, reduces inhibition, augments the appetite, increases digestive action, stimulates liver action, increases the action of the heart, stimulates blood circulation, dilates blood vessels, slightly increases body temperature, stimulates and enhances the performance of all bodily functions, exhilarates, intoxicates, increases cerebral activity, heightens sensory perception, and energizes mental activity.[9]

Though alcohol's activity is systemwide, its two most potent areas of activity are in the liver and brain. The liver is a remarkably comprehensive organ in its range of activity. As the eminent medical herbalist David Hoffmann observes:

> The liver serves to metabolize carbohydrates and store them as glycogen; metabolize lipids (including cholesterol and certain vitamins) and proteins; manufacture bile; filter impurities and toxic material from the blood; produce blood-clotting factors; and destroy old, worn-out red blood cells.[10]

The stimulation of the liver by alcohol results in more efficient and rapid activity in all those areas.

The effects of alcohol in increasing cerebral activity, heightening sensory perception, and energizing mental activity correlates to its long historical use by artists of all kinds. Its general effects of stimulating and enhancing bodily function correlate well to its long-ascribed healing and health-enhancing properties. Many indigenous cultures also are clear about the effects of alcohol on the mind. Among the Charoti of South America, the spirit of a plant attains its highest development and manifestation when fermented. This highly developed plant spirit fills the human that consumes it. Thus, they say that an intoxicated person has a *peyak nota nappibe*, "a good spirit in the forehead."[11] This good spirit fills them with strength and a resistance to evils of every kind.

The widely publicized negative effects of alcohol come from, as noted earlier, the separation of alcohol from its original plant context. In traditional fermentations and the cultures that use them, the negative side effects of alcohol are never found. The overuse of the separated pure, active constituent causes two primary physical side effects: the destruction of the liver and mental aberration. Interestingly, both occur in the primary areas positively enhanced by the use of traditional fermentations. The use of the separated toxic constituent of plant fermentation overloads all systems, those two first and foremost, and side effects, including death, that are never noted from the use of traditional plant fermentations, occur.

Alcoholism, solitary drinking, and the various diseases attendant with alcohol abuse do not exist in indigenous cultures, irrespective of the amount of fermentation and drunkenness they engage in. These problems come from alcohol's separation from its sacred and ritual context, its isolation from its plant matrix, and concomitants of civilization (most especially the scientific belief that the isolated "pure" substance in a thing is better than leaving it in its matrix of origin). In all things, it seems, our civilization has to encounter the shadow side of whatever we incorporate into it. We must feel the ice of its touch, the darkness of its gaze, the holocaust of its beliefs, and then (in horror of the shadow) try to remove it from our world. A foolish waste of time. We would do better to listen to Baudelaire when he speaks of the gift of fermentation.

> *I shall light up your aged wife's eyes,*
> *the old companion of your everyday cares and your oldest hopes.*
> *I shall soften her glance and drop into the pupil of her eye*
> *the lightning-flash of her youth.*

> *I shall sink into your bosom like a vegetable ambrosia.*
> *I shall be the seed that fertilizes the laboriously cut furrow.*
> *Our close reunion will create poetry.* [12]

SIX

The Fermentation and Sacredness of Grains

Are we to believe that the foundations of Western civilization were laid by an ill-fed people living in a perpetual state of partial intoxication?
—Paul Manglesdorf, 1991[1]

Only to him who stands where the barley stands and listens well, will it speak and tell, for his sake, what man is.
—Masanobu Fukuoka, 1985[2]

*M*OST BEERS AND ALES that we rec-
ognize as "beer" come from fermented grains. Unlike honey, the sugars in
grains are protected from yeasts—they have been converted to starch. As
a result, it is not so easy to make a beer from grain. A few other steps are
necessary. Luckily, nature was there ahead of us.

The starch, stored in the seed of a plant, is there to be used by the
new seedling when it begins to grow, but the seed can't use unconverted
starch, either. It needs to turn the starch back into sugar to use as an
energy source until its own abilities to transform sunlight and water and
carbon dioxide into sugar can begin. So, like much of life, it has an
enzyme for just that purpose.

When a seed gets wet and is kept warm, it begins to sprout. At that
moment, an enzyme is released that begins converting the starch in the
seed into sugar. A similar enzyme is present in mammal saliva. Since early
times, many cultures have masticated grains or starchy roots in order to mix
them with human saliva—thus beginning the same starch conversion.
Much later, human beings began to use the natural process of the seed germination—called "malting" by brewers. After a few days of germination, the
seed will have released the enzyme necessary for starch conversion. At that
point, the germinating seeds are dried and are stored for making beers and
ales. This is a tremendous accomplishment, and it is also much more labor-
intensive than other ways of producing sugar for fermentation. It began in
the areas of ancient Sumer (now Iraq) and Egypt some 10,000 years ago and
was developed into a high art by the Egyptians while the rest of the world
continued to ferment in other ways. In Greece, for instance, they still used
honey, grapes, and other fruits—easy sources of fermentable sugar.

For a long time archaeologists and scholars have insisted that the
domestication of grain was the beginning of civilization. They thought
that grain domestication came first, fermentation second. Evidence that
agriculture began even earlier and that maybe, just maybe, fermentation
came before grain domestication is a possibility that outrages many.

There is evidence that perhaps the earliest agricultural plant was the bottle gourd (*Lagenaria siceraria*). It was regularly cultivated in Africa at least 40,000 years ago and in South America 13,000 years ago. Barley, einkorn, and emmer wheat (all used to brew ancient beers) appeared later, not being intentionally grown and used in planned human food production until after the major land changes of the Pleistocene (about 11,000 years ago). These grains were first used in northern Africa. But there is evidence that wild grains were harvested for food for thousands of years prior to this time.[3] And though many researchers identify the first appearance of beer at this time in the areas we now call Egypt and Iraq, there is evidence that it also appeared in South America at virtually the same time.[4] Conventional scientific theory has it that grain was cultivated in order to provide food for a static, growing population, and that fermentation was a later, accidental discovery. However, a number of researchers, such as Solomon Katz and Fritz Maytag, have proposed that it was the discovery of grain malting and its subsequent fermentation that was the original motivation of societies to settle in one place and begin intentionally growing grains.[5] Some verification that this might be true can be found among the Chagga of Tanazania's Mount Kilimanjaro. Their extensive irrigation systems were developed in antiquity solely to provide sufficient water to grow millet, which is a beer crop and is rarely eaten.[6] And among the Lepcha of the Himalayas, millet (grown extensively) is so sacred that it is never eaten and is used only for fermentation.

It is an odd coincidence, to say the least, that the climate changes that led the two wheats and barley to immigrate to northern Africa and the Middle East occurred at the same time that beer fermentation is known to have begun there. Nearly all researchers of fermentation insist it happened accidentally, like the medicinal uses of plants. In their view, some woman left a pot of grain out in the rain, and it germinated and then fermented, and she bravely drank it and felt so good she informed the world of her wonderful discovery, which swept the human population. But there is evidence that honey was fermented long before grains, at least as long as

35,000 years ago. And examination of the oral traditions that remain that
tell about honey and mead insist that it was not an accidental cause-and-
effect discovery. Like the most ancient accounts of brewing grains, that
discovery is attributed to the intervention of sacred beings.

Probably the oldest *written* account of the discovery of grain fermentation is included in Rune XX of the Finnish epic, the *Kalevala*, circa
1000 B.C. Basically, the epic relates how a semidivine woman creates the
first fermentation of barley for human beings. She tries a number of
things: fir cones and pine seedlings, the saliva from enraged bears, and
finally a bee is sent to gather nectar from flowers. These are all added to
the barley and water; the final additive, from the bee, produces the first
fermentation of grain.

Louhi, hostess of Pohyola,
Hastens to the hall and court-room,
In the centre speaks as follows:
"Whence indeed will come
           the liquor,
Who will brew me beer from barley,
Who will make the mead abundant,
For the people of the Northland,
Coming to my daughter's marriage,
To her drinking-feast and nuptials?
Cannot comprehend the malting,
Never have I learned the secret,
Nor the origin of brewing."

Spake an old woman from the corner:
Beer comes from the barley,
Comes from barley, hops, and water,
And the fire gives its assistance.

Hop-vine was the son of Remu,
Small the seed in earth was planted,
Cultivated in the loose soil,
Scattered like the seed of serpents
On the brink of Kalew-waters,
On the Osmo-fields and borders.
There the young plant grew
           and flourished,
There arose the clinging hop-vine,
Clinging to the rocks and alders.

Man of good-luck sowed the barley
On the Osmo hills and lowlands,
And the barley grew and flourished,
Grew and spread in rich abundance,
Fed upon the air and water,
On the Osmo plains and highlands,
On the fields of Kalew-heroes.

Time had traveled little distance,
Ere the hops in trees were humming,
Barley in the fields was singing,
And from Kalew's well the water,
This the language of the trio:
Let us join our triple forces,
Join to each other's powers
Sad alone to live and struggle,
Little use in working singly,
Better we should toil together.
Osmotar, the [brew wife]
    beer-preparer,
Brewer of the drink refreshing,
Takes the golden grains of barley,
Taking six of barley-kernels,
Taking seven tips of hop-fruit,
Filling seven cups of water,
On the fire she sets the caldron,
Boils the barley, hops, and water,
Lets them steep, and seethe,
    and bubble,
Brewing the beer delicious,
In the hottest days of summer,
On the foggy promontory.
On the island forest-covered;
Poured it into birch-wood barrels,
Into hogsheads made of oak-wood.

Thus did Osmotar of Kalew
Brew together hops and barley,
Could not generate the ferment.

Thinking long and long debating,
Thus she spake in troubled accents:
"What will bring the effervescence,
Who will add the needed factor,
That the beer may foam and sparkle,
May ferment and be delightful?"

Kalevatar, magic maiden,
Grace and beauty in her fingers,
Swiftly moving, lightly stepping,
In her trimly-buckled sandals,
Steps upon the birch-wood bottom,
Turns one way, and then another,
In the centre of the caldron;
Finds within a splinter lying,
From the bottom lifts the fragment,
Turns it in her fingers musing:
"What may come of this I know not,
In the hands of magic maidens,
In the virgin hands of Kapo,
Snowy virgin of the Northland!"

Kalevatar, took the splinter
To the magic virgin, Kapo,
Who by unknown force and insight,
Rubbed her hands and knees together,
And produced a snow-white squirrel;
Thus instructed she her creature,
Gave the squirrel these directions:
"Snow-white squirrel, mountain jewel,
Flower of the field and forest,

Haste thee wither I would send thee,
Into Metsola's wide limits,
Into Tapio's seat of wisdom;
Hasten through the heavy tree-tops,
Wisely through the thickest branches,
That the eagle may not seize thee,
Thus escape the bird of heaven.
Bring me ripe cones from the fir-tree,
From the pine-tree bring
        me seedlings,
Bring them to the hands of Kapo,
For the beer of Osmo's daughter."

. . . [The squirrel searches, finds the
        cones and seedlings]
Brought them to the hands of Kapo,
To the magic virgin's fingers,
Kapo took the cones selected,
Laid them in the beer for ferment,
But it brought no effervescence,
And the beer was cold and lifeless.

Osmotar, the beer-preparer,
Kapo, brewer of the liquor,
Deeply thought long and considered:
"What will bring the effervescence,
Who will lend me aid sufficient,
That the beer will foam and sparkle,
May the ferment be refreshing?"

Kalevatar, sparkling maiden,
Grace and beauty in her fingers,

Softly moving, lightly stepping,
In her trimly-buckled sandals,
Steps again upon the bottom,
Turns one way and then another,
In the centre of the caldron,
Sees a chip upon the bottom,
Takes it from its place of resting,
Looks upon the chip and muses:
What may come of this I know not,
In the hands of mystic maidens,
In the hands of magic Kapo,
In the virgin's snow-white fingers.

Kalevatar took the birch-chip
To the magic maiden, Kapo,
Gave it to the white-faced maiden.
Kapo, by the aid of magic,
Rubbed her hands and knees together,
And produced a magic marten,
And the marten, golden-breasted;
Thus instructed she her creature,
Gave the marten these directions:
"Thou my golden-breasted marten,
Thou my son of golden color,
Haste thou wither I send thee,
To the bear-dens of the mountain,
To the grottos of the growler,
Gather yeast upon thy fingers,
Gather foam from lips of anger,
From the lips of bears in battle,
Bring to the hands of Kapo,
To the hands of Osmo's daughter."

... [*Thus the marten travels,*
Finds the bears in mountain wildness]
From their lips the foam was dripping,
From their tongues the froth of anger;
This the marten deftly gathered,
Brought it to the maiden Kapo,
Laid it in her dainty fingers.

Osmotar, the beer-preparer,
Brewer of the beer of barley,
Used the bear-foam as a ferment;
But it brought no effervescence,
Did not make the liquor sparkle.

Osmotar, the beer-preparer,
Thought again, and long debated:
"Who or what will bring the ferment,
That my beer may not be lifeless?"

Kalevatar, the magic maiden,
Grace and beauty in her fingers,
Softly moving, lightly stepping,
In her trimly-buckled sandals,
Steps again upon the bottom,
Turns one way and then another,
In the centre of the caldron,
Sees a pod upon the bottom,
Lifts it in her snow-white fingers,
Turns it o'er and o'er, and muses:
"What may come of this I
        know not,
In the hands of magic maidens,

In the hands of mystic Kapo,
In the snowy virgin's fingers?"

Kalevatar, sparkling maiden,
Gave the pod to magic Kapo;
Kapo, by the aid of magic,
Rubbed the pod upon her knee-cap,
And a honey-bee came flying
From the pod within her fingers.
Kapo thus addressed her birdling:
"Little bee with honeyed winglets,
King of all the fragrant flowers,
Fly thou whither I direct thee,
To the islands in the ocean,
To the water-cliffs and grottoes,
Where asleep a maid has fallen,
Girdled with a belt of copper;
By her side are honey-grasses,
By her lips are fragrant flowers,
Herbs and flowers honey-laden;
gather there the sweetened juices,
Gather honey on thy winglets,
From the calyces of flowers,
From the tips of seven petals;
Bring it to the hands of Kapo,
To the hands of Osmo's daughter."

... [*The bee finds the maiden*
        sleeping] ...
In the honey-fields of magic, ...
Brought the honey back to Kapo,
To the mystic maiden's fingers.

Osmotar, beer-preparer,
Placed the honey in the liquor;
Kapo mixed the beer and honey,
And the wedding-beer fermented;
Rose the live beer upward, upward,
From the bottom of the vessels,
Upward in the tubs of birch-wood,
Foaming higher, higher, higher,
Till it touched the oaken handles,
Overflowing all the caldrons;
To the ground it foamed and sparkled,

Sank away in sand and gravel.
Time had gone but a little distance,
Scarce a moment had passed over,
Ere the heroes came in numbers,
To the foaming beer of northland,
Rushed to drink the sparkling liquor,

Ere all others Lemminkainen
Drank, and grew intoxicated
On the beer of Osmo's daughter,
On the honey-drink of Kalew.[7]

This account is remarkable for three important reasons. First, Scandinavian brewers traditionally use evergreen boughs as an integral part of their beer—one of the few regions of the world to do so. They are used not only for flavor but for their antiseptic properties, which keep unwanted bacteria from infecting the beer. The use of evergreen (usually juniper boughs in Norway) is the first step in cleaning the vessels used for brewing. Second, barley cannot be fermented into ale until its starchy seed is converted to sugar. This is traditionally done by either germinating the grain (malting) or the use of saliva, which contains an enzyme that converts starch to sugar. An integral part of this first Finnish grain beer is the use of saliva from enraged bears. Third, it shows that honey beers—meads—predate the discovery of barley ales, because the essential element in starch conversion had not yet been discovered and had to be found; the grains still would not ferment without something in honey (it is to be remembered that heather plants include a fogg and wild yeast that will begin fermentation); and the use of the word "mead" shows that mead—fermented honey—already existed prior to the writing of the Kalevala.

The connection of sacred beings with grain and fermentation pervades all ancient cultures. And in many cultures the grain or starchy plant itself was seen as a physical manifestation of a particular sacred being—the grain growing from where their body was buried. Most often, the grain came first, fermentation after.

For instance, among the Lepcha, the gift of cereal grains came from Itpomu, the Mother of Creation.

> Mayel [known to many as Shangri-la], the legendary homeland of the first people [of the Lepcha], is said to lie somewhere behind Mount Kinchenjunga far up the Talung Valley. At one time, it is said, the road through the valley was open all the way to Mayel but it now no longer is passable. The immortal beings who live there are seven brothers, the progenitors and guardians of the Lepcha. This ancestral fraternity was created by Itpomu, the great creator deity or Mother of Creation. Each brother serves as the patron "saint" of a different type of grain—millet, rice, maize, etc.—which Itpomu placed in their charge when she created each of these cereals.[8]

The seven brothers had no wives, and each spring they would make love to the Earth, and in that place the particular grain that was theirs would grow. Though the Lepcha do plant seeds each spring, they surround the planting with ceremonies and prayers. These ceremonies bring the brothers to make love in the place where the grain seeds are planted. If the ceremonies have been done correctly, with the proper reverence, and the Earth has been kept healthy through proper prayers, ceremony and care, the insemination takes place and the grain grows well. (As mentioned earlier, the Lepcha are one of the cultures who never use their millet for food, only for fermentation.)

Among many of the indigenous cultures of Indonesia—Wemale, Balinese, Javanese, Sudanese, Bugis, and Flores—all the important plants used by human beings came into the world from the body of a sacred girl who died. This story from the Wemale is typical. Again, it has many connections to fermentation, grains, and the sacred.

In the long ago times the original nine clans of the human beings lived on the sacred mountain, Nunusaku. It was good then. There was plenty of game for all the people and everyone was happy. And among the people there was a great hunter named Ameta, who would often go into the forests and hunt food for them. It was upon one of these hunts that he found a thing he had never seen before. It was round, a little smaller than a human head, brown, and hairy all over. He didn't know what it was. But he thought that maybe he would take it and put it into a hole in the ground and see what would happen. As he patted the brown earth over the top of it, the ground began to tremble. And before his eyes a great tree rose up, one that he had never seen before. He walked all around, marveling at it, and he noticed that out of its side there was a little sap coming. Putting out his hand, he tasted of it and it was very sweet. He thought to himself that he would cut this tree down and collect the sap and maybe something good would happen. But as he began cutting the tree, he missed his aim and cut his finger. Before he could stop it, his blood dripped on the sap of the tree. As they mixed together, they began to change. There before him a tiny and very beautiful baby was born from the tree sap and the blood, and she began crying. He picked her up and thought she should have a name, and he gave her one—Hainuwele. Hainuwele grew very fast. By the time he got home, she was a little girl. The next morning she was even older, and by the third day she was a young woman just entering puberty.

Among the nine clans a special dance, the *maro*, was held each year for the young women just entering puberty. And it so happened that it was the time of the maro dance that Hainuwele came to be a woman. So it was that she went to dance with the other maidens of the clans. The dance was long, lasting nine days, and as the young men and women danced, they interwove together in a winding spiral. Each night the women were to give the men a gift of a betel nut. But Hainuwele, for the first time in the history of the nine clans, did something different. The first night she gave, like the others, the gift of betel. But the second she gave corals and the third porcelain. Each night she gave a gift more magnificent and beautiful than the night before. The men did not know why she was doing this, and they became afraid. So on the ninth night, before she could dance and give her gift, they dug a hole and, throwing her into it, buried her alive.

As it had been each day of the dance, Ameta waited for his daughter to return home. But on this ninth and final night she did not come, and becoming worried he went to search for her. By the time he came to the place of the dance, all the people had gone. He looked everywhere and could not find her. But after a while he found a fresh grave, and digging within it, he found his daughter, dead, where they had buried her. Ameta mourned the daughter he had known only a short while, born of his blood and the tree that he had never seen before. But as he sat mourning, his daughter's voice came to him, saying that he should take her body, cut it up, and bury the pieces all over the sacred mountain, that the clans should have the final and ninth gift of the maro dance that she had brought for them. And this he did. From each part of her body came one of the sacred plants of the nine clans: yams, taro, the coconut palm, bamboo, rice, the banana tree, and corn.[9]

Another grain story, of the Celtic corn goddess Cerridwen, has many connections to fermentation, grain, and the origins of poetry. It brings to mind some of the elements of the story of Odin and the Mead of Inspiration. One important point to remember is that when examining the ancient grain legends, the word corn means something different from the way we think of it. Corn, as we know it, was still "undiscovered" (i.e., in the Americas) when these legends were first told. Corn, in

A Mediaeval
Garden of Herbs
from Brunschwig's
Liber de Arte
Distillandi,
Strassburg,
Grüninger, 1500

ancient tradition, was not "corn"—that is, maize—but grain. Their Old
World word—corn—was attached to the grain that came from the New
World—maize—which is now the only grain known as corn. So any
stories about "corn" actually mean grain.

Cerridwen had two children, Crearwy, a beautiful, radiant, and warm
daughter, and Afagddu, a cold, dark, and ugly son. In order to make up for
her son's misfortune, Cerridwen decided to brew him a sacred drink—one
that would give him the gifts of inspiration and knowledge and impart to
him the ability to perceive all things: past, present, and future. The brew
would embody these qualities and impart them to the first one to drink of

it—whom she intended to be Afagddu. To make the brew, she gathered the sacred herbs and put two people in charge of the brewing. The first, Gwion Bach, a young boy, was to stir the brew for the time it needed to attain its powerful properties—a year and a day. The second, Morda, was an elderly blind man whose job it was to keep the fire going. All went well until the last day of the brewing. At that time three drops splashed out of the kettle onto Gwion Bach's thumb. Instinctively, he sucked his thumb, and, at this taste, all the properties of the brew went into him. He immediately knew his future—that Cerridwen would try to kill him—and he fled. When Cerridwen found the brew already used and thus worthless to Afagddu, she flew into a rage and began to hunt Gwion Bach. As she closed in on him, Gwion Bach changed himself into a hare to run the faster, but Cerridwen changed herself into a hound. He then became a fish, and dove into a river, but Cerridwen became an otter. Then he became a bird and Cerridwen a hawk. Finally Gwion Bach changed himself into a grain of wheat, thinking to hide himself in something so small it would be overlooked. But Cerridwen was not fooled. She changed herself into a hen and ate the grain. However, after returning home in her proper guise, she discovered she was pregnant. Nine months later she gave birth to Gwion Bach, who was so beautiful that she could not bring herself to kill him. Instead she sewed him in a bag and threw him into a river. The bag floated down the river and into the fishing nets cast by Elphin, a human being. On opening the bag, the baby's beauty caused him to exclaim, "Taliesin" (which means "radiant brow"), and this became Gwion Bach's new name. Taliesin, a contemporary of Myrddhin whom we call Merlin, grew into the most renowned poet, skald, and sage of his time.[10]

These stories have much in common, and they all bear similarities to many of the others in this book, such as those about honey, saguaro, and manioc. It is also interesting how many have somewhere in them reference to a sacred or fermented beverage that confers new abilities on those who drink it.

Grain itself, in ancient cultures, took on many of the characteristics of the sacred source from which it came. And in many societies, such as the Egyptian, it came to figure prominently in the culture's highly complex religious ceremonies. Grain, when viewed as sacred, becomes something like a zen *koan*. A koan is a question such as "What is the sound of one hand clapping?" In Buddhist traditions, it is given to people to think upon and to answer. The contemplation of such a seemingly unanswerable question can move the mind beyond linear articulations into deeper truths and awareness. Traditionally, in any culture that recognizes the sacredness of plants, certain people are called to "the path of plants." Because plants are created out of the sacred substance from which all matter comes, they partake of its essence. Thus, contemplation on plants in general or one particular plant species in particular can be a path to understanding the sacred in deeper ways and a way to learn about what it means to be a human being.

All the world's major religious texts contain innumerable instances where holy teachers have used the sacredness of plants as a teaching to help human beings understand the nature of the divine and their relation to it. As mentioned earlier, nonindustrial cultures typically experience all plants as possessing sacredness and a soul. That this was also believed during the development of cities can be seen in Greek, Egyptian, and Roman cultures. Exceptionally deep spiritual relationships were developed with plants that came to have particular and long lasting importance to human beings— such as rice, barley, maize, and trees. Each plant was felt to possess a particular sacred archetype, an intelligent awareness, or *logos*, and to possess meanings beyond that of plants in general. Relationship with and contemplation of this profound sacredness could offer profound teachings to human beings who wanted to deepen their relationship with the sacred. This kind of sacred contemplation and religious devotion was particularly true of barley in Egypt and, eventually, grain in Greece. To the Egyptians

> Osiris was the original John Barleycorn, the slain god
> whose body, the chaff, is scattered to the winds at

threshing time. Like his mythological descendant, Dionysus, Osiris also went to India, conquering by teaching art, sculpture, music, and the arts of beer- and wine-making. Osiris is sometimes portrayed with ears of wheat sprouting from him—a corn god.[11]

In the ancient Egyptian temple of Philae, Osiris is engraved on a sarcophagus, ears of wheat rising from his body. Below this, an inscription reads, "This is the form of the unmentionable, secret Osiris who is speeding upwards."[12] And in ancient Athens, initiates in the Eleusinian Mysteries were shown, at one point, "the mighty and marvelous and most complete epoptic mystery, an ear of grain reaped in solemn silence."[13] Initiates in the Mysteries participated in highly complex ceremonies that were originally held every five years. At the end of many days of ceremony and ritual, they engaged in the supreme act of the Mysteries: opening the *kiste*, working with its contents, and then drinking *kykeon*. The chest, kiste, held the tools needed to turn grain into kykeon, the sacred drink made from barley.[14] By taking the grain into their bodies, as food and fermentation, human beings brought into themselves the body of the sacred itself.

> By eating the body of the god [man] shares in the god's attributes and powers. And when the god is a corn-god, the corn is his proper body; when he is a vine-god, the juice of the grape is his blood; and so by eating the bread and drinking the wine the worshipper partakes of the real body and blood of his god. Thus the drinking of wine in the rites of a vine-god like Dionysus is not an act of revelry, it is a sacred sacrament.[15]

Such belief was based on a deep experience and perception of the sacredness inherent in the Earth and each part of it. Such feelings engendered a deep reverence for all life and took on special meaning when applied to plants that were especially important to human life. Eating such a plant was an occasion of great reverence, but bringing it together with water and the magic of yeast ceremonially allowed the unique qualities of the sacred to come into the body. "Thus wine or some other fermented beverage becomes 'the supreme symbol of unity between human and divine.'"[16] When taken in this context, human beings literally become "intoxicated with the god."[17]

The practicalities of obtaining sugar from plants, their conversion into fermented beverages, and the nutrition gained from that process was not lost on our ancestors. The conversion of barleylike grains, as I have said, entailed something relatively new in brewing history—germination of grain and the use of the subsequent malt that is created.

When using human saliva to convert starch to sugars, the enzyme in saliva, ptyalin, converts starch to glucose, the original sugar that plants create from photosynthesis. But in using germination for starch conversion, the grain is soaked until the seed head is saturated and then it is allowed to sprout. The sprouted grain looks much like a smaller version of alfalfa or bean sprouts. When the grain germinates, it creates an enzyme, diastase, that it uses to convert the starch stored in the seed to sugar. After it is dried as malt, in the later presence of warmth and water, it contains a sufficient quantity of diastase to convert the remaining starch in the seed to sugar.

To make beer from malted barley, the malt is roughly crushed, hot water (120 to 150 degrees F) is added, and the temperature is kept constant for an extended period of time, generally 1 1/2 to 8 hours. In this warm water, the enzyme diastase converts the starch in the grain to sugar. Then the water in which the malt has been sitting is slowly drained off. There is still some sugar in and on the malt, however, and to extract it, more hot water is added and it, too, is slowly drained through the malt, pulling the sugars along with it. What is obtained is a sweet solution that yeast will convert to alcohol and carbon dioxide.

Diastase is incredibly potent in converting starch to sugar. As little as 1 part diastase to 2,000 parts starch will result in complete conversion of the starch into sugar. For this reason, other, unmalted, grains (such as oats, wheat, and rye) can be added to soaking malt, and the diastase will be present in sufficient quantities to convert the starch in the unmalted grains to sugar. Most grains and some starchy roots, such as potatoes, can be malted. All have been fermented, as a result, at one time or another. However, barley contains the most diastase of any grains; processed rice contains none (which is why Asian fermentation processes are so different).

Malting a grain considerably enhances its nutritional qualities. Besides the sugars that are released, malting dramatically increases the ascorbic acid, vitamin B, and caloric content of the grain. As Mikal Aasved observes, "Sprouted maize, for example, contains three and one-half times the riboflavin of unmalted maize. Nicotinic acid, or niacin, is increased by a factor of 2 to 3.5; biotin, by 2.3; pantothenic acid, by 1.7; pyridoxin, by 1.2; folic acid, by 4; inositol, by 1.9; and the aneurin content is almost doubled."[18] The malt, or dried germinated barley seed, itself, contains starch, diastase, some maltose (sugar), numerous plant constituents, and dextrin (a gummy, water-soluble substance similar to gum arabic).

The sweet sugar solution obtained from the crushed malt (sometimes concentrated into a syrup called malt extract) has long been recognized as a beneficial substance in its own right and was used medicinally for centuries. In the nineteenth and early twentieth centuries it was considered demulcent, nutrient, mucilaginous, and tonic and used "in *anorexia, chronic bronchitis, phthisis, asthma, dyspepsia,* convalescence from exhausting maladies, and in all diseases accompanied by general debility, and impairment of the vital powers."[19] It is especially good for those with what they used to call "wasting diseases." Usually this referred to people who could eat but could not gain weight, usually because of digestive problems or general weakness. The enzyme, diastase, in malt extract or in the sweet wort itself helps the digestion of starchy foods by converting them into sugar in the stomach (or in the bowl before they are eaten), thus aiding digestion. The sugars in the malt or malt extract enter the bloodstream quickly, giving strength with less work, and the nutritive properties of the malt extract make it a high-yield food for those with debilities from illness.

The barley itself is considered highly nutritious and medicinal. It is nutritive, demulcent, mildly laxative, and possesses mild nervine properties similar to those of oats (in other words, it is a relaxant and mild sedative). Its demulcent qualities are imparted to the body by coating mucous membranes, thus soothing them if they are inflamed. Because it is also highly nutritious, it is a perfect food for the sick and convalescent. In traditional herbal and indigenous medicine, it has been used (internally) in febrile diseases, catarrh, dysentery, inflammation of the bladder, gonorrhea, and chronic mucous inflammations. Externally, moistened barley flour and cooked barley have both been used in making poultices for wounds and ulcers, its mucilaginous and demulcent qualities also soothing external inflamed tissues. When being used internally, barley was often used as barley water, a staple of traditional medicine.[20]

Barley Water

Take 2 ounces barley, wash thoroughly in cold water, then boil briefly in 1/2 pint water. Strain and discard the water (this cleans the barley grains for medicinal use). Add 4 pints boiling water, boil to 2 pints and strain. Alternatively, pearl barley (barley with the outer husk removed) can be used. Wash pearl barley, take 10 parts barley to 100 parts water, boil 20 minutes, strain.

The malt infusion or malt extract is, however, more effective than the barley itself for internal conditions.

But in spite of these beneficial nutritional and medicinal properties, it is the spirit in the fermented grain that has always held the most powerful sacred qualities for our ancestors. That the grain is also medicinally and nutritively active was only an inevitable characteristic of a plant made from the body of a god, a grain that, when fermented, brought into the world all the power of the sacred.

> After the harvest, the powerful, vital essence of these plant-spirits remains in the pulpy liquid of the fruit—or root, or grain, or sap, or flower, etc.—to attain its highest development during the miraculous process of fermentation. It is the spiritual power of these gods that changes the "water into wine" and that remains locked within the fermented beverage—the magical essence, the lifeblood of the plant. Thus, to tribal man, the spirituality of fermented beverages has a dual origin: it derives ultimately from the divine origin of the plants from which they are made and from the sanctity of the ancestral souls or other deities that animate them. Fermentation reawakens, amplifies, and unleashes the miraculous powers embodied in the plant—powers that are generated by a fusion of the divine essence of the Creator with that of the born-again ancestor-gods who have lain dormant for so long.[21]

SEVEN

Psychotropic and Highly Inebriating Beers

The ancient Egyptians brewed a mandrake beer, the American
Indians spiced up their maize beer (chicha) with coca leaves
(Erythroxylon coca), angel's trumpet (Brugmansia sp.), and
morning glory seeds (Ipomoea sp., Turbina corymbosa).
Oriental beer was often improved with hashish and opium, while
dried fly agaric mushrooms were crumbled into beer in Siberia. The
Gauls brewed beer from darnel (Lolium temulentum), . . . The
pagan "Mead of Inspiration" was no simple beer or mead, but must
have been a psychoactive beverage whose inebriating ingredients had
a stimulating effect upon creativity.

—Christian Ratsch, 1994[1]

The leaves and flowers of milfoil or yarrow, inebriate, and are used
by the Dalecarlians to render their beer intoxicating. Clary and saffron have the same effect. The last exhilarates the spirits to such a
degree, that when taken in large doses, it occasions immoderate mirth

*and laughter. Darnel, or lolium timulentum, which is vulgarly
known under the name of sturdy, when malted with barley, a process
which the seeds of it often undergo, causes the ale brewed from it to be
speedily intoxicating. . . . Among these inebriants the inspissated
milky juice of the common garden lettuce is considered as powerful in
its operation as opium itself.*

—W. T. Marchant, 1888[2]

*Now in the primeval silence of some unexplored tropical forest I
spread my feathery leaves, a giant fern, and swayed and nodded in
the spice-gales over a river whose waves at once sent up clouds of
music and perfume. My soul changed to a vegetable essence, thrilled
with a strange and unimagined ecstacy.*

—Fitzhug Ludlow, *The Hasheesh Eater*[3]

*O most powerful spirit
of the bush with the fragrant leaves
we are here again to seek wisdom
give us tranquility and guidance
to understand the mysteries of the forest
the knowledge of our ancestors*

—Amahuaca prayer when taking
aayahuasca, the vision vine[4]

*F*ERMENTATION IS INTIMATELY connected to traveling in sacred realms. The plants used in fermentation are sacred, and that sacredness changes those who ingest them, but in many cultures, for a variety of reasons, additional plants have also been added during fermentation. Some of these have been for medicinal or culinary reasons, but there are ancient traditions of sacred plants that, in themselves, significantly alter human consciousness. The most ancient of these is heather, used in heather mead, the Mead of Inspiration, but there are others—many of them European. Some are survivors of ancient Celtic and Druidic practice, others were commonly used in the Middle Ages. Many of the plants that were used, like yarrow, are innocuous or only mildly stimulating alone. When included in a fermenting beverage, however, their effects can increase dramatically. The inebriating herbs of the longest historical use in European brewing are heather and those that went to make up *gruit*. Gruit ale held sway over Europe for nearly 1,000 years, and heather mead and ale have been made in the area known today as Scotland for at least 4,000 years. But the use of such powerful herbs is undoubtedly much more ancient and has been an integral part of the magic of fermentation and herbal lore for millennia.

Plants used in fermentation (in this chapter) fall into two general categories: those that cause extreme inebriation and those that can be considered psychotropic. (Extreme inebriation means a high state of drunkenness, psychotropic means causing a chemically induced alteration in consciousness.) In the past, as both herbalist and writer, I have avoided dealing with these kinds of plants because mention of them generally causes an almost immediate Puritanitis—an inflammation or spasming of the Puritan reflex. To the attentive mind, *all* plants are psychotropic; they all change consciousness, awareness, understanding, and sense of self. There is, however, in the Western world, perhaps because of our overemphasis on material reality, a rather unhealthy fascination with intensely psychotropic and inebriating plants. It is as if having repressed natural contact with the nonmaterial world, such plants exert a disproportional influence on our culture and many of its members.

Frenzied antidrug hyperbole, dedicated use of psychotropics far beyond their proper sphere, and national concern with "the drug problem" are all manifestations of this repression. Thus, to discuss the subtle consciousness of plants in any context where their psychotropic properties are also discussed inevitably leads to a focus on the latter (and its particular can of worms), to the detriment of the former. It is, however, impossible to ignore the subject of psychotropic and inebriating plants; they have been an integral aspect of fermentation for thousands of years. Such plants are an irremovable part of the Earth ecosystem and are intimately bound up with the development of the human species. Much of our human exploration of the nature of consciousness and our relationship to the divine has centered around such plants. Their use, in many cultures, is often central to spiritual development—they open the doors of perception.

Except in certain specific ritual contexts, most spiritual disciplines view continued use of the key once the door is open at best as an indulgence, at worst as dangerous. Such plants can save your life, but they can also take it. Like all powerful things that are channeled for human use (and this includes science, human culture, and language) they have a shadow side. A number of the painful difficulties we are struggling with as a species come from assuming there is *only* a light or *only* a shadow side to some specific element of our lives—a regrettable tendency that we seem to engage in with monotonous regularity. Our culture's understanding of the place of psychotropic plants falls into this category. But it is clear from the pervasiveness of their use throughout human history that the use of powerful plants is the norm for our species. This brief era of prohibition, begun with the creation of the Food and Drug Administration in 1906, is the aberration, *not* the norm.

These plants do speak with loud voices—perhaps so that the nearly deaf among us can learn to hear something beyond the usual noises that deafen us. Used in fermentation, their voices sound even louder, with words that can also deafen in their turn. The spirits of these plants have long been understood to be powerful, in all cultures and times in which they have been known. Their teachings are also powerful, and like all plant teaching, they can point the way to a deeper spirituality in all life.

GRUIT ALE

Gruit (or sometimes grut) was, primarily, a combination of three mild to moderately narcotic herbs: sweet gale (*Myrica gale*), also called bog myrtle, yarrow (*Achillea millefolium*), and wild rosemary (*Ledum palustre*), also called marsh rosemary. Gruit varied somewhat, each gruit producer adding additional herbs to produce unique tastes, flavors, and effects. Other adjunct herbs were juniper berries, ginger, caraway seed, aniseed, nutmeg, and cinnamon (most, themselves, having psychotropic properties).[5] The exact formula for each gruit was, like that for Coca Cola, proprietary—a closely guarded secret.

It is important to keep in mind the properties of gruit ale: it is highly intoxicating—narcotic, aphrodisiacal, and psychotropic when consumed in sufficient quantity. Gruit ale stimulates the mind, creates euphoria, and enhances sexual drive. The hopped ale that took its place is quite different. Its effects are sedating and anaphrodesiacal. In other words, it puts the drinker to sleep and dulls sexual desire. That two so widely differing brews should be the accepted standards in ale and beer brings up the question of why such a marked change should happen in such a historically short time.

Gruit ale was *the* ale of Europe for at least 700 years, much as hopped ale or beer is throughout the world today. Hops were simply one of many plants that could be used or else were unknown to local brewers, and they were a fairly late addition. As Maude Grieve observes:

> Hops appear to have been used in the breweries of the
> Netherlands in the beginning of the fourteenth century.

In England they were not used in the composition of
beer till nearly two centuries afterwards. The liquor prepared from the fermented malt formed the favourite
drink of our Saxon and Danish forefathers. The beverage went by the name of Ale . . . and was either brewed
from malt alone, or from a mixture of the latter with
Honey and flavoured with Heath tops, Ground Ivy, and
various other bitter and aromatic herbs, such as
Marjoram, Buckbean, Wormwood, Yarrow, Woodsage,
or Germander and Broom.[6]

Hops, when they began to be suggested for use as a primary additive, in both Germany and England, were bitterly resisted. Those who
held a monopoly on gruit production in Germany and on pure ale in
England fought hop introduction through the legislatures, proclamations
of the royalty, writings of the day's medical practitioners, and through
Church edict. The struggle over what ingredients could be allowed in ale
lasted, in its most furious forms, for about 200 years. This fight occurred,
interestingly, simultaneously with the Protestant Reformation. The accu-
sations of the powerful interests opposing hops can still be found in governmental records in both England and Germany.

Brewers in England complained to the mayor of London about hops
and noted that there was

a deceivable and unholesome fete in bruying of ale
within the said citee nowe of late [that] is founde in
puttyng of hoppes and other things in the said ale, contrary to the good and holesome manner of bruynge of
Ale of old tyme used. . . . Pleas it therfore your saide
good lordshyppe to forbid the putting into ale of any
hops, herbs, or other like thing, but only licour, malte,
and yeste.[7]

In Germany, as John Arnold reveals:

> Hopped beers, not alone their manufacture but also their importation into the domains of the Archbishop of Cologne, were strictly prohibited in various edicts, and infractions threatened with severe penalties. The reason for this was two-fold. First, the manufacture of gruit was a privilege, exploited or granted by the archbishop and bishops, hence a source of large revenue for them, a veritable ecclesiastical monopoly. Second, "gruit" contained herbs and spices, meeting the taste of that time (and of succeeding centuries), its composition being a mystery for the common people, and in any event a trade secret for the privileged manufacturer. This privilege was now threatened in the highest degree by the hops and hopped beers which began to appear from different localities.[8]
>
> . . . How determinedly the archbishops for the reasons mentioned opposed the introduction of hopped beers [can be seen] from a decree issued, April 17, 1381, by Archbishop Frederick of Cologne, in behalf of the maintenance of the gruit monopoly, according to which not only the brewers, but also the clergy, the military and the civilians, in fact, anybody who wanted to brew beer were commanded to buy their gruit in the episcopal gruit-houses; furthermore, the importation of "hopped beer" from Westphalia was prohibited, and so was the brewing of such beers in Cologne itself, under pain of the severest penalties which the Church could inflict.[9]

Hops, until this time, were merely one of the plants used all along in the production of beer. The earliest mention of their use was probably in

Hildegard of Bingen's (1098–1179) *Physica Sacra*. However, hops were in no way accepted as a superior herb for use in beer production. In spite of such decrees as that issued in Cologne and complaints like that from the brewers of London, the assault on gruit and pure ale continued, and hopped ale slowly began to supplant gruit ale (or pure malt ale in England). Hops finally gained ascendancy in Germany at nearly the same time Martin Luther was excommunicated by the Catholic Church (1520). It is doubtful this is mere coincidence.

One of the arguments of the Protestants against the Catholic clergy (and indeed, against Catholicism) was their self-indulgence in food, drink, and lavish lifestyle. This behavior was felt to be very un-Christlike indeed. And it was this Protestant religious intolerance of Catholic indulgence that was the genesis of the temperance movement. (It would not stop, of course, with the assault on gruit production or gruit ales, but would continue on to include, by the twentieth century, ale itself and any kind of psychotropic or inebriating plants and drinks.) The Protestant reformists were joined by merchants and competing royals to break the financial monopoly of the Church. The result was, ultimately, the end of a many-thousand-years' tradition of herbal beer making in Europe and the narrowing of beer and ale into one limited expression of beer production—that of hopped ales or what we today call beer. The majority of historical beer writers insist that this was *only* because (after some 10,000 years) our ancestors accidentally discovered that hops were antiseptic enough to really preserve beer. But our ancestors were neither that blind nor that narrow in their empiricism. Hops kept the beer from spoiling, yes; however, a number of other herbs possess strong antibacterial properties and can help beer "keep."

Many of those herbs were commonly used in ale; for instance, wormwood and juniper. But hops possess two characteristics notably different from the herbs they replaced. They cause the drinker to become drowsy and they diminish sexual desire—quite the opposite of the other herbs used in beer and especially those used in gruit production. Yarrow, sweet gale, and marsh rosemary are highly inebriating and stimulating when used in ale, far out of proportion to their individual effects outside of fermentation. The literature of the time, denoting the "problems" associated with the gruit herbs, contradict contemporary beer historians and are in actuality some of the first drug control manifestos on record. The laws that eventually passed in the sixteenth to the eighteenth centuries are the first drug control laws on record. For instance, Odd Nordland, the Norwegian brewing historian, comments:

> At the time the decree of 1667 ordered an increase of cultivation of hops in Norway, the authorities in continental Europe were generally trying to abolish the use of *grut* and bog myrtle in brewing. The provincial laws of Bavaria, of 1533 and 1616, imposed severe penalties on anyone brewing ale with herbs and seeds not normally used for ale. Similar laws were passed in, for instance, Holstein in 1623, and here [Norway] the *Post* (bog myrtle) was expressly forbidden together with other "unhealthy material". As late as 1723, the laws of Brunswick-Luneburg made it a punishable offence for a brewer to have the dangerous *Post*, or other herbs imparting a dangerous potency to the ale, in his house. It is stated that, in spite of earlier warnings, this practice had continued to the peril of the lives and health of His Majesty's subjects.[10]

The historical record is clear that hops' supplantation of other herbs was primarily a reflection of Protestant irritation about "drugs" and the Catholic Church, in concert with competing merchants trying to break a monopoly and so increase their profits. The motivations were religious and mercantile, reasons not so different from the ones used to illegalize marijuana in the United States in the twentieth century.

The strong incentive for merchants to break the gruit monopoly can be seen from the legal structure affecting the brewing of ales at the time. There was a tax on gruit in addition to taxes on the ale subsequently brewed from them. "The gruit tax was independent of the beer tax. Everybody who brewed on his own account, was bound to pay the gruit tax upon the gruit bought at the gruit-house, while the brewers had, besides to pay the lawful beer tax, the excise tax."[11] And gruit producers had a monopoly. In many regions of Europe during the Middle Ages, those who made ale commercially *had* to use gruit in their ale and they had to buy it from licensed gruit producers.

The fight against hops, however, was a long one. It began about A.D. 1250 and continued well into the seventeenth century, about 400 years in all. Interdicts were placed on the use of hops in many parts of Germany until the sixteenth century, and it was not legal to even grow hops in England until an act of Parliament made it so in 1554. But in spite of the eventual ascendancy of hops, gruit did not entirely disappear. The brewers in "Bremen continued to employ gruit as well as hops until early in the eighteenth century, when a police mandate (1718) ordered that 'No brewer shall undertake to buy such herbs [marsh rosemary, etc.], no matter on what pretense.'"[12] Slowly the herbs used in gruit ale passed out of commercial use and into the hands of home and small village brewers. It held on longest in places far out of the mainstream, such as Iceland and rural Norway. But that wasn't destined to last; a number of researchers have noted that the strong Protestant temperance movements of the middle twentieth century were nearly the end of village and home brewing in rural Norway.[13]

I have separated the herbs used in gruit into their own categories, since they were also used individually to make ales. I also include here one traditional gruit ale that uses all three herbs. You can see from the descriptions of their individual effects that they must be potent when combined together. Yarrow is commonly available throughout the United States, both wild and as a common garden flower. *Myrica* is available through many homebrewing stores under the Brewers Garden brand name, though I have no idea how fresh the herb is. It generally comes pre-ground in two-gram packages. To date, I am unaware of any commercial source for marsh rosemary.

The following recipe is adapted from an early fourteenth-century recipe by John Harrison and members of the Durden Park Beer Club in England.

Gruit Ale

Ingredients

> 1 gallon water
> 1 3/4 pounds pale malt
> 1 1/2 pounds CaraPils (or crystal malt)
> 1 1/2 grams *Myrica gale*
> 1 1/2 grams marsh rosemary
> 1 1/2 grams yarrow
> yeast

> Heat water to 170 degrees, pour onto malted grains enough water to make a stiff mash. Let stand, covered, for three hours. Sparge slowly with 170 degree water until one gallon total liquid is acquired. Boil wort and herbs for 1 1/2 hours. Cool to 70 degrees F and strain. Pour into fermenter and add yeast. Ferment until completion. Prime bottles, siphon and cap. Store four months before drinking.[14]

MYRICA ALE

To add a strong flavour to the ale, and to make it heady, pors [Myrica gale] was put into it. This plant grows on the moors, close

> to some of the lakes. It was gathered in the autumn, and the leaves
> were also taken. When this plant was used the ale was strong. It went
> to one's head. They spoke of having a "Christmas head."
>
> —Odd Nordland, 1969[15]

Myrica, also called sweet gale and bog myrtle, was commonly used in ale production throughout Europe through World War II. It reached its height in the Middle Ages but was still to be found from time to time in the rural areas of England, Europe, and the Scandinavian countries until 1950 or so.

Myrica Ale

Ingredients

    5 pounds malted barley
    4 ounces fresh leaves and berries of *Myrica gale*
    4 gallons water
    yeast

> Malt the barley at 150 degrees F for 90 minutes. Sparge
> (run the rest of the heated water through the malt) and
> boil all together with 2 ounces of the *Myrica gale*. Strain
> and cool to 70 degrees F, pour into fermenter and add
> yeast. Hang the remaining 2 ounces of *Myrica* in a
> muslin bag in the fermenter. Ferment until complete,
> siphon into bottles, prime, and cap. Ready to drink in 10
> days to two weeks.

About Myrica Gale

Myrica gale

> It was said locally that when one drank much of it, it was strongly
> intoxicating, with unpleasant after effects.
>
> —Odd Nordland, 1969[16]

Myrica has been used throughout Europe for millennia in the brewing of ale. It was one of the most common herbs, after juniper, in traditional brewing in Norway; the ale was called *pors*. The stories of its intoxicating properties are legendary. In Norway "It was said locally that when one drank much of it, it was strongly intoxicating, with unpleasant after effects."[17] Many brewers both in Norway and throughout Europe commented that *Myrica* was used "to make the ale more intoxicating."[18] And "The famous Swedish botanist Linnaeus as well as the learned Norwegian bishop and scientist Gunnerus both mention the especially intoxicating effects of ale brewed with bog myrtle. The former recommends rapid boiling, the latter skimming the foam from the boiled ale, as counter-measures against these effects."[19] In spite of this, *Myrica* was still in common use as late as 1892 in Sweden, when the medical herbalist Millspaugh noted that "[T]he leaves [of *Myrica gale*] are said to be substituted for hops in Sweden, in the manufacture of beer."[20] Maude Grieve comments that its use was still common at the writing of her *A Modern Herbal* in 1931: "The branches have been used as a substitute for hops in Yorkshire and put into a beer called there 'Gale Beer.' It is extremely good to allay thirst."[21] *Myrica* was so important an item of commerce because of its use in ale that not only in Europe, but in Norway it could be used to pay taxes. *Myrica* or bog myrtle is mentioned in the 1300s in Norwegian legal proclamations stating that "rent for farms could be paid in bog myrtle, and that moors where bog myrtle could be gathered belonged to the farms in the same way as the right to coast-lines and fishing waters."[22]

Traditionally (or as Maude Grieve puts it so wonderfully, "in cottage practice"), sweet or *Myrica gale* has been used similarly to bayberry, though it is rarely used now in contemporary herbalism. Bayberry (*Myrica cerifera*) is one of the more important herbs in medical herbalism, and *Myrica gale* possesses many of its same properties, though in milder form. The leaves of *Myrica gale* are astringent, balsamic, bitter, with a strong, not unpleasant, rather spicy aroma. It possesses expectorant, sedative, fungistatic, and antiseptic properties, and relaxes bronchial tissue. It is also alterative and an effective stomachic. It can be used as a powder for skin sores and ulceration, its astringent and antiseptic actions effective in arresting those conditions. These actions also make it a primary remedy for inflamed and bleeding gums. The resins of the plant have a strong vasodilating effect and are more pronounced in the fresh herb. The fresh leaves of *Myrica gale* contain ".50% of a stupefying essence," and taken in large doses produce "a narcotic effect."[23] The bark of the root of the bayberry or wax myrtle is most often used in herbal practice, though, as mentioned, the fresh leaves of *Myrica gale* possess the same, though milder, properties. The berries of the bayberry plant (*Myrica cerifera*) are not really berries at all but are dense clusters of bony, globular nuts. These nuts appear more like berries in the wax myrtle because of their covering of wax, less so in sweet gale. In the bayberry or wax myrtle plant, the berries are covered with a white or grayish wax that can be used to make candles—the wax is obtained by boiling the berries in hot water, cooling, and skimming off the wax. The wax is also used in herbal medicine, having an astringent action useful in dysentery. *Myrica gale* possesses the same kind of nuts or tiny nut cones, though with a significantly smaller wax content. The wax and resins in these species are more easily soluble in an alcohol and water combination. The wax itself has also been found to possess narcotic properties.[24]

Myrica gale is a somewhat smaller species than bayberry. It is a shrub from one to six feet in height with long oval leaves lightly serrated at the ends. The nut cones are ovoid and resin coated. They form in the fall of the year on the tips of the branches and look something like an abortive scale or gall-like growth. The leaves and nut cones contain at least 41 compounds, few of which have been identified. It ranges throughout the northern part of the United States, often in bogs and wetlands—hence its name, bog myrtle—dipping south in the eastern U.S. as far as the Carolinas and Tennessee. The branches containing the nut cones should be gathered in fall and used fresh or recently dried. The older they are, the less vasodilating effect they possess, the resins deteriorating with time. It is likely that part of the effects of ales fermented with *Myrica gale* come from the plant's strong vasodilating action in combination with the narcotic and stupefying properties noted above. Because the resins dissolve more readily in alcohol, some of the fresh herb should be hung in the fermenter to work with the alcohol that the yeasts produce during fermentation.[25]

WILD ROSEMARY ALE

[I]n Westphalia and surrounding districts they used to brew a beer, called gruitbier, or gruehsing, which was made by mashing barley in water, and which had the distinguishing feature that it was made with the addition of a 'fermentum,' being boiled and cooked up with it, and that this 'fermentum' consisted of the blossoms and seeds of the rosemary cilvestris [wild rosemary—now denoted as Ledum palustre], which previously had been treated in a certain way. This plant, it says, grew in Westphalia in profusion.

—John Arnold, 1911[26]

Like bog myrtle, wild rosemary's use was pervasive throughout Europe in brewing, and its cousin, Labrador tea (*Ledum glandulosum*), was used to some extent in the seventeenth and eighteenth centuries in Canada in the same manner. Some researchers have suggested that the similarity between *Myrica gale* and wild or marsh rosemary in areas of growth, coloring, shape, and spicy smell led to confusion between the two, causing *Myrica* to become an additive in ale instead of what they really wanted— marsh rosemary. This seems farfetched. Both plants offer pleasant taste, narcotic activity, and a certain bitterness to infusions.

The species available in the United States are *Ledum glandulosum* (formerly *L. latifolium*), or Labrador tea, and *Ledum groenlandicum*, a variety of *Ledum palustre*. Labrador tea, while not as strong in its effects as wild rosemary, may still be used similarly both in brewing and in herbal practice.

Wild Rosemary Ale

Ingredients

> 5 pounds malt
>
> 1 pound dark brown sugar
>
> 4 ounces wild rosemary or Labrador tea, fresh flowering tops
>
> 5 gallons water
>
> yeast

> Mash malt with water at 150 degrees F for 90 minutes. Boil remaining water and sparge mash. Boil all with 2 ounces flowering tops of wild rosemary. Let cool to 70 degrees F, place in fermenter, and add yeast. Place the final 2 ounces of wild rosemary flowering tops into a muslin bag and lower into the wort in the fermenter. You will need to place a small stone in the bag to make sure it sinks. Allow to ferment until complete. Prime bottles, fill, and cap. Ready to drink in two weeks.

ABOUT WILD ROSEMARY

Ledum palustre

> *Wild Rosemary grows in swamps and wet places of northern Europe, Asia, and America, and on the mountains of southern districts. The leaves are reputed to be more powerful than those of* Ledum latifolium *[Labrador tea], and to have in addition some narcotic properties, being used in Germany to make beer more intoxicating.*
>
> —Maude Grieve, 1931[27]

A member of the *Ericaceae*, or heath, family, wild rosemary, like many of its relatives, possesses narcotic properties. Mention of its powerful effects abound in the literature of brewing and herbalism. Millspaugh (1892) notes that "Marsh Tea, [is] used in dysentery, diarrhea, tertian ague, and in some places to render beer heady, though it is said to bring on delirium."[28] Christian Ratsch comments that "Wild Rosemary contains a volatile oil (ledum oil) that has strong inebriating effects and that in high doses produces cramps, rage, and frenzy. . . . A number of experiments with wild rosemary beer have demonstrated that the inebriating effects of alcohol are increased, and people get drunker quicker."[29] And Michael Moore notes that "Ledol [*Ledum camphor*], one of the aromatics found in the spicy oils [of Labrador tea], is somewhat toxic in excess, but it is not water soluble. It is a sedative and slightly narcotic substance and, like camphor, can cause palpitations and cerebral irritation in large amounts."[30] Rafinesque observed in 1830 that the plant was said to be "narcotic and phantastic,"[31] and the United States National Dispensatory "records that the leaves in full doses cause headache, vertigo, restlessness, and a peculiar delirium. [It] augments a secretion of saliva, of perspiration, urine, and dilates the pupil of the eye."[32] Both wild rosemary and Labrador tea have been used similarly in herbal practice.

Lloyd and Felter comment that

> *Ledum latifolium* is pectoral and tonic, and, in small doses,
> is useful in *coughs, irritations of the pulmonary membrane*,
> and in *dyspepsia*. It increases the urinary flow. Reputed
> also to possess similar, but less energetic, properties than
> the *Ledum palustre*, which is supposed to possess narcotic
> powers. An infusion of the leaves has been successfully
> employed in decoction in *pertussis, dysentery*, and to allay
> *pruritic irritation in exanthematous diseases*. In *leprosy, itch*,
> and *several diseases of the skin*, the decoction internally
> and externally has been beneficially used. . . . Dose of
> the infusion of either of the above plants, from 2 to 4
> fluid ounces, 3 or 4 times a day.[33]

Maude Grieve cautions, however, that "Overdoses [of the infusion] may cause violent headache and symptoms of intoxication."[34] Historically, both marsh rosemary and Labrador tea have been used in chronic bronchitis, coughs, as a digestive aid, as a diuretic, and as an antiscorbutic. Externally they were used as vulneraries (to heal wounds), and for itchy skin conditions, scabies, and leprosy. Indigenous peoples in the Americas used the plants for healing burns and ulcers, stomach pains, rheumatism, as a blood purifier, for asthma, coughs and colds, fevers, chills, as a general tonic, and as a narcotic.[35]

Felter and Lloyd make an interesting observation about the higher levels of ledum oil in the flowering tops of marsh rosemary.

> Its chief proximate principles are: (1) *Ericolin*, a resinous, bitter glucosoid . . . ; (2) *leditannic acid*; (3) volatile oil containing crystallizable *ledum camphor* melting at 105 degrees C (221 F). 0.7 percent of the oil was obtained by Hjelt and Colan (1882) from the herb grown in wet localities. The flowering tops yielded 1.2 percent of the oil, while the non-flowering shrub yields only about 0.35 percent.[36]

The traditional use of the fresh flowering tops of wild rosemary indicates that ancient brewers knew of this increased potency and were specifically attempting to enhance their beers. That ledum oil is not water soluble accounts for the use of the fresh tops in the fermenting beverage itself and not alone in the water and barley malt extract.

Generally, the *Ledums* are low-growing bushes or shrubs, rarely reaching six feet in height. Like bog myrtle, they like marshy, swampy areas. The leaves are long elliptics with white, feltlike hairs underneath. The leaves tend to curl along the margins and are generally a bright evergreen color. The lower leaves tend to be brownish, and all, when crushed, give off a particularly *Ledum* spicy smell. They grow in wet places in the mountains from British Columbia south to the Sierra Nevadas of California, and in northeastern Oregon, central Idaho, and northwestern Wyoming.

YARROW BEER

*According to Linneaus, it was used by the people of Lima in
Dalecarnia, instead of hops, when they brewed for weddings: ". . . so
that the guests become crazy." Linneaus called the plant* galentara,
*"causing madness", and this plant "which the people of Lima some-
times use in their ale stirs up the blood and makes one lose one's balance.". . . Yarrow is in no way innocent when mixed with ale. It has
a strong odour and flavour, and well deserves the name Linnaeus gave
it, to indicate the frenzy that was said to result from it. Like* Ledum
palustre, skvattram *adds poisonous after-effects to the influence of
the alcohol. Thus yarrow must contain substances which increase the
effect of the alcohol, and bring about special sensations and feelings
when added to ale. According to Linnaeus, it is significant that it was
used to arrive at a state of complete and immediate intoxication.*

—Odd Nordland, 1969[37]

The brewers in the Scandinavian countries commonly used yarrow for brewing, though it was also used extensively in Europe both alone and as part of
gruit. Yarrow's connection to ale and beer can be traced through the many
brewing-related names given to it. Throughout Scandinavia it is called *jordhumle*, "earth hop." In Denmark it is also associated with hops, being called
variously *backhumle, akerhumle*, and *skogshumle* (*humle* meaning "hop"). In
Jutland it is called *brygger* and *gjedebrygger*, "brewer" and "goat brewer." And
in Iceland, *vallhumall* and *jardhumall*, "meadowhops" and "earth hops." In one
part of Norway, yarrow is called *hardhaus*, "hardhead," because of its intense
effects when added to ale. It was used in Norway and Denmark alone and in
conjunction with other herbs such as St.-John's-wort and juniper in ales
using malt and, in some instances, to brew a potent fermented beverage
without any malt.[38] Maude Grieve notes its intoxicating effects and comments that "It is said to have a similar use in Africa."[39] Yarrow is still used to
some extent in Europe and the Scandinavian countries to brew ales.

Yarrow Beer

Ingredients

> 5 pounds malted barley
>
> 3 ounces recently dried yarrow (plant and flowers)
>
> *or* 6 ounces fresh flowering tops
>
> 6 gallons water
>
> yeast

Mash malt with water at 150 degrees F for 90 minutes. Boil remaining water and sparge mash. Boil all with 1 1/2 ounces dried yarrow or 3 ounces fresh plant. Let cool to 70 degrees F, place in fermenter. Put remaining 1 1/2 ounces of dried yarrow (or 3 ounces fresh) in muslin bag and hang in fermenter; add yeast. Allow to ferment until complete. Prime bottles, fill, and cap. Ready to drink in two weeks.

Alternative Method: Instead of malt, use 6 pounds brown sugar to make the wort. Follow the rest of the recipe above, except add all the fresh yarrow to the wort itself. Do not boil the yarrow, allow to steep until cool.

ABOUT YARROW
Achillea millefolium

> *The Navajo Indians esteem the plant for its aphrodisiac properties.*
> —Christian Ratsch, 1997

Yarrow is probably one of the most widely used herbs in the world, known to all indigenous peoples and folk herbalists who have access to it. More than 58 indigenous tribes regularly used it for medicine in North America, and it has been well known throughout Europe since the beginning of recorded history. Its use is perhaps one of the oldest recorded, having been found, along with other medicinal herbs, in the grave of a Neanderthal Man buried some 60,000 years ago in Iraq.

Yarrow is innocuous—a small, feathery, almost fernlike plant with a large flowering top in season. It grows in profusion wherever it takes root, one plant often leading to scores of others.

Yarrow has been extensively studied in recent years; more than 120 active compounds have been identified. Its uses, however, were empirically discovered thousands of years ago in every culture in which it grew. Its effectiveness lies in three primary areas: colds and flus with associated fevers, bleeding, and digestive problems.

Yarrow is highly aromatic and in addition contains substances found to be antiseptic, antimicrobial, antibacterial, anti-inflammatory, and spasmolytic. Used as a steam for upper respiratory infections, it helps alleviate coughing, soothes and shrinks inflamed bronchial passages, and offers antibacterial, antiseptic, and antimicrobial actions, especially against staph and strep. Use of the tea along with the herbal steam lowers fevers (one of its primary historical uses) through both diaphoresis and direct action. It is analgesic, somewhat milder than aspirin, offering relief from the pains associated with flu and cold symptoms.

Its use to staunch bleeding is ancient. The herb, fresh or recently dried and placed as a poultice on bleeding wounds, slows or stops bleeding and alleviates the natural inflammation associated with such wounds. To many contemporary herbalists yarrow is thought of more as a simple herbal "band-aid"—an herb to reliably staunch bleeding—than a serious healing herb. It is actually much more powerful, as both historical and contemporary use shows.

The current Latin name, *Achillea millefolium*, means the thousand-leaved plant of Achilles. Achilles, the great warrior, used the plant for wounds from battle for himself and all his men. Both the ancient Romans and the Teton Dakota (as Matthew Wood observes) recognized the value of the herb for serious traumatic wounds. The Romans called it *Herba militaris* (soldier's grass) and the Dakota called it *tao-pi pezu'ta* (medicine for

Yarrow (Achillea millefolium)

the wounded). Even the common name for the plant—yarrow—comes from its powerful action for wounds. It is derived from the Old English *garwe* or *garwela*, meaning "spear well" or "to make well from spears." The names are suggestive. All four are connected to war and healing the wounds of war. It heals penetrations of the flesh from technology—arrows, swords, knives— all deep cuts. Contemporary practition- ers have noted that serious wounds, even to the bone, if treated with yarrow heal rapidly with little scarring. This is so even with wounds that normally would be stitched, such as large, deep wounds. The herb, dry powdered root or crushed fresh plant, when placed in such wounds immediately staunches bleeding and causes the wound walls to begin drawing together and knitting. Additionally, its analgesic action helps reduce the pain of the wound, and its antibacterial, antimicrobial, and antiseptic actions help prevent infection.

Though (as a practitioner) I have never used it with women's men- strual cycles, it has a long history of use for menstrual irregularity. Michael Moore reports good success in stemming occasionally heavy flows through yarrow's hemostatic activity, noting that it helps regularize chronic congested, extended, and dull-pain menses.

Yarrow is a reliable digestive bitter and tonic. Effective in aiding upset stomach or indigestion, it is better in combination with poleo or peppermint (half and half, as a tea or tincture), as its bittering action can stimulate stomach acid secretion and exacerbate the problem. The addi- tion of one of the mints produces a degree of relief attainable with neither alone. Yarrow is effective in dyspepsia, helping to tonify the stomach and normalize digestion.

Yarrow is also sometimes used in the treatment of urinary tract infections (UTI). The plant contains compounds with proven effectiveness against a number of organisms that are associated with UTI: *Candida albicans, Escherichia coli,* and *Streptococcus faecalis.*[40]

It is specific against the *Shigella* bacteria that causes dysentery,[41] and that action, combined with its natural astringency, makes it a natural and effective agent for bacillic dysentery. In vitro studies have found that an aqueous solution possesses antibacterial activity against *Staphylococcus aureus.*[42] Like many plants traditionally used for fevers, some of yarrow's constituents have been found to be similar to quinine in their effectiveness, making it a useful adjunct treatment for malaria.

Comments regarding its effects as a narcotic and inebriant have not been confined solely to Linnaeus (though every herbalist for the past 250 years has, seemingly, quoted him). Rafinesque (1830) observes that yarrow is a "bitter . . . tonic, restringent, and vulnerary, but subnarcotic and inebriant."[43] Mockle (1955) comments that in folk usage in Canada, it is used as a bitter tonic, inebriant, and hemostatic in hemorrhages, wounds, hemorrhoids. It is also a vulnerary and anthelmintic."[44] Several contemporary herbalists have told me that yarrow whose leaves are darker in color and with larger, whiter flower heads, possess the greater narcotic activity. Christian Ratsch notes (*Plants of Love,* Ten Speed Press, 1997) that the greater the intensity of sunlight that the plant receives the higher the content of aromatic oils and thus increased aphrodisiac and inebriating activity. Matthew Wood notes that in his experience the plants that grow on soils that are sandy, gravelly, stony, and light are the more potent medicine. He uses the fresh spring or fall leaves or the mature summer flower head.

Kindscher (1992) notes the presence of thujone in yarrow, the same substance so strongly present in wormwood (see "About Wormwood"). Thujone is considered to be "an active narcotic poison" by the Food and

Drug Administration[45] and is considered to be the reason absinthe has such a terrible reputation with regulators and such a good one with writers.

Yarrow brings both a complementary bittering action to ales and preservative action through its antimicrobial, antibacterial, and antiseptic properties. Its taste is not overwhelming and is quite delicious in brewing, especially if the aromatics are brought into the ale. The aromatics are especially strong in the flowering plant (the tannins and astringent action being stronger in the leaves). To preserve the aromatics, which will boil off, the plant should both be boiled and added to the fermentation to infuse over time, as in the yarrow beer recipe, or else simply steeped in the hot wort as it cools.

Yarrow grows throughout the northern continents in all types of terrain: meadows, prairies, open woods, and heavy forests. It tolerates both wet and dry conditions and flowers from late April through October, depending on the area.

WORMWOOD ALE

There fell a great star from heaven, burning as it were a lamp. . . .
And the name of the star is called Wormwood.

—Rv 8:10, 11

When there is a Scarcity of Hops; the End of Hops being only to
allay the exceeding lusciousness of the Malt by their Bitterness,
whereby both uniting themselves together, becomes a Savory and
Wholesome Drink for Man's Body; Now this may be in every
respect as well performed with Wormwood, *and in some Sense more*
agreeable, for Wormwood *is endued with many vertuous Qualities;*
It Strengthens the Stomach, Resists Putrefaction, Prevents
Surfeits, Strengthening both the Retentive and Expansive
Faculty, and many more, *as may be seen in every Herbal; when as*

to Hops we do not attribute one half the Vertues: 'tis true they purge the Belly of Choler: And thus appears the wholesomeness of Beer above Ale, as Parkinson *saith; but however we are speaking of their scarcity, when* Wormwood *is generally at all Times found in the field or High-ways. But here some may object, and say, That* Wormwood *will make Drink too bitter: But in answer to this I say, That we must learn to know the Qualities of Things; for as we have said in the* Britannean Magazine of Wines, *one handful of* Wormwood *goes farther than three of other Herbs, nay than five of some sort, especially when it seeds, for therein consists the most oleous Parts; and as the End is only to Mitigate the sweetness of the Malt, therefore you may take such a Proportion as will only mitigate, and yet not let the bitter Quality be predominant, beginning with small Quantities, and when by several Tryals, you have hit the pondus, let that be your guide in Brewing.*

—Dr. W. P. Worth, 1692[46]

Wormwood has a long tradition of use in brewing. Nordland comments on its use in Norway and in antiquity when he says

The *grabone*, reported from Herefoss, E. Agder, "to add colour to the ale" must be *Artemisia absinthium*, wormwood. Wormwood is among the herbs mentioned by Placotomus in connection with the preparation of ale for medicinal purposes, but it must also have had its use in ordinary beverages. Henrik Wergeland also recommends *grabo* to add strength to the ale.[47]

Millspaugh notes (1892) that "Brewers are said to add the fruits [of wormwood] to their hops to make the beer more heady; and rectifiers also to their spirits."[48] And Lloyd and Felter observe that "In Germany it is employed as a substitute for hops in the making of *Wermuth beer*."[49]

Interestingly, *Wermuth* means "preserver of the mind," reputedly from wormwood's virtues as a mental restorative and nervine.

Wormwood is extremely bitter and needs to be used with a judicious hand, as Dr. Worth cautioned in 1692. The plant hasn't changed much since then. I originally used 3/4 ounce in the following recipe and found it too bitter for my taste, though people with a tendency toward gustatory sadomasochism, tongue flagellation, or those who enjoy the taste of ear-wax might find it pleasant. But then, I have never cared much for bitter beers. Used with a lighter hand, however, the taste is pleasant and a fine complement to the heaviness of the flavor of malt.

> *He hath made me drunken with wormwood.*
>
> —Lam 3:15

Wormwood Ale

Ingredients

    4 pounds malt extract

    1 pound raw wildflower honey

    1/2 ounce wormwood (*Artemisia absinthium*)

    4 gallons water

    yeast

Bring the water to a boil, add wormwood, simmer one hour. When cooled to 160 degrees F, strain over malt extract and honey in fermenting vessel. Cool to 70 degrees F. Add yeast. Allow to sit in fermentation vessel until fermentation is complete (about six or seven days). At that point nothing but a few isolated specks of foam should be visible on the surface of the fermenting beer. It should be bottled before all trace of the honey has disappeared. Put 1/2 teaspoonful of sugar in each bottle, pour in the beer, and cap. Ready to drink in 10 days to two weeks.

Wormwood ales were frequently used for illness with attendant feverish conditions, i.e., colds and flus, malarial attacks, and other infectious diseases producing fever. John Bickerdyke (1890) lists the ingredients in a wormwood ale for fevers commonly prescribed in the Middle Ages. It's not one I have yet tried—I can't quite figure out what "githrife" is.

Wormwood Ale for Fevers

Fever patients are recommended to drink during a period of thirty days an infusion of clear ale and wormwood, githrife, betony, bishop-wort, marrubium, fen mint, rosemary and other herbs.[50]

About Wormwood
Artemisia absinthium

The Juice, the distill'd Water, the Syrup, the fixed Salt, and the Oyl of it are used; but the Wine or Beer seems to be the best. It strengthens the Stomach, creates an Appetite, opens obstructions, and provokes Urine.
—John Pechet, 1694[51]

Wormwood's use as an herbal medicine is extremely ancient. But it has not only been highly thought of in medicine; it has also been considered a plant possessing powerful sacred properties. It is connected, by many cultures, to the realm of the gods. In the *Herbarium* of the Greek Apuleius, wormwood is said to have been a gift of Diana, goddess of the hunt.

Of these worts that we name Artemisia, it is said that Diana did find them and delivered their powers to Chiron the Centaur, who first from these Worts set forth a leechdom, and he named these worts from the name of Diana, Artemis, that is Artemisias.[52]

The connection between the *Artemisias* and the sacred is pervasive in all cultures in which *Artemisia* grows. It has been traditionally used in sweat-lodge ceremonies throughout North America and is felt to be one of the primary herbs that dissipates evil influences. Delores LaChappelle in her *Sacred Land, Sacred Sex, Rapture of the Deep* (Silverton, CO: Finn Hill Arts, 1988) quotes Herbert Wright on the prevalence of sagebrush throughout human history. Wright notes that North Africa, Spain, Italy, Greece, Iran, and Syria were originally dominated primarily by the *Artemisia* species sagebrush. LaChappelle remarks:

> In Southwestern Asia, as well, there was a domi-
> nance of sagebrush steppe in this same Pleistocene
> period. . . . [A]s the human race began during
> Pleistocene times in Africa, the odor of sage was every-
> where present. The persistent odor of sage accompanied
> humans as slowly, over generations, they moved further
> north and into the Paleolithic cave areas of Spain and
> France. Then, as the climate changed, the persistent
> odor of the sage steppe moved further north into the
> areas where humans later learned to grow cereal grains.
> Throughout all this period of human development, sage
> was always present.
>
> No wonder that Artemis, one of the most important
> Greek goddesses, has the same name as this plant. . . .
> [*Artemisia*] grew abundantly on Mt. Taygetus, the favorite
> haunt of Artemis. . . . Artemis means bear. . . . Here again
> we have a herb which bear first showed to humans.[53]

As the human species developed over time with this pervasive plant, *Artemisia* was absorbed into similar rituals throughout the world. The Egyptians, Greeks, Romans, and Chinese all used it, for medicine and for sacred ceremonies. Pliny the Elder notes that a draught of the herb was given to "the winner of a ritual, four-horsed chariot race on the Capitoline Hill at Rome."[54] And *Artemisia* species are used religiously in Nepal and India. Trilock Chandra Majupuria and D. P. Joshi note in their *Religious and Useful Plants of Nepal and India* (Lalitpur Colony, India: Craftsman Press, 1989) that *Artemisia* has traditionally been used for many ceremonies.

> The leaves of this plant are offered to Shiva after chanting various *mantras*. In the month of *shravana* (July to August) the flowers of this plant are offered to Vishnu and Surya. After funeral ceremonies Hindus also use either flowers or leaves of this plant. The fragrance of this plant has also been said to be used by several religious people to avoid letharginess and yawning.[55]

The similarity of use of the *Artemisias*, not just for medicine, but for the same kinds of ceremonies and rites among disparate and unconnected cultures, strikes many researchers as amazing. Chase Stevens comments that

> In the New World, as in the Old, the lives of the natives were intimately and vitally related to the plant population, and it need not surprise us that our Indians put the indigenous *Artemisias* to much the same medicinal uses as the early Europeans and Asiatics did theirs; but that our Indians should have, as they did, the same kind of superstitions about the *Artemisias* and use them in similar rites and ceremonies, with confidence in their magic powers, is amazing.[56]

But it is clear that any examination of the *Artemisias* (and the *Salvias*, the true sages, with whom they are sometimes confused and that are used in similar ways) reveals that there is a deeper and more sacred aspect to them than can be accounted for by science alone (though many researchers might now begin to offer the opinion that it is the *Artemisias'* inebriating qualities that explains it).

As an inebriant, wormwood used in beers does not receive the acclaim the herbs used in gruit do, though the comments about headiness and strength coming from its addition indicate that it does increase beer potency. Wormwood is known best for its use in absinthe, a highly alcoholic drink popular throughout Europe until the early twentieth century. The real thing is now illegal everywhere except the Czech Republic, though several countries sell a poor mimicry of it. Absinthe, bottled at between 120 and 160 proof, is extremely strong and bitter, usually being diluted and sweetened before consumption. The liquors now available that are called absinthe are actually aniseed knockoffs. Absinthe fell to the antialcohol and antidrug Protestant temperance movements in the early twentieth century. Anecdotal evidence of the time indicated absinthe was a central nervous system poison and antiabsinthe fervor (much like the drug hysteria of today) swept the world. It is now legal in the Czech Republic because of their antipathy to overly active governmental intervention in individual life decisions—a not unsurprising position, given their recent history.

Artemisia absinthium does contain thujone, which is classified as a narcotic poison by the FDA; and absinthe was historically thought to cause irreversible nervous system damage. The best treatment on the history and effects of absinthe (and thus of wormwood) is Dale Pendell's remarkable *Pharmako/poeia* (San Francisco: Mercury House, 1995). There is little actual evidence that wormwood, even used to excess, will produce the kind of toxic effects that caused the banning of absinthe; however, there is plenty of evidence that it is mildly narcotic and psychotropic (probably the real reason it was banned). A number of cultures smoke *Artemisia*, and Pendell comments that research by Jonathan

Ott noted psychoactive effects from such smoking, an effect with which Pendell agrees. (I have smoked it and found it quite calming but certainly not psychoactive.) Though wormwood was blamed for the toxic effects of absinthe, real absinthe contains a number of other herbs—hyssop, lemon balm, fennel, anise, sweet flag, coriander, veronica, marjoram, nutmeg, oregano, angelica, mint, chamomile, parsley, and juniper. Many of these herbs contain turpenes with effects similar to thujone, particularly hyssop, fennel, and anise.

The thujone is concentrated, however, in the essential oil of wormwood, and only a little of the oil is necessary to produce toxic effects. Felter and Lloyd note that it acts as a nerve depressant on human beings.

> Less than drachm doses produced on rabbits and dogs
> tremors, spasmodic muscular action of a clonic character,
> intoxication, and loss of sensibility. Larger doses (from 1
> to 2 drachms) produced violent epileptoid seizures, in
> some instances resulting fatally. Small doses adminis-
> tered to man act as a gentle stimulant, larger doses pro-
> duce headache, while still larger doses induce cerebral
> disturbances and clonic hysteroidal convulsions.[57]

There are still occasional news reports about people who end up seriously ill trying to make absinthe by using the essential oil of wormwood. Similar reports exist for the ill-considered use of pennyroyal oil and a few other essential oils. Wormwood itself, however, is still used in standard medicine practice in Germany and among herbalists everywhere.

Wormwood has been traditionally used in nearly the same manner as yarrow, though it is much more powerful in its action. Its name refers to its ability to expel intestinal worms (usually round worms or thread worms), though few use it for such in contemporary practice. It is of interest that like many plants useful for fevers, wormwood is especially effective in the treatment of malaria (one of its historical uses). Malaria, like thread- or roundworms, is caused by an invading parasite, *Plasmodia* spp., and is increasingly resistant to standard practice pharmaceuticals. Long thought conquered, malaria is making a strong resurgence around the globe, sickening half a billion people per year and killing 3 million of them. Rare in the United States for the past 50 years, it is now showing up in places like New York City and Minnesota. In an inexorable growth curve, the number of cases is increasing at a tremendous rate, 1,200 cases (half the estimated actual cases) being reported in the United States in 1996.

As malaria is increasingly resistant to antibiotics, a number of herbs once used for malaria are being rediscovered. One such is the traditional Chinese herb *Artemisia annua* which is now being used in clinical practice throughout the world, under the auspices of the World Health Organization, to treat resistant malaria, with excellent results. A major component in all the *Artemisias* is artemisinin, which has been thought by many researchers to be the active constituent in those herbs that act as antimalarials. However, extracts of *Artemisia annua* that contain no artemisinin have been found to be as effective in the treatment of malaria as artemisinin extracts though at twice the dosage. These results indicate that, like herbs in general, the whole plant is much more effective than any isolated component alone. *Artemisia absinthium*, wormwood, has also been found to possess antimalarial activity in vivo and in vitro, though I can find no evidence of clinical trials using it for malaria.[58] Wormwood also contains absinthin, perhaps the bitterest substance known, and, as such, it is an excellent digestive bitter. In stimulating the liver, the gallbladder, and digestive juices, it is much more powerful than yarrow. It possesses antimicrobial, antifungal, and anti-inflammatory properties. It is diaphoretic, stimulating sweating.

Wormwood is a member of the same family that contains chamomile, tansy, and yarrow—all herbs reputed to possess mild narcotic properties and to increase inebriation when used as an adjunct in brewing.

SAGE ALE

*Sage is much used of many on the moneth of May fasting, with butter
and Parsley, and is held of most much to conduce to the health of
man's body. It is also much used among other good herbes to bee tund
up with Ale, which thereupon is termed Sage Ale, whereof many barrels
full are made, and drunke in the said month chiefly for the purpose
afore recited: and also for teeming women, to helpe them the better forward in their childebearing, if there be feare of abortion or miscarrying.*
— Parkinson, 1629[59]

Sage ale was one of the primary ales brewed throughout the Middle Ages
and was considered highly medicinal and wholesome. Gerarde, in 1597,
observed that "No man needeth to doubt of the wholesomenesse of *Sage
Ale*, being brewed as it should be with Sage, Scabious, Betonie, Spikenard,
Squinnette (Squinancywort) and Fennell Seedes."[60] It is a pleasant-tasting
ale, but like clary, sage ale was thought to be especially inebriating. *The
Universal Herbal* (1820) observes that "The leaves, flowers, and seed, put
into a vat with ale, while fermenting, greatly increase inebriating quality."[61]

Sage Ale — *A Modern Recipe*

Ingredients

> 4 pounds malt extract
>
> 2 pounds brown sugar
>
> 4 ounces fresh culinary sage (*Salvia officinalis*)
>
> 2 ounces licorice root
>
> 4 gallons water
>
> yeast

Bring the water to a boil, add 2 ounces sage and
licorice root, simmer one hour. When cooled to 160

degrees F, strain over malt extract and sugar in fermenting vessel, stir until sugar and malt are dissolved. Cool to 70 degrees F. Add yeast. Add final 2 ounces sage to fermenter. Ferment until complete (about the sixth or seventh day). At that point nothing but a few isolated specks of foam should be visible on the surface of the fermenting beer. Put 1/2 teaspoonful of sugar in each bottle, pour in the beer, and cap. Ready to drink in 10 days to two weeks.

Sage Ale — *A Nineteenth-Century Recipe with Hops*

Ingredients

- 5 pailsful water
- 1 quart hops
- 1/2 pint rye meal
- 2 quarts molasses
- 1 handful fresh sage
- 1/2 pint yeast

To five pails of water put one quart bowl of hops, and one large handful of sage. Add half a pint of rye meal, and let all boil together three hours. Strain it through a sieve, while it is scalding hot, upon two quarts of molasses. There should be about four pails of the liquor when it is done boiling; if the quantity should be reduced more than that, add a little more water. When it is lukewarm, put to it a half pint of good yeast; then tun it into a keg and let it ferment. In two days or less it will be fit to bottle.[62]

S a g e   A l e — *An Eighteenth-Century Recipe*
Ingredients

> 3 gallons water
> 1 gallon fresh red or garden sage
> juice of 6 lemons
> 6 pounds sugar
> ale yeast

> Take three gallons of water and Six pound of Lofe Sugar
> boyle the water and Sugar together and as the Scum rises
> take it of and when it is well boyled put it into a Clean
> Tubb. Have ready in the Tubb one gallon of Sage Leaves
> free from the stalks. So let it then Stand till it be almost
> cold then Put to it the Juice of 6 Lemmons beat them with
> a litle Ale yest brew it well together cover it very close that
> no Aire come in let it Stand 48 hours full and when it hath
> don working Stop if very close and let it Stand three
> weeks or a month before you bottle it. Putting into each
> bottle A litle lump of lofe Sugar this wine is best kept a
> quarter of a year or longer before it is Drankt.[63]

CLARY ALE

*Clary is included also among "herbez for the coppe [cup]" in a fif-
teenth-century manuscript. A slightly later manuscript states: "Some
brewers of ale doe put it in their drink to make it more heady, for to
please drunkards."*

—Margaret Freeman[64]

Clary sage, like culinary sage, was used both in beers and wines. Unlike
the *Artemisias*, with whom they are often confused, the true sages are
milder in their bitterness and delectable as culinary spices.

Clary Ale — *A Variation of an Early Seventeenth-Century Recipe*

Ingredients

- 10 gallons water
- 16 egg whites
- 1 pint clary flowers
- 13 pounds sugar
- 1 pint ale yeast

Ten gallons of water, thirteen pounds of sugar, and the whites of sixteen eggs well beat. Boil it slowly one hour and skim it well. Then put it into a tub till it is almost cold. Take a pint of clary flowers with the small leaves and stalks, put them into a barrel with a pint of ale yeast, then put in your liquor and stir it twice a day until it has done working. Put into each bottle a little lump sugar.[65]

Clary Ale — *A Modern Recipe*

Ingredients

- 4 pounds malt extract
- 2 pounds brown sugar
- 4 ounces fresh clary sage
- 4 gallons water
- yeast

Bring the water to a boil, add 2 ounces sage, simmer one hour. When cooled to 160 degrees F, strain over malt extract and sugar in fermenting vessel, stir until sugar and extract are well dissolved. Cool to 70 degrees F. Add yeast. Add final 2 ounces of sage to fermenter. Allow to ferment until complete (about the sixth or seventh day). At that point nothing but a few isolated specks of foam should be visible on the surface of the fermenting beer.

Put 1/2 teaspoonful of sugar in each bottle, pour in the
beer, and cap. Ready to drink in 10 days to two weeks.

ABOUT SAGE

Salvia spp.

> *Waller (1822) states [clary sage] was also employed in this country
> as a substitute for Hops, for sophisticating beer, communicating con-
> siderable bitterness and intoxicating property, which produced an
> effect of insane exhilaration of spirits, succeeded by severe headache.
> Lobel says: "Some brewers of Ale and Beere doe put it into their drinke
> to make it more heady, fit to please drunkards, who thereby, accord-
> ing to their several dispositions, become either dead drunke, or foolish
> drunke, or madde drunke."*
>
> —Maude Grieve, 1931[66]

The sages are used throughout the world for healing and in ritual. The
famous culinary sage, *Salvia officinalis*, is a European native and is what
was traditionally used in medicine and ales. Sages are, however, ubiquitous native plants throughout the world and can be used interchangeably
for culinary and ritualistic purposes. Sagebrush is an *Artemisia* species (see
"About Wormwood"), and though used interchangeably with true sages
for their spiritual properties in indigenous cultures, the two do differ
botanically. The taste difference between sage and wormwood is tremendous—one is good, one is, well dreadful. Sage can be used in food (which
Artemisia cannot) and in much greater quantities in ales.

Like the *Artemisias*, the *Salvias* grow throughout the Mediterranean
region and the world, and they, too, are felt to have beneficent spiritual
properties. The name *Salvia* means "to save" or "to heal" and comes from
the Latin *salvus* (*salvere*)—"to make healthy" or "to make safe." *Salvia officinalis* was at one time known as *Salvia salvatrix*—"Sage the Savior." And
there is a saying of the ancients: *Cur moriatur homo cui Salvia crescit in*

Sage (Salvia *spp.*)

horto?—"Why should a man die whilst sage grows in his garden?" Sage has long had a reputation as an herb that mitigates mental and bodily grief, heals the nerves, counteracts fear, and protects human beings from evil influences, spiritual and physical.

Sage is highly antibacterial and has been medicinally used for thousands of years as an antibacterial healer. As a smudge it protects against infection, and in teas and alcoholic tinctures it has been used in infections of all kinds. It is antibacterial, antimicrobial, and antiseptic.[67] Sage has also been found to possess a number of compounds active against *Candida albicans*, *Escherichia coli*, and *Klebsiella pneumoniae*, all implicated in urinary tract infections (UTI) as well as other diseases. The antibacterial activity has been shown to be especially effective against *Staphylococcus aureus*.[68] This makes sage especially useful in infectious diseases. The tea or powdered herb is good for skin infections and wounds, UTI, yeast infections, colds, sinusitis, otitis media, etc.

British researchers have found that sage inhibits a primary enzyme linked to Alzheimer's disease. John Gerarde in 1597 noted its efficacy for these kinds of memory disorders, recommending it to "helpeth a weak braine or memory." Sage has been confirmed as possessing compounds effective in the treatment of asthma, and researchers have also identified six anti-inflammatory compounds in sage. It also possesses tannins, and they, along with the antibacterial and anti-inflammatory compounds in sage, make it an excellent remedy for gingivitis and tonsillitis; it is official for this purpose in Germany. Its effectiveness against *Candida* also makes it useful as a douche for *Candida* vaginal infections.[69]

Sage dries up secretions; thus, it slows or stops sweating, lactation, and menstruation—all traditional uses of the plant. It has been shown to possess estrogenic properties, which gives it a place in the treatment of menopausal hot flashes.[70] Sage has also been used for a long time in the treatment of nervous disorders and to fortify a debilitated nervous system. It also contains thujone, the same volatile oil in wormwood, though not to the same degree. The thujone is probably one of the reasons why the sages have a reputation for increasing the inebriating effects of the ales in which they are used.

The volatile oils in sage are not especially water soluble and need alcohol to extract them from the plant. Sage ales benefit from adding some sage to the fermenter so that as the yeasts produce alcohol, the more active constituents of the sage are extracted into the ale.

BROOM ALE

Before the introduction of Hops, the tender green tops were often used to communicate a bitter flavour to beer, and to render it more intoxicating.
—Maude Grieve, 1931[71]

Broom, as its name implies, was traditionally used for making brooms. It possesses long, green, slender, tough branches with few leaves. The branches grow in bunches, which were cut and bound together to make brooms before industrial manufacturing came into vogue. Broom has also been long used as a medicinal herb and in the making of ales and beers.

Broom Ale
Ingredients

　　　4 pounds malt extract

　　　2 pounds dark brown sugar

　　　1 1/2 ounces dried (or 2 1/2 ounces fresh) broom, flowering tops

　　　4 gallons water

　　　yeast

Boil water and broom for one hour and strain. Add malt extract and sugar to cooling wort and stir until completely dissolved. Cool to 70 degrees F, pour into fermenter, and add yeast. Ferment until complete. Prime bottles with sugar, bottle, and cap. Ready in one to two weeks.

Broom Ale for Dropsy—1695

Ingredients

Three handfuls of broom tops

1 quart Rhenish wine

3 ounces elecampane root

2 ounces horseradish

3 ounces agrimony

3 ounces polipody

3 1/2 gallons good ale

Take three handfuls of the tops of Broom, (Green Broom is the best) and Boyl it five Hours in two Quarts of good Ale, adding thereto (after one Hours Boyling) a Quart of Renish Wine, and three Ounces of Elecampane Root; when it has Boyled so long, take it off the Fire, and strain it through a Linnen Cloth, and put the Liquor into an Earthen Vessel, and put therein two Ounces of Horse-Radish sliced, Agrimony, and Polipody of each three Ounces, let it stand three Weeks and pour it into three gallons of Ale, and it will be an excellent drink against the Dropsy.[72]

ABOUT BROOM

Cytisus scoparius or *Sarothamnus scoparius*

> *Shepherds have long been aware of the narcotic properties of Broom, due to Sparteine, having noticed that sheep after eating it become at first excited and then stupefied, but the intoxicating effects soon pass off.*
>
> —Maude Grieve, 1931[73]

Broom, also called Scotch broom, is a profusely blooming shrub of up to 10 feet in height. Originally a native of Europe, it has escaped gardens in the United States and found it likes its freedom. Thought of as a pest by state agricultural management agencies, it has taken over many areas that were formerly open prairies and sparse woodlands.

Broom has long enjoyed a reputation in folklore as a magical plant that imparts amorousness and euphoria to those who ingest it. It is found in the oldest European herbals and enjoyed a wide use throughout its range. Broom flowers from April to July, the yellow flowering tops are used in herbal medicine and brewing, and the flower buds, pickled or fresh, are used in salads much like capers. The flowers, early in their season, are thought to be stronger; they do not keep their properties well upon drying. Broom contains tannins and is thus astringent. It is considered to be a cardioactive diuretic, hypertensive, a peripheral vasoconstrictor, and an emetic. The actions of broom are thought to come primarily from two of its constituents, scoparin and sparteine. Scoparin is diuretic and purgative; sparteine is a narcotic, bitter alkaloid.

The bitterness of broom, of course, makes it useful in ales, which always benefit from some bitter agent to balance the sweetness of the malt. The tannins are additionally of benefit in brewing flavor, especially in mead fermentation. Ingestion of sufficient broom results in inebriation, staggering gait, and impaired vision. Greater amounts result in vomiting and profuse sweating.

Broom has traditionally been used for a weak heart, which results in the accumulation of fluid in the lower extremities (dropsy). The herb stimulates the heart to more efficient and strong beating and provokes urine (the loss of water from the body), directly affecting the condition. It also constricts blood vessels, making it effective for low blood pressure. Its astringent properties are useful in excessive menstruation and in external application for wounds. It is rarely used in herbal practice now, though it was official in many medical pharmacopeias until after World War II. Too large a dose is unpleasant, as it creates almost the opposite effects of more moderate doses. In overdose, it weakens the heart, lowers blood pressure, and depresses the system, somewhat like hemlock in its actions. The seeds may be used much as the flowering tops are employed.[74]

HENBANE ALE

That there really were [ale] mixtures which might have dangerous effects is shown by the Eichstatt police regulations, in which the use of seeds of the narcotic henbane is mentioned. The botanists of the sixteenth century also mention henbane, darnel, and woody vine as dangerous herbs mixed into ale.

—Odd Nordland, 1969[75]

References to henbane surface in historical ale literature like the momentary appearance of a great whale coming up for air. You have a sense of something huge just beneath the surface, something to which there is a great deal more, but only a little of it can be seen before the writer moves on and it drops back and is obscured from view.

Henbane is known under a variety of names in middle Europe: *bilsa, Pilsen, pilsenkrut,* and (commonly in Germany) *Bilsenkraut.* The original pilsner beer (brewed in Pilsen in the Czech Republic) was made from henbane and got its name from the local name for henbane—*pilsen* (as presumably did the town).

The following recipe is from Christian Ratsch's *Urbock* (AT Publishing, 1998, 199) a large book that is, regrettably, not yet available in English. He notes that if desired the *Myrica gale* can be omitted from the recipe.

Henbane Ale
Ingredients

2.6 pounds barley malt extract

2 pounds honey

1.43 ounces (40 grams) henbane seed (dried)

5 grams *Myrica gale*

(5 grams) dried yeast

6 gallons water

Take the henbane (finely ground) and 1 quart of water and mix together (if you desire to add the *Myrica* do so at this time). Bring to a boil, remove from heat, and let sit until cool to the touch. Then take malt extract and honey and 2 quarts of hot water and mix well (until the sugars are dissolved) in a fermentation vessel that has been sterilized. Add the henbane (and *Myrica*) mixture and stir well—do not strain. Then add 6 gals of cool water. Check the temperature, making sure it is in the 68–76 degrees F range and then sprinkle yeast on top. Let ferment until complete, then siphon into primed bottles, and store for two weeks in a cool place.

ABOUT HENBANE
Hyoscyamus niger

> *In low doses, beer brewed with henbane has an inebriating effect; in moderate doses, it is an aphrodisiac. (Henbane is the only beverage that makes you more thirsty the more you drink! This is due to the dehydrating effects of the tropane alkaloids.) In high doses, it leads to delirious, "demented" states, confusion, disturbances of memory, and mad behaviors having no apparent cause.*
>
> —Christian Ratsch, 1994[76]

Henbane, like jimson weed (*Datura stramonium*), mandrake (*Atropa mandragora*), and bittersweet (*Solanum dulcamara*), some of the other members of the deadly nightshade family, has an imposing, beautiful, and cautionary presence. Henbane, as jimson weed does, exudes an almost forbidding and intelligent presence to any sensitive enough to feel it. It should not be underestimated nor used indiscriminately. A sacred herb of the Celts, it is a powerful narcotic poison; unlike mescaline or psilocybin, it is not gentle in its effects.

Henbane has been used in herbal medicine for at least 5,000 years. It, generally, is a biennial plant growing to three feet tall. The stalk and leaves are hairy and dark green, the flowers an eerie pink at the top of the stalk. In small doses henbane is strongly sedative and analgesic. It was commonly used for pain relief, even for surgical operations. In larger doses it produces giddiness; too large a dose produces intense terror, inability to move the body, extreme visual distortion, acute physical pain, spontaneous random movements, memory loss, and delirium. Death, though rare, can occur.

Henbane is primarily narcotic, anodyne, calmative, and antispasmodic. It has been traditionally used for the treatment of pain for patients who have disagreeable reactions to opium. It is an excellent anti-spasmodic

in the treatment of asthma, bronchitis, whooping cough, and internal muscle spasming. It has been used for insomnia, neuralgic pain, and for calming hysterical states. However, the efficacy of its effects are directly related
to the amount used. The plant is so powerful that minute dosage alterations often produce significantly different effects. It is easy to go beyond
the hallucinogenic narcotic stage with a slightly too large dose, resulting in
strong negative side effects. The plant, in large doses, does not produce a
lightness of spirit.

Gustav Schenk, a German writer who experimented with henbane, comments that the giddy effects he experienced were accompanied with extreme terror and almost complete bodily dysfunction.
"The gray misery that fills the mind is enhanced by the precarious
state of the body and the derangement of the senses. Sight, hearing,
smell and touch do not obey the will and seem, still entirely under the
influence of the henbane, to be going their own way."[77] Memory is
impaired, agitation and restlessness take over, and the hallucinations
attendant to taking henbane are frightful when the dosage is even
slightly too high.

Like jimson weed, henbane is not an emotionally soft-and-fuzzy
plant, happy at last to be in contact with human beings. There is almost a
wild coyote laughter that one can hear in the back of the mind when
encountering jimson weed—a laughter that threatens to break out also
with its cousin henbane. Unless treated with extreme respect, it is not a
"nice" or helpful plant. And this essential nature infuses its narcotic
effects. Schenk comments on this aspect of henbane (and indeed all
plants) when he notes that

> When we partake of a plant, we absorb its physical
> constituents, its substances. But we take into our bod-
> ies more than its material elements. Though this may
> sound like mysticism, it is nonetheless a fact that in

addition to the physical substances of the plant we also absorb its life forces, the particular qualities of strength and tenacity with which it confronted and mastered life. . . . We can see clearly that a plant has a life of its own, a life very different than ours. If we take a large quantity of this alien life into ourselves while we are well, it may act as a poison and over-power us with fatal consequences.[78]

Though used as a powerful sacred plant by the Celts and Wiccans throughout Europe, henbane's use was attended with a great deal of knowledge of the territory it opened to the quester. Like jimson weed, use of henbane without knowledge precipitates one into frightful terrain. Henbane is a native of Europe now quite thoroughly naturalized in the United States.[79]

MANDRAKE BEER

The ancient Egyptians brewed a mandrake beer.

—Christian Ratsch, 1994

Among the most sacred herbs of the Druids were mandrake, mead-owsweet, water mint, vervain, mistletoe, henbane, sage, heather, ivy, and selago. (The most sacred trees were the oak, holly, birch, and rowan.) Of these, mandrake was considered especially potent. Mandrake has been used for thousands of years in ceremony and for medicine throughout its range. That it was used in ales like its cousin, henbane, is certain. Oddly, little real lore about mandrake, given its importance in sacred European ceremonials, has survived to the present day.

Unfortunately, I have not been able to meet the *Mandragora* in person; this recipe is equivalent to the dosages used in the Middle Ages.

Mandrake Beer

Ingredients

    4 pounds malt extract

    2 pounds dark brown sugar

    1/2 ounce dried mandrake root

    4 gallons water

    yeast

Boil water and mandrake root for one hour and strain. Add malt extract and sugar to cooling wort and stir until completely dissolved. Cool to 70 degrees F, pour into fermenter, and add yeast. Ferment until complete. Prime bottles with sugar, bottle, and cap. Ready in one to two weeks.

The root of the mandrake was said to bear the likeness of a human form and to screech when being uprooted.

About Mandrake

Atropa mandragora or *Mandragora officinarum*

> *The Hebrew word for mandrake means love-plant, and in Genesis both of Jacob's wives—unable to have children for different reasons—became pregnant after acquiring the herb. It has long been considered a powerful aphrodisiac: the ancient Egyptians called it the "phallus of the field."*
>
> —Rob Talbot and Robin Whiteman, 1997[80]

Mandrake, now known as *Atropa mandragora* and formerly as *Mandragora officinarum*, is one of the most sacred of European herbs. Its name, *Mandragora*, is a combination of the Latin *mens*, meaning "mind," and *dragora*, meaning "dragon"—thus, the "dragon-mind." *Atropa* is derived

from the name of the Greek goddess Atropos, one of the three sacred
beings (the Fates or Destinies) who control human destiny. Atropos (her
sisters are Clotho and Lachesis) is keeper of the shears that cut the thread
of life. So the entire meaning of the name is "the dragon-mind that holds
the shears that cut the thread of life." Mandrake is of extremely ancient
use in the Mediterranean region; a *Mandragora* wine was given to
Odysseus' companions by Circe in the *Odyssey*. And in fact, mandrake
was known to writers of antiquity as *Kirkaia*, the plant of Circe.

Unlike henbane, mandrake does not rise up but remains a basal
rosette of leaves. Also unlike henbane, which is often a biennial plant,
mandrake is perennial and may live to a great age. The leaves are not as
dark nor as hairy as henbane's, but the flowers nod in a knowing manner
(even when encountered in a painting), and I wonder if it was they, not
opium, that lulled Odysseus' companions into eternal dreamland. Like
many of the deadly nightshade family, mandrake has its own eerie quality. Unlike many of its cousins, I feel strongly drawn to mandrake (the
other that calls me is bittersweet, *Solanum dulcamara*, a lovely, delicate,
vining plant with striking, delicate, violet-yellow flowers. Bittersweet possesses the same energetic properties as mandrake, though in milder form).

Mandrake, in many respects (though not in medicinal action), is much
like the American herb buffalo gourd, *Curcurbita foetidissima*. Buffalo gourd
was one of the most sacred herbs of the Plains Indians, the root growing as
large as a human being and weighing up to 200 pounds. Buffalo gourd
grows the same size and shape as a human being—head, arms, legs, body.
The herb was considered a gift of the Great Spirit to the tribes, and when
dug, the root had to remain unharmed and be removed whole and intact.
These same harvesting beliefs are present in all cultures that used mandrake.

Mandrake root is smaller than buffalo gourd, though still large. The
smaller species grow to two feet in length, the larger four to five. Like
many perennials, the older the plant the larger its roots become. The roots
will often take on the appearance of a human being in their shape, the
above-ground plant being considered the head by the ancient writers. But

there is more to this, I think, than mere physical similarity. Mandrake, like buffalo gourd and ginseng, can live to great age. Great forests, when they attain a certain age, take on an inhabited state. That is, there is a conscious and living presence in the forest. This does not occur in young forests and any forest that is extensively logged will lose this living presence. Humans have grown as a species in long relationship with this forest presence—a presence that possesses intelligence, awareness, and consciousness—and we are immediately aware of it whenever we encounter it. (The loss of the great forests thus deprives us of something deeply necessary to our humanity.) Though "old growth" buffalo gourd is still somewhat common, the same cannot be said for ginseng and mandrake. Like the great forests both these plants were known for becoming "inhabited" when they reached a certain age. It is the appearance of this consciousness that, in part, explains the pervasive attribution of human form to the plant. And these plants, the inhabited old growth grandmothers and grandfathers, do indeed posses great power as medicine and spiritual teachers. Unfortunately there are probably none of the age necessary for this inhabitation to occur still left in the world.

Because of the power of the plant the ancients were aware that mandrake must be harvested with a special attentiveness of mind. Like buffalo gourd, it was felt that it must be dug whole without any damage to the root. Harming the root in excavation, with both plants, was felt to be highly disrespectful and would result in misfortune to whoever harmed it. Mandrake harvesting was deeply ceremonial in nature; the plant was never gathered without attentive mind. Though all indigenous cultures know that plants can speak with humankind, mandrake is almost the only plant from indigenous European practice about which this belief is still extant. Throughout its Christian European history, it has been believed that when mandrake was harvested, the root would scream, and that the sound would drive the harvester mad. The pre-Christian users of mandrake believed that if the proper ceremony was observed and the spirit of the plant was asked to come and aid humankind, the plant would not cry out.

The root's power caused it to be highly sought after, even after the demise of pre-Christian religious practices. Throughout the Middle Ages the plant was hunted eagerly. Though the original sacred connection of the indigenous European peoples had been lost by that time, the root was still believed to possess powers beneficial to those who could obtain one. Mandrake roots commanded extremely high prices, and the demand nearly decimated the wild species. Eventually, fake mandrake roots, made of bryony, were either carved or force grown to resemble the mandrake in shape, and they, too, commanded extremely high prices, as much as 30 gold pieces each during the Middle Ages.

Mandrake is indigenous to southern Europe, North Africa, Asia Minor, and the Himalayas. Because the plant was at one time fairly common in England, it is thought that there might have been a native species there that could endure cold better than the North African/southern European variety. This species, if species it was, no longer can be found. In any event, the southern variety was extensively transplanted throughout England where it enjoyed great popularity. And apparently at one time there were extensive wild populations of this species there and in France. However, the southern species does not like extremely cold weather, and often will not survive below-zero weather. Gardeners frequently take it indoors in colder climes until the winter has passed.

The leaves of mandrake are dark green, a foot or more in length, and five to six inches in width. They spread out and lay upon the ground, taking up a circle sometimes up to three feet in diameter. From among the leaves the flowers unfold on stalks four or so inches high. The flowers may be lavender or whitish tinged with purple. The flowers give way to the distinctive yellow fruits, which are smooth, round, apple-like, and apple-scented. Throughout its range mandrake has been consistently used for its aphrodisiac, fertility, and consciousness expanding effects. Every culture in which mandrake grew described it as a plant that would assist in stimulating sexual desire and countering infertility, effects which were described at some length in the Bible (Gen. 30: 14–17).

Like wild American ginseng in the United States, and for much the same reasons, mandrake is very uncommon in the wild. The dried root can sometimes be purchased through English herbalists, though even they seldom use it. In its effects it is nearly identical to henbane, though the root, instead of the seeds, is used. However, historically mandrake is considered to be more human friendly than henbane to those who can make a relationship with it. Like henbane, it has a history of use of at least 5,000 years. The American mandrake, *Podophyllum peltatum*, should not be confused with the European mandrake—they are entirely different in action and appearance. Unlike henbane, mandrake was exceptionally rare by the time of European settlement of North America and was never naturalized here.[81] However, unbeknownst to most of America, *Mandragora* is slowly being planted in record numbers in the United States. A representative of Horizon Seeds, a company actively working to bring back the *Mandragora* from its endangered state, told me that whenever they finally get mandrake seeds, their stock sells out almost immediately. That Druidic consciousness just keeps on and on, doesn't it? Horizon can be reached at (541) 846-6704.

DARNEL BEER

Darnel, or lolium timulentum, which is vulgarly known under the name of sturdy, *when malted with barley, a process which the seeds of it often undergo, causes the ale brewed from it to be speedily intoxicating. It produces the same effect when mixed with bread and eaten hot. Many stories are told of its effects, some of which are sufficiently amusing, but not exactly suited to this essay.*

—W. T. Marchant, 1888

Darnel has long been reputed to possess the capacity to inebriate. John Gerarde observed that "the new bread wherein Darnel is eaten hot causeth drunkenness."[82] It is a grass from which a grain like wheat is harvested. The inebriating qualities are ascribed, by some, to an ergot growing on the plant. Others feel that the plant itself, which possesses an alkaloid, temuline (from the Latin for "drunkenness")—the only member of the grass family to do so—is what causes the effects associated with darnel.

Darnel Beer

Ingredients

> 5 pounds pale malt
> 1/2 pound darnel seed, malted
> 1 pound brown sugar
> 4 gallons water
> yeast

> Malt the darnel seed. Combine it with the pale malt and add enough water at 170 degrees F to cover it. Leave for 90 minutes. Sparge until 4 gallons of wort are obtained. Cool to 70 degrees F, pour into fermenter, add yeast, and ferment until complete. Siphon into primed bottles and cap. Ready to drink in one to two weeks.

About Darnel

Lolium temulentum

> *When Darnel has been given medicinally in a harmful quantity, it is recorded to have produced all the symptoms of drunkenness: a general trembling, followed by inability to walk, hindered speech, and vomiting.*
>
> —Maude Grieve, 1931[83]

Darnel is a member of the grass family, like most crops grown for bread flour. Its Latin name, *temulentum*, means "drunkenness," attesting to the ancient reputation it has for causing inebriation. The common name, darnel, comes from the French *darne*, signifying "stupefied." It grows throughout the world, though much more commonly in Europe and the Mediterranean region, and has occasioned significant problems whenever it intermingles with wheat. Maude Grieve comments that one of the common names for darnel was "cheat," from its use as an adulterant of malted wheat and barley. A custom that, she notes in 1931, "has not been entirely abandoned."[84] Its uses were known in antiquity, the Romans, Greeks, and authors of the Bible all commenting on its effects, all ancient cultures having used it for both brewing and medicine. It is regarded as anodyne and sedative and has been traditionally used for pain relief and as a relaxant in nervous conditions. It is rarely used in herbal medicine now, and few in the United States have heard of it. Overdoses can be quite uncomfortable and can lead, though rarely, to death. It possesses large quantities of starch in the seeds (which look much like wheat berries) and it malts well. When used historically as a malt, darnel made the ale or beer cheaper. Less malted barley or wheat needed to be used—the inebriation came from the darnel, not the alcohol content, which was quite low.[85]

SAFFRON ALE

In England, Clary (Salvia sclarea) *is said to give an intoxicating quality to beer. Saffron also—the dried stigmas of the Crocus* sativus, *has a similar effect.*

—J. Johnston, 1879[86]

Saffron, from which the red/orange/yellow stigmas of the flowers are harvested for use, is a typical member of the crocus family. It is one of the most ancient and most expensive of spices used by humankind. Four thousand three hundred and twenty flowers are harvested to produce one ounce of dried saffron. Saffron has a penetrating and wonderful fragrance and a bitter taste. It grows wild throughout the world and is commercially grown in both Europe and the Far East. The best saffron is thought to come from Spain.

Saffron Ale

Ingredients

> 12 ounces molasses
>
> 8 ounces brown sugar
>
> 1/2 ounce saffron
>
> 1 gallon water
>
> yeast

> Boil molasses, brown sugar, and water; stir well. Add saffron, stir, cover, and let stand three hours. Pour into fermenter, add yeast at 70 degrees F, and ferment until complete. Siphon into primed bottles, cap, and store. Ready to drink in one to two weeks.

ABOUT SAFFRON
Crocus sativa

> *[Saffron] exhilarates the spirits to such a degree, that when taken in large doses, it occasions immoderate mirth and laughter.*
>
> —W. T. Marchant, 1888

Saffron was official in a number of Western pharmacopeias until this century. It fell out of use in many respects because of its high cost. Saffron was often adulterated in the past, though it is unlikely that will be the case now due to its infrequent use. It can be bought in most stores that carry culinary spices.

Saffron was used primarily as an emmenagogue and diaphoretic. It reliably stimulates menstruation when used in small quantities; the average dose is five drops of the tincture two times per day. It was used as a diaphoretic to stimulate the eruption of sweat in feverish conditions, primarily with children. Recent research has found that saffron contains a blood pressure lowering chemical called crocetin that is quite effective. Its presence in saffron may explain the low incidence of high blood pressure in Spain, where saffron is consumed in quantity.

The narcotic properties of saffron were apparently unknown to Western medical herbalists but are well documented in the East, where it is sometimes used to produce narcotic inebriation. Christian Ratsch notes that saffron contains "an essential oil that has psychoactive and stimulating effects and evokes long, distinctive orgasmic sensations." The Greeks felt that this effect was markedly pronounced in women, and saffron does have distinctive effects on women's reproductive systems. Both traditional Nepalese and Indian herbal practice consider saffron to be indicated for fevers, melancholia, and enlargement of the liver. It is considered a stomachic in catarrhal afflictions, and a stimulant, narcotic, nerve sedative, and emmenagogue. Externally it is used for bruises, sores, rheumatism, and neuralgic pain. It is used as a dye throughout India and Nepal and is considered one of the most sacred of their herbs. It is an integral part of many Hindu and Buddhist ceremonies, the forehead streak often being prepared from saffron.[87]

WILD LETTUCE ALE

Among these inebriants [when used in beer] the inspissated milky juice of the common garden lettuce is considered as powerful in its operation as opium itself.

—W. T. Marchant, 1888

Lettuce has long had a reputation as a feeble opiate. Marchant is talking about garden lettuce, but all the species may be used similarly. Lettuce, though sweet to eat when young, generates a bitter, milky-white sap when it puts out its flowering stalk. This milky sap, collected and concentrated, was a part of standard practice medicine throughout the Western world until World War II. Unless you are a gardener, wild, or prickly, lettuce is your best source for lettuce ale.

Wild Lettuce Ale

Ingredients

> 1 gallon water
>
> 12 ounces molasses
>
> 8 ounces brown sugar
>
> 1 ounce prepared wild lettuce sap
>
> yeast

> Boil molasses, brown sugar, and water; reduce to 70 degrees F, and pour into fermenter. Chop the prepared lettuce sap (see "About Wild Lettuce") into small pieces and add to the fermenter. Add the yeast. Allow to ferment until complete. Siphon into primed bottles, cap, and store. Ready in two weeks.

ABOUT WILD LETTUCE

Lactuca spp.

> *Figure a yield of about 2-3 grams from a four foot plant after it has been systematically bled until reduced to a one-foot-tall, headless pygmy and the latex dried down in a shady but breezy place until it resembles a mixture of butterscotch pudding, dried library paste, and tubercular phlegm.*
>
> —Michael Moore, 1979[88]

Wild, or prickly, lettuce is a rather prolific, unpleasant two-to-four-foot weed covered with small spines that have the persistent property of insinuating themselves into the skin without the grace to be easily seen or extracted. The leaves grow haphazardly up the spindly, tough stalk, and the whole plant is topped by a rather disgraceful bunch of small dandelion-like flowers waving about on a thin profusion of branching floral stems. These give way to numbers of small, bulbous seed pods in late summer or fall.

The plant can easily take over any region in which it is established and loves disturbed ground. The leaves do look something like non–head lettuces. Wild lettuce is, however, quite bitter, especially late in the season. It can be eaten in early spring when the plants are quite new and used as a pot herb if the water is changed, but it is not a food plant to excite the inner child. It has long been used in indigenous medicine and clinical herbal practice for its feeble opiatelike effects. Some people respond to these effects, while others notice nothing and believe that its reputation is a product of unrestrained, perhaps hopeful, imaginations. However, its long use in indigenous cultures throughout the world for pain relief indicates that it can be reliably used as a feeble opiate for *some* people. There is some indication that, like many herbs fermented in ales and beers, this opiatelike activity is enhanced during brewing. Again, the bitter principles of wild lettuce are useful in brewing for the same reason that those properties are sought after by the users of hops.

The milky-white sap is usually collected from the plant and prepared for storage and eventual use. In this prepared form it is called lactucarium and was formerly an official medical composition in many countries. Basically, producing lactucarium is a tedious task, best conducted in company, like corn shucking, or alone if in a manic episode of herbal fanaticism.

During early flowering, confront a large grouping of plants with shears in hand, somewhat like Jason in *Friday the 13th* (the hockey mask is not necessary) or an herbal Atropos. Decapitate 20 three-to-four-foot-tall plants by cutting all the flowers from each. Throw those away. Allow the milky sap to ooze out and dry a bit, then scrape it off in a bowl. Taking shears in hand, snip another half inch off the same stalk, allow the sap to bubble out and dry a bit, and scrape it off into the bowl. Continue until the plants are a foot or so tall. Allow the collected sap to dry and attain the appearance described by Michael Moore (the first to accurately describe this harvesting process).

You now are in possession of lactucarium, or "inspissated" lettuce sap, to use in your ale. In the old days, when this was an important item of commerce, lactucarium could be bought in dried chunks and prepared by the individual physician for use—few doctors were excited by the process of making it and were just glad to have it on hand. Unfortunately, it is no longer a part of commerce; if you want it, you must make it yourself. Some herbalists swear the seeds are as strong in their effects as the sap, some use the whole herb, a few use the lactucarium, and many skip the plant altogether.

Lactucarium does taste and smell like opium (which it is not), and it does have enough feeble opiatelike effects for herbalists to keep it part of phytomedical tradition. Though some work has been done attempting to identify the active constituents of lettuce, none discovered so far explain its actions. In traditional medicinal herbal practice it has been used as a calmative, hypnotic, sedative, and analgesic. Animals such as dogs tend to respond to lactucarium quite strongly, much more so than people. The strongest plant sap is reputed to be that of *Lactuca virosa*, followed by the wild, or prickly, lettuce, *L. serriola*. It has been used most effectively with those who are in some degree of constant pain (from severe coughing, for instance) and need a sedative, relaxant, and pain reliever. It tends to quiet coughing in children, alleviate sleeplessness and general irritability, and calm the unsettled and hysterical.[89]

EIGHT

Beers and Ales from Sacred and Medicinal Trees

Just as the seed contains the tree, and the tree the seed, so the hidden world of God contains all Creation, and Creation is, in turn, a revelation of the hidden world of God.

—Roger Cook, 1974[1]

Most of the important action in our lives is hidden from view, taking place on the spiritual plane, for what we do there affects events far beyond the areas our limited physical minds can grasp. We have to preserve our physical world—the environment our bodies need to survive on this earth. But we also must preserve the secret and invisible world—the environment our spirits need to survive in eternity. The tree is essential to one, and the symbol of the tree is essential to the other. The physical tree sustains our bodies with its fruit, its shade, its capacity to reproduce oxygen and to hold the fertile soil safe. The mythic tree sustains our spirit with its constant reminder that we need both the earth and the sunlight—the physical and the spiritual—for full and potent life. The tree gives us a sense of quiet continuity, for its life is long compared with ours, and it is not inconceivable that we might sit in the shade of the same tree to contemplate the meaning of life that Shakespeare himself sat under to compose Hamlet.

—Moyra Caldecott, 1993[2]

JUNIPER BEER AND ALE

Juniper ale and beer is traditionally brewed in the Scandinavian countries: Norway, Finland, and Sweden. The best, and almost only, source in English for in-depth information on the traditional beers of the Nordic countries is the remarkable *Brewing and Beer Traditions in Norway* by Odd Nordland. Published in 1969 by the Norwegian Research Council for Science and the Humanities in association with the Norwegian Brewery Association, it is, regrettably, out of print. Some additional material (primarily describing the juniper beers of Finland) is available in volume 17, number 4 of *Zymurgy* magazine. Nordland's book, though focusing on Norway, notes throughout his text that many of the processes for making juniper beer are common also in Finland and Sweden, and Maude Grieve in her *A Modern Herbal* (New York: Dover, 1971) comments that "In Sweden a beer is made that is regarded as a healthy drink [from juniper berries]."[3]

Like many traditional beers that rely on local brewmasters or household brew wives, juniper beer is not nearly as common now as it once was. Large industrialized breweries, temperance movements, increasing technology, and commercial advertising have largely eroded their traditional base.

Juniper plays a major role in the craft of beer making and, indeed, life in Norway. Juniper extract (a concentrated tea made from juniper branches and berries) has long been used for washing and cleaning in Norway, representing a deep and long-standing knowledge of its antiseptic properties. Though hops are often used in beers in the present day along with juniper, juniper is the most ancient herb in use in traditional beer making in Norway and the Scandinavian countries, and its antiseptic or preserving properties predate the advent of hops.

Juniper is the primary tree herb used in Scandinavian brewing, though alder is also frequently used. Birch, too, has been used, followed by occasional use of other trees such as spruce, fir, hazel, oak, willow, and rowan. Oddly enough, given the widespread use of spruce beer in the United States, many people in the Scandinavian countries avoid these trees, feeling that spruce and fir are not really good for beer because of the strong resins they contain.

Generally, after malting the barley (though sometimes oats are also used in "poorer" beers), the beer is prepared in Norway (and Finland and Sweden) in the following manner.

The malt is soaked in a hot liquid—just enough to cover the malt (and it is frequently checked to make sure that as the malt absorbs liquid, the level of liquid does not fall below the top of the malted grains—if it does, more liquid is added). The liquid used is either water or juniper extract. The juniper extract is simply water boiled with a quantity of juniper branches— the amount and strength of this infusion being determined by the taste of the individual brewer and the region in which he or she lives. The soaking malt (the mash) is then allowed to sit for some period of time, from one hour to several days, usually in a barrel covered with blankets to keep it warm. This releases the sweet sugar from the malted barley into solution. At that point the liquid is drawn off and saved (the brewer can usually tell how good the beer will be simply from tasting this initial wort—the sweet barley water mixture). The wet malt that remains is carefully ladled into another, specially prepared container (called the *kuurna* in Finland). This container, usually a barrel with a hole and spigot (or tap) at the bottom edge, is prepared by crosshatching layers of straw and juniper branches—basically a gridwork, straw north and south, juniper east and west, and so on. Usually straw is the first to be laid down, with the juniper branches next. The straw is often boiled first to make sure it does not carry with it any unwanted bacteria. Usually the bottom layers of straw and juniper are somewhat large, with smaller twigs of juniper being placed on the higher levels. If other types of trees are used (usually alder), those are substitued for the juniper (or the juniper and straw) or added as a final top layer. If only alder is being used, the bark is shredded in a thick mass and then smaller branches of alder are placed on top of that.

The wort that is originally drawn off the mash is saved and added to more hot juniper extract or water, and the resulting liquid is poured extremely slowly over the mash in the barrel. The straw, juniper twigs, and alder create an efficient strainer, allowing the sweet wort to pass through the barrel and leave all particulate matter behind. In many instances the juniper branches that are boiled in the water are not removed but are simply poured with the juniper extract directly onto the mash—both the mash and the branch-strainer filtering them out. The juniper and alder branches that make up the strainer also add fresh flavor and a deeper color to the hot wort as it passes through them.

Sometimes this first draw of the sweet wort is boiled again, this time with hops in those regions that use them, and poured once more over the mash. The final wort is then placed in a fermenter, and allowed to cool to the proper temperature. Yeast is then added, and the mixture is allowed to ferment. Not too different, really, from beer making by homebrewers in the United States and Europe at this time. The primary difference is in the use of juniper and the amazing ingenuity of the juniper and straw strainer.

If hops are added to the final draw of the wort and the two are boiled together, the wort has to be strained again. Though a number of strainer types are traditionally used, the two most common, and most interesting, are made with small split branches of juniper (sometimes from fine rootlets of local plants) or from long, braided strands of women's hair. Both of these strainer baskets look like many of the handwoven African or South American baskets found in craft stores throughout the United States and Europe. The weave is tight enough to keep any particulate matter out but still allow a good flow of the hopped wort. Quite often the strainer baskets are attached to a stick frame at the basket's top. The sticks protrude far beyond the sides of the basket and rest on the fermentation vessel, the basket hanging below, to free the hands to pour the hopped wort through the strainer.

There are basically seven methods in use in Norway for brewing juniper ale: boiled mash and wort, boiled mash and wort with repeated pourings, the wort boiled but not the mash, mash and some of wort boiled, mash boiled but not the wort, some wort boiled but not the mash, and neither mash nor wort boiled (raw ale).

BOTH MASH AND WORT BOILED

This means that either boiling water or a boiling juniper extract is poured over the mash, the mash is allowed to sit, and then the remainder of the boiling water or juniper extract is poured slowly through the mash to produce the sweet wort. (In some instances, the malt itself is boiled with the juniper extract or water, allowed to cool, and the liquid is poured off—a heretical notion among current brewing practitioners in the United States because it is not the most efficient manner of extracting the sugar from the malted barley, and in fact [they insist], may damage it.) After being drawn off, the sweet wort is boiled. In this process hops may or may not be added. The boiling of the wort tends to produce a sweeter wort, as some of the water in the wort is evaporated during boiling.

> Generally 18–20 litres of juniper extract were used with about 17 litres of malt. It was kept covered in the filter-vat for 1 1/2–2 hours before tapping. The wort had to flow slowly, and it was always tasted and discussed. Good wort should be slightly sweet.[4]

The mash is sometimes used a second time with about the same amount of juniper extract in order to produce a second-grade or light ale. A third run is sometimes (rarely) produced, though this is not fermented. It is used as a thirst-quenching beverage for the men working in the fields. Though the amount of hops used in Norway, as is always true elsewhere, is a matter of both the regional and individual brewer's tastes, for the recipe above about .4 kilograms of hops are used per 60 liters of wort.

BOILED MASH AND WORT WITH REPEATED POURINGS

For this type of ale, the process outlined above is followed with one difference. After the wort is drawn off and boiled, it is once again poured over the mash, or the entire mash and wort are boiled together one more time. Depending on the individual brewer, this process might be repeated two, three, or four times. If hops are to be added, at the last boiling of the wort, the desired quantity is added, boiled with the wort, and then poured over the mash.

> They took about 100 litres of juniper extract to half a barrel of malt. Then they tapped the wort (sometimes called *rosten*), heated it to boiling point, and poured it over the mash. This was repeated three to four times. The wort was tapped into wooden buckets, and the wort for strong ale would be dark brown. It was remembered as being delicious before the hops were added.[5]

Again, second run-throughs are common to make a light ale. Hops are added to taste in both, approximately 1 kilogram for the recipe above.

WORT BOILED BUT NOT THE MASH

In this process, the juniper extract is boiled but allowed to cool before being poured onto the mash. After the wort is drawn off, it is boiled, and if hops are to be added, they are added at this time. This process might only be done once, or the boiled wort might be allowed to cool and be poured over the mash one or more times. Except for repeated boilings, this type of brewing is most similar to that commonly followed in home-brewing in the United States.

All the wort was boiled, and poured onto the hops. It was best if the hops had been soaked in advance, and they were then put into a bag of coarse cloth for boiling with the wort. One-fourth kg of hops were used to 180 litres of wort and 45 litres of malt. The hops could also be boiled in the juniper extract, and then mixed with the wort. Especially in summer, when the cows were at the mountain outfarm, ale was often drunk with porridge. For this purpose, ale without hops was best. It did not taste so bitter. This ale was mixed with sugar. It was also the custom to cut up pieces of bread, and mix them with the ale into a kind of soup.

Strong ale was made by using 10–15 litres of water to five litres of malt, but it is a long time since such strong ale was used here.

The most common mixture is 20 litres of water to 5 litres of malt. The mash in the filtre-vat was "watered" two, three or four times, according to the strength desired. The final tapping, to which yeast and hops had been added, was called spesill, and was used as a refreshing drink.[6]

ALL THE MASH AND SOME OF THE WORT BOILED

In this process the boiling juniper extract or water is poured on the mash for the first run-through of the wort, or else the mash and water/juniper extract are boiled together. However, only a portion of the wort is then reboiled (usually with hops) and then either again poured over the mash or poured directly into the cooling wort from the first run-through. Second run-throughs using this method are also done to produce a weaker, light ale.

They stirred it with a long stick, the mash-stick, *meiskeren*. To the wort they added hops which had been boiled, and strained through the hop strainer, in which they were left. Then water was added. First they tapped the "good ale", *godt ol*, and then the "thin ale", *tunol* or *spassol*. They had two barrels for this. Some of the wort was tapped into ladles and wooden cups, and tasted. The wort had to be sweet and thick. Then hops were boiled in some of the wort, and water added. If many hops were used, the flavor of the hops was too strong, *humlebramt*. They worked according to a specific measure: equal amounts of wort and water were taken, corresponding to the amount of malt.[7]

SOME WORT BOILED, BUT NOT THE MASH

In this process, hot water or juniper extract is poured over the mash and some of the drawn wort is then boiled with hops. Sometimes, in this process, cold water is used as the last liquid through the mash, sometimes being left to stand for a day before being drawn off.

To 100 kg of malt, about 200 liters of juniper extract are used, and this makes 200 litres of good ale. The strength of the ale depends on many factors: good malt and good yeast, and the fact that "not too much was taken", as they put it. [Author's note: This means that the brewer did not try to get all the sweetness out of the malt but settled for the best, and first, run-through.] The different kinds of ale were called "good ale" and "thin ale", *godtol* and *tynning*. They did not always tap the thin ale.

They boiled juniper extract and wort with hops, and tapped it into small tubs. If they poured too much juniper extract on to the mash, the ale became weak, and a certain strength was thought desirable.

Some of the wort was boiled with the hops, and then strained into the rest of the wort. Strong ale was made by adding more malt to each measure of wort.[8]

NEITHER MASH NOR WORT BOILED—RAW ALE

In this type of traditional brewing, it is believed that any boiling (except of hops) would interfere with successful beer making, and also that raw ale is stronger than boiled ale. The water or juniper extract is simply heated, not boiled, and then poured over the mash. As in all of these traditional Norwegian brewing methods, the hot liquid and malted barley are allowed to stand for from 1 to 24 hours before the wort is drawn off. Once drawn off, the wort is not heated or boiled again but is put into the fermentation vessel. If hops are to be added, they are boiled separately, poured into the wort, and yeast is added immediately.

When strong ale is made, the measure of ale should be equal to the measure of malt. The wort flowed slowly, and was regulated by a small chip put in alongside the tap. Everybody had to taste the wort, and the adults discussed its quality, and how the ale might turn out. The wort should be sticky to the touch. It was tapped into a shallow cup which was emptied into the tub. The hops were boiled separately. After the extract had been poured into the tub, the wort was again tasted and discussed. Sometimes more hops might have to be boiled.[9]

Another form of juniper ale, usually made by poor students or young men, is a simple drink prepared from water, juniper branches with berries, sugar, and baker's yeast. This is called *sprakol,* the word means simply "juniper" (*sprake*) "ale" (*ol*).

FINNISH SAHTI

Some updated recipes have been collected in the *Zymurgy* previously mentioned (volume 17, number 4). Similar to the processes in Norway, these recipes are typical of Finland and Sweden. You can see how a number of these recipes fit into the various categories outlined above.

S a h t i — 1 9 0 1 (*Adapted from a 1901 cookbook recipe*)
Ingredients for 5 gallons

> 11 pounds malted barley
> 1 pound malted rye
> 8 gallons water
> a fistful of hops
> juniper branches [amount undefined]
> brewing yeast

Moisten malts with cold water, mix, cover and let sit overnight. In the morning add two scoops of hot water to the malt. Boil the remainder of the water and add a scoopful at a time to the malt, mixing well, until the mash has the consistency of porridge. Add the remainder of the water and allow the mash to stand for one hour.

Bring the clear portion of the mash to a boil four to six times by alternating between two kettles and adding the porridge at the conclusion of each boil. Mix, allow the grains to settle, and pour off the clear wort and reboil.

During the final boil prepare a container with a hole and plug near the bottom. Rinse rye straw with boiling water, place a layer on the bottom of the barrel, dump the porridge on the straw and pour liquid from the final boil on top of it. Let the wort flow through the tap into a fermenting vessel. Pour clean juniper water, made by boiling juniper branches and berries in water, over the porridge, and through the tap. Boil the liquid with hops. When cool, add yeast and ferment.

To make juniper berry Sahti, take one-half gallon (2 liters) of cleaned juniper berries per quarter gallon (liter) of liquid, macerate in cold water for 10 hours and use this liquid to moisten the malt. Follow the remainder of the procedures above.[10]

Pohjanmaan Sahti

Ingredients for 5 gallons

    2 1/5 pounds malted barley
    4/5 pound rye flour
    2 pounds dark brown sugar
    1 juniper branch 6–8 inches long
    ale yeast

Add malt and flour to 1 gallon of water heated to 140 degrees F. Mix well, cover the container with a towel or blanket and let stand for four to five hours. Bring the mash to a boil for five minutes. Transfer to a sanitized plastic fermenter. Add sugar to 4 gallons boiling water. Stir well, add to the fermenter and stir again. Add the juniper branch. After the wort has cooled to pitching temperature, transfer liquid off the sediment and pitch ale yeast. Original specific gravity: 1.038, final specific gravity: 1.004.[11]

Sysma-Style Sahti

Ingredients for 5 gallons

17 1/2 pounds pale barley malt

1 pound dark rye malt

long, thick pieces of straw

juniper twigs with berries

(Note: both straw and juniper twigs should be strong enough to
   support the weight of the hot mash)

ale yeast

Heat 2 gallons of water to about 170 degrees F. Transfer to a large container, add malt and mix well. At 30 minute intervals add 1 to 2 quarts of progressively hotter water, mixing after each addition. This is done 10 to 12 times. Cover the mixing container to retain heat. By the last addition the water should be boiling. Transfer (by siphoning) the clear portion of the mash to a kettle and bring to a boil.

Prepare a filter bed in the *kuurna* with straw and juniper twigs over wooden sticks. Run the thicker part of the mash over the bed and collect the runnings. If necessary, run boiling water through the *kuurna* until 5 gallons of wort are collected.

Pour off about two quarts of wort, cool to 93 degrees F and add yeast. When the remainder of the wort has cooled to 70 degrees F, add this starter back to the fermenting vessel. Ferment for two or three days. Rack to a wooden keg and move to a cooler place after one day. The sahti is ready to drink when fermentation is complete.[12]

BREWING GOTLANDSDRICKA

Gotlandsdricka is an ancient brew of Gotland, a large island off the coast of Sweden. The primary sugar source is a smoked malted barley extract. The malted barley is prepared by steeping barley for three days in water. It is then drained, left to rest for one day, and then germinated on the floor in four-inch layers for about a week. It is then kilned in woodsmoke, generally from burning birch logs, for another six or seven days.

The malt is then crushed and placed in a barrel (a mash tun) with a false bottom built up from layers of old juniper sticks, fresh juniper branches (including berries), and straw. Fresh juniper branches with berries are boiled with water for an hour and the hot liquid (enough to cover the malt) is poured over the crushed malt. It usually is allowed to sit for anywhere from one hour to overnight. After testing the sweetness of the wort, the remaining liquid (still hot) is sparged over the malt and is drained slowly through the layers of sticks, straw, and juniper branches. The wort is placed in a fermenting vessel, allowed to cool, and the yeast is pitched. Sometimes a portion of the wort is boiled with hops or honey for additional sweetness and then poured back in with the rest of the wort.

Gotlandsdricka — *A Modern Version*

Ingredients for 5 gallons

> 5 pounds home-smoked barley malt (some brew stores now carry a
>   smoked malt)
> 1 pound honey
> 4 pounds juniper branches with berries
> 1/3 ounce Perle hops
> bakers or brewers yeast

> Boil 8 gallons of water with juniper for one hour. Mash
> the smoked malt for 90 minutes at 154 degrees F with

enough liquid to cover the malt then sparge with the juniper-infused water. Boil sixty minutes with hops. Primary ferment for one week at 56–68 degrees F. Secondary fermentation is optional.[13]

Gotlandsdricka — *Another Modern Recipe*

This is one I used to make a hearty juniper beer. It possesses a citruslike resiny flavor and took nearly a month to carbonate in the bottles.

Ingredients

5 pounds two-row malted barley

2 pounds juniper branches with berries

7 gallons water

yeast

Boil the juniper branches for 60 minutes in 7 gallons water and remove branches—do not worry about remaining bits of juniper in the infusion; they will filter out during sparging. Mash the malted barley with 2 gallons juniper water for 90 minutes. Sparge with the remaining juniper water, then boil the wort until the quantity is reduced to 5 gallons. Cool to 70 degrees F, pour into fermenter, and add yeast. Ferment until complete, prime bottles, fill, and cap. Ready in one month.

ABOUT JUNIPER
Juniperus spp.

Juniper is felt to possess powerful sacred and spiritual qualities throughout the world. Ethnobotanists, in studying plant usages throughout the world's indigenous cultures, typically cross-reference plant usage among many cultures. If usnea (*Usnea* spp.) is commonly found to have strong antibiotic properties throughout the world's cultures, ethnobotanists tend to think that some aspect of usnea has been transculturally discovered and suggest conducting laboratory studies to try to verify its medicinal effects. However, when faced with universal attribution of nonphysical activity by a plant, they are usually not so bold. The esteemed herbalist, Michael Moore, comments succinctly on this phenomenon.

> The aromatic properties of all parts of juniper plants have been used against bad magic, plague, and various negative influences in so many cultures, from the Letts to the Chinese to the Pueblo Indians, that there would seem to be some validity to considering the scent as beneficial in general to the human predicament. Overlapping traditions are useful in triangulating valid functions in folk medicine. If unrelated traditions say that Yarrow clots blood, it is easy to admit that such is probably the case; if they say that juniper clears bad "vibes," many of us will back off and start to twitch skeptically. Our mechanistic approach to "primitivism" is too selective, accepting the possibility of drug effect on the one hand and nervously rejecting something as "subjective" as the warding off of bad influences on the other. In most non-Western peoples the two go hand in hand.[14]

As Moore notes, juniper is used extensively throughout the world for its capacity to ward off negative influences. In many instances, the juniper needles or laden branches are burned and the smoke is used as a smudge. Many cultures believe that this act keeps negative influences from traveling through the air to infect participants in ceremonies—as good a description (as Rob McCaleb, president of the Herb Research Foundation, noted) of antibiotic activity to combat airborne bacteria as anything Western physicians might say. Nevertheless, there seems to be something to a number of plants, among them juniper (which includes cedar), the *Artemisias*, and sage, in that wherever they occur, indigenous peoples recognize in them effects that go beyond the material and embrace potent spiritual activity, usually in cleansing or counteracting spiritual negativity and fearful emotions.

Juniper (Juniperus *spp.*)

The terms cedar and juniper are often interchangeable, many being *Juniperus* species. The juniper with which I am most familiar, the Rocky Mountain juniper, is also known as western red cedar and is the source for the tremendously aromatic wood used in cedar chests. The cedar found in old-growth forests and the source for the cedar used in home building is another tree. In spite of that, *all* juniper and cedar species are used in the same manner throughout the world. Daniel Moerman, who has done the most to try to correlate all the data available from early ethnobotanical accounts of plant usage in Native North America, has collected extensive accounts of traditional usage of eight juniper species. In all cases the uses are remarkably similar, among those is the use of the plant in sweat baths or as smoke to cleanse negative influences or fear.[15] This most basic aspect of the spiritual activity of juniper and cedar is echoed in deeper traditions the world over.

In the American Indian Osage traditional creation myths, "cedar is associated with the creation of the human race"[16] and it is, among the

Osage, like so many other cultures, the Tree of Life. It is told that at the giving of the cedar to human beings, the tree said to the people:

> I stand here on this cliff so that the Little Ones may make of me their medicine. Look at my roots, a sign of my old age. When the Little Ones make me their symbol they, too, will live to see their toes gnarled with age. Look at my branches, how they bend. With these as symbols the People will live to see their own shoulders bent with age. Look at the feathery tips of my branches. When the Little Ones make these their symbols, they will live to see their own hair white with age as they travel the Path of Life.[17]

Other legends about cedar tell that the thunder birds or beings (powerful sacred beings in many American Indian cultures) live in a vast forest of cedars. Interestingly, throughout Europe and Northern Africa, cedar is associated with the Tree of Life and was believed by the ancients to be representative of the essence of *incorruptibility* and to preserve all things with which it came into contact—it being a tree of youthfulness—ever green.[18] Also of interest is that Gilgamesh, in his search for the powerful gods to question them about the mortality of humankind, found their home to be, like that of the thunder beings, in a great cedar forest.

Melvin Gilmore comments in his *The Uses of Plants by the Indians of the Missouri River Region* (Lincoln: University of Nebraska Press, 1977) that "[t]he cedar, appearing to be withdrawn into lonely places, and standing dark and still, like an Indian with his robe drawn over his head in prayer and meditation, seemed to be in communion with higher powers."[19] This perspective about juniper and cedar is echoed in Jeffrey Hart's *Montana—Native Plants and Early People.*

Charles Sitting Man, a Cheyenne, said that the Great Spirit has much respect for juniper because it seems to never grow old and remains green the year round. It therefore represented youthfulness, and they accordingly placed it centrally in many of their holy rites and purification ceremonies. Indians also admired it for the aromatic fragrance of its needles, which they burned as sacred incense; for the durability of its wood, which they found desirable for lance shafts, bows, and other items, and for the dark red seemingly dyed-in-blood color of its wood.[20]

The spiritual cleansing properties of juniper and cedar have corresponding physical elements as well, having traditionally been used antiseptically, antibacterially and for viral infections.[21] Oddly, little research has been done on the antiseptic and preserving properties of juniper and cedar, though a great deal of other research has been done on these trees. Some research, however, has noted juniper's antiseptic properties,[22] and the herbalist Wade Boyle notes:

Juniper berries are not really berries but rather fleshy cone scales which easily pass for berries. They were official in the United States Pharmacopoeia from 1820–1936. They are rich in volatile oils with names like pinene, thujine and terpenine which give them their antiviral, antibiotic and antifungal properties. In the old days . . . doctors used to chew them when treating epidemic infections as an antiseptic barrier.[23]

However, Boyle gives no citations for his assertions of these medicinal effects, and I have not seen any research material for information on pinene, thujine, and terpenine. But juniper berries' long-standing use in botanical medicine as an antiseptic effective for treating urinary tract infections points to its possessing antiseptic and antibiotic properties.[24] Additionally, its long duration of use in American Indian botanical practice for colds, coughs, sore throats, influenza, respiratory infections, and as a wash and disinfectant for sores and vaginal infections, along with traditional use for urinary tract infections, indicates a broad-spectrum use for many thousands of years for bacterial and viral infections[25] and seems to bear out Boyle's comments. This traditional use in North America echoes the traditional Norwegian use of juniper extract (infusion) as a general antiseptic to be used in washing and cleaning.

Interestingly, juniper berries have been found to contain up to 30 percent dextrose, also known as grape sugar, an easily fermentable sugar.[26] The presence of such a large amount of dextrose may account, in part, for the use of juniper and juniper berries as an integral part of Norwegian brewing. A number of people who met and talked with Nordland noted that the use of juniper made the malt "go further." And though his book is not clear on this point, it seems to indicate in a number of sections that juniper beer was sometimes made with juniper, water, and yeast only—no other source of sugar being used.

Juniper has been used in traditional eclectic botanical practice as a stimulant, carminative, and a diuretic. The oil of juniper, used in a specially prepared electic medical salve was used for eczema and in the healing of ulcers.[27] Juniper, juniper berries, and oil of juniper from various species have also been used to help with rheumatic pains, as a diaphoretic, and an emmenagogue to stimulate menstruation.[28] Chancel Cabrera, the Canadian herbalist, reports clinical data supporting use of juniper berry or oil for "renal hyperemia; chronic nephritis; catarrh of the bladder; chronic pyelitis; after acute nephritis; scarlet fever; oil is used in non-inflammatory prostatorrhea and gleet; chronic arthritis; chronic gout; tendopathies; myogeloses; chronic low-grade irritation of urinary tract; renal congestion; depressed, chronic kidney disease; dysuria and polyuria, especially during menopause; renal atony with catarrh."[29] Boyle also notes consistent use of juniper berries in stomach complaints (echoed in the traditional use by American Indians for those conditions). Fritz Weiss, the noted German botanical physician, found juniper berries useful "for chronic arthritis, gout, neuralgia and rheumatism."[30] The berries were found by Boyle and others, notably Father Kneipp, to produce marvelous effects in the treatment of disease relating to food absorption problems. Boyle comments that this is "because they improve nutrition via their action on the stomach and because they enhance detoxification through the kidney."[31]

Given the antiscorbutic properties of spruce and pine, it seems likely that juniper would also possess this property, but nothing I have read has noted it in any juniper species. Generally, juniper and juniper berries are contraindicated in acute kidney infections or "renal disease, gastric inflammation, pregnancy, and acute UTI."[32]

The medicinal properties of juniper were noted by numerous people interviewed by Nordland in his book on Norwegian brewing. Many mentioned the medicinal effects of juniper ale or the juniper wort before it was fermented. Some commented that it was medicinal without attributing any specific qualities to it. Others were more specific, making such comments as, "It was especially good for gallstones."[33] Or that "some of the wort was saved, and used as a tonic for people who were weak after a long illness."[34] The amount of juniper used in the extracts in Norway for drawing off the wort and brewing is enough to produce medicinal effects in those drinking the ale as part of a regular diet. It would be interesting if Nordland or some other researcher would look into the commonness (or lack thereof) of diseases for which juniper is specific in the population who uses juniper ale as a regular part of its culture.

Generally, juniper is a marvelous herb to use in brewing, and the taste of juniper ale is good and very refreshing. Given the many benefits from the herb, as a preservative and a medicine, especially on nutrition and digestive health and as a potentially useful herb in the treatment of colds and flu, it seems an excellent herb to use in ales and beers.

ABOUT ALDER
Alnus spp.

> *The wood resists water, and has been much used for posts and piles, for wet situations, the wood becoming hard and durable. It was formerly employed in making water-pipes, pump trees, and reservoir conduits.*
> —Felter and Lloyd, 1895[35]

Alder is rarely used in botanical medicine at this time, though it is a powerful remedy for a number of conditions. It is strongly astringent, the leaves and bark containing 16 percent tannin. As such, it is an excellent remedy when an astringent is needed. Traditionally, alder has been used as a vulnerary (wound healer) and stomachic. It tonifies the stomach and small intestine, helping improve food absorption and fat metabolism. It is also a bitter and stimulates gastric secretions. Traditionally, alder has been used with great effectiveness in eye infections, sore throats, mouth infections, stubborn and bleeding wounds, diarrhea, and skin ulceration. Felter and Lloyd call it a "positive anti-putrefactive agent," and a number of traditional medical herbalists note its effectiveness in treating gangrene. The comprehensive recommendation for its use in bacterial infections (mainly of the skin), especially ones of long duration that have resisted alternative treatments, indicate an antibacterial activity to the herb, though I have been unable to find *any* clinical trials on alder or its constituent properties that might verify this. Its astringent activity is responsible for much of its reputation—both for internal and external afflictions— its main drawback being that it stains the skin and (some) people find its taste unpleasant.[36]

BIRCH BEER

A beer is made with the decoction, also with the sap, which is sweet
like maple sap and can become syrup and honey by boiling.

—C. S. Rafinesque, 1828[37]

When the stem of the tree is wounded, a saccharine juice flows out which
is susceptible, with yeast, of vinous fermentation. A beer, wine, spirit,
and vinegar are prepared from it in some parts of Europe. Birch Wine,
concocted from this thin, sugary sap of the tree, collected from incisions
made in the trees in March, honey, cloves, and lemon peel being added
and then the whole fermented with yeast, makes a very pleasant cordial,
formerly much appreciated. From 16 to 18 gallons of sap may be
drawn from one large tree, and a moderate tapping does no harm.

—Maude Grieve, 1931[38]

Of all the ancient tree beers, the names of only two, spruce and birch
beer, remain, if somewhat vaguely, in the common consciousness. (In
many respects, juniper ale is only a cultural variation of spruce beer.)
Birch sap, like maple, was one of the staples of American settlers. Also
used a great deal in Northern Europe, it was used as a refreshing drink,
for beer and wine, and as a syrup for cordials and sweetening foods. Not
easily accessible now, it has a light and fresh flavor and was the original
source for wintergreen flavoring. Most original root beers were made
with a wintergreen extract made from birch sap or the birch sap itself.
The tree used for sap harvesting was generally not the paper birch,
which has a low sugar concentration in the sap, but the black birch.
Because birch sap flowed longer than the maple, the maples were often
tapped first, then the whole operation moved to the birch groves. Most
traditional recipes used sugar as an additive because of the labor involved
in making birch sap sweet enough to provide enough sugar for fermentation by itself. Birch sap is much less sweet than that of the maple tree. To

make a syrup, maple sap must be boiled down 40 to 1, that is, 40 gallons of sap make 1 gallon of syrup. Birch sap must be boiled down 150 to 1. This was sometimes done, but often birch sap was used for birch beers with a sweetener added: honey, maple syrup, or sugar. The use of the young twigs will impart both the flavor and medicinal activity of birch to beer—the sap is not necessary, though it was traditionally used.

Birch Beer — *Two Recipes from 1978*

Ingredients

>   4 gallons birch sap
>   1 gallon honey
>   4 quarts birch—budding twigs
>   yeast and nutrient

>>   Boil the sap for ten minutes and remove from heat, add the honey. Put the four quarts of budding twigs into the birch/honey mixture, allow to cool to 70 degrees F. Strain into fermenting vessel, add the yeast. Allow to work until fermentation is complete (this will take longer than with malt or sugar—not quite as long as with honey only), add 1/2 tsp of sugar to each bottle, bottle and cap. Ready to drink in 10 days to two weeks.[39]

As birch sap and the necessary quantity of twigs are somewhat hard to come by, an alternative recipe that will taste very similar is:

Ingredients

>   4 1/2 gallons water
>   1 quart maple syrup
>   2 1/2 quarts (5 pounds) honey
>   2 ounces wintergreen extract
>   yeast

Melissa officinalis

Published by W.Woodville June 1.1792.

B A L M

Melissa officinalis

Sambucus Ebulus

Published by W. Woodville, 1792.

E L D E R

Sambucus Ebulus spp.

M A N D R A K E

Atropa mandragora

Hypericum perforatum
Publish'd by D.r Woodville Feb.r 1. 1790.

ST.-JOHN'S-WORT

Hypericum perforatum

Heat water hot enough to dissolve honey and maple syrup. Cool to 70 degrees F. Pour into fermenter and add yeast. Ferment until done, prime bottles, fill, and cap. Ready to drink in two weeks.

Birch Beer—1824

Ingredients

    1 gallon birch sap

    2 pounds sugar

    yeast

The mode of extracting the juice is very simple; it is done by boring a hole in the trunk, and then stopping it with a cork, through which, when a quill, open at both ends, is thrust, the juice passes at the rate of a large drop every second. Amidst the immense forests that darken the mountains of Norway, great quantities may easily be obtained in this way. The inhabitants manufacture it as follows: To a given quantity of juice is put a proportion of sugar, mostly two pounds to every gallon. These are boiled together until all the impurities rise to the top, and are skimmed off. To the remainder, when properly cooled, is added a little yeast to promote fermentation. About three or four days complete the whole of this process. Among some of the better class, wine and lemons are used in the making of this liquor.[40]

Birch Beer—Ca. 1600

Ingredients

    1 gallon birch sap

    1 pound powdered sugar

    yeast

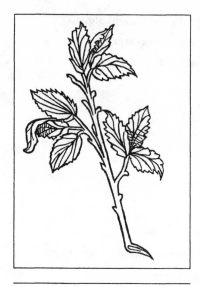

Birch (Betula fontinalis)

First make an incission & an hole through ye bark of one of ye largest birch tree bows, & put a quill therein, & quickly you shall perceive ye juice to distill. You may make incission into severall bowes at once, which water ye receive into whatever vessill you pleas. It will continew running 9 or 10 days, & if yr tree be large, it will afford you gallons. Boyle it will, as you doe beer, but first put to every gallon, one pound of white pwdered sugar. When it is well boyled, take it of the fire, & put in A gilefate with yeast, as yu doe to ale or beere, & it will worke in the same mannor. After 4 or 5 days, bottle it up in the thickest bottles you can get, for fear of bursting. & then at 8 or 9 weeks end, you may drink it, but it is better if you keep it older. This drink is very pleasant and allsoe physicall, first for procuring an appetite, & allsoe it is an antydote against gravell and the stone. This liquor must be procurd & make up in march, which is ye onely time, and not at the latter end of march neyther, for then the trees will not run soe well & freely as at ye beginning of the moneth.[41]

The wonderful Russian herbalist, Rita Bykhovsky, recently shared with me her experiences with birch beer. In the 13-house village where she lived, her husband would make large quantities of this beer every spring. They considered it a refreshing spring tonic beer and wonderful thirst quencher. She calls it a traditional Russian kvass (from the same root word as Kvaser from whose blood the Mead of Inspiration was made) as it was made from birch sap, fresh mint leaves, and yeast.

ABOUT BIRCH
Betula fontinalis

> *This Tree, in the beginning of Spring, before the Leaves come forth, being pierced, yields plentifully a sweet and potulent Juice, which Shepherds, when they are thirsty, often drink in the Woods. Tragus, Helmont, Charleton, and others commend the Virtue and Efficacy of this Liquor, and not undeservedly, for the Stone in the Kidnies and Bladder, for Bloody Urine and the Strangury. This Tree begins to yield its Juice about the Middle of February, and sometimes not till the Beginning of March. Tragus also commends it for the Jaundice. Some wash their faces with it, to take off Spots, and to beautifie. Dr. Needham cured Scorbutick Consumptions with it: He used to mix with it good wine and honey.*
>
> —John Pechet, 1694[42]

The birch is one of the most ancient of sacred trees. In many traditions a birch was planted on the graves of deceased relatives when they were buried so that as the tree grew, they would be able to climb toward heaven. Among the shamans of Siberia, it was the practice during ceremonies to climb a birch tree. They felt the birch to be the guardian of the door to the sky—a manifestation of the world tree that gives access to the realms of the sacred. Any time spent in a birch forest brings a strong sense of the sacredness of these trees to the visitor, and it is understandable that to many indigenous peoples, the birch is a powerful and moving tree.

Methyl salicylate, the main active constituent of birch sap and the herb wintergreen, has the delicious and easily recognizable taste we call "wintergreen." Our ancestors discovered this flavor long ago and incorporated it into "diet" drinks of the time. Methyl salicylate is similar to aspirin. It is strongly analgesic and anti-inflammatory, being therefore of use internally in decoction for treating arthritic and rheumatic conditions. It has also been a part of standard practice medicine for topical application for rheumatic and arthritic swelling of the joints. Birch twigs and sap contain a large quantity of this substance, and both were used in medical herbal practice. Additionally, both sap and bark are diuretic, antiscorbutic, antiseptic, and strongly astringent. Internally the herb was used for diarrhea, dyspepsia, and lack of tone in stomach and small intestine, much like alder. Externally, it was used for wound healing and for the same complaints as alder.[43]

MAPLE BEER

As to the water of the maple which is the sap of that same tree, it is equally delicious to French and Indians, who take their fill of it in the spring. It is true also that it is very pleasing and abundant in Gaspesia, for, through a very little opening which is made with an axe in a maple, ten to a dozen half gallons may run out. A thing which seemed to me very remarkable in the maple water is this, that when by virtue of boiling it is reduced a third, it becomes a real syrup, which hardens to something like sugar, and takes on a reddish colour.

—Christien LeClercq, 1691[44]

Sugar maple sap is virtually the only tree sap still used in the United States. Originally, the Indians tapped not only all the maples (six species) and birches (six species), but also butternut and hickory trees. Though the northern Indian tribes do not appear to have fermented maple sap (even though they fermented a number of plant berries from tribe to tribe), the American settlers did.

Maple Beer—1846
Ingredients

> 4 gallons water
>
> 1 quart maple syrup
>
> 1 tablespoon spruce essence
>
> 1 pint yeast

> To Four gallons of boiling water, add one quart of maple molasses, and a small tablespoon of essence of spruce. When it is about milk warm, add a pint of yeast; and when fermented bottle it. In three days it is fit for use.[45]

Maple Beer—*A Traditional New England Recipe*
Ingredients

> 2 gallons fresh maple sap
>
> yeast

> Boil the maple sap to 1/2 its volume. Cool to 70 degrees F, pour into fermenter and add yeast. Ferment until completion, prime bottles, fill, and cap. Ready to drink in two weeks.

Maple Beer—*A Modern Equivalent*
Ingredients

> 3 pounds maple syrup
>
> 1 gallon water
>
> yeast

> Heat water until maple syrup will dissolve. Cool to 70 degrees F, pour into fermenter, add yeast, and ferment until complete. Prime bottles, fill, and cap. Ready to drink in seven days.

ABOUT MAPLE

Acer saccharum

> *Sugar Maple. 1. Decoction of the inner bark is used for diarrhea. 2.*
> *The sap is boiled in making sugar and syrup. 3. The wood valued for*
> *making arrow shafts. Black maple, sometimes used as sugar maple. The*
> *sap flows fast from the tree and drunk causes the urine to flow fast also.*
> —W. J. Hoffman, 1885[46]

Maple is now rarely used in herbal practice, but during maple sap gathering, early New Englanders often drank the fresh sap as a spring tonic. It does possess expectorant, diuretic, and astringent properties and is excellent in cough syrups. Above all, however, maple syrup is one of the most complete nutrient foods known. A common question on winter survival tests is about the importance of maple syrup to survival. With only maple syrup, as with honey, it is possible to live many weeks without adverse physical effects. Maple syrup is high in calories (though not as high as sugar), calcium, potassium, phosphorus, and vitamin B_{12}. It also contains significant amounts of many other B vitamins and iron. Indigenous cultures have traditionally used maple (sap and bark) for skin conditions such as hives and stubborn wounds, as a wash, a decoction for kidney trouble, as a cough remedy, as a diuretic, for cramping, as a blood purifier, as a tonic, and as an astringent for bleeding. Oddly, in spite of the pervasiveness and importance of this tree, there is less information on its medicinal use than any other American herb I know of.[47]

SPRUCE BEER

> *The utilization of the resin of the pine and spruce seems to be very*
> *ancient. It is also mentioned in song XX of the old Finnish epic*

*"Kalevala". When he was brewing for the wedding of Ilmarinen,
the hero, the brewer added spruce cones and pine twigs, to start the
ale fermenting.*

—Odd Nordland, 1969[48]

Spruce beer is probably the one herbal beer that most people have heard
of and remember. It was of primary importance to American colonists and
explorers in preventing scurvy. Made correctly, it is a pleasing and
refreshing drink. A spruce beer does not produce drowsiness like hopped
beers but rather invigorates the spirits and uplifts the energy.

Charlie Millspaugh's Spruce Beer—1892

Spruce beer is an American beverage, made by Indians
with twigs and cones of spruces, boiled in maple syrup.
Now it is chiefly made with molasses and yeast; when
no spruce is put in, it is only molasses beer. The proper
spruce beer is a palatable and healthy drink, powerfully
antiscorbutic. The discoverers of Canada were cured of
the scurvy by it, since which it has become in common
use in Canada, the Northern States, and even in Europe.
The essence of Spruce (a concentrated aqueous decoction of the young twigs) is an article of exportation,
used as naval stores; spruce beer may be made by it in a
short time, and anywhere.

Ingredients

1 gallon water

1 ounce Spruce essence

7 ounces molasses

yeast

Spruce beer may be made from the extract as follows: Take one part essence of spruce and seventy-six parts of water, boil, strain, allow to cool, and add ninety-six parts warm water, seven parts molasses and one part of yeast. Allow the mixture to ferment, and bottle strongly while fermenting.[49]

Felter and Lloyd's Spruce Beer—1895

An aqueous decoction of the young branches, strained and concentrated, forms the well-known Essence of Spruce, which enters into the formation of Spruce Beer, an agreeable and salutary summer beverage, possessing diuretic and antiscorbutic properties, and valuable on board ships.

Ingredients

    2 ounces gingerroot
    2 ounces sassafras bark
    2 ounces guaiacum
    4 ounces hops
    10 ounces essence of spruce
    14 gallons water
    3 quarts molasses
    12 fluid ounces yeast

Spruce Beer may be made as follows: Take of ginger, sassafras bark, and guaiacum shavings, each, 2 ounces; hops, four ounces; essence of spruce, 10 ounces; water, 4 gallons; mix them and boil for 10 or 15 minutes, then strain. Add 10 gallons of warm water, 3 quarts of molasses, and 12 fluid ounces of yeast, and allow it to ferment. While the fermentation is going on, put the fluid in strong bottles and cork them well.[50]

Spruce Beer—1796

Ingredients

17 gallons water

1/2 pint yeast

8 ounces spruce essence in 1 quart water

2 gallons molasses

4 ounces hops

Take four ounces hops, let them boil half an hour in one gallon of water, strain the hop water then add sixteen gallons of warm water, two gallons of molasses, eight ounces of essence of spruce, dissolved in one quart water, put it in a clean cask, then shake it well together, add half a pint of emptins, then let it stand and work one week, if very warm weather less time will do, when it is drawn off to bottle, add one spoonful of molasses to every bottle.[51]

Spruce Beer—*A Modern Recipe*

Ingredients

2 pounds molasses

2 gallons water

6 ounces fresh spruce boughs

yeast

Boil water and spruce boughs for one hour. Take from heat and remove spruce boughs. Add molasses and stir well to dissolve. Allow to cool to 70 degrees F, pour into fermenter, add yeast, and ferment. When complete, prime bottles, siphon spruce beer into them, and cap. Ready to drink in 10 days.

ABOUT SPRUCE
Abies nigra

> In the seventeenth century, Josslyn wrote [1672] that "the tops of Spruce-boughs, boiled in bear [beer] and drunk, is assuredly one of the best remedies for the scurvy; restoring the infected party in a short time." . . . It is notable that "spruce beer" was one of the antiscorbutics used on Captain Cook's voyage of 1776–1780, and that spruce tea was drunk by the California gold-rushers of 1849 in order to prevent scurvy.
>
> —Virgil Vogel, 1970[52]

To make spruce essence, take the green shoots of black or red spruce (blue spruce can be used, but it is much stronger in taste), cover with water, and boil until the water is pungent, strongly flavored, and reddish brown. Strain and boil the liquid down to half its original volume. It can be bottled and kept year-round for use. It is strongly preservative, like juniper, and is strongly antiscorbutic. Felter and Lloyd describe it as "a viscid, molasses-like liquid, having a somewhat sour and bitterish, astringent taste."[53] Spruce has been traditionally used by indigenous peoples for coughs, colds, and flu as an infusion or in sweat baths, and the inner bark has been applied to stubborn skin infections. They have also used it for kidney infections, much like juniper. I have used a syrup made only from spruce on pancakes, which is traditional in Alaska, and found it delightful. It also keeps well.

Given its history, remarkably little is available on the medicinal activity of spruce. Though primarily known for its antiscorbutic properties, spruce has been used extensively as a diaphoretic (inducing sweating), to break up kidney stones and flush them out of the system, to relieve rheumatic complaints, as an antiseptic wound healer, and as a diuretic.[54]

PINE ALE

A Decoction or Infusion of the Tops in Beer, or some other proper
Liquor, is reckon'd very good for the Stone of the Kidnies and Bladder,
and for the Scurvy, and Diseases of the Breast.

—John Pechet, 1694[55]

A few brewers in Norway used parts of the pine for brewing ale and beer. Odd Nordland quotes Colerus as recommending pine chips "for keeping the ale from turning sour."[56] And "In one of his table conversations, Plutarch maintains that the pine was sacred to Dionysus because its resin was used for flavoring and preserving wine."[57]

Pine Ale — 1770

Ingredients

> 1 quart whole maize kernels
>
> 7 gallons water
>
> 1/2 pound pine tops
>
> 1/2 pound China root
>
> 1/2 pound sassafras bark
>
> 1 gallon molasses
>
> 1 pint yeast

> Place all ingredients in the water and boil until the liquid is reduced to 5 gallons or the kernels crack open. Cool to 70 degrees F and strain. Add molasses and stir

until dissolved, pour into fermenter and add yeast. Ferment until completion, prime bottles, fill, and cap. Ready to drink in 7 to 10 days. (The original recipe used only 3 pints molasses and was to be "bottle[d] when fermentation begins." It was, in fact, really a "root beer" recipe used as a "diet drink" for spring or winter consumption—an antiscorbutic and medicinal beer with low alcohol content.)[58]

ABOUT PINE
Pinus spp.

The Nuts have a delicate Taste, and are good for Coughs and Consumptions, and for heat of Urine. They increase Milk, and Provoke Venery.

—John Pechet, 1694[59]

To the Indian everything in nature is alive. Plants, like human beings, have souls, otherwise they could not live and grow. Many are supposed to talk and sing and to feel joy and pain. For instance, when in winter the pine-trees are stiff with cold, they weep and pray to the sun to shine and make them warm. When angered and insulted, the plants take their revenge.

—Carl Lumholtz, 1902[60]

Pine has long been one of the world's sacred trees. The rod of Moses was formed of a unique tree that grew from three seeds: cypress, pine, and cedar. They intertwined as they grew, forming one tree from which the rod was made. The pine also holds a prominent place in Chinese tradition as a symbol of the individuation of and unique contribution to creation by each human soul.

᧬

It is said in an old Chinese tale that once a carpenter and his apprentice were passing an ancient pine of great girth standing next to an Earth altar.

The apprentice was taken by the tree and remarked on its great age. But his master dismissed it, saying, "Yes, it is old, but it is good for nothing. It is no good for ship building or for tools. Ignore it in your craft."

That night the old tree came to the carpenter in his dream. "You have demeaned me," it said, "and failed to see my true nature. The trees you admire and use all die young, taken by men for building or tools. Look at me. Do you think I would have reached this age if I had been considered useful to men? Do you think I am fulfilling no purpose? I stand next to the Earth altar; have you not understood what that means?"[61]

As in this ancient Chinese tale, the pine is rather brusquely dismissed by many of today's herbalists. It is rarely used, generally unrecognized for its healing virtues, passed over for "sexier" herbs. But, still, even unnoticed, it stands next to the Earth altar.

Pine needles are strongly antiscorbutic and impart a pleasing taste to tea. They also possess expectorant, diuretic, and antiseptic activity as well. The resin is the most strongly expectorant element of the plant; for this purpose, an amount about the size of a raisin is chewed and swallowed. Pine helps soften bronchial mucous and move it out of the system through expectoration. In any condition where the lungs are congested without fruitful expectoration, it is useful. As a diuretic and antiseptic, it is useful for urinary tract infections. Pine is strong, and as a result, it is easy to take too much, which can aggravate active kidney and urethral inflammation. The bark is fairly high in tannins and mucilaginous constituents. These combined with its antibacterial activity make it a highly useful herb for external wound poultices, as it will help stop bleeding, help damaged tissues bind together, soothe inflamed tissues, and help prevent infection. These same actions make it useful in stomach ulceration and especially in cough syrups for upper respiratory infections. Though used fairly regularly in the Hispanic communities in the southern United States, few others use it in contemporary herbal practice. In traditional medical herbalism, pine bark or resin has been used as a stimulant, laxative, expectorant, diuretic, pectoral, vermifuge, detergent, balsamic, and vulnerary. Indigenous practice has used it frequently for colds and flus, sore throats, stubborn wounds, sores or ulcers, inflammations, and rheumatism. It was one of the most important herbal medicines for the Menominee Indians of North America.[62]

FIR ALE

The Branches and Tops are infus'd in Diet-drinks, for the Scurvy, with very good success.

—John Pechet, 1694[63]

Throughout Europe and North America, fir trees were used much like pine and spruce in beers and ales—mainly as antiscorbutics. John Arnold, the beer historian, comments that in Georgia "settlers of German extraction made a beer from molasses, sassafras and the tops of fir trees."[64]

Fir Ale
Ingredients

    1 1/2 gallons water
    24 ounces molasses
    1 ounce sassafras root bark, dried
    2 ounces fresh fir bough tips
    yeast

    Boil water, molasses, sassafras, and fir for 45 minutes. Cool to 70 degrees F, strain into fermenter, and add yeast. Ferment until complete (about one week), siphon into primed bottles. Ready to drink in one to two weeks.

ABOUT FIR

They make a kind of spruce beer [in North America] of the top of the white fir which they drink in summer; but the use of it is not general and it is seldom drunk by people of quality.

—Peter Kalm, 1752[65]

It is said that the fir received its name from the word *fire,* being "firewood," the most common wood used for heating and cooking in homes in ancient times. Unlike other evergreens, several species of fir, notably Douglas, contain a fairly high concentration of sugar. In hot weather they will sometimes secrete a white crystalline sugar, composed primarily of a rare trisaccharide, melezitose. For this reason they are of especial benefit when used in fermentation.

Like cedar, fir has been traditionally used in many indigenous cultures as a spirit medicine. It is commonly used in sweat lodges and for its antiscorbutic actions. It is also a traditional indigenous medicine for high fever, weight loss, anemia, and lack of energy and appetite.[66] It possesses many of the same properties as pine, spruce, and juniper, being antiscorbutic, diuretic, astringent, expectorant, and antiseptic. It has been traditionally used for urinary tract infections, coughs and colds, external wounds, asthma, and as an analgesic for wounds, burns, sores, and ulcers. Like pine, it is strong and may irritate mucous membranes.[67]

AN IMPORTANT NOTE
ABOUT EVERGREEN TREES AND BEER

If you look you will notice that the new spring shoots on the branch tips of most evergreen species are a lighter and more vibrant green than the older growth. If you taste these and compare them to the older needles you will find a significant difference in taste. (All the species will possess distinct astringent action, puckering the mouth, pine being the most astringent.) The new spring growth in every species possesses a distinct citrus flavor, the older growth tends to lack this in the same degree and to be more bitter. I suspect that the new growth possesses more vitamin C, though I have seen nothing on this in the literature. What is certain, however, is that (though you can use older branches if desired) the fresh spring tips were generally used in making evergreen beers.

OAK BARK ALE

In lung disease a man is to "withhold himself earnestly from sweet-ened ale," to drink clear ale, and in the wort of the clear ale "boil young oak-rind and drink."

—John Bickerdyke, 1890[68]

They still make an oak wine for sale in England, though it is somewhat uncommon (they also have mistletoe wine if you take the time to look for it).

Oak Bark Ale
Ingredients

    1 1/2 gallons water

    2.2 pounds pale malt extract

    2 ounces oak bark

    yeast

Boil water, malt extract, and oak bark for 45 minutes. Cool to 70 degrees F and strain into fermenter. Add yeast and ferment until complete, 7 to 10 days. Siphon into primed bottles, cap, and store for one to two weeks before drinking.

ABOUT OAK

Q*uercus* spp.

> *The whole Oak is astringent, but especially the Bark. A Decoction of*
> *it is given for the Bloody-Flux, and for Spitting of Blood. The*
> *Acorns are Diuretick. The Water distill'd from the Leaves of a young*
> *oak, cures the Whites.*
>
> —John Pechet, 1694[69]

The oak was perhaps the most sacred tree of the Druids. Each month, six days after the crescent moon, the Druidic priests would search out an ancient sacred oak upon which grew mistletoe. When it was found, offerings would be made to the tree, then the Druidic priest would climb and cut the mistletoe with a ceremonial golden knife and the herb would fall into the white robes of the head priest, never being allowed to touch the ground. This specially harvested mistletoe played a central part in the most important Druidic ceremonies, and it was considered to possess qualities not present in mistletoe growing on other types of trees. It was named *gui*—"all heal." Oak mistletoe is extremely rare, and this rarity accounts, in part, for the place it held in Druidic ceremonies. One researcher commented in 1884 that he could only verify eight instances of mistletoe on oak since 1630. It has been speculated that it is a different species of mistletoe that grows on oak (and also that it was a different species of oak upon which it grew), which accounts for its modern rarity. After the domination of the Celts by Christianity, converts assiduously hunted all mistletoe that grew on oaks and killed both tree and herb as a means of destroying this most potent symbol of the ancient Earth practice. However, even after the destruction of Druidic practice, oaks were held in great esteem in England. Many of the great poems, decisions, and agreements of England were made under the spreading canopy of ancient oaks.

The power of old growth and ancient oak has long infused the psyche of humankind, and the use of oak for doors is significant. As Moyra Caldecott comments: "Behind a door of oak we are safe in our world of ordinary objects and events, but through it we glimpse the splendors and terrors of the unknown. Dare we step through?"[70] So, too, through the ancient oak we glimpse the sacred terrors and splendor of the unknown. On this side we are safe. Dare we step through?

Oak is extremely long lived and slow growing. British oaks from 1,000 to 2,000 years of age were at one time fairly common in England. The largest of these had a circumference of 90 feet at the base and spread more than 300 feet above. At maturity an oak adds less than one inch a year to its circumference.

Oak is primarily an astringent. The bark is usually used, though the galls are much stronger. For bleeding, externally or internally, oak is one of the prime herbs of choice. It is exceptionally useful in diarrhea and dysentery, and is often used as an enema for these conditions, though a tea will also work. In traditional practice it was considered to be astringent, antiseptic, and hemostatic. It stops bleeding, tones tissues, helps bind wounded skin, and decreases secretions. It was used as a gargle for sore throats, for inflamed gums, as a poultice for wounds, and as a tea or enema for dysentery and diarrhea. Its huge tannin content gave it a traditional place in the tanning of leather.[71]

Some brewers suggest adding oak chips to the fermenting vessel— one to four ounces of chips per five gallons of wort—and leaving the brew to ferment until the chips sink to the bottom of the fermenter (about eight days). (They, of course, suggest steam sterilizing the chips in a pressure cooker for 20 minutes first.) Other brewers simply make an "oak bark tea" by boiling one cup of roughly ground oak bark in two cups of water for 20 minutes and adding this to the fermenter. As they say, "This imparts an oak character."

NINE

Beers and Ales from Sacred and Medicinal Plants

Here give me leave to tell you, that there are a great number of brave Herbs and Vegitations that will do the business of brewing, as well as hops, and for many Constitutions much better; for 'tis Custom more than their real virtues that renders Hops of general Use and Esteem; they are an excellent Herb, and would be much better, if they were or could be dried in the Sun. Some other Herbs I shall here mention, for to be made use of in Drinks.

Peny Royal and Balm are noble Herbs, and of excellent use in Beer or Ale. They naturally raise and cheer the drooping Spirits, and open and cleane the passages after a friendly way, and with a mild Operation. And also they add great strength and fragrancy, and makes brave, well tasted Drink, good to prevent and cure all, or most of those Diseases which the wise Ancients have appropriated that Herb unto. The like is to be understood of Mint, Tansie, Wormwood, Broom, Cardis, Centuary, Eye-bright, Betony, Sage, Dandelion, and good

Hay; also many others, according to their Natures and Qualities, and for those Diseases to which they are respectively appropriated. But note, that all and every of these Herbs ought to be gathered in their proper Seasons, and dryed and preserved as we have given Directions in our Way to Health, for you ought not to use any Herb or Vegitation in Beer or Ale whilst they are green, except there be a necessity.

—Thomas Tryon, 1691[1]

The richer sort [of Americans] generally brew their small-beer with malt, which they have from England, though they have as good a barley of their own as any in the world, but for want of convenience of malt-houses the inhabitants take no care to sow it. The poorer sort brew their beer with molasses and bran; with Indian corn malted by drying in a stove(!); with persimmons dried in cakes and baked; with potatoes; with the green stalks of Indian corn cut small and bruised; with ponpions, and with the Batates canadenses, or Jerusalem artichoke, which some people plant purposely for that use, but this is the least esteemed of all the sorts before mentioned.

—Roger Beverly, ca. 1700[2]

NETTLE BEER

Nettles were once tithed, they have so many uses: medicine, food, fodder, fertilizer, beer, dye, fiber for thread, nets, durable cloth, paper, hair restorer, aphrodisiac, and smoke!

—Susun Weed, 1989[3]

For thousands of years, as the young nettles began to sprout forth from the Earth in the spring, our ancestors would eagerly seek them out as one of the first green foods of the new year. Stinging nettles grow in abundance wherever they find suitable ground, and when harvested, usually by people wearing gloves, they were steamed or boiled for eating, a process that deprives them of their "sting." Before the kind of food preservation we now enjoy, winter meals were usually limited to meat and stored grains, and dried plants and fruits. Scurvy was thus a recurring problem in many northern cultures. The early dark green nettle plants have always been thought of as a spring tonic and antiscorbutic remedy and were an important part of traditional diets. Nettles fulfill not only this important dietary function but are also extremely tasty, being similar to spinach, though better in flavor. It is not surprising, then, to find that nettles have also been used in beers in many cultures. Once upon a time, especially in England, they were a standard tonic beer for spring and summer use.

There are many historical records of beers made from nettles. Here is one from the United States found in Catherine Ferns' *The Kitchen Guide* (*Chester* [*Pennsylvania*] *Times*, 1925).

Catherine Fern's Nettle Beer—1925
Ingredients

> 5 gallons water
>
> 2 pounds sugar
>
> 1/2 peck nettles
>
> 1 pint yeast or 5 yeast cakes

> [Take] 5 gallons water, 2 pounds sugar, 1/2 peck nettles, 1 pint yeast or 5 yeast cakes. Boil the nettles 15 minutes, strain, sweeten and add the yeast; then let it stand 12 hours; skim and bottle.[4]

Gabrielle Hatfield, exploring traditional remedies of rural England, observes that in East Anglia, nettle beer was extremely common and considered to be a primary medicinal beer of the region. "Among the plant remedies recorded by Taylor is beer from nettles. This according to Dr. Randall of Boston, Lincolnshire, was regarded as a 'specific' for tuberculosis."[5] One of her sources shares his memory of his grandmother's nettle beer.

> To keep blood clear, in the early summer my grandmother would brew up what was called "nettle beer". This consisted of nettles and cleavers or goosegrass (*Galium aparine*) which with possibly some ground ginger were covered in boiling water and steeped for several days. It was then strained and some yeast and sugar added to work it for a few days. The result was a pleasant, slightly fizzy drink which my brother and I enjoyed drinking.[6]

Maude Grieve, in her famous herbal (originally published in 1931), describes a traditional English nettle beer.

Maude Grieve's Nettle Beer—1931

Ingredients

    2 gallons cold water
    one pailful of nettles
    3 or 4 handfuls dandelion
    3 or 4 handfuls cleavers

2 ounces bruised gingerroot

2 cups brown sugar

yeast

> The Nettle Beer made by cottagers is often given to their old folk as a remedy for gouty and rheumatic pains, but apart from this purpose it forms a pleasant drink. It may be made as follows: take two gallons of cold water and a good pailful of washed young Nettle tops, add three or four large handfuls of dandelion, the same of Clivers (Goosegrass) and 2 oz. of bruised whole ginger. Boil gently for 40 minutes, then strain and stir in 2 teacupfuls of brown sugar. When lukewarm place on the top a slice of toasted bread, spread with 1 oz. of compressed yeast, stirred till liquid with a teaspoonful of sugar. Keep it fairly warm for 6 or 7 hours, then remove the scum and stir in a tablespoonful of cream of tartar. Bottle and tie the corks securely. The result is a specially wholesome sort of ginger beer. The juice of two lemons may be substituted for the Dandelion and Clivers. Other herbs are often added to Nettles in the making of Herb Beer, such as Burdock, Meadowsweet, Avens, Horehound, the combination making a refreshing summer drink.[7]

A recipe for nettle beer from brewer and author C. J. J. Berry is as follows.

C. J. J. Berry's Nettle Beer—1963

Ingredients

1 gallon young nettles

1/4 ounce root ginger

4 pounds malt

1 level teaspoonful granulated yeast

2 ounces hops

4 ounces sarsaparilla

2 gallons water

1 1/2 pound sugar

2 lemons

Choose young nettle tops. Wash and put into a saucepan with water, ginger, malt, hops and sarsaparilla. Bring to a boil and boil for a quarter of an hour. Put sugar into a large crock or bread pan and strain the liquor on to it. Add the juice of two lemons. Stir until the sugar has dissolved, and allow to cool to 70 degrees F, keeping pan covered, in a warm room for three days, then strain the beer into bottles, cork, and tie down or wire the corks. Keep the beer in a cool place for a week before drinking—and keep and eye on the corks! This makes an excellent summer drink and should be made in May.[8]

Another, and more recent, recipe is contained in Richard Mabey's excellent herbal, *The New Age Herbalist* (New York: Simon and Schuster, 1988).

Richard Mabey's Nettle Beer—1988

Ingredients

1 pound young nettles

4 ounces dandelion leaves

4 ounces fresh, sliced or 2 ounces dried burdock root

1/2 ounce root ginger, bruised

2 lemons

1 gallon water

1 pound plus 4 teaspoons soft brown sugar

1 ounce cream of tartar

brewing yeast

Put the nettles, dandelion leaves, burdock, ginger and thinly pared rinds of the lemons into a large pan. Add the water. Bring to a boil and simmer for 30 mins.

Put the lemon juice, 1 lb sugar and the cream of tartar into a large container and pour in the liquid through a strainer, pressing down well on the nettles and other ingredients. Stir to dissolve the sugar. Cool to room temperature.

Sprinkle in the yeast. Cover the beer and leave to ferment in a warm place for three days. Pour off the beer and bottle it, adding 1/2 teaspoon brown sugar per pint.

Leave the bottles undisturbed until the beer is clear—about 1 week.[9]

Perhaps the strongest contemporary advocate of the medicinal use of nettles is the Wise Woman herbalist, Susun Weed. In her book, *Healing Wise*, she shares her recipe for nettle beer (which she calls "One of the most delightful medicines for joint pain I've ever taken").[10]

Susun Weed's Nettle Beer — 1989

Ingredients

1 pound raw sugar

2 lemons

1 ounce cream of tartar

5 quarts water

2 pounds nettle tops

1 ounce live yeast

> Place sugar, lemon peel (no white), lemon juice, and cream of tartar in a large crock. Cook nettles in water for 15 minutes. Strain into crock and stir well. When this cools to blood warm, dissolve yeast in a little water and add to your crock. Cover with several folds of cloth and let brew for three days. Strain out sediment and bottle. Ready to drink in eight days.[11]

Nettle beer is indeed one of the sublime herbal beers. The taste really is indescribable, being a blend of a number of flavors, a veritable gustatory extravaganza. In general, the nettle tops are gathered in the early spring as soon as they are a foot or so tall. Some of the lower leaves should be left on the growing plant stalk to facilitate regrowth. The nettles can be harvested several more times throughout the year for more beer. My rule of thumb is one pound of nettles per gallon of water. You want to cook the nettles until they are about the consistency of those green beans our grandmothers used to cook—no vitamins or minerals should be left in them. I cook them 40 minutes to one hour. Set the nettles aside to cool and then wring them out; there is quite a bit more water in them that contains that fresh, wonderful nettle taste. I also add one tablespoon of lemon juice per gallon of water and (often) 1/4 ounce fresh ginger per gallon. It is crucial to use either brown or raw sugar. White sugar is simply dreadful for nettle beer.

ABOUT NETTLES
Urtica dioca

> *If they would eat nettles in March, and drink mugwort in May,*
> *so many fine maidens would not go to the clay.*
>
> —Funeral song of a Scottish mermaid[12]

Nettle stems have been used for centuries to produce fiber for weaving and as cordage. Many people have thought that the use of nettles as material for nets might have been the origin of their name (though some think that perhaps the word *nettle* is a corruption of *needle*, a reference either to the sharp stinging hairs that nettle possesses or else its common use in sewing). Nettle stalk is extremely fibrous and strong; it was made into thread and rope, and then woven into nets (as well as cloth and sails in some cultures). This use of nettle stalks to make fishing nets was widespread in the ancient world, even among indigenous cultures.

The Algonquin Indians tell how the Creator, Sirakitehak, after watching the spider spin, taught human beings to make nets from nettles. Antoine Raudot, in 1709, commented that "[the Indians] have on this subject a story that a certain Sirakitehak, who they say created heaven and earth and who is one of their divinities, invented the way of making nets after having attentively considered the spider when she worked to make her web to trap flies. They make these nets of nettles or wild hemp, of which there is much in moist places, and the women and girls spin and twist these on their bare thighs. . . . It is with these nets that they take all sorts of fish."[13] Too, nettles were felt to be a strongly beneficent plant among indigenous cultures, able to protect those who used them from many of the bad things of the world: illness, evil intent of others, difficulties of the human condition.

Urtica dioica

Nettle (Urtica dioca)

Nettle also produces a very fine cloth when woven, a durable paper, a colorful green dye, powerful fertilizer, and an extremely nutritious fodder for animals. According to many sources, cows who are fed a diet of nettle produce better milk and meat, and chickens who are fed nettle lay more and stronger eggs. Nettle also contains a strong coagulant and has long been used as a rennet substitute in the making of cheese.

Medicinally, nettle possesses astringent, tonic, antiseptic, depurative, hemostatic, and diuretic properties. It has been used in traditional botanical medicine for diarrhea, dysentery, scurvy, hemorrhages, kidney stones, liver problems, bowel problems, skin diseases such as eczema, and rheumatic problems. Nettle is often used to help heal kidney and adrenal problems, restore digestive tone, strengthen the lungs, help with symptoms of menopause, reduce likelihood of heavy bleeding in childbirth, and help prevent hair loss and nourish skin and hair. Most of these uses are traditional in European and American botanical and folk medicine and are found independently among all indigenous peoples where nettle grows.[14]

For rheumatic and arthritic problems, the fresh plants are vigorously rubbed over the affected area. This seems hopelessly old-fashioned and painfully masochistic to us now. However, there is more to this remedy than first meets the eye.

The "sting" of the nettle is produced by small hollow hairs that cover the surface of the plant and that are filled with a pressurized fluid. When the hairs are broken by an animal or human brushing over them, the fluid is forcibly ejected. In the case of unprotected skin, the hairs act like miniature hypodermic needles, and the fluid is injected just under the surface of the skin. This fluid contains histamines, acetylcholine, and formic acid. Acetylcholine, also found in bee venom, plays a crucial role in the transmission of impulses from one nerve fiber to another across synaptic junctions, making it highly useful in the treatment of Alzheimer's disease, Parkinson's disease, and multiple sclerosis. Bee venom has been used quite successfully in the treatment of arthritis and rheumatism. And formic acid is one component of ant venom, which has also been used in the treatment of rheumatic and arthritic complaints

NETTLE IS ALSO a potent source of "minerals, vitamins, amino acids, and protein building blocks."[18] Susun Weed comments that it is high in calcium (2900), magnesium (860), trace minerals, chlorophyll, chromium (3.9), cobalt (13.2), iron (41.8), phosphorus (447), potassium (1750), zinc (4.7), copper, sulphur, thiamine (.54), riboflavin (.43), vitamin A (15,700 IU), niacin (5.2), protein (10.2%), manganese (7.8), selenium (2.2), silicon (10.3), tin (2.7), ascorbic acid (83), sodium (4.9), and vitamins D and K.[19]

with great success in clinical trials.[15] This fluid in nettle stings is specific for arthritis and rheumatic conditions, and though painful, has been found to be extremely successful in treating those conditions. This use is common among all indigenous peoples and folk practitioners where nettle grows—the anecdotal evidence is consistent and overwhelming. Unfortunately, I have been unable to find any extensive analysis of the constituents of the nettle's stinging fluid, any extensive comparison to bee venom, or any clinical trials of its use for arthritic complaints. But I have used it myself.

Having suffered from arthritic conditions in my hands from years of using hammers and typewriters, I have found a periodic use of nettles in this manner (every five years or so) alleviates all the symptoms I have suffered. When made into beer or tea, the fluids contained in the fresh stinging hairs dissolve in the water, and when consumed produce the same effects.

Recent studies in other areas of medicinal activity have shown nettle to be a potent antihistamine and exceptionally effective in the treatment of hay fever, bronchitis, and asthma,[16] an assertion made by Nicholas Culpepper 400 years ago. Nettles have also shown reproducible clinical activity in the treatment of kidney stones, a use for which the German Commission E botanical monographs specifically recommends them.[17] Many of nettle's ancient medicinal uses have been verified in clinical trial and are documented in James Duke's easily accessible *The Green Pharmacy* (New York: Rodale Press, 1997). Duke also comments that application of fresh nettles to the body may be of possible benefit in the treatment of multiple sclerosis (MS) because of their high acetylcholine content, present, as I noted earlier, in bee venom. Nettle contains many of the same substances produced by a bee's sting, and as Duke observes, the bees die, but the nettle can be used many times, making nettle a renewable resource. His speculation about MS is interesting in that many indigenous cultures also recommended nettle for paralysis and nervous system disorders.

Nettle also contains 47 parts per million of boron (dry weight). The Rheumatoid Arthritis Foundation has found that 3 milligrams of boron, taken daily, can be helpful in treating rheumatoid arthritis and osteoarthritis. A 100-gram serving of steamed nettle contains significantly more than this amount. This may be part of the reason why eating fresh nettles or drinking nettle beer helps reduce arthritis symptoms. Nettle is also effective in the treatment of osteoporosis, because boron helps the body retain calcium and raises estrogen levels in the body.[20]

Traditional nettle beers, as you might have noticed, use a rather large quantity of nettles. These recipes produce a tremendously strengthening and tonic beer, especially good in the spring after poor winter diets and extended lack of sunshine.

ABOUT BURDOCK
Arctium lappa

> [Burdock] seed is an excellent Lithontripick, being powder'd, and taken in Small Beer or Posset-drink.
>
> —John Pechet, 1694[21]

Burdock is a primary nutritive and restorative herb. It cleanses the blood (alterative) and is diuretic and diaphoretic. Clinical study has shown that the herb has marked effects on restoring liver function and helping the gallbladder. It has been found to have antibiotic and antifungal effects, one clinical study has shown antitumor activity, and it is extremely effective in scrofula, scurvy, and skin eruptions.[22] It has also shown antiseptic activity.[23] Burdock has been found, as well, to be effective in the treatment of diabetes. It contains inulin (as does dandelion), which exerts a beneficial effect on normalizing blood sugar levels.[24] It is also useful in alleviating rheumatic complaints, is effective in all types of skin conditions, such as psoriasis, eczema, dry and scaly skin, and has been shown to have antimicrobial actions.[25] Recent research has noted that burdock has shown test-tube activity against HIV.[26] Burdock, a European plant

Burdock (Arctium lappa)

now naturalized in the United States, has been used among North American indigenous cultures similarly to the way it has been used in Europe, and for similar complaints.[27]

The similarity of effect of nettles, burdock, sarsaparilla, and dandelion (as you will see) make them an ideal combination for a spring tonic beer or herbal preparation. The beer would help cleanse toxins from the blood, reduce or alleviate rheumatic problems, help clear up skin conditions, increase strength of the immune system, normalize digestion, restore liver and gallbladder function, and normalize pancreatic function. It is no wonder then that burdock, as well as these other herbs, is often added to nettle beer.

DANDELION BEER

The dried Dandelion leaves are also employed as an ingredient in many digestive or diet drinks, and herb beers. Dandelion Beer is a rustic fermented drink common in many parts of the country and made also in Canada. Workmen in the furnaces and potteries of the industrial towns of the Midlands have frequent resource to many of the tonic Herb Beers, finding them cheaper and less intoxicating than ordinary beer, and Dandelion stout ranks as a favourite. An agreeable and wholesome fermented drink is made from Dandelions, Nettles, and yellow Dock.

—Maude Grieve, 1931[28]

Another early spring plant, dandelion is also used as a traditional spring food and tonic herb. In spite of dandelion's being an introduced species, the American Indians quickly recognized its medicinal value and developed wide-ranging uses for it.[29]

Although the flowers are still made into wine in some parts of the country, dandelion is now rarely used to make herbal beers in America.

Maude Grieve's Dandelion Beer—1931

Ingredients

    2 ounces dried dandelion herb
    2 ounces dried nettle herb
    1 ounce dried yellow dock root
    1 gallon water
    2 pounds sugar
    2 tablespoons dried powdered ginger
    yeast

Take two oz. each of dried Dandelion and Nettle herbs and 1 oz. Yellow Dock. Boil in 1 gallon of water for 15 minutes and then strain the liquor while hot on 2 lbs of sugar, on the top of which is sprinkled 2 tablespoons of powdered Ginger. Leave till milk-warm, then add boiled water gone cold to bring the quantity up to 2 gallons. The temperature must then not be above 75 degrees F. Now dissolve 1/2 oz. solid yeast in a little of the liquid and stir into the bulk. Allow to ferment 24 hours, skim and bottle, and it will be ready for use in a day or two.[30]

C. J. J. Berry's Dandelion Beer—1963

Ingredients

    1/2 pound young dandelion plants

    1 pound Demerara sugar

    1 lemon

    1 gallon water

    1/2 ounce root ginger

    1 ounce cream of tartar

    yeast

This is a pleasant drink and is said to be good for stomach disorders. The young plants should be lifted in the spring, and well washed. Leave the thick tap roots but remove the fibrous ones. Put the plants, the well bruised ginger and the rind of lemon (excluding any white pith) in the water and boil for 20 minutes. Strain onto the sugar, the juice of the lemon, and cream of tartar, and stir well until all is dissolved. Cool to 70 degrees F, add yeast, and ferment (covered) in a warm place for three days. Bottle in screw-topped bottles.[31]

Susun Weed's Dandelion Beer—1989

Ingredients

- 1 pound sugar
- 1 ounce cream of tartar
- 1/2 ounce ginger
- 1/2 pound dandelion
- 5 quarts water
- 1 cake or 1 tablespoon yeast

Wash well a large non-metal fermentation vessel. Put sugar and cream of tartar into vessel. Wash dandelion (use any mix of roots and leaves) and chop coarsely. Boil 10 minutes with grated ginger and water. Strain through cloth into fermenting vessel. Stir well until sugar is completely dissolved. When cooled to blood temperature brew is ready for yeast. Dissolve yeast in water and add to vessel. Cover the lot with a clean cloth and let it ferment for three days. Siphon off into sterile bottles and cap. Store bottles on their sides for a week before opening. Tastes best well chilled.[32]

ABOUT DANDELION

Taraxacum officinale

You see here what virtues this common herb hath, and that is the reason the French and Dutch so often eat them in the spring; and now if you look a little farther, you may plainly see without a pair of spectacles, that foreign physicians are not so selfish as ours are, but more communicative of plants to people.

—Nicholas Culpepper, 1651[33]

Dandelion, like the other herbs in nettle beer, acts primarily as a blood purifier. As Daniel Mowrey comments, it acts "by straining and filtering toxins and wastes from the blood stream."[34] Dandelion is an example of a plant whose parts offer different, and specific, effects. The root is a powerful liver herb, the leaf is a powerful diuretic. Several studies have shown that dandelion root corrects chronic liver congestion, is effective in treating hepatitis, swelling of the liver, jaundice, and dyspepsia with deficient bile secretion. Some evidence exists that use of dandelion stimulates the flow of bile to the same extent that injections of bile into the liver also

Dandelion (Taraxacum officinale)

accomplish. Dandelion reduces bile duct inflammation and gallstone formation. Severe gallstone problems have been alleviated with the use of preparations containing dandelion, and detailed studies have shown that it increases the concentration and secretion of bilirubin in the duodenum.[35] A number of clinical trials have shown dandelion to be effective in treating pneumonia, bronchitis, and upper respiratory infections.[36] Many herbalists also note its calming effects as a tea, commenting that it has a slight (minimal) narcotic effect.[37] It combats uric acid accumulation in the body and is thus effective in the treatment of gout.[38]

Dandelion is a bitter (like hops) and stimulates digestion. While the leaf is one of the best diuretics available, it also contains large amounts of potassium (which the root does not). Excessive urination depletes the body of potassium, which is why many physicians prescribe potassium supplements with any diuretics they dispense. Dandelion leaf replaces all the potassium that is lost through its diuretic action.[39]

Dandelion is also highly nutritive. It contains significant amounts of iron, manganese, phosphorus, protein, aluminum, vitamin A, chromium, cobalt, magnesium, niacin, potassium, riboflavin, silicon, sodium, tin, zinc, and vitamin C.[40] It is a good source of silicon and also contains 125 parts per million of boron (which helps the body retain calcium and raises estrogen levels in the blood) and 20,000 ppm of calcium. This makes it useful in the treatment of menopausal symptoms and osteoporosis.[41]

CHINA ROOT ALE

China Ale, however, was not a term applied by wits to tea, as has been suggested, but was composed of ale flavoured with China root and bruised coriander seed, which were tied up in a linen bag, and left in the liquor until it had done working. The ale then stood fourteen days, and was afterwards bottled.

—John Bickerdyke, 1890[42]

China root is an Oriental species of *Smilax* commonly known as sarsaparilla but known now more often simply as smilax. It is used quite regularly in contemporary herbal practice and has a good and pleasant flavor.

China Root Ale
Ingredients
    2 gallons water
    4 pounds malt extract
    4 ounces china root or other dried *Smilax* species
    1/2 ounce coriander seed, powdered
    ale yeast

Boil water with 2 ounces china root and 1/4 ounce coriander seed for one hour. Cover and let stand overnight. Strain and reheat enough to dissolve malt extract. Cool to 70 degrees F and pour into fermenter. Place remaining China root and coriander seed in muslin bag and hang in fermenter; add yeast. Let remain in fermenter three weeks. Prime bottles, fill, and cap. Ready to drink in two weeks.

ABOUT CHINA ROOT

Smilax spp.

> *It is reckoned a great sweetener of the blood.*
> —Nicholas Culpepper, 1651

Smilax species were known to the herbalists and brewers of antiquity, though most medicinal species are from the New World. The species itself was named for a maiden of antiquity, Smilax. Her love being spurned by the young Crocus, she transformed into the plant that bears her name. (The plant from which saffron comes was named for Crocus.) Smilax has a long history of ceremonial use, especially those ceremonies relating to fermentation: throughout Roman times garlands of the plant were worn by the common people at yearly festivals for the wine god Bacchus.

Smilax (or sarsaparilla) has enjoyed a long history of use (and popularity) in herbal medicine. In 1831, for instance, it was in such demand that 176,854 pounds of the root were imported to England for use in standard practice medicine. It has a long history of use in American medicine, being listed in the *U.S. Pharmacopeia* until 1950. It is still official in Belgium, China, Japan, and Portugal.

One note on China root: Some researchers insist that the plant was actually a tuber-shaped fungus, *Poria cocos*, long used in traditional Chinese medicine. Most researchers however, believe it (as do I), to be a true *Smilax*, *Smilax China*. All the *Smilax* species are used interchangeably in herbal medicine. Like wild sarsaparilla (see "Wild Sarsaparilla Ale") with whom it shares many properties and a similar taste, *Smilax* species were commonly used in many ales and beers. The *Flora Medica* (1838) comments, "From the tubers, with maize, sassafras and molasses the negroes of Carolina manufacture a very pleasant beer."[43]

Smilax is similar in its actions to, though somewhat weaker than, burdock. As Werbach and Murray note in their groundbreaking *Botanical Influences on Illness* (Tarzana, CA: Third Line Press, 1994):

> Sarsaparilla species have been used all over the world in many different cultures for the same conditions, namely gout, arthritis, fevers, digestive disorders, skin disease, and cancer. Sarsaparilla contains saponins or steroid-like molecules that bind to gut endotoxins. This effect may support the plant's historical use as a "blood purifier" and tonic in human health conditions associated with high endotoxin levels, most notably psoriasis, eczema, arthritis, and ulcerative colitis.[44]

In general the herb is a tonic for the whole body. It has been found to possess antibiotic and antimicrobial activity and is useful in digestive complaints, for fevers, as a diuretic, and for hypertension.[45] Related species have been used for thousands of years among the North American indigenous cultures for similar complaints.[46]

Smilax has been, however, considered to be, primarily, an alterative and tonic herb. This means that the herb, after prolonged use, begins to move the body toward a more optimum level of health, correcting organic tendencies toward disease in a number of organ systems. This kind of "medicine" is not well understood in contemporary Western medical practice, though such action has been recognized throughout the world for millennia. Wood's *Therapeutics* (1883) put the action of *Smilax* (and alteratives) most succinctly.

The curative effect of sarsaparilla is very slow, because the alterative change of tissue upon which its efficacy probably depends, is also slow; and this very slowness may constitute one of its real merits; as it seems difficult seriously to abuse a remedy of such feeble physiological action. But gradually, under its use, the appetite often improves, the secretions assume their normal state. . . . A new and healthy tissue has taken the place of the old and diseased.[47]

WILD SARSAPARILLA ALE

The roots are also nutritious . . . a kind of beer can be made with them. The berries give a fine flavor to beer, and a wine similar to elder wine can be made with them.

—C. S. Rafinesque, 1828[48]

The following recipe is adapted from the *Canadian Pharmaceutical Journal* of 1876. It was known as "New Orleans Mead." The original recipe was a "root" beer and may have been referring to *Smilax* and not the wild sarsaparilla I am using here. However, wild sarsaparilla has identical actions to *Smilax*, even though it is an entirely different species of plant Wild sarsaparilla was, however, used extensively in root beers of that time, and is a quite delicious and highly medicinal herb.

Wild Sarsaparilla Ale
Ingredients

    8 ounces fresh sarsaparilla root
    8 ounces fresh licorice root
    8 ounces fresh cassia root

8 ounces fresh gingerroot

2 ounces cloves

3 ounces coriander seed

12 pints corn sugar syrup

4 pints honey

8 gallons water

yeast

"Take 8 ozs. each of the contused roots of sarsaparilla, licorice, cassia, and ginger, 2 ozs. of cloves and 3 ozs. of coriander seeds. Boil for fifteen minutes in eight gallons of water; let it stand until cold . . . Then strain through flannel onto syrup 12 pints (thick sugar syrup) and honey 4 pints," stir until dissolved, heating again if necessary. Cool to 70 degrees F and pour into fermenter. Add yeast. Ferment until complete. Prime bottles, fill, and cap. Ready to drink in 7 to 10 days.[49]

ABOUT WILD SARSAPARILLA
Aralia nudacaulis

The dark berries are made into a kind of wine by the Montagnais and used as a tonic. . . . The same is done by the Penobscot. The berries are put into cold water and allowed to ferment in making the wine referred to.

—Frank Speck, 1917[50]

Wild sarsaparilla, *Aralia nudicaulis,* is a member of the ginseng family and was commonly used, like *Smilax* species, during the latter part of the nineteenth century—a veritable herb-of-the-day, much as *Echinacea* is used now. Considered a blood tonic and system strengthening herb, wild sarsaparilla was used in herbal medicines and "root" beers throughout America.

Wild sarsaparilla roots have a wonderful aromatic, almost balsamic odor and a familiar and pleasant ginseng taste, being somewhat sweet in flavor.

Wild Sarsaparilla is considered to be a reliable substitute for any of the *Smilax* species. The root is alterative, was used in pulmonary complaints, as a general tonic, for lassitude, general debility, stomachaches, and as a wash for shingles and indolent ulcers of the skin in primary nineteenth-century herbal practice. In folk practice it was used as a diuretic and blood purifier, for stomachaches, fevers, coughs, and to promote sweating. American Indians used it in virtually the same ways for hundreds of years.[51]

Wild Sarsaparilla
(Aralia nudacaulis)

GINGER BEER

There were times in the country's history before the introduction of lager beer when the commercial sale of ginger beer exceeded both hopped beer or cider.

—Sanborn Brown, 1978

Ginger beer is the original form of the drink now known as ginger ale, and as you might have noted, ginger is included in many of the recipes for nettle and dandelion beer. In some respects, you could, sort of, consider all those beers a variety of ginger beer (as Maude Grieve comments about her nettle beer).

Widely valued as a flavoring and as medicine, ginger is one of the oldest spices known. It was so popular in beer in America at one time that, as Sanborn Brown observes, "[t]here were times in the country's history before the introduction of lager beer when the commercial sale of ginger beer exceeded both hopped beer or cider."[52] Because of its prevalence and popularity in brewing history, there is good reason to suppose that all original ginger "ales" were alcoholic.

References to ginger beer abound in beer and herbal literature. Cindy Renfrow has done a remarkable job of collecting many old brewing recipes in her *A Sip Through Time* (n.p.: Renfrow, 1995). I first found a number of the following ginger beer recipes in her book.

This early ginger beer is included in *The Family Receipt Book, Containing Eight Hundred Valuable Receipts in Various Branches of Domestic Economy; Selected From the Works of the Most Approved Writers, Ancient and Modern; and from the Attested Communications of Scientific Friends*, originally published in 1819.

Ginger Beer—1819

Ingredients

> 1 gallon water
>
> 1 ounce gingerroot
>
> 1 pound sugar
>
> 2 ounces lemon juice
>
> yeast
>
> isinglass

> To every gallon of spring water add one ounce of sliced white ginger, one pound of common loaf sugar, and two ounces of lemon juice, or three large tablespoonfuls; boil it near an hour, and take off the scum; then run it through a hair sieve into a tub, and when cool (viz. 70 degrees) add yeast in proportion of half a pint to nine gallons, keep it in a temperate situation two days, during which it may be stirred six or eight times; with a spoon. In a fortnight add half a pint of fining (isinglass picked and steeped in beer) to nine gallons, which will, if it has been properly fermented, clear it by ascent. The cask

must be kept full, and the rising particles taken off at the bung-hole. When fine (which may be expected in twenty-four hours) bottle it, cork it well, and in summer it will be ripe and fit to drink in a fortnight.[53]

From *The American Frugal Housewife* (1832) comes this one:

Ginger Beer—1832
Ingredients

- 1 cup gingerroot
- 1 1/2 pails water
- 1 pint molasses
- 1 cup yeast

Most people scald the ginger in half a pail of water, and then fill it up with a pailful of cold; but in very hot weather some people stir it up cold. Yeast must not be put in till it is cold, or nearly cold. If not to be drank within twenty-four hours, it must be bottled as soon as it works.[54]

The Young Housekeeper's Friend, or a Guide to Domestic Economy and Comfort, published in 1846, offers this recipe.

Ginger Beer—1846
Ingredients

- 1 1/2 ounces ginger
- 1 ounce cream of tartar
- 2 lemons sliced
- 1 pound brown or white sugar
- 4 quarts water
- 1 cup yeast

Take one ounce and a half of ginger, one ounce cream
of tartar, one pound of brown sugar, four quarts of boiling water, and two fresh lemons, sliced. It should be
wrought in twenty-four hours, with two gills of good
yeast, and then bottled. It improves by keeping several
weeks, unless the weather is hot, and it is a delightful
beverage. If made with loaf instead of brown sugar, the
appearance and flavour are still finer.[55]

And finally from Renfrow's book, she notes this one for a "Superior
Ginger Beer" from *Miss Beecher's Domestic Receipt-Book: Designed as a
Supplement to her Traetise on Domestic Economy*, originally published in 1857.

Ginger Beer—1857

Ingredients

    3 pints yeast
    1/2 pound honey
    1 egg white
    1/2 ounce lemon essence
    10 pounds sugar
    9 gallons water
    9 ounces lemon juice
    11 ounces gingerroot

Boil the ginger half an hour in a gallon of water, then add
the rest of the water and the other ingredients, and strain
it when cold, add the white of one egg beaten, and half
an ounce essence of lemon. Let it stand four days then
bottle it, and it will keep good many months.[56]

This next recipe comes from *King's American Dispensatory*, perhaps
the finest botanical work on the medicinal use of herbs ever published in

the United States. It was originally published in the latter part of the nineteenth century. Since it does not mention yeast, the authors either must be allowing a wild yeast to naturally begin fermentation or they neglected to mention it.

Ginger Beer—1898

Ingredients

> 2 pounds white sugar
>
> 14 drachms lemon juice or cream of tartar
>
> 12 1/2 drachms honey
>
> 13 drachms ginger
>
> 2 gallons water
>
> white of one egg
>
> 24 minims essence of lemon
>
> [yeast]

> A good ginger beer may be made as follows: Take of white sugar, 2 pounds; lemon juice or cream of tartar, 14 drachms; honey 12 1/2 drachms; bruised ginger, 13 drachms; water, two gallons. Boil the ginger in two pints of water for 1/2 hour; add the sugar, lemon juice, and honey, with the remainder of the water, and strain; when cold, add the white of an egg, and 24 minims of essence of lemon; let it stand for 4 days, and then bottle.[57]

C. J. J. Berry's Ginger Beer—1963

Ingredients

> 1 ounce root ginger
>
> 1/2 ounce cream of tartar
>
> 1 pound white sugar
>
> 1 lemon

1 gallon water

yeast and nutrient

> The ginger should be crushed and then placed in a bowl
> with the sugar, cream of tartar and lemon peel (no white
> pith). Bring the water to the boil and pour it over the
> ingredients. Stir well to dissolve the sugar, then allow to
> cool to 70 degrees F before adding the lemon juice,
> yeast and nutrient. Cover closely and leave in a warm
> room for 48 hours, then stir, strain into screw-stopper
> flagons and store in a cool place. The beer is ready to
> drink in three to four days.[58]

This next recipe is from the 1970s and is included in the interesting
Home Brew by Bertrand Remi. A fairly common title for a book on brewing, until you note the book was published in English in Nepal and was
never published in the United States. The book contains a remarkable
number of beers learned during Remi's travels around the world.

Bertrand Remi's Ginger Beer—1976

Ingredients

    1 1/2 ounces ginger

    1 tablespoon cream of tartar

    12 ounces brown sugar

    1 gallon water

    yeast and nutrient

> Bring crushed ginger to a boil (in all the water). Add
> sugar and cream of tartar. Strain. When cool add yeast
> and nutrient. Ferment to completion.[59]

And finally, Sanborn Brown offers a ginger beer made from malt extract instead of sugar (the rice is added to increase the head or foam on the beer—the same effect being created by the cream of tartar in the other recipes):

Sanborn Brown's Ginger Beer—1978

Ingredients

>   2 ounces ginger
>
>   3 pound can malt extract
>
>   6 cups white sugar
>
>   1/4 cup rice
>
>   5 gallons water
>
>   yeast and nutrient

> Crush the ginger and boil it and the rice in 1 gallon of water for one hour. Strain. Add malt extract and sugar and mix until dissolved. Cool to 70 degrees. Pour into fermentation vessel and add yeast and nutrient. Allow to ferment until fermentation is complete (three to six days), rack into bottles, prime with 1/2 tsp sugar and cap. Ready to drink in two to three weeks.[60]

Ginger beer is truly one of the great refreshing beers that exist and I wish some of the microbrews would begin making it commercially. Oddly, it is cooling and deeply thirst quenching in the summer and warming to the body during the cold of winter. Because of ginger's stimulation of peripheral circulation, I consider it to be one of the best winter drinks. It significantly helps the body stay warm. Generally, I feel that 1 1/2 ounces of fresh grated ginger per gallon of water with brown sugar as the only sugar source produces the best beer.

ABOUT GINGER
Zingiber officinale

> *A native of tropical Asia, ginger or zingiber, was widely used by the*
> *Greeks, as well as the Romans who brought it to Britain.*
>
> —Talbot and Whiteman, 1997[61]

Though ginger did not originally grow in North America, those cultures
in which it was available early recognized its powerful medicinal and
spiritual qualities. Many nonindustrial cultures, as the writer Stephen
Fulder notes, recognized the potency
of ginger and regarded it "as a vehicle
of magical force and power."[62] And
though the wild ginger of North
America, *Asarum canadense*, is not
botanically related to ginger, it has
been traditionally used in many of the
same ways and possesses many of the
same properties as ginger. It was even
used traditionally in beers in North
America by European settlers (in much
the same manner as ginger was then
used in Europe), as Rafinesque notes in
his journals from 1828. "A grateful
wine or beer may be made by the infusion of the whole plant, in fermenting

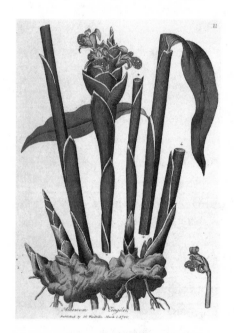

Ginger (Zingiber officinale)

wine or beer."[63] Rafinesque comments
that the taste is intermediate between
ginger and Virginia snakeroot (*Aristolochia Serpentaria*) and was used by
both Indians and European immigrants in much the same manner as ginger. Oddly, stories of European ginger and the origin stories of wild

ginger among the indigenous peoples of North America connect both
children and rapid activity. This Hupa story of the origin of wild ginger
is typical of those in North America.

> Out east in the corner of the world, a maiden lived
> all alone. She saw nobody, not even the tracks of people
> did she see. But after awhile, without reason, she became
> pregnant. And yet she had seen nobody.
> And so she thought, "Where is it from that this
> baby has come?"
> Eventually it was time for her to begin birthing that
> baby. And so she did, from her that baby came.
> She thought to herself, "I will pick up that baby."
> But it dodged away from her. She kept trying to
> pick it up but always it dodged. Finally, it tumbled
> down from the sky, and toward the west it went, get-
> ting so close it seemed about to tumble into the water.
> But close to the beach it stopped and where it stopped
> the plant grew. At the base of the plant it stopped, and
> when it did that plant became medicine. Then the
> woman came to the baby and broke off the medicine.
> With it she picked him up. Then, back to the corner of
> the world, in the east, she took him. She took the medi-
> cine and steamed the baby with it and the baby grew
> fast and healthy.[64]

It is interesting that there is a persistent relationship between children's quickness of movement and ginger, whether wild American or
commercial ginger. As Fulder points out in *The Ginger Book* (New York:
Avery Publishing, 1996), in European tradition ginger is often connected to children, as, for example, in the story of Hansel and Gretel,

in which a brother and sister, lost in the wildness of a forest, are enticed into the gingerbread house by a witch. And in another common European story, a gingerbread boy, being baked by a cook, leaps off the baking tray and runs so fast that no one can catch him. The commonality of these stories is interesting to me, because ginger stimulates more vigorous movement, it "quickens" the blood, and stimulates peripheral circulation. And among all cultures, ginger is a medicine used to produce these effects. With both types of ginger it is the root that is used.

This action of ginger on the blood and peripheral circulation is helpful in the treatment of sexual dysfunction, both for men and women. Clinical study has shown that for men it helps stimulate erection, and for women it increases sexual desire. It also alleviates morning sickness in pregnancy and will promote delayed or scanty menstruation. It has traditionally been a primary herb of choice for treating colds and flu in children, in that it is effective and sure in its actions, safe in large quantities, and yet tastes quite good.

Ginger is foremost a circulatory herb with pronounced effects on the heart and blood. Japanese researchers have found that ginger causes the heart to beat more strongly and slowly and that blood pressure lowers by 10 to 15 points after ginger is ingested. The blood vessels relax and expand, lowering blood pressure and allowing the heart to beat more slowly to pump the blood throughout the body. This, combined with a stronger beat of the heart, means that the blood is pumped more efficiently throughout the body. Indian researchers have found that ginger is also effective in removing cholesterol from both the blood and liver. Ginger was found by Dutch researchers to be efficient in preventing the blood from clotting, similar in its effectiveness as aspirin. Ginger also soothes the stomach, helping digestion. It relieves gas, flatulence, and cramping, and facilitates the breakdown of food in the stomach and the absorption of food in the small intestine. A number of researchers have found that ginger is highly effective in alleviating motion sickness, nausea, and vomiting, being more effective than Dramamine, the usual drug of choice for those conditions. It has also been shown to be quite effective for morning sickness. Though it does stimulate circulation and thus could be considered to be contraindicated for pregnancy (stimulation of circulation can cause the fetus to abort), the quantity in which ginger is taken to alleviate morning sickness is too small to negatively affect pregnancy. Ginger also has the property of lowering body temperature, thus being helpful in feverish states. It is also of use in rheumatic or arthritic complaints. Numerous studies have shown that ginger not only alleviates the symptoms of arthritis but in many instances apparently cures the problem.[65] Ginger's various isolated components also possesses anti-inflammatory, antiviral, diuretic, antifungal, antiseptic, antibiotic, and narcotic properties.[66] It has been found effective in the treatment of cataracts, heart disease, migraines, stroke, amenorrhea, angina, athlete's foot, bursitis, chronic fatigue, colds and flu, coughs, depression, dizziness, fever, infertility and erection problems, kidney stones, Raynaud's disease, sciatica, tendonitis, and viral infections, among other things.[67] Because of its ability to stimulate circulation, ginger is especially effective in any condition where hands or feet are cold. Interestingly, many people who suffer cold hands and feet also experience migraine headaches and (if female) painful menstruation. Ginger is equally applicable in all those conditions, making it the elegant choice for such a complex of conditions. And as I explored in chapter four in the section on chang, ginger contains a naturally occurring *Aspergillus* fungi that converts starch to sugar, allowing the beginning of fermentation. It is a primary ingredient in the yeast cakes used for making chang and saki. The simple addition of crushed gingerroot to any cooked starchy grain will result in starch conversion and the subsequent growth of *Saccharomyces* yeast and the beginning of fermentation. Truly a synergistic action of ginger, yeast, and grain resulting in biological enoblement.

CORIANDER ALE

For if we add but a few Coriander-Seeds, gently infused in a small quantity of Wort, and afterward wrought in the whole, it will make a drink like Chinay-Ale.

—Dr. W. P. Worth, 1692[68]

There is at least one commercial ale on the market made similarly to this recipe. Called Belgian White Ale, it is produced by Blue Moon Brewery in Denver, Colorado, and is fairly easy to find. It has a wonderful floral taste that is the trademark of coriander seed.

Coriander Ale
Ingredients

> 2 pounds malted grain
> 1/4 ounce coriander seed, powdered
> 4 ounces honey
> 1/2 ounce orange peel
> 1 gallon water
> yeast

> Pour water at 170 degrees F over malt. Let stand 90 minutes and sparge. Boil the coriander seed and orange peel in the wort for half an hour. Cool to 70 degrees F, pour into fermenter and add yeast. Ferment until complete. Prime bottles, fill, and cap. Ready to drink in 7 to 10 days.

ABOUT CORIANDER

Coriandrum sativum

> *Coriander, native to the Mediterranean and eastern European regions,*
> *is mentioned in the Egyptian Ebers Papyrus, circa 1500 B.C.*
>
> —Richard Mabey, 1988[69]

Coriander, a native of Italy, is an annual plant about 12 to 18 inches in height when mature. It now grows throughout Europe and Asia and is used primarily as a culinary spice. The seeds are carminative, aromatic, mucilaginous, and contain a volatile oil and tannin. It was used extensively in nineteenth-century herbal practice as a carminative and stimulant. The volatile oil in coriander seed is only partially water soluble and is extracted more readily by alcohol. (Thus, adding the seeds to the fermenting wort will extract more of it.) The volatile oil is carminative, aromatic, and anodyne and has been used in medical herbal practice for neuralgia, rheumatic pain, flatulent colic, and cramps. It aids in the production of digestive juices and stimulates the appetite. It was traditionally added to herbal compounds that were prescribed for constipation. Its action in the bowels as an antispasmodic herb offsets possible cramping from herbal laxatives, particularly senna.[70]

SASSAFRAS BEER

> *Leaves and buds [of sassafras are] used to flavor some Beers and Spirits.*
>
> —C. S. Rafinesque, 1828[71]

Sassafras is a uniquely American herb. Its strong medicinal qualities and wonderful taste helped it to quickly attain national prominence, especially

in drinks. William Penn, writing circa 1685, comments on the local alcoholic beverages in Pennsylvania: "Drink has been Beer and Punch, made of
Rum and water. . . . but beer was mostly made of Molasses, which well
boyld, with Sassafras or Pine infused into it, makes very tolerable drink."[72]

Sassafras was the original herb used in all "root" beers. They were all
originally alcoholic, and along with a few other medicinal beers—primarily
spruce beers—were considered "diet" drinks, that is, beers with medicinal
actions intended for digestion, blood tonic action, and antiscorbutic properties. The original "root" beers contained sassafras, wintergreen flavorings (usually from birch sap), and cloves or oil of cloves. Though Rafinesque notes the
use of leaves and buds, the root bark is what is usually used, both traditionally
and in contemporary herbal practice. Both of the following recipes use sassafras and wintergreen herb. I have found that, in my experience, that the
bark, root or tree, is just too astringent for my taste. What really makes a
wonderful "root" beer using sassafras is the flowers. They add that incredible
wintergreen taste without the need for wintergreen and without the "I am
sucking all the moisture out of your body" experience that the bark creates. I
would substitute it for bark in any sassafras recipes.

Sassafras Beer—*A Recipe from 1846 Using Hops*

Ingredients

> 5 pailsful water
>
> 1 quart hops
>
> 1/2 pint rye meal
>
> 2 quarts molasses
>
> 1 quart sassafras roots, 1 quart checkerberry (wintergreen)
>
> 1/2 pint yeast

> To five pails of water put one quart bowl of hops, and . . .
> about two quarts of sassafras roots and checkerberry,
> mixed. . . . Add half a pint of rye meal, and let all boil
> together three hours. Strain it through a sieve, while it is
> scalding hot, upon two quarts of molasses. There should be

about four pails of the liquor when it is done boiling; if the quantity should be reduced more than that, add a little more water. When it is lukewarm, put to it a half pint of good yeast; then turn it into a keg and let it ferment. In two days or less it will be fit to bottle.[73]

The following recipe was not originally intended to be a beer—it was a corrupted "diet drink," a twentieth-century nonalcoholic "root" beer using carbonated fountain water for carbonation. Besides sassafras, it originally contained a wintergreen essence instead of wintergreen herb. I have altered the recipe somewhat for a true root beer in the recipe that follows.

Sassafras Beer—1925

Ingredients

   2 gallons water

   6 cloves

   3 pints molasses

   2 ounces sassafras bark

   2 ounces wintergreen herb

   1 pinch each: cinnamon powder, grated nutmeg

   1 1/2 quarts honey

   1 heaping tablespoon cream of tartar

   yeast

   Purchase from the druggist five bunches of sassafras roots, scrape [bark from roots—use 2 ounces root bark] and cover with two quarts boiling water, [adding wintergreen herb], a pinch each of powdered cinnamon and grated nutmeg; cover closely, and when of the desired strength, strain through cheesecloth, stirring in three pints of New Orleans molasses, a [quart] and a half of strained white honey and six whole cloves. Place in a saucepan and bring slowly to the boiling point, allowing it to simmer for about ten minutes; again strain and add a heaping tablespoon of cream of tartar. [Add remaining water, cool to 70 degrees F, and pour into fermenter. Add yeast and ferment until complete. Prime bottles, fill, and cap. Ready to drink in 7 to 10 days.][74]

ABOUT SASSAFRAS

Sassafras officinale or *Sassafras albidum*

> *Sassafras, called by the inhabitants Winauk, a kinde of wood of most pleasant and sweet smel: and of most rare vertues in phisick for the cure of many diseases.*
>
> —Thomas Harriot, 1590[75]

The sassafras tree has been used for healing by American Indians for hundreds if not thousands of years, being one of the primary remedies of the continent. It grows throughout the eastern United States as far west as Texas. The American colonists agreed with the indigenous inhabitants' assessment, and sassafras became one of the major herbal medicines of the European immigrants. Though all parts of the tree have been used in herbal practice, the most effective (in American practice) was considered to be the bark of the root. It was used in standard nineteenth-century herbal medicine as a tonic and blood purifying herb, an aromatic stimulant, warming, diaphoretic, diuretic, and alterative. The root was used primarily as a "spring tonic and blood purifier." Like many herbs classified as such,

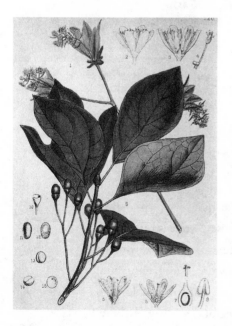

Sassafras (Sassafras officinale)

it helps liver function, helps cleanse the bloodstream of accumulated toxins from a monotonous winter diet, and provides a warming stimulation
to all parts of the body. The pith of the tree was also used. Having a
high mucilaginous content, sassafras pith was used externally for application to wounds and inflammations of the eyes. Internally, the pith was
used as a demulcent drink for any disorders that respond to mucilaginous
herbs: disorders of the chest, bladder, kidneys, and bowels. The root
bark contains about 9 percent of a volatile oil that is generally considered to be the primary active compound in sassafras. In the latter part of
the twentieth century, the FDA determined that the dominant chemical
in the volatile oil, safrole (which comprises about 80 percent of the oil),
was carcinogenic and banned its use in the United States. Sassafras root
bark that is now purchased is stamped prominently "for external use
only." However, the tribes in whose regions sassafras grows used it
extensively, and there are few if any historical accounts of cancer among
them. Cancer is a disease of industrialized man and is rarely present in
indigenous cultures. Steven Foster and James Duke in their somewhat
overreactive but still useful *Peterson's Field Guide to Eastern/Central
Medicinal Plants* (Boston: Houghton Mifflin, 1990), however, do not
extend much credence to the FDA's perspective (unusual given the
alarmist content of that book). Duke notes that "the safrole in a 12-
ounce can of old-fashioned root beer is not as carcinogenic as the alcohol (ethanol) in a can of beer."[76] The FDA ban is thus, like many FDA
bans, absurd.

Oil of sassafras has been found to be antiseptic, stimulant, diuretic,
carminative, alterative, and diaphoretic. Due to the FDA ban, little
research can occur on sassafras, and no practicing herbalist can legally
use it clinically. Both these conditions preclude its being a part of the
current herbal renewal. I use it personally and find it a delightful herb.
Practically the only material available that can be viewed as "clinical" trials is the long historical use by indigenous cultures. Throughout the
range of its growth it was used for colds and flu, as a tonic, as a blood

purifier, for circulatory conditions such as high blood pressure, as a vermifuge, for fevers, and for rheumatic and arthritic aches and pains. More work with this herb should certainly be done. It is possible to buy an "oil of sassafras" for use in root beers. However, the safrole has been removed (which, remember, constitutes 80 percent of the real sassafras oil). Thus, the product you can buy, while it may taste like sassafras, is not sassafras. Finally, the leaves of the plant are highly mucilaginous and are excellent as poultices. It is my belief that all parts of the plant possess antibacterial and antifungal properties (though not as strongly as many other plants) and are, in general, excellent for wounds of any sort. The leaves are traditionally used in Creole cooking to thicken soups. Their flavor is enjoyable and they thicken liquids well.[77]

WINTERGREEN ALE

The people inhabiting the interior colonies [of North America] steep both the sprigs and berries [of wintergreen] in beer, and use it as a beverage.

—J. Carver, 1779[78]

As I previously noted, there is much reason to believe that "root beer" flavoring was originally intended for a fermented beer and only later adapted to its present use in a nonalcoholic beverage. Originally made from field-gathered plants, "root" beer eventually was made only from their essential oils. A traditional recipe for concocting root beer flavoring is: "Oil of Wintergreen 4 drachms; Oil of Sassafras, 2 drachms; Oil of cloves, 1 drachm, alcohol 4 ounces. Mix and dissolve."[79] A drachm is about equal to 1/8 ounce, or 4 milliliters. The original flavoring called "wintergreen" came either from concentrated birch sap, which has a light wintergreen flavor, or the plant known as wintergreen. Originally many root beers were made from concentrated birch sap *or* the wintergreen herb; sassafras leaves, buds, or bark; and cloves. For the following recipe, use the root beer essence described above (you will have to buy a sort-of sassafras oil that is sort of the real thing . . . kind of . . . or else buy a ready-made "root beer" essence):

Wintergreen Ale

Ingredients

> 4 gallons water
>
> 3 pounds brown sugar
>
> 12 ounces molasses
>
> 2 ounces root beer essence
>
> yeast

> Boil water, molasses, and sugar. Let liquid cool to 70 degrees F, pour into fermenter, then add root beer essence and yeast. Do not add root beer essence to hot wort as the heat will cause the essential oils to "boil off." Ferment until complete, bottle, and cap, adding 1/2 teaspoon of sugar to each bottle. Ready to drink in a week or two.

Here is a more original recipe, made from the plants themselves. You can add cloves if desired to mimic the taste of "root beer."

Another Wintergreen Ale

Ingredients

> 1 gallon water
>
> 1.5 pounds malt extract
>
> 2 ounces dried wintergreen herb
>
> 1 ounce sassafras root bark
>
> yeast

Boil wintergreen herb and sassafras root bark in 1 gallon water and let liquid cool to 70 degrees F (overnight). Strain and add malt extract, stir until well dissolved, heating slightly if necessary. Pour into fermenter when still cool (70 degrees F); add yeast. Allow to ferment in fermentation container until fermentation is complete. Bottle and cap adding 1/2 teaspoon of sugar to each bottle. Ready to drink in 7 to 10 days.

ABOUT WINTERGREEN

Gaultheria procumbens

Berries, used in home beer in the North, gives it a fine flavor, they are a good antiscorbutic, invigorate the stomach, &c.

—C. S. Rafinesque, 1828[80]

The wintergreen plant grows throughout the United States. Though its leaves are much larger, the appearance of the plant, its size, berries, and flowers, and many of its medicinal actions are quite similar to uva-ursi (*Arctostaphylos Uva-ursi*), which grows throughout the western and northern latitudes of the United States. Uva ursi, however, does not possess the particularly "wintergreen" taste of wintergreen. Wintergreen is said to have a *mild* astringency; however, I find it to be stronger, slightly less than that of uva-ursi (which is used in the Scandinavian countries to tan leather). The astringency is from the tannins in the plant (from which comes the phrase to "tan" leather). The astringency makes it of use in diarrhea and externally for wounds to help stop bleeding. Wintergreen is also diuretic, emmenagogue, antibacterial, anodyne, and stimulant. It was most often used in nineteenth-century medical herbal practice for urinary tract infections such as cystitis (as was uva-ursi) and as a stimulant in cases of debility. The plant contains methyl salicylate, an analgesic somewhat like aspirin, useful for the pain of rheumatism and inflamed joints. It can be used topically (its usual application) or taken internally. Methyl salicylate is the persistent odor that we call "wintergreen." The volatile oil of wintergreen is the source of commercial oil of wintergreen and is almost pure methyl salicylate. This oil has also been extracted from eight other plants. Though useful medicinally and quite tasty (and commonly used in root beer recipes for more than 100 years) the oil is toxic when taken in too large a dose. As little as .5 ounce of the oil has produced death.

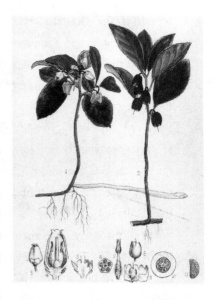

Wintergreen (Gaultheria procumbens)

Wintergreen is a member of the heath family but does not seem to possess the same psychotropic properties that many of the heath family members possess. (Even so, it has been used as an anodyne, for neuralgia, and as a stimulant—all general actions of narcotics.) While the plant itself is benign in large doses, the oil should be used with caution.[81]

LICORICE ALE

John Josselyn gives the recipe for a beer which he used to brew for the Indians when they had bad colds. It was strongly flavoured with elecampane, liquorice, anis seed, sassafras, and fennel.

—Maude Grieve, 1931[82]

Licorice has been used for hundreds of years in beers, as a sweetener, coloring agent, and medicinal. Maude Grieve notes its use in beer in 1931 as a coloring agent: "Liquorice is also largely used by brewers, being added to porter and stout to give thickness and blackness,"[83] properties for which it is still used. Commercially, licorice is added to beers and ales to increase the foam or head on the beer—one-third of an ounce per five gallons of wort—and to add color and sweetness to the body of the beer. Licorice contains a saponin glycoside, glycyrrhizin, that is 50 times sweeter than sugar. Non-fermentable it remains in the beer and adds a sweetness that really is quite wonderful in some beers. However, it is also quite medicinal and adds a particularly nice taste to beer, and, no, it doesn't taste like those rubberoid black things that are sold as licorice—they generally contain no licorice, their flavor coming from anise or fennel.

John Josselyn does mention one recipe that may be the one Maude Grieve is speaking of in his *New England Rarities Discovered* (originally published in London in 1672), but it is somewhat different than Mrs. Grieve indicates. He did publish another work, *An Account of Two Voyages to New England Made During the Years 1638, 1663*, which was originally published in London in 1664. Recently *Rarities* was reprinted by Applewood Books of Bedford, Massachusetts; I have been unable to find the second. Josselyn's recipe is as follows:

> Oak of *Hierufalem* (Jerusalem) is . . . excellent for stuffing of the Lungs upon Colds, shortness of Wind, and the Ptifick [physic]; maladies that the Natives are often troubled with: I helped several of the *Indians* with a Drink made of two Gallons of *Molosses wort*, (for in that part of the Country where I abode, we made our Beer of Molosses, Water, Bran, chips of *Sassafras* Root, and a little Wormwood, well boiled,) into which I put Oak of *Hierufalem*, Catmint, Sowthistle, of each one handful, of *Enula Campana* [elecampane] Root one Ounce, Liquorice scrap'd brused and cut in pieces, one Ounce, Sassafras Root cut into thin chips, one Ounce Anny-seed and

sweet Fennel-seed, of each one Spoonful bruised; boil
these in a close Pot, upon a soft Fire to the consumption
of one Gallon, then take it off, and strein it gently; you
may if you will boil the streined liquor with Sugar to a
Syrup, then when it is Cold, put it up into Glass Bottles,
and take thereof three or four spoonfuls at a time, letting
it run down your throat as leasurely as possible you can;
do thus in the morning, in the Afternoon, and at Night
going to bed.

As it reads it could be made a number of ways: a molasses water mixture in which the herbs listed are boiled until a syrup results that is then
trickled slowly down the throat for healing; a beer wort that is not fermented that is made from molasses, water, bran, sassafras, and wormwood
into which is added the remaining herbs and the whole thing cooked down
into a syrup; or a beer made as he described into which the herbs are put
and cooked down into a syrup. I do not read it as being a beer made from
all the ingredients listed. In spite of this it would be *very* interesting making
a beer from the ingredients listed. And it would be quite good for colds.

Here is a recipe for a licorice ale made with malt extract:

Licorice Ale
Ingredients

> 5 pounds malted barley
> 4 gallons water
> 2 pounds brown sugar
> 4 ounces licorice
> yeast

Mash the barley in water at 150 degrees F for 90 minutes. Sparge with boiling water until a total of 4 gallons

is drawn off. Boil the 4 gallons water with the licorice one hour. Strain and add brown sugar and stir until dissolved. Cool to 70 degrees F and pour into fermenter; add yeast. Ferment until complete, approximately one week, siphon into bottles primed with 1/2 teaspoon sugar, and cap. Ready to drink in 10 days to two weeks.

Here's another made with brown sugar:

Licorice Ale

Ingredients

    1.25 gallons water

    1 pound brown sugar

    2 ounces ground licorice root

    yeast

Boil water, sugar, and licorice for 40 minutes. Let cool to 70 degrees F, strain into fermenter, and add yeast. Ferment until complete. Siphon into primed bottles and cap. Ready to drink in one to two weeks.

ABOUT LICORICE
Glycyrrhiza glabra

The root of this plant is deservedly in great esteem, and can hardly be said to be an improper ingredient in any composition of whatever intention.

        —Nicholas Culpepper, 1651[84]

The Dakota name for licorice is *wi-nawizi*—"jealous woman"—because it is said to take hold of a man. As among the American Indians, licorice is a major herb in any herbal repertory. It is broad in its application, having benefit in four primary areas: lungs, adrenals, stomach, and the female reproductive system.

Within the lung system, licorice provides several important actions. It is antispasmodic, helping to reduce coughing, an expectorant, helping to move phlegm up and out of the lungs, an anti-inflammatory, helping to reduce lung inflammation suffered during onset of a cold, and a demulcent, helping to soothe and coat inflamed mucous passages.[85]

For people who have burned the candle from both ends, drinking huge amounts of coffee, constantly tense with an activated "flight or fight" response, and perhaps using

Licorice (Glycyrrhiza glabra)

cocaine or amphetamines, the usual result is exhausted adrenal glands. Since the adrenals are also the sight of production for sex hormones, exhausted adrenals may lead to decreased libido. The adrenals also supply the substances that help facilitate healthy body repair and growth to bodily tissues. Exhausted adrenals can lead to longer healing time and a lack of vitality in body tissues. Licorice supplies many substances that can be used by the body as a substitute for the substances produced by the adrenals. Using licorice in conjunction with reducing stress and coffee or tea intake can allow the adrenals to rest and recuperate. In cases of adrenal exhaustion, licorice should usually be taken three times per day, 30 drops (one dropperful) per 150 pounds of weight for three to six months.[86]

Licorice also finds strong application in treatment of ulceration in the stomach. The dried herb, powdered, should be used. If the ulceration is present in the stomach, one ounce of the powdered herb should be added to any suitable liquid and drunk each morning. If the ulceration is in the duodenum, which lies just below the sphincter muscle of the stomach, which releases food into the intestines, the powdered herb should be placed in capsules and taken, two capsules, three times per day. The powdered herb forms a thick mass at the entrance to the duodenum, and when the sphincter opens, it falls, fairly intact, into the ulcerated area.[87]

Licorice is quite high in phytoestrogens, plant precursors to estrogen. I have found the herb to be very effective in the treatment of menopausal symptoms. Usually I combine it with other herbs high in plant estrogens such as hops and black cohosh. However, taken alone in sufficient dosage, it can be quite effective on its own. I suggest one dropperful six times per day to start, and the dose to be adjusted as needed.[88] Overuse in men, especially in combination with other phytoestrogen-rich herbs, can stimulate breast growth—a somewhat painful experience. The breasts do not grow much, just enough to cause pain, nipple sensitivity, and attendant nervous fright from those conditions. Avoidance of the herb for a few weeks quickly brings things back to their normal state.

Licorice is antibacterial (against Gram-negative bacteria) and antimicrobial. It also possesses antiviral properties and stimulates interferon production in the body. Licorice has shown effectiveness against bacteria that are resistant to standard antibiotics.[89] Further, licorice seems to enhance the action of other herbs taken in conjunction with it. Thus *Echinacea*, when taken with licorice, produces immune-enhancing actions far beyond what it accomplishes on its own. Interestingly it has been shown that licorice root, traditionally used in root form as a tooth brush for at least 5000 years (the end is chewed until it resembles a brush), is strongly inhibitory to plaque-forming bacteria in the mouth.

Licorice should not be used in any sustained dosages or for extended periods by people who suffer from high blood pressure or active liver disease.

ST.-JOHN'S-WORT BEER

It happened that someone added a little hypericum, especially if they wanted really intoxicating ale.

—Odd Nordland, 1969[90]

St.-John's-wort (*Hypericum*) has been traditionally used in brewing beer in Norway and to some extent in Europe. It was used for this purpose often enough in the Scandinavian countries that a number of the common names for St.-John's-wort reflect that historical use, *erthopfe, veltehope, jordhumle, strandhumle,* and *olkong* being a few (veltehope, for instance, means "field hop"). Some Norwegian brewers used St.-John's-wort in conjunction with yarrow to create the filtering system described under "Juniper Beer" (see chapter 8): "[we] put them [St.-John's-wort and yarrow] in layers with the malt into the filter-vat, now and then adding a juniper twig, until all the malt was in the vat."[91]

The fresh, flowering plants were used, and were considered to give a good color to the ale and to help the ale flow easily.

A Traditional Norwegian St.-John's-Wort Ale

Ingredients

> 4 gallons water
> 6 1/2 pounds malted barley
> 2 pounds fresh, flowering St.-John's-wort
> yeast

> Place 1 pound of flowering St.-John's-wort criss-cross in the bottom of the mashing tun. Mash the barley in 150 degree F water (which has all been placed on top of the St.-John's-wort) for 90 minutes. Sparge the malt with the remaining water, in which the remaining 1 pound of

St.-John's-wort has been boiled for 45 minutes. Cool to 70 degrees F. Place in fermenter and add yeast. Rack off after three days into secondary fermenter; allow to complete fermentation. Prime bottles, fill, and cap. Ready to drink in 10 days to two weeks.

St.-John's-Wort Ale — *Another Recipe*

Ingredients

- 3 gallons water
- 2 1/2 pounds light barley malt extract
- 1 pound brown sugar
- 1 pound fresh, flowering St.-John's-wort
- yeast

Boil water, remove from heat. Add St.-John's-wort, cover, and let steep overnight. Strain water to remove St.-John's-wort. Bring to a boil, then allow to cool to 150 degrees F and add malt extract and sugar. Allow to cool to 70 degrees F and pour into fermenter; add yeast. Ferment to completion, 7 to 10 days. Prime bottles, fill, and cap. Ready to drink in one week.

ABOUT ST.-JOHN'S-WORT

Hypericum perforatum

> *This is a most excellent Herb for Wounds, if you boil it in Whitewine and drink it, or make an Oil or Ointment of it or a Bath or Lotion; tis very effectual in Bruises or Wounds, and strengthens feeble Members.*
>
> —*An English Herbal*, ca. 1690[92]

On St. John's Eve every man's house was decorated with green birch,
long fennel, orpine, white lilies, and, of course, St. John's wort. Its other
name of hypericum comes from a Greek word meaning "to protect."
—Lesley Gordon, 1985[93]

St.-John's-wort has been used for at least 2,000 years as a primary herbal medicine, though its history of use is undoubtedly much older. The first historical record of its use is in the writings of Euryphon, a Greek physician practicing about 288 B.C. It's name, *Hypericum*, is generally thought to be derived from *yper* ("upper") *eikon* ("an image"), meaning a heavenly image or spirit that watches over human beings. Its common name, St.-John's-wort, is obviously Christian in genesis and is thought to derive from the small pinprick holes in the plant's leaves that bleed red when the hypericin content is at its strongest. In Christian thought, this is the sign of the stigmata, or the bleeding of Christ from the nails in his hands and feet. St. John, in the Christian tradition, bears the light of Christ and watches over Christ's followers to protect them from harmful influences. Thus, the plant continues to hold in its common name the original meaning of the Greek word *hypericum*.

St.-John's-wort is best known now for its antidepressant effects. Recent television, magazine, and radio reports on its effectiveness as a natural antidepressant have driven its use to record levels in the United States. These reports were sparked by European research that showed the efficacy of the herb in treating clinical depression. American physicians, taking notice of these trials, then began prescribing it for Americans. As many antidepressants have undesirable side effects, which St.-John's-wort does not, the herb was an instant success when it was finally noticed by standard practice American medicine. St.-John's-wort has, beyond its antidepressant effects, two other major areas of action: wound healing and antiviral activity.

Its main antidepressant use, as Michael Moore observes, is primarily for people whose life has fallen apart and who are having difficulty dealing with it. Depression from such a major life shift is common, and the herb can help until innate resources come back on line. It is remarkably effective for this. Additionally, though it is not thought to be as effective in other depressive conditions, I used it for a decade with good success in my own clinical psychotherapy practice for people whom conventional psychiatric physicians expected to be medicated for life. An increasing number of Americans (some figures put it at 1 in 10) expect to be on Prozac throughout their lifetime, a practice that I think bodes ill for our national character. St.-John's-wort has proven extremely effective as both an alternative to pharmaceutical antidepressants and as a bridge between prescription antidepressants and none at all.

As to other medicinal actions, clinical trials have shown that St.-John's-wort is remarkably effective as a wound and burn herb. It possesses stronger antibacterial action than sulfanilamide.[94] St.-John's-wort thus helps prevent infection in wounds and burns. Additionally, the use of the herb in such conditions helps prevent the formation of scar tissue, keloids, and, in clinical trials, speeds healing by a factor of three. It also possesses strong anti-inflammatory and antimicrobial activity. I have found that the addition of St.-John's-wort and bloodroot (*Sanguinaria canadensis*) to conventional herbal skin salves make a wound salve that no other combination of herbs can rival. Healing is indeed extremely rapid and scarring minimized. Anecdotal evidence and homeopathic practice suggest that the use of St.-John's-wort is also of benefit for nerve damage caused by physical trauma.

The plant has also been found to "strongly inhibit a variety of retroviruses *in vitro* and *in vivo*."[95] This has promising applications for HIV infection and other emerging retroviruses. The combination of antibacterial, antidepressant, and antiviral properties make it a good herb to use in HIV and full-blown AIDS, along with pharmaceuticals. Use of the herb in the winter when both depression and respiratory infection are highest has produced a marked decrease in seasonal affective disorder (SAD) and winter flus and colds.

The herb is useful in stomach ulceration and chronic gastritis— probably attacking the bacteria responsible for stomach ulceration, though I have been unable to find clinical studies of *Hypericum's* activity on the *Helicobacter* bacterium that causes stomach ulceration. It is, however, recommended for this use in standard practice European medicine. It is also diuretic, and soothes smooth muscle cramping and reduces nerve pain; consequently, it is a traditional herb for treatment of sciatica and neuralgia.

St.-John's-wort is a native of Europe and Asia that hitchhiked over with European immigrants. It is now well established in North America and can be found throughout the country. When established, it grows unabashed, often dominating entire ecosystems. For this reason it has been identified as a noxious weed by most states, and strong eradication procedures have been implemented. In spite of this, it can still be found without too much work, and once it is found, there is usually a lot of it. The fresh, flowering tops are gathered at midsummer. The tincture, oil, and tea of the fresh, flowering tops all become dark red from the hypericin constituent of the plant, which is produced at flowering. Ancient herbalists also recommended its harvesting at this time. Dried St.-John's-wort rarely produces this red coloration and rapidly loses its effectiveness. Herbal preparations and beers and ales should be prepared using the fresh plant.[96]

SWEET FLAG OR CALAMUS ALE

Calamus imparts at once an aromatic taste and an agreeable bouquet or odor to the liquid in which it is infused. It is used by the rectifiers to improve the flavor of gin, and is largely employed to give a peculiar taste and fragrance to certain varieties of beer.

—A. H. Church, 1879[97]

Sweet Flag Ale

Ingredients

> 3-pound can malt extract
>
> 4 gallons water
>
> 2 pounds brown sugar
>
> 1 1/2 ounces sweet flag, dried root
>
> yeast

> Boil the 4 gallons water with 1 1/2 ounces sweet flag,
> malt extract, and sugar for one hour. Strain, cool to 70
> degrees F, and pour into fermenter; add yeast. Ferment
> until complete, approximately one week, siphon into
> bottles primed with 1/2 teaspoon sugar, and cap. Ready
> to drink in 10 days to two weeks.

ABOUT SWEET FLAG

Acorus calamus

> *The rhizomes are used by confectioners as a candy, by perfumers in
> the preparation of aromatic vinegar, by rectifiers to improve the flavor
> of gin and to give a peculiar taste to certain varieties of beer.*
>
> —Lewis Sturtevant, 1919[98]

Sweet flag, or calamus, is one of the seven primary sacred herbs of the
Penobscot Indians and is perhaps their most important sacred plant. The
following story retells how, like all plants, it was given to the Penobscot
peoples by the Creator through a dream.

It is said that in the old days, the Penobscot peoples were suffering from a
great plague. Many were ill, many had died. One of the Penobscot lead-
ers, severely troubled about the illness sweeping his people, prayed to the
Creator for help. That night the Muskrat appeared to him in his dreams.

"You have prayed for help for your people," said the Muskrat, "and I have come to help you. Look carefully and remember."

The man looked closely and saw the Muskrat turn himself into a plant. He examined the plant closely until he knew it well, knew he would remember how it looked and in what kind of terrain it liked to grow. He looked deeper and saw that the spirit and power of the Muskrat was contained within the *root* of the plant and thus knew that this was the part of the plant he was to use.

When he awoke he dressed and traveled to the place where he had been shown the plant would be found. There he dug it up and made medicine for his people. In this way the Penobscot people were healed and sweet flag, muskrat root, came to the people.

Nearly every Penobscot family kept the dried root of sweet flag hung in their homes for use as medicine. The root was burned as a smudge in all homes to protect them from sickness, in the sweat lodge for healing, and chewed for personal healing and as a preventative. It was considered to be a general panacea.

It was used throughout the indigenous world in North America, all the tribes having access to it considering it a powerful medicine. Generally, it was used in colds and flus, infectious diseases, wound treatment, and digestive complaints. In all cultures, it is the root of the plant that is used.

Sweet flag grows throughout the world. It is considered to be a powerful sacred and medicinal plant to both Hindus and Muslims and to other indigenous tribes throughout its range. Many texts of the Middle Ages refer to the use of "rushes" as a floor covering. This refers to the sweet flag plant, which looks a great deal like iris. The long leaves were picked and strewn fresh on floors in both homes and commercial buildings. Sweet flag has a wonderful, spirit-gladdening scent, and was used in many Christian churches for its cleansing smell.

It was also used in standard practice American medicine, being official in the *U.S. Pharmacopeia* well into the twentieth century. It has traditionally been used as a tonic for the intestinal tract. It possesses both bitter and mucilaginous properties, making it well suited for such use. It soothes and coats the stomach and stimulates digestion. It has also been used throughout the world for fevers, infectious diseases, and indolent ulcers. English herbalists in the twentieth century recommended it for the treatment of malaria, even when quinine was ineffective, and typhoid. I have been unable to find much current research on the plant, but its historical use for all those conditions suggest it possesses antibacterial properties. It has been traditionally used in dysentery, diarrhea, bowel problems, fevers, externally for stubborn infected ulcers, and for nervous disorders. It is considered carminative, tonic, and excitant. It has been used extensively for flatulence and intestinal colic. Its use as tea or tincture produces relief from indigestion, hiatus hernia pain, and colon cramping. It has also shown a consistent antihistamine-like effect that makes it useful in helping the stuffiness that accompanies head colds and hay fever.[99] Some indigenous tribes, notably the Cree, assert sweet flag has psychotropic properties. Modern research has verified this, noting that the root oils contain asarone and beta-asarone and are thought to produce strong visual hallucinations when taken internally.[100]

The pleasant odor, so noticeable in the plant, becomes even more pronounced when the root is dried. The root should be harvested in either spring or fall and dried before use. The dried leaves are a wonderful smudge. Sweet flag has a spicy flavor and has often been used as a substitute for ginger, nutmeg, and cinnamon. In the treatment of digestive disorders it has often been combined with meadowsweet.[101]

MEADOWSWEET ALE

Meadowsweet *was also formerly much in favour [in herb beers]. The mash when worked with barm made a pleasant drink, either in the harvest field or at the table. It required little sugar, some even made it without any sugar at all.*

> *Another favourite brew was that of armsful of Meadowsweet, Yarrow, Dandelion, and Nettles, and the mash when "sweetened with old honey" and well worked with barm, and then bottled in big stoneware bottles, made a drink strong enough to turn even an old toper's head.*
>
> —Maude Grieve, 1931[102]

There is some evidence that meadowsweet gained its name from its use in ales and beer. Maude Grieve comments that "In the fourteenth century [meadowsweet was] called Medwort, or Meadwort, i.e. the mead or honey-wine herb, and the flowers were often put into wine and beer."[103] The herb has a delightful smell and invigorating quality, much like sweetgrass, and I often use it in sweat lodges for the same purpose sweetgrass is used.

M e a d o w s w e e t   A l e — *Maude Grieve's Recipe*

Ingredients

> 2 ounces meadowsweet
>
> 2 ounces dandelion
>
> 2 ounces agrimony
>
> 2 gallons water
>
> 2 pounds white sugar
>
> 1/2 pint yeast

> Dandelion, Meadowsweet, and Agrimony, equal quantities of each, would also be boiled together for 20 minutes (about 2 oz. each of the dried herbs to 2 gallons of water), then strained and 2 lbs of sugar and 1/2 pint of barm or yeast added. This was bottled after standing in a warm place for 12 hours. This recipe is still in use.[104]

I actually prefer a sugar source other than white sugar, which is too cidery in taste for me; I like a heavier body. The following brew alters

Grieve's recipe by using a different base of sugar and one different herb—lavender. Lavender (*Lavandula* spp.) is a mild nervine and relaxant herb, and the resultant beer produces an interesting state of mind after consumption. This beer is very relaxing and possesses a somewhat flowery taste that explodes on the tongue and then diminishes rapidly. The lavender taste is quite strong—I would suggest using only one ounce of lavender to begin with.

Meadowsweet Ale—*A Variation*

Ingredients

    1 pound brown sugar

    12 ounces molasses

    2 ounces meadowsweet (dried)

    2 ounces agrimony (dried)

    2 ounces lavender flowers (dried)

    2 1/2 gallons water

    yeast

Boil water, sugar, molasses, and herbs for 30 minutes. Cool to 70 degrees F, and strain (to remove herbs) into fermenter. Add yeast. Ferment until complete, prime bottles, fill, and cap. Ready in one week.

ABOUT MEADOWSWEET

Spiraea Ulmaria

The leaves and floures of Meadowsweet farre excelle all other strowing herbs for to decke up houses, to strawe in chambers, halls and banqueting-houses in the summer time, for the smell thereof makes the heart merrie and joyful and delighteth the senses.

—John Gerarde, 1597[105]

Meadowsweet is not much used in American herbal practice, though it has a long tradition in England. Its smell really is uplifting to the heart and does ease the melancholy soul. It was one of the most sacred of herbs to the Druids, probably for its heart-uplifting, sweet nature, and was most likely used much as sweetgrass is used by American Indians. The plant is considered aromatic, astringent, alterative, stomachic, tonic, antirheumatic, anti-inflammatory, antacid, and antiemetic. The herb is highly useful in stomach ulcerations, coating and soothing the stomach and reducing the production of stomach acid. Upset stomach and nausea respond well to its use. The presence of a number of salicylate compounds (similar to aspirin) in the plant make it effective for joint or rheumatic pain. These same compounds also make it effective for use in fevers. It was used with some effectiveness by nineteenth-century medical herbalists for the treatment of cystitis.[106]

BORAGE ALE

The use of Borage in cups [beer] is very ancient, and old writers have ascribed to the flower many virtues. In Evelyn's Acetaria *it is said "to revive the hypochondriac, and cheer the hard student." In Salmon's* Household Companion *(1710) Borage is mentioned as one of the four cordial flowers; "It comforts the heart, cheers melancholy, and revives the fainting spirits."* . . . *[Borage] gives to cups a peculiarly refreshing flavour which cannot be imitated.*

—John Bickerdyke, 1890[107]

Borage (Borago officinalis)

Borage is a relative of comfrey (*Symphytum officinale*) and looks much like it, though its leaves are not nearly so dark a green. Formerly, it was frequently used in herbal practice but is only now becoming commonly known to this new generation. It is a very refreshing plant, and I can understand its frequent use in ale in the Middle Ages.

Borage Ale

Ingredients

>   3 pounds brown sugar
>   4 gallons water
>   3 ounces fresh borage
>   yeast

Boil water, sugar, and herb for 30 minutes. Cool to 70 degrees F, strain, and pour into fermenter; add yeast. Ferment until complete, approximately one week, siphon into bottles primed with 1/2 teaspoon sugar, and cap. Ready to drink in 10 days to two weeks.

ABOUT BORAGE
Borago officinalis

> *Syrup made of the floures of Borage comforteth the heart, purgins melancholy and quieteth the phrenticke and lunaticke person. The leaves eaten raw ingender good bloud, especially in those that have lately been sicke.*
>
> —John Gerarde, 1597[108]

Borage is highly nutritive, traditionally used much like comfrey as a spring food and tonic herb. It is mucilaginous, expectorant, diaphoretic, tonic, calmative, antidepressant, diuretic, and anti-inflammatory. It is especially effective whenever the body has been highly stressed over a long period of time. David Hoffmann suggests its use as a restorative for the adrenal glands after long periods of stress. The leaves, flowers, and seeds are high in gamma-linolenic acid, a potent anti-inflammatory, thus making the herb or expressed fresh juice effective in any inflammatory condition. Selena Heron uses borage in her quite sophisticated (and effective) herbal endometriosis protocol and notes that it has shown significant hormonal activity. She suggests using the fresh expressed herb to minimize loss of nutrients during drying.[109] Its calming and antidepressant activity has been found effective in the treatment of attention deficit disorder (ADD).[110] The mucilaginous content of borage is soothing to mucous membrane tissues of the stomach and throat and externally inflamed wounds. The relatively new research showing its calming and antidepressant activity verifies Gerarde's observations of 1597 and that of later practitioners.

HOREHOUND ALE

Horehound is sometimes [traditionally] made into a "beer for coughs."
—Gabrielle Hatfield, 1994[111]

Horehound is one of the bitterest herbs in common use. Primarily it is included in cough syrups, and a little goes a long way. I don't use it often, but many herbalists swear by it. The following recipe, which I haven't made, will almost certainly be extremely bitter, as gentian, calumba, and horehound are all tremendously bitter. In cough syrups I generally use 1 1/2 ounces of horehound per gallon of syrup, and that is almost too bitter for me. Calumba is an African plant, *Jateorhiza calumba*, and I have never seen it for sale in the United States. It is a standard herb, however, in English herbal practice, that probably being how C. J. J. Berry's friend obtained some for this recipe. Calumba is a bitter tonic mostly used for helping digestive weakness. Thus, this horehound ale would certainly be excellent for poor digestion and a general rundown condition from colds or flu (if you could drink it).

Horehound Ale

Ingredients

4 ounces horehound

4 ounces gentian root

1 lemon

3/4 pound Demerara sugar

1 gallon water

1/2 ounce capsicums

2 ounces calumba root

yeast and nutrient

This recipe from a Lancashire brewing friend, makes, he says, an excellent tonic beer. Put the horehound, bruised capsicums, gentian, calamus root and lemon peel (omitting any white pith) into a polythene bucket and pour over them the water, boiling. Cover and leave for 12 hours. Put the sugar into a boiler, strain the liquid on to it, and heat and stir until all sugar is well and truly dissolved. Cool to 70 degrees F, transfer to fermenting jar, and add yeast and nutrient. Ferment in warm room for three days, then siphon carefully into quart screw-stopper flagons. Store in cool place for a week before drinking.[112]

Horehound Ale — *Another Recipe*

Ingredients

2 pounds dark malt extract or molasses

1 1/2 ounces horehound

1 gallon water

yeast

Boil the horehound in the water for one hour. Remove from heat and let cool. Strain and add malt extract. Reheat if necessary to dissolve extract. Cool to 70 degrees F and add yeast. Ferment until complete, prime bottles, fill, and cap. Ready in one week.

ABOUT HOREHOUND

Marrubium vulgare

> *The Juice of it mix'd with Hony is good for those that have Coughs, and are Consumptive. . . . Take of the Syrup of White Hore-hound two ounces, of Oyl of Tartar per deliquium one Scruple; mix them: Let the Sick take often of it, a spoonful at a time.*
>
> —John Pechet, 1694[113]

Horehound is an indigenous European plant now naturalized throughout the United States. It was esteemed among the Egyptians, who called it the Seed of Horus, and both the Romans and the Greeks valued it for its medicinal properties. It has been traditionally used for pectoral complaints, especially coughs. It clears up lung congestion, stimulates expectoration, alleviates coughs, produces sweating, is diuretic, diaphoretic, and stimulates stomach secretions. Felter and Lloyd note that "its stimulant action upon the laryngeal and bronchial mucous membranes is pronounced" and feel it influences respiratory function.[114] In standard practice herbal medicine it was used in coughs and colds, asthma, bronchitis, bronchial congestion, and weak digestion. Its primary use today is in cough syrups to help stimulate the clearing of congestion in the lungs. It stimulates expectoration, softens up and helps move mucous trapped in the lungs, relaxes the smooth muscles of the bronchial tract, and promotes sweating, which helps shorten the duration of colds and flu. Its antispasmodic properties (relaxing smooth muscle) helps alleviate uncontrolled coughing. Horehound cough lozenges can still be bought and are a remnant of nineteenth-century American herbal medicine.[115]

CALENDULA (MARIGOLD) ALE

It hath pleasant, bright and shining yellow flowers, the which do close at the setting downe of the sunne, and do spread and open againe at the sunne rising.

—Dodoens-Lyte 1578[116]

Marigolds, now generally referred to as calendula in herbal practice, have been used throughout history for their healing, nutritive, and coloring properties. Marigold wine was not uncommon—made from the flowers, like dandelion wine, it was said to possess a wonderful color and taste. The recipe that follows was intended to be more of a wine recipe; I have altered it slightly.

Calendula Ale—*A Variation of a Seventeenth-Century Recipe*

Ingredients

>   2 gallons water
>   Juice of one lemon
>   1 peck (8 quarts) fresh (or 4 quarts dried) marigold flowers
>   4 pounds sugar
>   3 spoonfuls yeast

>   Take 2 gallans of spring water too which is put 4 pound
>   of Lofe sugar, and Lett them boyle gently one houer
>   then take a peck of flours bruse them in a Morter, and
>   when the Liquor is blood warm put the flouers into it
>   with the Juce of a Lemon then take 3 spunfulls of yeist

with 6 spunfulls of the Liquor and beat it well together, then put it to the other Liquor and Lett them stand five Days, then strain it out hard and put it into a barrell, after it is done working stop it Close and Lett it stand a month or more then draw it into bottells with a little Lofe sugar, after 6 weeks boteling it will bee fitt to drinke, keep it a year or Longer, the larger the quantity is made at a time the beter it will be.[117]

ABOUT CALENDULA (MARIGOLD)
Calendula officinalis

> *Conserve made of the flowers and sugar, taken in the morning fasting, cureth the trembling of the harte, and is also given in the time of plague or pestilence. The yellow leaves of the flowers are dried and kept throughout Dutchland against winter to put into broths, physicall potions, and for divers other purposes.*
>
> —Stevens, 1699[118]

Calendula, more famous as marigold, is a ubiquitous garden flower grown throughout the world for its beauty. It also has a long duration of medicinal use in both standard practice medicine and folk herbalism. It has been shown to be active as a menstrual tonic, useful in dysmenorrhea, metrorrhagia, amenorrhea, and as an emmenagogue. It is an anti-inflammatory both externally and internally, and has been shown to possess cytotoxic, antitumor, and antiviral activity against specific agents. The flowers and essential oil are antibacterial, immune stimulating, and antifungal. Calendula is antispasmodic and useful in treating wounds, being vulnerary with antiseptic and hemostatic properties.[119] In fact, calendula is most often used in conventional herbal medical practice for wound healing (vulnerary). Its anti-inflammatory, hemostatic, and antibacterial actions combine together as a potent wound healer. It stops bleeding (hemostatic), prevents infection (antibacterial), and reduces swelling and redness (anti-inflammatory). Clinical trials have shown that it possesses definite antiulcer activity and that it alleviates the symptoms of hypersecretory gastritis (chronic stomach inflammation). I have never used it as a menstrual normalizer, but it has a good reputation for that use backed up by impressive clinical research. A number of clinicians and folk herbalists are beginning to use it as an internal herb in the treatment of bacterial infections such as strep throat and stomach ulceration with good success.[120]

ELDER ALE

English summer arrives with the elder and departs with the ripening of its berries, and like the rowan, it, too, was a guardian tree.
—Lesley Gordon, 1985[121]

For centuries, elder was often used throughout both Europe and the United States in the making of ales and wines and in herbal remedies. It is still used occasionally for wine, mostly for jams and pies among some rural folk, but it has fallen out of common knowledge and use in the past 30 years.

Elder flower ale was incredibly popular both in the United States and Europe at the time of the American Revolution. Elderberries, though used mostly in wine, were also used to make a special barley wine (sometimes ale) called ebulon, which was stored up to a year before drinking and was felt to be as good in flavor as port wine.

ELDERFLOWERS

Small ale in which Elder flowers have been infused is esteemed by many so salubrious that this is to be had in most of the eating houses about our town.
—John Evelyn, 1664[122]

Ale was also infused with Elder flowers.

—Maude Grieve, 1931[123]

There was a pleasant country belief that if the flowers were put into ale, and a man and woman drank it together, they would be married within a year.

—Lesley Gordon, 1985[124]

A Modern Elderflower Beer — 1963

Ingredients

> 1 pint fresh elderflowers (not pressed down) or 1/2 pint dried flowers
>
> 1 gallon water
>
> 1 lemon
>
> 1 pound sugar
>
> yeast and nutrient

> Squeeze out the lemon juice and put into a bowl with the elder florets and sugar, then pour over them the boiling water. Infuse for 24 hours, closely covered, then add yeast. Ferment for a week in a warm room, then strain into screw-stopper flagons. Store in a cool place for a week, after which the beer will be ready for drinking.[125]

A number of herbs, among them elderflower, juniper berry, and yarrow, have a traditional use as fermented beverages without the addition of any sugar or yeast. I haven't yet tried this and (to my Germanic interior voice) it hasn't made much sense. But several herbalists have remarked to me that they ferment an elderflower beer (they call it a champagne) and that, indeed, they use no additional sugar or yeast. They feel it reaches its peak at one year though one person told me she has kept it as long as five years. I have been told that it ages well and does not spoil.

Anecdotally, the making of this elderflower champagne is as follows: Take a quart of fresh elderflowers, let sit in a closed glass container with a gallon of water over a long summer day, strain and press the flowers and put the resulting liquid into a glass carboy with a fermentation lock. Apparently the flowers have a naturally occurring yeast on them and the sugar content of the flowers is enough to lead to a mild (2% or so) alcohol content. Let the elderflower water ferment until complete, bottle (prime with a little sugar if carbonation is desired or bottle while fermentation is still occurring), and let age for anywhere from one month to five years.

ELDERBERRIES

Ebulon, which is said to have been preferred by some people to port, was made thus: In a hogshead of the first and strongest wort was boiled one bushel of ripe elderberries. The wort was then strained and, when cold, worked (i.e., fermented) in a hogshead (not an open tun or tub). Having lain in a cask for about a year it was bottled. Some persons added an infusion of hops by way of preservative and relish, and some likewise hung a small bag of bruised spices in the vessel. White Ebulon was made with pale malt and white elderberries.

—John Bickerdyke, 1890[126]

Elderberry Ale
Ingredients

    1 gallon water
    2 cups fresh elderberries
    2 pounds malt extract
    yeast

Place elderberries and 1 quart water in blender and puree. Slow-boil elderberry puree and remaining water for one hour, cool to handling temperature, and strain (and press) through a sieve. Add malt extract. Pour into fermenter and add yeast at 70 degrees F. Ferment until completion. Prime bottles, fill, and cap. Like many wines, elderberry beer is felt to attain a better flavor when stored a long time. However, this recipe can be drunk after one to two weeks.

Maude Grieve's Version of Ebulon—1931

Ingredients

    1 gallon fresh elderberries

    1 quart damson plums or sloes

    6 quarts water

    6 pounds white sugar

    2 ounces ginger

    2 ounces allspice

    1 ounce hops

    yeast

Get one gallon of Elderberries, and a quart of damsons, or sloes; boil them together in six quarts of water, for half an hour, breaking the fruit with a stick, flat at one end; run off the liquor, and squeeze the pulp through a sieve, or straining cloth; boil the liquor up again with six pounds of coarse sugar, two ounces of ginger, two ounces of bruised allspice, and one ounce of hops; (the spice had better be loosely tied in a bit of muslin); let this boil above half an hour; then pour it off; when quite cool, stir in a cupful of yeast, and cover it up to work.[127] When fermentation is complete, prime bottles, fill, and cap.

Dr. John Harrison of the Durden Park Beer Club, in his *Old British Beers and How to Make Them* (London: Durden Park Beer Club, 1991), has a number of useful and interesting old English beer recipes (most with hops). Here is the one he calls "Ebulum." It is adapted from a recipe he found dating to 1744.

John Harrison's Recipe for Ebulon—1976

Ingredients

> 1 gallon water
>
> 4 pounds pale malt
>
> 1 1/2 pounds ripe fresh elderberries
>
> yeast

> Heat water to 170 degrees F. Pour enough water on malted barley to make a stiff mash. Let stand, covered, three hours. Sparge, bring the liquid up to one gallon by adding more water if necessary. Boil wort with elderberries for 20 minutes, cool and strain. Cool to 70 degrees F, pour into fermenter, and add yeast. Ferment until complete. Prime bottles, fill and cap. Store at least six months.[128]

ABOUT ELDER
Sambucus spp.

> *The flowers discuss, mollifie, and dissolve, and are Sudorifick and Anodine. Vinegar, wherin the Flowers have been infus'd, is very agreeable to the Stomach, and excites Appetite; and it cuts and attenuates gross and crude Humours. The Berries are Alexipharmick and Sudorifick. The Spirit drawn from the Berries, provokes Sweat, and therefore good in Fevers. The Wine made of the Juice*

of them, or Juice mix'd with White or Rhenish-Wine, does much good in Dropsies.

—John Pechet, 1694[129]

The elder is a common perennial bush or tree that grows from three to 30 feet in height. I had been told it never surpasses 15 feet and believed my sources until I met the 30-foot old-growth Elder elder, an imposing tree that grows on our land in Washington State.

The primary species used in historical European herbalism is the black elder, *Sambucus nigra*. Another European species, *Sambucus Ebulis*, is the source of the name of elderberry beer—ebulon—and was perhaps the species of berry more commonly used in beers and wines. *Ebulis* comes from the Latin *ebullire*—to boil out. Ebullient also comes from this word—bubbling or boiling over with excitement or enthusiasm. And this is interesting because the word "elder" has been traced to not only the Old English word *eldo* meaning "old age" but also the Old English *aeld* meaning "fire," another form of boiling or bubbling. This perhaps touches on its use in beers and wines that bubble from the fermenting yeasts but it might also be, as the wonderful herbalist Matthew Wood remarks, because elder is so potent a medicine for the fires of fever that often accompany colds and flu. In any event, the knowledgeable use of elder causes the fires of life to "boil over with enthusiasm" in the people who use it for medicine.

The genus name, *Sambucus*, comes from "sambuca," now generally thought of as an ancient Asian triangular stringed instrument. But of more ancient derivation it also means the panpipes used by ancient peoples throughout the world, in this instance particularly the panpipes of Greece. From one point of view, the herb was named thus because the stems of the bush or tree are easily hollowed out to make the pipes. However, the deeper meaning is that the tree itself is "sambuca"—the pipe of Pan—and it is his spirit blowing through this most sacred tree that enters the world (and the sick body) to heal and teach humankind. In fact, elder is viewed in all ancient texts as a panacea, a cure-all. Pan is the sacred power of forest and animal, the Lord of the Hunt, Guardian of Forest and Animal. The exact meaning of panacea is "to be healed or cured by Pan, the deepest sacred power of forest." When the tree is used for medicine the sacred power of Pan is evoked through this, his most sacred healing plant. It has been set down in all ancient oral traditions that those who truly use the power of the elder for their medicine shall all grow old, becoming in their turn an elder, that, in fact, it will cure all ills that humankind encounters if one calls on its power properly.

In European tradition it is the wife of Pan—the Lady of the Underworld—who guards access to the spiritual power of the plant and, subsequently, to Pan himself. This lady, it is to be remembered, has two faces—that of Spring and that of Winter. She is of both life and death and either of her aspects can affect human beings. This lady, called the Elder Mother in many herbal traditions, is she to whom prayers are addressed before the plant itself can be harvested. In harvesting the plant, her name is invoked and access to the power of the plant and Pan himself is requested. Her reply is "why should you be granted access to these things?" The answer is, "Elder Mother, in time I will come to you, my body will be returned to the Earth and in that time will I pay for this bounty and help I request." It is at this time that she will allow the sincere person to harvest the elder and the power of Pan to be approached. Once this access is granted, not only the power of the plant itself is awakened, but to those who understand the deep power of old-growth forest and of Pan himself can be awakened in the herb.

One of the most potent forces of Earth is thus activated for help in human healing. Because of the powerful beings who are touched upon in using elder, the plant has long been viewed as not only a portal for life but also for death. For the healer who uses elder *all* realms are accessed: life and death, male and female, secular and sacred, gentle and harsh. The plant expresses the opposites of Universe in balance within itself. Through the plant either pole can be accessed or even the balance of polar opposites in dynamic tension.

The elder plant, because it is a portal for the power of Pan, is also considered to be a powerful teacher for other plants in its area or in any garden in which it is planted. In this way it is an "elder" to other medicinal plants in the gardens and fields in which it grows. When used as medicine with other plants, it "teaches them where to go and what to do." Thus it facilitates the action of other herbs.

The American elders are, generally, of two varieties: *Sambucus race-mosa* which is quite poisonous and can be identified by its red berries, and the medicinal elder of choice *Sambucus canadensis*. This elder, called American elder or, sometimes, red elder, has berries that are darkish purple, becoming nearly black when ripe. The berries grow in profusion, and it is quite easy to harvest many pounds of them without much effort. Their natural sugar content and general abundance make them of especial use in beers and wines. And, of course, they have long been used in jams, jellies, and pies.

The flowers of elder grow in a flattish cluster of small white blooms, each cluster about the size of a man's palm. The European black elder was also known as the "stinking elder" from the somewhat disagreeable scent of the black elderflowers. I don't like it myself but I do love the scent of the American elder which is delicate, wholesome, and healthful. The flowers are a traditional staple food in many countries when dipped in an egg and flower batter and deep fried. Some people like the flowers cooked fresh in pancakes. In Germany, the oil in which they are fried is saved and used for ear infections and stubborn wounds.

The elder has often been likened to a complete herbal pharmacy in itself. The flowers and leaves (as an ointment or decoction) are applied to large wounds as an emollient and vulnerary. The leaves have shown antibacterial activity and help the cell walls of the skin to bind together during healing. The flowers in a warm infusion are considered to be a stimulant, in cold water a diuretic, alterative, and laxative. The flowers are considered strongly anticatarrhal. The bark is a purgative and emetic, as are the leaves when taken internally. The berries have laxative properties.

The leaves and flowers are used for wounds, sprains, and bruising. Elderflowers are excellent for upper respiratory problems such as colds and flu and will help clear up problems such as hayfever. For internal use, generally a tea or tincture of the flowers is used medicinally, two tea-spoons dried or fresh flowers steeped in hot water for 15 minutes, or 15 to 30 drops of the tincture. This hot infusion of the flowers is considered a certain remedy for difficult fevers and flu. It will stimulate sweating to break the fever, clear the lungs, calm the patient, and provide antiviral and antibacterial action.

The bark and leaves are generally considered too strong for use without experience. As few as five drops of the leaf tincture can stimu-late strong sweating and begin the early symptoms of imminent vomit-ing. However with judicious practice extremely small dosages (one to five drops) of the leaf tincture can be used reliably for colds and flus, to stimulate sweating in hot dry fevers, and as a reliable calmative for the nervous system. The flowers are more often used for this and it is to be stressed that the flowers possess reliable calmative or mild nervine properties. Because the fresh flowers can still possess emetic activity, the dried flowers are most often used; the purgative action is lost upon drying. Matthew Wood notes elder's historical use for "wild ravings," wakefulness, and epilepsy, confirming its nervine properties. The power of the plant in this area is for wild mood swings from one polar opposite to the other with shortness of breath and feelings of terror or deep fear and hysteria. Its use in epilepsy—for "shorting" out of the nervous system of the brain is indicated for those for whom epilepsy is accessing multiple realms of reality with attendant feelings of terror, fear, and hysteria.

Elderflower will break fever, calm the nerves, stimulate deeper and easier breathing, open up congestion in the lungs, move mucous up and out of the bronchial passages, stimulate the immune system, and directly attack both viral and bacterial infections. Recent clinical trials found a tincture of the berries to be both antiviral and antibacterial.

Two tablespoons of the tinctured berries were given twice a day to people infected with the influenza virus. Healing time was three days.[130]

Elder ales, because they are generally made from the flowers and berries, are extremely good ales for colds and flu, immune stimulation, antiviral and antibacterial action, and rheumatic complaints.

SCURVY GRASS ALE

Such kind of Plants grow in every Region, by the Appointment of God Almighty, which most agree with the People and Animals that are there bred. [Solenander] says he could tell what were the Diseases of any Country, by seeing the Herbs that were most common in it. As, Among the Danes and Dutch, with whom Scurvy is very frequent, Scurvy-grass grows plentifully.

—John Pechet, 1694[131]

Europeans, especially the British, once suffered mightily from scurvy, a deficiency of vitamin C. A number of ales and beers were made specifically to combat that disease, most especially scurvy grass ale in Europe and spruce beer in North America. Regrettably, I have not been able to find scurvy grass to make any of these ales (not surprising, considering its range of growth—i.e., not around here).

The first recipe seems impossible to me to get into five gallons of ale; the first three herbs total four gallons by themselves. It seems a more likely recipe for 32 gallons or even a hogshead—63 gallons (though sometimes I have seen a hogshead referred to as 54 gallons). However, the second recipe below seems to be an adapted form of this one, and it too uses five gallons. This brings up interesting and impossible images in my mind. (The recipe does say "tun" it up. Generally this means to put it all in a cask. A tun, however, was a quantity considered to be 216 gallons.)

Scurvy Grass Ale—1651

Ingredients

5 gallons ale wort

1 peck (2 gallons) fresh scurvy grass

1 gallon fresh watercress

1 gallon brooklimes

4–6 ounces fresh agrimony

4–6 ounces tamarisk or ash bark or buds

1 pound raisins

1/2 pound licorice root

1/4 pound fresh pithed fennel roots

1/4 pound fresh parsley roots

1/4 pound aniseed

1/4 pound fennel seeds

yeast

> Make your scurvye-grasse Drinke in this manner: Take
> a peck of Scurvie-grasse, and a gallon of Water-cresse,
> and a gallon of Brook-limes, one handfull of
> Egremony, one handful of Tamariske, or the buds or
> barke of the Ashe, Raysons of the Sunne, stoned a
> pound, of Licorish halfe a pound, contused Fennell
> roots peethed, and Parsley roots, Annis-seeds, and
> Fennell seeds a quarter of a pound, put all these into a
> thin Bagge, in five gallons of Beere or Ale, put the
> Bagge into the Barrell when the drinke is ready to be
> tunned, with a stone in the bottome of the bagge, let it
> hang within three or foure inches of the bottome of
> the Barrell, let this drinke worke with these ingredients
> in it, then stop it close, and at eight or ten dayes drinke
> of it and none other (except a little at meate) untill the
> Party be well; most especially in the morning drinke a

pint, and exercise until the party is ready to sweat, and keep him warme after it.[132]

Scurvy Grass Ale—1692

Ingredients

>   5 gallons strong ale wort
>   8 quarts fresh scurvy grass
>   3 quarts fresh watercress
>   1 1/2 quarts brooklime
>   6 ounces English rhubarb, fresh
>   4 ounces fresh horseradish
>   1 ounce aniseed
>   1 ounce caraway seeds
>   1 ounce sena
>   4 ounces polypody of the oak
>   8 ounces raisins
>   8 ounces figs, stoned
>   yeast

A Compound Physical Ale, good against the
Scurvy, Dropsy, and other Diseases

Rx. Of Scurvygrass one Peck, Water cress twelve Handfuls, Brooklime six handfuls, English Rhubarb six ounces, Horse Radish four ounces, Anniseeds and Caraway Seeds of each one ounce, Sena one ounce, Polipody of the Oak four ounces, Raisins stoned and Lent Figs, of each eight ounces, New Ale five gallons; Make it S.A.[strong ale].[133]

This next recipe is, again, a variety of the last one. And, again, I cannot figure out how they are getting all this into the amount of ale wort specified. Surely, one of them must have really made this ale.

Scurvy Grass Ale—1695

Ingredients

> 2 gallons ale
>
> 4 quarts scurvy grass
>
> 1 quart watercress
>
> 3/4 quart brooklime
>
> 3 ounces horseradish
>
> 2 ounces fennel seeds
>
> 2 ounces sena
>
> 4 ounces figs

Scurvy Grass Ale After the Best Manner

Take Scurvy-grass half a Peck, Water-creases four Handfulls, Brooke-lime three Handfulls, Horse-Radish three Ounces, Sweet Fennel-Seeds and Sena, of each 2 Ounces, Figs four Ounces, bruised, and new Ale 2 Gallons; put them into an Earthen Pot well stopt, and let it stand for use. As you increase the Quantity of the Liquor increase likewise the ingredients.[134]

The following is a famous medicinal ale, Butler's Ale, which was sold throughout Britain for many generations. Taverns that offered it, like today's bars and their use of the trademark signs of well-known beers, posted a cutout or painting of the good doctor's head outside to advertise that they had it on tap. This is supposedly the original recipe. (And I still can't figure out how they are doing it; this one has even more ingredients per gallon than those above.)

Butler's Ale

Ingredients

> 4 gallons of good ale
>
> 8 quarts (sea) scurvy grass

8 quarts (garden) scurvy grass

4 ounces sena

4 ounces polipody of the oak

6 ounces sarsaparilla (*Smilax* spp.)

1/2 ounce caraway seeds

1/2 ounce aniseeds

2 ounces licorice root, fresh

3 ounces agrimony, fresh

3 ounces maidenhair fern, fresh

A Purging Ale by Dr. Butler, *Physician to King James*

Take Sea and Garden Scurvy-grass, of each a Peck, Sena and Polipody of the Oak, of each four Ounces, Sarsaparilla six ounces, Caraway-seeds and Anni-seeds, of each half an Ounce, Liquoras two Ounces, Agrimony and Maiden-hair, of each two indifferent handfuls, cut the Sasparilla, scrape and slice the Liquoras, then let them be all together grosloy beaten, then put a Gad of Steel into the bottom of a Canvas Bag to make it sink, and upon that all the former ingredients, and hang it in a Vessel of a fit size, and Tun upon it four Gallons of good Ale, after four or five Days you may drink of it and when it begins to grow stale draw it into Bottles and Cork it close, and set it in a Cool Cellar upon the stones or in sand. If you would have more purging, increase, or double the Proportion of Sena.[135]

ABOUT SCURVY GRASS
Cochlearia officinalis

Scurvy: A condition due to the deficiency of vitamin C in the diet and marked by weakness, anemia, spongy gums, a tendency to mucocutaneous hemorrhages and a brawny induration of the muscles of the calves and legs. It oftenest affects mariners and those who use salted meats and few or no vegetables. The use of fresh potatoes, scurvy grass, and onions as food, and especially the drinking of lime juice, are preventative and remedial measures.

—Dorland's Illustrated Medical Dictionary, 1964[136]

[This Herb] cures those Diseases that proceed from too great a quantity of fixed Salts, but especially the Scurvy; upon which it is called in English, Scurvy-grass. . . . The Scurvy is a Disease very frequent among those that live on the Sea-shore, especially in the North; and among such as feed chiefly on Salt-fish.

—John Pechet, 1694[137]

Scurvy grass is a relative of horseradish, *Cochlearia Armoracia*. It is described in *King's American Dispensatory* as an "acrid, bitterish, pungent plant when fresh." The authors go on to note that it is "sometimes used as a salad. It is stimulant, antiscorbutic, and diuretic. It is very valuable in scurvy when eaten fresh, and the juice in water makes a good wash for *spongy gums* and *buccal ulcerations*."[138] It grows primarily in the British Isles, the seacoasts of northern and western Europe, and in the European mountains.

GROUND IVY ALE

The women of our Northern parts, especially Wales and Chesire, do turn Herbe-Ale-hoof into their ale.

—John Gerarde, 1597[139]

Historically, ground ivy was one of the primary herbs used in ale and beer in Europe. Its frequent use in beer can be seen in its common names:

gill-go-over-the-ground, tunhoof, alehoof, and alehove ("gill" is said to come from the French *guille*, meaning to ferment, and the Old English word *gyle* was another word for wort). The three great herbalists of England—Gerarde (1597), Culpepper (1651), and Grieve (1931)—all comment on its use in ale. Culpepper insists that "It is good to tun up with new drink, for it will clarify it in a night that it will be fitter to drink the next morning; or if any drink be thick with removing or any other accident, it will do the like in a few hours."[140] Maude Grieve is somewhat more comprehensive when she comments in *A Modern Herbal* that

> It was one of the principle plants used by the early Saxons to clarify their beers, before hops had been introduced, the leaves being steeped in the hot liquor. Hence the names it has also borne: Alehoof and Tunhoof. It not only improved the flavour and keeping qualities of the beer, but rendered it clearer. Until the reign of Henry the VIII it was in general use for this purpose.[141]

Ground Ivy Ale

Ingredients

> 5 pounds malted barley
> 4 gallons water
> 2 pounds brown sugar
> 3 ounces ground ivy
> yeast

> Mash the barley in water at 150 degrees for 90 minutes. Sparge with boiling water until a total of 4 gallons is drawn off. Boil the 4 gallons water with 3 ounces ground ivy for one hour. Strain, add brown sugar, and stir until dissolved. Cool to 70 degrees F and pour into fermenter;

add yeast. Ferment until complete, approximately one
week, siphon into bottles primed with 1/2 teaspoon
sugar, and cap. Ready to drink in 10 days to two weeks.

ABOUT GROUND IVY

Glechoma hederacea or Nepta glechoma or Nepta hederacea

> *The decoction of it in wine drank for some time together, procureth
> ease unto them that are troubled with the sciatica, or hip gout; as also
> the gout in the hands, knees or feet; if you put to the decoction some
> honey and little burnt alum, it is excellent good to gargle any sore
> mouth or throat.*
>
> —Nicholas Culpepper, 1651[142]

As you can tell from the name, ground ivy is an ivy-type plant, covering
the ground, and sometimes walls and hedges in a thick mat. It is fairly easy
to gather, as it grows in abundance. The running vines break off easily
from their roots, and you can easily gather it up by the handful. It is the
above-ground plant that is used in brewing and herbal medicine. The taste
of the plant is (to me) pleasant, and though considered a bitter for beer
use, I find it only mildly so. Its taste reminds me of black tea. It has a strong
"black tea" aftertaste that fades into a general dryness in the mouth from
the tannins in the plant. However, Felter and Lloyd comment that the
leaves "have an unpleasant odor, and a harsh, bitterish, slightly aromatic
taste."[143] So it might be, as with many herbs, a matter of individual taste.

Medicinally, ground ivy is diuretic, astringent, tonic, a gentle stimulant, a digestive aid, and specific for coughs, especially those of long
standing. It was often used for those with tuberculosis and concomitant
severe coughing. It is decent as a gargle to alleviate a sore throat and to
tone and strengthen soft gums that easily bleed. In this it is like oak and
relies for these actions on its tannin content. Its bitter components help
stimulate digestion, and it has been traditionally used throughout history

as a stomach tonic. Historically it has been considered a tonic for the kidneys and effective as a blood purifier. Unfortunately, little research has been done on ground ivy, and it is now rarely used in clinical herbal practice. Ground ivy grows mainly in Europe, to which it is native, and is naturalized throughout the eastern United States.

The beer is, however, delicious, with a unique taste all its own. If this plant grows near you, you may find it worthwhile to rediscover it. Ground ivy is generally gathered in late summer. It takes about four quarts of fresh plant to make an ounce of dried leaves for use in beer.[144]

CARAWAY ALE

Caraway has from the earliest times been used in Europe for flavoring ale. It is recorded among the items in stock at the "grut house" in Cologne, as early as 1393.

—Odd Nordland, 1969[145]

Caraway is a traditional ingredient (though somewhat uncommon) in Norwegian ales. It grows wild in Norway and is used in many traditional foods: cheese, bread, cooking, spirits, and ale. Most often the seeds were used for cooking, and the plant, as dried straw, in the filtervat, for a special, added flavor. The use of caraway in ale is very old; Nordland notes its use in European ale houses from at least 1393, and a number of the recipes in this book from the Middle Ages include it.

To make a caraway ale, it is better to use a heavy malt and end up with a flavor somewhat like bread in which caraway seeds have been cooked. As you can imagine, it can be quite tasty when properly prepared.

Caraway (Carum carvi)

Caraway Ale

Ingredients

    3 pounds dark malted barley

    1 pound unmalted dark rye

    2 gallons water

    1/2 ounce caraway seeds

    yeast

Mash the barley in water at 150 degrees F. Boil the unmalted rye for 30 minutes and add to the barley mash. Let both steep for 90 minutes. Sparge with boiling water until a total of 2 gallons is drawn off. Boil the wort with 1/2 ounce caraway seeds for 30 minutes. Cool to 70 degrees F and pour into fermenter; add yeast. Ferment until complete, approximately one week, siphon into bottles primed with 1/2 teaspoon sugar, and cap. Ready to drink in 10 days to two weeks.

ABOUT CARAWAY

Carum carvi

The Seed is Stomachick, and Diuretick: It expels Wind, and helps Concoction; provokes Urine, and strengthens the Brain. 'Tis of great Use in the Cholick, and for Giddiness in the head, and the like. 'Tis much us'd in the kitchin; for it is baked in Bread, and mix'd with Cheese, and boyl'd in Broths. 'Tis sold in the Shop Candied. The Root, when it is tender, it as effectual as the Seed, and eats more pleasantly than Parsnips.

—John Pechet, 1694[146]

Caraway has been used by human beings for at least 5,000 years, fossilized seed having been found at Mesolithic sites. The ancient Egyptians valued it both for culinary and medicinal use. At huge Roman feasts, caraway was an integral dish—served dipped in sugar, caraway "comfits," were used to aid digestion and relieve flatulence between courses. It was often used by Arabian physicians, they giving it the name *karawya* from which "caraway" comes. Caraway is indigenous to most of the world and has hitchhiked to the rest. Throughout its range of growth it is used mostly for culinary purposes. The seeds are high in protein, fat, and a volatile oil that is used in the liqueur industry, mostly in Russia and Germany. Caraway is considered to be aromatic, gastrointestinal tonic, stimulant, and carminative. Its primary use, like that of many of its relatives (dill, fennel, etc.), is to relieve flatulence and bloating. It is quite useful in indigestion and helps restore tone and function to the stomach. It possesses calming qualities and has been used historically for treatment of hysteria. Modern research has shown that the seeds possess carminative, anticramping, and antinausea properties. It has also been shown to possess phytochemical antagonists specific against two microorganisms: *Candida albicans* and *Escherichia coli*.[147]

WILD CARROT SEED ALE

Mr. Boyle, in his Book of the Usefulness of Natural Philosophy, says, That discoursing once with an eminently learned and experienc'd Physician of the Antinephristical Virtue of the Seed of this Carrot, fermented in Small Ale, he smilingly told him, That he found it's Efficacy but too great; for, having prescrib'd it to some of his rich Patients, who were wont frequently to have recourse for the Stone and after the Use of this Drink for a pretty while, he seldom heard of them any more. (Mr. Boyle prescribed one Ounce and an half of this Seed to a Gallon of Ale.)
—John Pechet, 1694[148]

Wild carrot seed has been used for many centuries in ale and beer. Maude Grieve notes that "They communicate an agreeable flavour to malt liquor, if infused in it while working in the vat, and render it a useful drink in scorbutic disorders."[149] I can concur.

Wild Carrot Seed Ale—1744

Ingredients

> 1 gallon water
>
> 2 pounds malt extract
>
> 1 1/2 ounces wild carrot seeds in muslin bag to hang in fermenter
>
> yeast

An Ale Which Will Taste Like Apricot Ale

Take to every gallon of ale one ounce and a half of wild carrot seed bruised a little, and hang them in a leathern bag in your barrel until it is ready to drink, which will be in three weeks; then bottle it with a little sugar in every bottle.[150]

ABOUT WILD CARROT SEED

Daucus carota

> *The Seeds of it infus'd in Beer, and drunk, is much commended by some Modern Authors, especially by* Charleton, *for the Strangury, and the Stone in the Kidnies.*
>
> —John Pechet, 1694[151]

Wild carrot, also known as Queen Anne's lace, is a member of the *Umbelliferae* family, the same as caraway. Like many plants in that family, the seeds of wild carrot are effective in the treatment of flatulence, intestinal cramping, and colic. The volatile oil in carrot seed and root is antiseptic and antibacterial. It is excreted by the body and thus is useful in the treatment of urinary tract infections. It is considered specific for kidney stones and has been for at least a millennium.[152] The seed has been traditionally used to promote menstruation and as a "morning after" herb. Indian researchers have found that the seed does prevent implantation of the fertilized ova in laboratory animals. Members of the carrot family, including wild carrot, have been found to possess phytochemical correlates of calcium channel blockers that are effective angina medications. Vegetarians have an extremely low incidence of heart disease, partly due to their low fat intake, but also due to the heart enhancing activity of the carrot family herbs. Wild carrot and the familiar garden carrot are the same plant, though one is domesticated and one is not. A significant amount of research has shown that carrot, both wild and domestic, plays a significant preventative role in cancer, cardiovascular disease, and cataracts. Wild carrot seed and root also contain phytochemical compounds that lower blood pressure.[153]

Wild carrot seed (Daucus carota)

Much of the research on carrot has been concerned with the domestic root. It is high in nutritive compounds that have been found to play a significant role in health. Less research has been conducted on the wild carrot, Queen Anne's lace, or the seeds of either domestic or wild carrot. However, the seeds contain many of the same compounds as the root, and more research should be conducted. In general, the seed of wild carrot is considered effective for promoting delayed menstruation, for treatment of urinary tract infections and kidney stones, and for flatulence and intestinal cramping.

DOCK ALE

*Infus'd in Beer, [it] is excellent for the Scurvy, and the Jaundice. The
Powder of the Seeds strengthen the Liver and stop all Fluxes of the Belly.*

—John Pechet, 1694[154]

The following recipe is really a treatment for scurvy, and again uses scurvy
grass. It also calls for pine or fir boughs, also powerful antiscorbutics, which
were used more often in Europe (along with juniper) than in North
America, where the preferred tree was spruce. I haven't made this recipe,
but I imagine that horseradish, fresh above-ground plant, would provide a
somewhat similar taste and effect to the scurvy grass. As sharp-pointed
dock, the dock called for in this recipe, is somewhat hard to find, yellow
dock, the dock of herbal commerce, could be substituted. Basically, the
recipe calls for making a pine or fir ale, then allowing the worked ale to sit
for a week with the herbs infusing in it in a muslin bag. The bag would be
withdrawn, and the bottles would be primed, filled, and capped. The beer is
ready to consume when the yeast has finished carbonating the bottled ale.

Dock Ale—1694

Ingredients

> 4 gallons water
> 4 pounds malt extract
> 3 handfuls new pine *or* fir, spring growth
> 3 handfuls scurvy grass *or* horseradish, above-ground plant
> 4 ounces sharp-pointed *or* yellow dock root, dried and ground
> peels of 4 oranges
> yeast

> Provide four Gallons of Small Ale; instead of Hops, boyl
> in it three Handfuls of the Tops of Pines, or Firr; after it
> has done working in the Vessel, put into a Canvas-bag

three Handfuls of Scurvy-grass, four Ounces of the Root
of Sharp-pointed Dock prepar'd, and the Peels of four
Oranges; hang the bag in the Vessel, with something to
sink the Bag: After it has stood a Week, and is clear,
drink of it for your ordinary Drink. This is frequently
used for the Scurvy, and is an excellent Diet-drink.[155]

ABOUT DOCK

Rumex acetus

> *Both the Swedish and English settlers are in the spring accustomed to
> prepare greens from [*Rumex spp.*]. . . . I must confess that the dish
> tastes very good.*
>
> —Peter Kalm, 1749[156]

The species in the preceding recipe is the sharp-pointed dock, *Rumex
acetus*, not the more commonly used yellow dock, *Rumex crispus*, though
either species would probably work as well. Sharp-pointed dock is better
known for treatment of scurvy, blood, and skin problems—yellow dock
for treatment of blood, skin, and liver problems. All the *Rumex* species,
however, are fairly high in the ascorbic acid content of their leaves. It is
odd, given that (and their effects were known in 1694), that Pechet
would use the root and not the leaves in his ale. However, yellow dock
and sharp-pointed dock can be used interchangeably, and both roots
have been used in the treatment of scurvy. The root has a marked effect
on liver function, increasing the liver's ability to detoxify the blood. The
root is high in iron and has been a traditional herb for treatment of iron
deficiency. It is used to clear the skin and is antibacterial. The root is
effective in the treatment of jaundice, promotes healthy liver and gallbladder function, and reduces glandular swelling and inflammation.
Dock root has been shown to be especially effective in the treatment of
skin conditions such as eczema, acne, and psoriasis.[157] The herb has mild

laxative properties, is tonic, bitter, and antibiotic.[158] Dock's primary use in contemporary practice herbal medicine is in the treatment of constipation, chronic skin complaints, and the liver.

COWSLIP ALE

Among the various beverages which good house-wives deemed it their duty to brew were Elderberry Beer, or Ebulon, Cowslip Ale, Blackberry Ale, China Ale, and Apricot Ale. Their names indicate to a great extent their composition.

—John Bickerdyke, 1890[159]

For about 300 years cowslip ale and wine were two of the most popular drinks throughout Europe. To my regret, I have not yet been able to find fresh cowslip flowers. Of all the ales I have read about, this is the one I wish the most to make.

Cowslip Ale—1674

Ingredients

    6 gallons water
    12 pounds sugar
    1 pint white wine
    1/2 peck cowslip flowers
    12 ounces citron or lemon juice
    1 or 2 lemons, halved
    yeast

> To every gallon of water add 2 pound of good whit shuger, boyle them together at Lest an houer, then taking of the scum, sett it too Colle till it bee hardly blood warme, then take too evry gallan 2 oz of Cittorn or Lemon, which must bee well beaten, with a quantity of

yeist fitt to sett it at worke, too 6 or 7 gallans I think wee us to put in 1/2 a pint, but of that more Less too youre Discretion or acording as the yeist is new or stale make a great brown toast hot spred over with yeist—putt the toast with the syrrup and yeist, beaten as a fore said into the Liquor and so Lett it stand and work 2 days and a night or 2 According as you find it worke if you find it worke not kindly stur it about with a ladell very well for a qr of an houer which will very much help it, after it hath stood the time to worke Take too 6 gallan 1/2 a peck of Couslip flouers put into a bagg fitt for the purpose made of Corse white Cloath Called bollster put it into a well sesoned vessell, if it hath had Latly wine in it the better, with a waite a bout 3 or 4 pound in the bottom of the bagg too keep the flouers downe, then put in the Liquor, to which add to over a gallan a pint of white wine, then put to it a Lemon or 2 Cutt in 1/2 then bung up the Caske, Close, Leving only a Littell vent hole open on the top of the Caske nere the bung and so Lett it stand a month or 5 weeks then draw it out into bottells, and Lay it up in the sand, in bottelling of it wee use to put in a Lumpe of sugger about as bigg as a large nuttmegg in to eatch bottell, this will keep good 9 or 12 months but may be drunke of in a weeke or tow.[160]

Cowslip Ale—1695

Ingredients

- 3 gallons water
- 5 pounds white sugar
- 4 quarts fresh cowslip flowers
- 1 pound syrup of lemons
- 2 spoonfuls ale yeast

How to make Cowslip Beer

Take three gallons of fair Water, and five Pound of Loaf-sugar, and Boil them for half an Hour, and scum it well, then let it stand till it is almost cold; then put in four Quarts of pickt Cowslips, gently bruised with two spoonfuls of Ale-yeast, and one Pound of Syrup of Lemons beaten with it, and let them stand close stopped three Days in Fermentation; then drain away the Liquor from the Herbs, and put it into a barrel, give it just room to Work, and so let it remain one month; then draw it off into Bottles upon a little Loaf-sugar, Cork it, and tie it down close, and it will keep a Year. The like may be done with Primroses, or any other Flowers.[161]

Cowslip Ale—1744

Ingredients

    1 bushel fresh cowslip flowers
    1 barrel ale

In the *London and County Brewer* (1744), is this receipt for Cowslip Ale: Take, to a barrel of ale a bushel of the flowers of cowslip pick'd out of the husks, and when your ale hath done working put them loose in the barrel without bruising. Let it stand a fortnight before you bottle it, and, when you bottle it, put a lump of sugar in each bottle.[162]

Cowslip Ale—Ca. 1900

Ingredients

    9 pints water
    1 quart fresh cowslip flowers
    2 pounds sugar
    2 spoonfuls yeast

Nine pints of water, two pounds of sugar. Boil and skim well. Pour it hot on one quart of picked cowslips. Next day strain and add two spoonfuls of yeast. Let it stand in an earthen pan a fortnight to work, covered close and stirred three times a day for the first three days. Then drain it into bottles with a little sugar and stop it tight. It will keep a year.[163]

ABOUT COWSLIPS
Primula veris

The flowers, when fresh, have a sweetish taste, and an odor suggestive of honey.
—Felter and Lloyd, 1895[164]

Like pink lady's slipper (*Cypripedium acaule*) in the United States, the English herb cowslip was highly overharvested. Though it still can be found in profusion in some parts of England, in other areas it is now scarce in the wild. I have never seen it used in American herbalism, but some English herbalists still use it as an important part of their practice. In appli-

cation its actions are much like those of pink lady's slipper. It is primarily a mild sedative and nervine. It relaxes and is highly effective in the treatment of stress, nervous excitation, tension, and insomnia. It is a reliable and gentle relaxant. It is also an expectorant and is quite useful in the treatment of all pectoral complaints. It relaxes the bronchus and helps move mucous trapped in the lungs up and out. It has been traditionally used in bronchitis, coughs, and colds.

Cowslip sends up a flowering stalk between March and May, and this is generally what is harvested for use in herbal medicine and in beers and

Cowslip (Primula veris)

ales. The flowering stalk should be dried quickly in the shade. From what I understand, it imparts a wonderful taste to beers and ales, but due to its scarcity, it should only be gathered if there is a profusion of plants, and the root, which possesses the same properties as the flowers, should never be gathered. Harvesting the flowering stalks allows the plant to continue to grow and propagate. Only one of every four flowering stalks should be gathered, the rest being left to seed.[165] In spite of its scarcity in the wild, it is often grown in England as a garden flower, and these domestic species should certainly be the ones used in ales.

PENNYROYAL ALE

Peny Royal *and* Balm *are noble Herbs, and of excellent use in Beer or Ale. They naturally raise and cheer the drooping Spirits, and open and cleane the passages after a friendly way, and with a mild Operation. And also they add great strength and fragrancy, and makes brave, well tasted Drink, good to prevent and cure all, or most of those Diseases which the wise Ancients have appropriated that Herb unto.*

—Thomas Tryon, 1691[166]

Pennyroyal is quite aromatic and imparts a refreshing bitterness and flavor to ales and beers.

Pennyroyal Ale
Ingredients
> 3 pounds brown sugar
>
> 24 ounces molasses
>
> 4 gallons water
>
> 3 ounces pennyroyal herb, dried
>
> yeast

Boil sugar, molasses, and herb for 30 minutes. Cool to 70 degrees F, strain into the fermenter, and add yeast. Ferment until complete, approximately one week, siphon into bottles primed with 1/2 teaspoon sugar, and cap. Ready to drink in 10 days to two weeks.

ABOUT PENNYROYAL
Mentha pulegium

> *It is of subtle, warm, and penetrating parts; it is also opening, discussive, and carminative; it promotes the menses, and loche, and prevents the flour albus.*
>
> —Nicholas Culpepper, 1651[167]

Pennyroyal has an extremely long history of use in herbal medicine. The European pennyroyal, *Mentha pulegium*, and its American cousin, *Hedeoma pulegioides*, possess similar properties and action. It is an annual herb with a branching square stem somewhat like mint, 6 to 12 inches high, with a profusion of small, light blue flowers. The above-ground herb is used in brewing and herbalism. It is best known for its action in starting delayed menstruation, and has been traditionally used as an abortifacient in large doses. The oil that is sometimes used for this is very strong, and toxic reactions are common from its use. Its use is not suggested. The herb also possesses strong relaxant properties and has been traditionally used in the treatment of anxiety. Part of this action is attributable to the wonderfully aromatic volatile oil pennyroyal possesses. It reduces flatulence and intestinal cramping and relaxes smooth muscle

Pennyroyal (Mentha pulegium)

contractions. Pennyroyal is a diaphoretic, promoting sweating, is a stimulant to low energy, and helps relax nervous states. It is thus of good use in colds and flus, where it helps lower fever. Its primary use, however, is in the treatment of delayed menstruation in women with pallor and lassitude, and who catch cold easily. Because of its action in promoting delayed menstruation, it should not be used during pregnancy.[168]

BETONY ALE

[Those Herbs] add great strength and fragrancy, and makes brave, well tasted Drink, good to prevent and cure all, or most of those Diseases which the wise Ancients have appropriated that Herb unto. The like is to be understood of Mint, Tansie, Wormwood, Broom, Cardis, Centuary, Eye-bright, Betony, Sage, Dandelion, and good Hay; also many others, according to their Natures and Qualities, and for those Diseases to which they are respectively appropriated.

—Thomas Tryon, 1691[169]

I am a particular fan of betony. It is a generous herb, quite giving of itself and its properties. I use the American betony in a great many herbal preparations and miss it greatly; it does not grow near my home in Washington State, as it did in Colorado, my former home. Its taste is quite agreeable.

Betony Ale

Ingredients

> 3-pound can dark malt extract
>
> 4 gallons water
>
> 2 pounds brown sugar
>
> 4 ounces betony herb, dried
>
> yeast

Boil the malt extract, sugar, and herb for 30 minutes. Cool to 70 degrees F and strain into fermenter; add yeast. Ferment until complete, approximately one week, siphon into bottles primed with 1/2 teaspoon sugar, and cap. Ready to drink in 10 days to two weeks.

ABOUT BETONY

Pedicularis spp.(American), *Betonica officinalis* (English)

> *The Leaves are Aromatick, and of a pleasant Taste, and agreeable to nature in Food and Physick. Counterfeit Tea, made of Sage, Betony, and Ground-pine, sweetened, and drank hot, is very good for the Gout, Head-ach, and Diseases of the Nerves; and eases Pain, occasioned by these Diseases.*
>
> —John Pechet, 1694[170]

The American betony is a somewhat fernlike plant standing to three feet in height. It tends to grow in clusters in wet, shady, sometimes marshlike locations. Various members of the *Pedicularis* family can be found throughout the United States. The European wood betony is a different species; however, all possess similar actions. The traditional herb used in beers and ales is the European species *Betonica officinalis*, which possesses a somewhat different taste than the American species. It is the above-ground herb that is used. Primarily betony is a skeletal muscle relaxant. It also possesses sedative and tranquilizing properties. It is extremely useful in nervous tension and stress where the muscles are stretched like a guitar string. Like cowslip and a number of other relaxant herbs traditionally used in beers and ales, betony enhances the relaxant properties of alcohol, producing a highly effective ale for nervous stress.[171]

MUSTARD ALE

They used to be a lot of ague in them days in the marshlands, Marsh Fever as they used to call it, but I have not heard of a case for many a year, except in men comen home from India or some such part. The cure was hot beer with mustard seed boiled in it, which was counted a fine powerful remedy.

—Gabrielle Hatfield, 1994[172]

This really sounds terrible to me, and I can't make myself try it or even imagine a recipe—you are on your own with this one. I suppose it must be something like ginger beer. However, I ran across references to it time and time again. It apparently was a common remedy in England, at least up until World War II. One fascinating thing is that some mustard seeds have a wild yeast that naturally occurs on them that will begin fermentation in beer. In many of the old herbal brewing recipes it is suggested that the brew be inoculated with a little mustard seed spread on toast and floated on the wort.

ABOUT MUSTARD

Brassica nigra or *B. alba*

Mustard groweth in Gardens and Corn-fields, hot and dry in the 3rd degree, and it under Mars. 'Tis excellent for cold Stomachs and cold Diseases, and as bad for the hot and cholerick; it resists Poysen, and strengthens the Heart; 'tis excellent for the Falling-sickness, Lethargy, Sneezing, and prevents an Ague, Sciatica, stoppage of Urine, Toothache, Bruises, Morphew; by gargling it preserves the Palate, Palsie of the Tongue: By steeping it in Ale and drinking it, the Louzey-Evil and Dropsy are cured.

—*An English Herbal*, 1690[173]

Mustard seed, white (*B. alba*) or black (*B. nigra*), is well known primarily as a culinary herb. The plants are indigenous to Europe but are naturalized in the United States and can be found wild. Mustard seed was formerly used in standard practice medicine in mustard plasters. Equal parts mustard seed, wheat flour, and lukewarm water were mixed and placed in gauze, and the whole was applied to the skin. Mustard plasters are extremely strong, producing ulceration if left on too long. They were, however, a reliable rubefacient (stimulating local blood supply in the skin) and used for many centuries. James Duke recommends their use in treatment of Raynaud's disease. Raynaud's disease is a cold condition of the fingers and hands, the fingers often turning blue-white from lack of peripheral circulation. Mustard plasters stimulate the blood supply in the hands. Duke recommends mixing four ounces mustard seed with enough water to make a paste, then applying it to the fingers. Mustard plasters have also been found effective in the treatment of sciatica and rheumatism.[174] Mustard is warming, like a number of herbs, and stimulates peripheral circulation when taken internally. It is also useful as a bronchial and sinus decongestant. If you have ever tried hot mustard and found your nose running immediately afterward, you can understand its usefulness for congestion.

GROUND PINE ALE

The parts used are the leaves and tops, which have a slightly terebinthinate, not unpleasant smell, and a rough taste, which properties are imparted to diluted alcohol.

—Felter and Lloyd, 1895[175]

Again, I haven't worked with this one. The following recipe is analytically stimulating, but, well, I can't summon up the enthusiasm to make it, and not having any ground pine, a native of Europe, nor scurvy grass either, I have a good excuse. The recipe must be exceptionally bitter, however, from the amount of wormwood and sage in it—adding to those the "rough taste" of the ground pine, it must be something to experience.

Ground Pine Ale—1694

Ingredients

    5 gallons middling ale
    10 handfuls scurvy grass
    2 handful fresh ground pine herb
    2 handful fresh wormwood herb
    6 handfuls sage herb
    6 oranges sliced
    2 parts barley meal
    1 part rye meal

To treat Gout and Scurvy

Take of Ground-pine and Wormwood, each two Handfuls; of Scurvy-grass ten Handfuls, of Mountain-sage six Handfuls, six Oranges sliced; put all into a Pye, made of two parts of Barley-meal, and one of Rye; bake it, and after shred it all small; then put it into a Bag, and hang it in five Gallons of Midling Ale: After six days, drink of it for your ordinary Drink.[176]

ABOUT GROUND PINE

Ajuga chamaepitys

> Ground Pine is a martial plant, hot and dry, warming and strengthening the nerves.
>
> —Nicholas Culpepper, 1651[177]

Ground pine is a European plant, used to some extent in historical herbal medicine, though never a major herb. It has an aromatic, somewhat turpentine-like smell. Historically it was considered specific for gout and rheumatism and stimulating delayed menstruation. It is diuretic, stimulant, and emmenagogue. Because of its strong diuretic action, it was used in dropsy (a condition of weak heart that causes fluid retention in the lower extremities). It is rarely used now.[178]

HOP BEER

They preserve Beer, and make it more wholesom and better tasted; and render it Diuretick. Beer, purges the Blood, is good in the Jaundice, and for Hypochondriack Diseases.

　　　　　　　　　　　　　　　　　　—John Pechet, 1694[179]

Hops rather make beer a physical drinke to keepe the body in health, than an ordinary drinke for the quenching of our thirst.

　　　　　　　　　　　　　　　　　　—John Gerarde, 1597[180]

Hops transmuted our wholesome ale into beer, which doubtless much alters its constitution. This one ingredient, by some suspected not unworthily, preserves the drink indeed, but repays the pleasure in tormenting diseases and a shorter life.

　　　　　　　　　　　　　　—John Evelyn, *Pomona*, 1670[181]

I explore some of the historical reasons that hops displaced the (formerly) amazing number of herbs in ales and beers in chapter 7 in the section on gruit. Because I like the underdog, it is hard for me to summon up much enthusiasm for hops as an additive in fermented beverages, but I suppose that hops themselves are not really at fault.

Historically beer was a barley ale with hops added. Ale, in England, was a fermented barley beverage with *no* herbal additives. On the Continent, ales were fermented barley malts with the addition of herbs other than hops. Meads, of course, would simply be metheglins if you added herbs, hops or not, and not really beers.

The great argument, for some 400 years, was whether or not to allow hops to gain ascendancy as an ale adulterant or additive. The supporters of hops brought forth three primary arguments for their use: (1) hops were a great preservative for ale; (2) hops were good for health; (3) hops were *the* antidrug (as in drug abuse) additive for ale (see "Gruit Ale" in chapter 7). Hop detractors, of course, argued that hops were not good for health, other preservatives worked just as well, and who wanted to go to sleep every time they drank ale? The argument was eventually settled after some 400 years of often rancorous debate. Part of the outcome was the passage of the world's first drug control laws in Germany in 1516. Ostensibly beer purity laws, one of their main purposes was to prevent the use of adulterants in beer that might have especially inebriating effects. Hops sedate the user, while being an excellent preservative, and seemed ideal. The domination of hops in beer wasn't final until World War II, though for all practical purposes, the contest was over by 1785.

In spite of my prejudice, hops are a good bitter and preservative for use in ale and beer. Here are three recipes for three different kinds of hopped fermentations. There are, of course, thousands more available in hundreds of beer publications.

A Simple Fermentation of Hops—1963

Ingredients

> 1 gallon water
>
> 1/2 ounce hops
>
> 1 pound white sugar

1/2 teaspoon caramel

1/2 ounce fresh gingerroot, crushed

yeast

> Boil all the ingredients except yeast in the water for an
> hour, and then make up to one gallon as necessary.
> Strain, cool to 70 degrees F, and add yeast and nutrient.
> Leave 48 hours in a warm place, closely covered, then
> siphon off (without disturbing yeast deposit) into screw-
> stoppered flagons, standing them in a cool place. Ready
> to drink in a week.[182]

A Light Lager

Ingredients

3 pounds dried malt extract

5 gallons water

2 ounces hops

1/2 ounce finishing hops

2 1/2 pounds corn sugar

1 1/2 teaspoons salt

2 teaspoons yeast nutrient

1/2 teaspoon citric acid

2 cups strong tea

lager beer yeast

> Boil 2 gallons water. Add malt extract, 2 ounces hops,
> corn sugar, salt, and citric acid. Boil for one hour, stir-
> ring constantly. At the same time, make 2 cups strong
> black tea (Lipton is fine). For the last 10 minutes of
> boil, add the final 1/2 ounce hops. Take from heat, let
> cool, and strain. Add wort, remaining water, and tea to

fermenter. When cooled to 70 degrees F, add yeast and
nutrient. Ferment until complete. Prime bottles, siphon,
and cap. Ready in 10 days.

Medieval Household Beer—1512

Ingredients

    1 gallon water

    2 1/4 pounds pale malt

    1 1/4 pounds amber malt

    1/5 ounce hops

    ale yeast

Mash grains for 2 hours with 170 degree water. Sparge
until one gallon liquor is obtained. Boil with hops for 2
hours. Cool and strain. Pour into fermenter, add yeast at
70 degrees F. Ferment until complete. Prime bottles,
siphon and cap. Age four months.[183]

ABOUT HOPS

Humulus lupulus

*Now as to the Nature of Hops; there is in them a most excellent
glance or friendly opening quality, more especially if they were
dried in the Sun, which is to be preferred before the Host or Kill; for
the spirituous part of this Plant is so nice, that it cannot endure
any violent heat without prejudice to its fine Virtues. . . . Hops naturally purge powerfully by Urine, if prepared and used with
understanding, so that they are unjustly charged to breed the Stone;
for on the contrary, they are a special Remedy against it, if ordered
with judgement, and as they ought to be; but as every thing consists
of Contraries, they may, and do occasion the Stone, and other*

*Diseases by accident, but it is only when they are abused, and after
their good Virtues are drawn off, or evaporated by the force of Fire,
as boyling, and the like, which is done in a trice, for no Herbs that
have been dried as they ought, will endure the Fire, or Boyling
without manifest prejudice to the best Virtues; but it is a gentle
Infusion that will naturally, and without violence to Nature,
extract or draw forth all that is desired in Hops, or any other dried
or prepared Herbs; but 'tis true, it will not rouze nor infect your
Liquor with their original harsh, bitter, fulsome, keen, hot
Properties, which too many, for want of distinguishing the
Principles of Nature, call Virtue and Strength; indeed Strength and
Fierceness it is, but far from Virtue in respect of Humane Bodies,
nothing fearce being more inimical and injurious thereunto, which
evil Properties in every thing are the more drawn forth and
increased by over much boyling, especially in Herbs and
Vegitations which have been already firmented and digested by the
Influences of the Sun and Elements, whereby the gross phlemy parts
are opened, and the Spirits set upon the wing ready to come forth
upon any gentle summons.*

—Thomas Tryon, 1691[184]

The hop plant is a meandering, clinging vine, and with sufficient water
will cover anything that will support its weight. It was introduced into
the United States from Europe for use in beer making and now grows
wild throughout the country. The part used in both brewing and herbalism are the hop cones or strobules. They look somewhat like small green
pinecones. They are about an inch long and three quarters of an inch in
diameter. Unlike pinecones, they are a light green, and the petals that
make up the cones delicate. Conventional brewers make a great deal of
the kind of hops they use, the amount of bitterness they possess, and
where they come from. Not being a fanatic, I find the wild ones sufficient

for home use. Hops are used in standard practice herbal medicine in three ways: as a soporific (sleep inducer), as a diuretic (promoting urine flow), and for menopause—they contain a high level of phytoestrogens and are a reliable alternative for pharmaceutical estrogen. Their strong antibacterial action makes them useful in wound powders and salves, but they are not often used for such conditions. Hops do possess tannins, from which beer benefits in flavor, and this lends hops a natural astringency, another positive factor for their use in treating wounds. The estrogenic activity of hops makes any use of the herb an anaphrodisiac for men who use them—that is, hops decrease sexual drive, erection, and desire. There is a well-known condition in England called Brewer's Droop. Both brewers and bartenders, from long-term exposure to the estrogenic properties of hops, eventually have difficulty sustaining erection.

Hops (Humulus lupulus)

The relaxant qualities of hops seem to negatively enhance depressive states and should only be used for sleep and nervous tension treatment in the absence of depression. The strong bitter action of hops stimulates gastric secretions and helps in feeble stomach conditions. Hops have been traditionally used to stuff pillows, hop pillows, to promote sleep. Hops are quite effective for this, but using a hop pillow can lead to a drugged feeling when you do finally wake up. I have used hops both in the treatment of menopause and endometriosis and found it remarkably effective for these conditions.[185]

BUCKBEAN (OR BOGBEAN) ALE

In Sweden the leaves are often used in brewing; two ounces of which
are said to equal a pound of hops, for which they are substituted.

—Charles Millspaugh, 1892[186]

I haven't yet been able to find this herb, but the proportions in this recipe
match its use in herbal practice, though going by Millspaugh's comparison to hops, it should be much less.

Buckbean (or Bogbean) Ale

Ingredients

> 5 pounds malted barley
>
> *or* 3-pound can dark malt extract
>
> 4 gallons water
>
> 2 pounds brown sugar
>
> 1 1/2 ounces bogbean herb, dried
>
> yeast

> Mash the barley in water at 150 degrees F for 90 min-
> utes. Sparge with boiling water until a total of 4 gal-
> lons is drawn off. Boil the 4 gallons water with the
> herb one hour. Strain and add brown sugar and stir
> until dissolved. Cool to 70 degrees F and pour into
> fermenter; add yeast. Ferment until complete, approxi-
> mately one week, siphon into bottles primed with 1/2
> teaspoon sugar, and cap. Ready to drink in 10 days to
> two weeks.

> Alternative Method: Or boil 1 gallon water, add 3-
> pound can of malt extract and 2 pounds sugar, stir until

dissolved, and allow to cool while you are boiling remaining 3 gallons of water with the herb. Cool both to 70 degrees F, strain, and pour both solutions into fermenter and continue as above.

ABOUT BUCKBEAN (OR BOGBEAN)

Menyanthes trifoliata

They are sometimes, among the common people, fermented with malt liquors for an antiscorbutic diet drink.

—William Lewis, 1791[187]

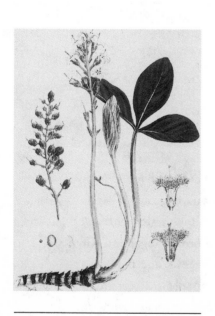

Buckbean (Menyanthes trifoliata)

Bogbean is a bitter, like so many other herbs used in ale, and thus stimulates stomach secretions, making it helpful in feeble gastric conditions. It is also a diuretic, stimulating urine flow, a cholagogue (producing gallbladder contraction), and an antirheumatic. It is a perennial plant, growing about a foot high and possessing leaf stalks with three leaves at the terminal end (*trifoliata*). Both the leaves and root can be used medicinally, though the leaves are generally more common in practice. Bogbean is indigenous to both the United States and Europe and likes boggy, marshy conditions (hence its name, *bog*bean). It has generally been used as a stomach tonic and for its anti-inflammatory properties in treatment of rheumatism.[188]

TANSY ALE

When you infuse in your Beer or Ale Wormwood, Broom,
Tansey, Cardis, or any other herb which exceeds in bitterness, you
ought not to let them lye in your Wort above half an hour, or if you
put in a good quantity, a quarter of an hour will be enough.

—Thomas Tryon, 1691

Tansy was called *olkall*, "ale man," in some parts of Norway and was also used from time to time in Europe. Thomas Tryon in his *The Art of Brewing Beer and Other Sorts of Liquors* (London, 1691) mentions it several times. Tansy is very bitter and, like wormwood, should be used with a light hand.

Tansy Ale

Ingredients

    5 pounds malt extract (two-row)

    4 gallons water

    2 pounds brown sugar

    1/2 ounce tansy herb, dried

    yeast

Mash the barley in water at 150 degrees F for 90 minutes. Sparge with boiling water until a total of 4 gallons is drawn off. Boil the 4 gallons water with the herb one hour. Strain, add brown sugar, and stir until dissolved. Cool to 70 degrees F and pour into fermenter; add yeast. Ferment until complete, approximately one week, siphon into bottles primed with 1/2 teaspoon sugar, and cap. Ready to drink in 10 days to two weeks.

ABOUT TANSY

Tanacetum vulgare

> *It is an agreeable bitter, a carminative, and a destroyer of worms, for which a powder of the flowers should be taken from six to twelve grains at night and morning.*
>
> —Nicholas Culpepper, 1651[189]

Tansy looks somewhat like yarrow, the leaves and flowers being used in standard practice herbal medicine. Traditionally, tansy has been used for expelling worms from the digestive tract, as a digestive tonic, and to stimulate delayed menstruation. It possesses a strong volatile oil that can be toxic in large doses. The oil has sometimes been used as an abortifacient with disastrous results. The plant is safe when used with discretion but is not now much used in standard practice herbalism. Like all bitter herbs, when tansy is used for fermentation, a little goes a long way. Like wormwood, the volatile oil of tansy is high in thujone and most likely would produce a high state of inebriation when used in beers and ales. It is moderately high in tannins and vitamin C. The tannins would help in the ale's flavor, the vitamin C being useful in the treatment of scurvy. Because of the tannin content and the volatile oil, which possesses antibacterial properties, the herb would be of some use in the treatment of wounds as a poultice or wound powder. Tansy has traditionally been used to repel insects and contains a number of insect-repelling compounds. During the Middle Ages, its aromatic smell (from the volatile oil) and its insect-repelling properties caused it to be a common herb strewn on floors. It kept down insect infestations and brightened the smell of the home.[190]

CARDAMOM SEED ALE

*Cardamoms are used in England to give strength to spirits and beer,
and are extensively mixed with gin, in conjunction with Capsicum
and Juniper berries, which, however, is an illegal practice.*

—Mrs. R. Lee's *Trees, Plants, and Flowers*, 1824[191]

Cardamom is a member of the ginger family and is used throughout Asia,
the Middle East, and South America as a culinary spice.

Cardamom Seed Ale

Ingredients

- 3 pounds brown sugar
- 4 gallons water
- 1 teaspoon cardamom seed, powdered
- yeast

Boil sugar, water, and herb for 30 minutes. Cool to 70
degrees F and pour into fermenter; add yeast. Ferment
until complete, approximately one week, siphon into
bottles primed with 1/2 teaspoon sugar, and cap. Ready
to drink in 10 days to two weeks.

ABOUT CARDAMOM

Elettaria cardamomum

*In Great Britain and the United States Cardamoms are employed to a
small extent as an ingredient of curry powder, and in Russia, Sweden,
Norway, and parts of Germany are largely used for flavoring cakes
and in the preparation of liqueurs, etc. In Egypt they are ground and*

put in coffee, and in the East Indies are used both as a condiment and
for chewing with betel. Their use was known to the ancients.

—Maude Grieve, 1931[192]

Cardamom is warming, somewhat pungent, and aromatic. Though considered carminitive, stimulant, and aromatic, it has been used primarily to relieve flatulence and is of use, like coriander, as an anticramping and carminitive herb and as a flavoring. It has been found helpful in indigestion. The volatile oil is more completely soluble in alcohol than water and is thus more effectively extracted by placing the seeds in the fermenting vessel than simply boiling them with the wort. It is not much used in herbal practice now, being more of a culinary spice. However, cardamom seed has been found to have specific antibacterial activity against *Candida albicans* and *E. coli*, both of which have been shown to play a part in urinary tract infections (UTI). Further, clinical examination has shown that the seeds also possess laxative, diuretic, stomachic, and antiasthmatic effects.[193] The laxative and anticramping effects make it a good herb to use in any herbal treatment for constipation, while the diuretic action and its activity against UTI organisms make it a useful adjunct in herbal treatment of UTI infections. However, treatment of UTI with cardamom would probably be most efficacious if cardamom were simply added to the diet.[194]

COW PARSNIP ALE

The people of Polonia and Lithuania used to make a drinke with the
decoction of this herbe, and leven or some other things made of meale,
which is used instead of beere and other ordinarie drinke.

—John Gerarde, 1597[195]

Cow parsnip is a common herb throughout the world and has found its use in traditional indigenous cultures wherever it grows. It takes some time to get to know it (and few herbalists make the time), but it repays friendship well.

Cow Parsnip Ale

Ingredients

> 3-pound can dark malt extract
>
> 3 gallons water
>
> 3 ounces cow parsnip root, dried
>
> yeast

> Boil malt extract, water, and herb for 30 minutes. Cool to 70 degrees F, strain into the fermenter, and add yeast. Ferment until complete, approximately one week, siphon into bottles primed with 1/2 teaspoon sugar, and cap. Ready to drink in 10 days to two weeks.

ABOUT COW PARSNIP

Heracleum lanatum

> *The seed is of a sharp cutting quality, and is a fit medicine for a cough and shortness of breath, the falling sickness and jaundice. The root is available for all the purposes aforesaid.*
>
> —Nicholas Culpepper, 1651[196]

Cow parsnip is another member of the *Umbelliferae* family, and like the others (fennel, caraway, etc.) it is highly effective in treating flatulence, indigestion, heartburn, and nausea. The plant grows throughout the United States and is considered a problem weed by most states, who try their best to eradicate it. The plant is large, often four feet or more in height, with huge leaves and hollow stems. The root is acrid, with a particularly cow parsnip smell when fresh, and should be dried before use. It looks something like a parsnip, whitish with a longish branching root, hence the "parsnip" part of its name (I don't know where the "cow" part came from). Michael Moore has suggested its use (it is a traditional Hispanic remedy) in the treatment of the pain of hiatus hernia. I have suggested its use in this condition a number of times and found its effects immediate and sure. The root and seeds possess similar properties and can be used interchangeably. It is bitter and so stimulates gastric secretions; it also possesses antibacterial, antiseptic, analgesic, and antispasmodic activity. I have used it in gum inflammations for both its analgesic and antiseptic properties. I don't much care for the taste, but it does work. It is a perennial plant that tends to grow in profusion and can be gathered easily when found. The root can be dug at any time of the year, but I tend to prefer it in the spring when it is larger. The leaf stems look much like celery and were traditionally eaten as a spring food by indigenous peoples. The outer skin is peeled off—it possesses a bitter white sap that can cause dermatitis—and the inner core is eaten like celery. The roots were also cooked fresh, the initial water discarded and the roots eaten after a second boiling in clean water. Both root and stems were dried and saved for inclusion in soups later in the year.[197]

MUGWORT ALE

The Mugwort is said to have derived its name from having been used to flavour drinks. It was, in common with other herbs, such as Ground Ivy, used to a great extent for flavoring beer before the introduction of hops. For this purpose, the plant was gathered when in flower and dried, the fresh herb being considered unsuitable for this object: malt liquor was then boiled with it so as to form a strong decoction, and the liquid thus prepared was added to the beer. Until recent years, it was still used in some parts of the country to flavour the table beer brewed by cottagers.

—Maude Grieve, 1931[198]

Mugwort is a member of the same genus as wormwood, *Artemisia absinthium* (see chapter 7), but its effects are much milder.

Mugwort Ale

Ingredients

>   3 pounds brown sugar
>
>   24 ounces molasses
>
>   4 gallons water
>
>   2 ounces dried mugwort herb
>
>   yeast

Boil sugar, molasses, water, and herb for 30 minutes. Cool to 70 degrees F, strain into fermenter, and add yeast. Ferment until complete, approximately one week, siphon into bottles primed with 1/2 teaspoon sugar, and cap. Ready to drink in 10 days to two weeks.

ABOUT MUGWORT

Artemisia vulgaris

Its tops, leaves and flowers are full of virtue; they are aromatic, and most safe and excellent in female disorders.

—Nicholas Culpepper, 1651[199]

Mugwort is one of the primary sacred herbs of the ancient Europeans and is noted as one of the nine sacred herbs in the *Lacnunga*, a Wessex writing of the tenth century. Remains of smoked mugwort wreaths have been found in ancient Irish archeological sites. One of the most ancient pre-Christian lays about mugwort comments on its powerful attributes.

Have in mind, Mugwort, what you made known,
What you laid down, at the great denouncing.
Una your name is, oldest of herbs
Of might against thirty, and against three,
Of might against venom and the onflying,
Of might against the vile She who fares through the land.

Like all members of this family, mugwort has been traditionally used throughout the world in sacred ceremonies, by indigenous peoples as smudge and in sweat lodges, and for offerings.

First and foremost, mugwort has long been considered a sacred woman's herb, used particularly for female reproductive disorders. It has also been traditionally used for aiding digestion. Its bitter constituents stimulate digestion and tone the stomach. It is a mild nervine used in mild cases of nervous tension and depression. It has also been used as an emmenagogue (stimulating menstruation) to regularize menstrual cycles. It contains small amounts of thujone, listed as a narcotic poison by the FDA, tannins, bitter principles, inulin, and other constituents. Inulin helps maintain blood sugar levels in the body and has been shown to be of use in the treatment of diabetes. Mugwort, like all the *Artemisia* species, contains artemesinin, though less than the other members of the family. It has been shown in vitro to possess antimalarial activity, though weak. It has also shown reliable antibacterial activity against *Staphylococcus aureus*, to possess antimicrobial activity, to be antifungal and anthelmintic. It has shown antibacterial activity against *Pseudomonas*, *Escherichia coli*, *Klebsiella*, *Streptococcus mutans*, and others.[200] Laboratory studies have shown a consistent, though weak, uterine stimulant action by mugwort. Traditional folk herbalists in more than 50 countries have used mugwort consistently for regularizing menstruation (used both to stimulate scanty menstruation or slow excessive bleeding—either after childbirth or during menstruation), to calm hysteria and for nervous disorders, as a tonic, to expel worms, and as a poultice for wounds. Primarily it has been used in gynecological disorders (usually scanty or excessive bleeding) with attendant nervous conditions.[201]

GENTIAN ALE

Before the introduction of hops, Gentian, with many other bitter herbs, was used occasionally in brewing.

—Maude Grieve, 1931[202]

Gentian is tremendously bitter and is a traditional ingredient in "bitters." I use its American relative a fair amount, though almost never as a bitter. Having a surplus of stomach secretions, I view the production of more with a kind of mild horror. Gentian extract is available from most health food stores and, yes, it is strong enough to flavor this recipe quite nicely. It could easily be substituted for hops in its degree of bitterness. I found the following recipe to be quite palatable.

Gentian Ale—1829

Ingredients

> 3 pounds molasses
>
> 6 gallons water
>
> 1 pint beer yeast
>
> 2 ounces gentian extract
>
> grated gingerroot to taste

> Boil, for twenty minutes, three pounds of molasses, in from six to eight gallons of soft water, with . . . a little extract of gentian. When cooled in the tub, add a pint of

good beer-yeast, or from four to six quarts of fresh worts from the brewer's vat. Cover the beer (and all fermenting liquids) with blankets or coarse cloths. Pour it from the lees and bottle it. You may use sugar for molasses which is lighter. This is a cheap and very wholesome beverage. A little ginger may be added to the boiling liquid if the flavour is liked.[203]

ABOUT GENTIAN
Gentiana lutea

[Gentian] strengthens the stomach exceedingly, helps digestion, comforts the heart, and preserves it against faintings and swoonings.

—Nicholas Culpepper, 1651[204]

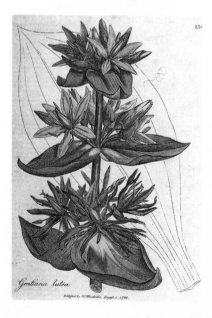

Gentian (Gentiana lutea)

Gentian is primarily a digestive bitter and stimulates gastric secretions and function. It is one of the oldest digestive tonic herbs. Its American relative, *Swertia radiata*—green gentian or cebadilla, is used similarly, being somewhat stronger and more energetic in its actions. The root of the plant is used and is indicated in all conditions of feeble digestion. Additionally, it is a mild stimulant to the circulation and warming to the body. I have rarely worked with the English plant and have come to use somewhat regularly the American version. I have found it easily throughout the Rocky Mountains. It is a biennial plant, the second year putting up a fairly tall (three to four feet) stalk covered with one of the few green flowers I know of. The flowers are remarkably beautiful, the entire plant quite lovely. The American root is useful as an antifungal, though somewhat mild in its effects. I have found it to be too weak for athlete's fungus without other herbs in addition. Its most interesting property is its antitumor activity, for which it has been traditionally used in Mexico and southern New Mexico. The dried root is powdered, mixed with Vaseline into a thick paste, and placed on skin tumors for 72 hours, covered with a gauze bandage. At removal, the tumor is shrunken and often comes off with the bandage. I have seen this work, though I am unaware of any research on this aspect of the plant. I have never heard of the English plant being used in this manner. In its traditional use in beers and ales, the English plant offers itself primarily as a stomach tonic and bitter. The English gentian contains a fermentable sugar that would be of use in ales and beers and is somewhat mucilaginous, which would also help to coat and soothe the stomach. [205]

LESSER BURNET ALE

It gives a grace in the drynkynge.

—John Gerarde, 1597[206]

I have never found lesser burnet, nor am I sure that it is much used anymore in herbal practice. But I have come across references to it many times, enough to indicate it was held in high esteem in ales and beers for many years. From the amount used in traditional herbal preparations, the amount for the following ale should be about right. A more easily found herb that may be substituted for it is angelica (see appendix 3). Angelica was used to some extent in medicinal ales and beers (see appendix 2); it has a quite agreeable taste and smell in ales.

Lesser Burnet Ale

Ingredients

5 pounds malted barley

or 3-pound can malt extract

2 pounds brown sugar

4 gallons water

3 ounces dried burnet herb

yeast

Mash the barley in water at 150 degrees F for 90 minutes. Sparge with boiling water until a total of 4 gallons is drawn off. Boil the 4 gallons water with the herb for one hour. Strain and add sugar; stir until dissolved. Cool to 70 degrees F and pour into fermenter; add yeast. Ferment until complete, approximately one week, siphon into bottles primed with 1/2 teaspoon sugar, and cap. Ready to drink in 10 days to two weeks.

Alternative Method: Or boil 1 gallon water, add 3-pound can of malt extract and sugar, stir until dissolved, and allow to cool while you are boiling remaining 3 gallons of water with the herb. Cool both to 70 degrees F, strain, and pour both solutions into fermenter and continue as above.

ABOUT BURNET

Pimpinella saxifraga

> *Turner advised the use of the herb, infused in wine or beer, for the cure of gout and rheumatism.*

> —Maude Grieve, 1931[207]

Burnet was used commonly in standard practice medical herbalism in Europe for a long time. Felter and Lloyd comment that this perennial "has a pungent, biting, balsamic, sweetish, and bitterish taste."[208] Traditionally, it was used as a diaphoretic, diuretic, vulnerary, and salad herb.[209]

ELECAMPANE ALE

The roots and herbes beaten and put into new ale or beer and daily drunk, cleareth, strengtheneth and quickeneth the sight of the eyes.
—Nicholas Culpepper, 1651[210]

Elecampane roots have a good taste. I have used them for years in cough syrups. There is something wholesome and uplifting about this plant.

Elecampane Ale
Ingredients

   3-pound can malt extract
   2 pounds brown sugar
   4 gallons water
   3 ounces dried elecampane root
   yeast

Boil sugar, malt extract, herb, and water for 30 minutes. Cool to 70 degrees F, strain into fermenter, and add yeast. Ferment until complete, approximately one week, siphon into bottles primed with 1/2 teaspoon sugar, and cap. Ready to drink in 10 days to two weeks.

Elecampane (Inula helenium)

ABOUT ELECAMPANE

Inula helenium

The Root is very thick, without brown, within white, and of an Aro-
matick Taste, and smells sweet and pleasantly, especially when dried.

—John Pechet, 1694[211]

Elecampane's Latin name, *helenium*, comes from Helen of Troy. The plant
is said to have grown wherever her tears fell (she cried a lot). The roots of
elecampane have enjoyed a strong place in herbal medicine for millennia.
It is expectorant, antitussive, diaphoretic, and antibacterial.[212] Clinical trial
has shown it to possess effectiveness in chronic bronchitis and to possess
stomachic and analgesic properties.[213] Research on its constituents have
shown that some of them possess powerful antibacterial, antifungal, and
sedative properties.[214] Its primary use in herbal medicine has been to soften
bronchial mucous, stimulate expectoration, and to calm chronic coughing.
It is quite effective for these conditions and is commonly used in cough
syrups in standard medical herbal practice. Its antibacterial action would
make it indicated in these conditions when the respiratory infection has
bacterial roots.[215] It has also been found to possess powerful antiamoebic
activity and is useful for the treatment of amoebic dysentery and gastrointestinal amoebic disorders.[216] In addition, elecampane contains inulin,
which has been found to exert a significantly beneficial effect on blood
sugar levels, making it a good herb to use in the treatment of diabetes.[217]

EYEBRIGHT ALE

[Eyebright] tunned with strong beer that it may work together and
drunk, or the powder of the dried herb mixed with sugar, a little mace,

fennel seed and drunk, or eaten in broth; or the said powder made into an electuary with sugar and taken, hath the same powerful effect to help and restore the sight.

—John Gerarde, 1597[218]

Eyebright can be found, from the Middle Ages, as an ingredient of many ales, beers, and meads. A highly respected herb of its time, it is still in common use in herbal practice in the United States and standard practice medicine in Europe.

Eyebright Ale

Ingredients

> 5 pounds malted barley
>
> 2 pounds brown sugar
>
> 4 gallons water
>
> 4 ounces dried eyebright herb
>
> yeast

Mash the barley in water at 150 degrees F for 90 minutes. Sparge with boiling water until a total of 4 gallons is drawn off. Boil the 4 gallons water with the herb for one hour. Strain, add 2 pounds sugar and stir until dissolved. Cool to 70 degrees F and pour into fermenter; add yeast. Ferment until complete, approximately one week, siphon into bottles primed with 1/2 teaspoon sugar, and cap. Ready to drink in 10 days to two weeks.

Eyebright
(Euphrasia officinalis)

ABOUT EYEBRIGHT

Euphrasia officinalis

> *The name Euphrasia is of Greek origin, derived from* Euphrosyne
> *(gladness), the name of one of the three graces who was distinguished
> for her joy and mirth.*
>
> —Maude Grieve, 1931[219]

Eyebright is an annual plant one to five inches in height. The herb itself is used and has had a history of use in eye complaints for some 2,000 years, hence its common name, eyebright. There is also a tradition of its brightening the spirit, causing the eyes to brighten as a result, that gave rise to its Latin name from the Greek goddess of gladness. The leaves possess a somewhat bitter, astringent taste. The bitter principle is soluble in water and imparts its flavor to beers, ales, and herbal preparations. It is anticatarrhal, astringent, and anti-inflammatory. It is extremely useful in hay fever and acute sinusitis, helping to reduce inflammation of the sinus cavities. It has long been used as a strong tea to wash the eyes in the treatment of eye infections such as conjunctivitis. Its astringent action from the tannins in the plant can be useful in external applications for wounds, but the herb is most often employed for eye inflammations. Little research has been conducted on eyebright, but clinical trials, especially on inflamed eyes with irritation, stinging, and watery discharge, and in conjunctivitis, have borne out the herb's traditional use for these conditions. I have used it successfully in the treatment of acute sinusitis and hay fever in combination with ephedra (*Ephedra vulgaris*) and ambrosia (*Ambrosia artemisiifolia*) with excellent results. The internal use of the herb in eye complaints seems to also bear good results.[220]

CHAMOMILE ALE

The whole plant is odoriferous and of value, but the quality is chiefly centered in the flower-heads or capitula, the part being used medicinally, the herb itself being used in the manufacture of herb beers.

—Maude Grieve, 1931[221]

Chamomile has risen to fame in our time as an herbal tea. Not much thought on by most of us, it has begun to find its place as more than just a quaint tea from the past. It has a historical reputation of increasing the inebriating quality of fermentations in which it is included, but in a kind, mild, chamomile sort of way.

Chamomile Ale—*A Variation of a Seventeenth-Century Recipe*

Ingredients

   2 gallons water

   Juice of one lemon

   8 ounces dried chamomile, whole plant

   2 pounds sugar

   yeast

Boil chamomile and water for one hour, cool, strain, and pour over sugar. Stir until sugar is dissolved, cool to 70 degrees F, pour into fermenter, and add yeast. Ferment until complete. Prime bottles, siphon, and cap. Ready in one week.

Chamomile (Matricaria chamomilla)

ABOUT CHAMOMILE
Matricaria chamomilla

> 'Tis a great Cordial, giveth ease and causeth Sweat if the Flowers
> and green Tea boil'd in Water of Wine and drank; it sweats
> strongly, eases Pain at the Stomach, and cures Agues. . . . In any
> sort of Ague, boil a handful in a pint of Ale till half be consum'd,
> then strain and drink it before the Fit comes, and sweat; do this three
> times, and it cures.
>
> —An English Herbal, 1690[222]

Chamomile is one of the most famous of herbs. Its botanical name,
Matricaria, comes from the word *mater*, meaning "mother," and refers to
its use as an herb that can relieve cramping in the uterus. It is a spindly
plant, one to two feet tall, with small, lacy leaves and the familiar yel-
low-and-white flower heads. It is indigenous to Europe; however, its relative, garden chamomile, *Anthemus nobile*, is grown throughout America
and possesses similar properties. The flowers are traditionally used in
herbal medicine, though, as Maude Grieve notes, the whole above-
ground plant was used in brewing. Chamomile has a recognizable, fragrant odor that is quite enjoyable. It is a mild yet reliable herb in its
actions. It possesses mild sedative properties, making it extremely useful
for children suffering from coughs or colds, helping them relax and
sleep. It lowers fevers, stimulates sweating, and its antispasmodic action
helps in soothing coughs. Its anti-inflammatory action helps in the
treatment of bronchitis and gastritis.[223] It also possesses antimicrobial
and vulnerary properties.[224] These in combination with its anti-inflammatory action make it an excellent herb for use in wound powders and
salves for abrasions, cuts, and infections.[225]

In cases of severe skin problems, such as acne, eczema, and psoriasis,
a wash of the herb helps reduce inflammation and infection. Clinical trials
in Europe have noted in addition an antiallergenic aspect of the herb and

have borne out uses of chamomile for skin conditions.[226] It is antispasmodic and carminative and thus of benefit in flatulence and intestinal cramping and colic. It has been found to have a definite antiulcerogenic action. This in combination with its anti-inflammatory and antispasmodic properties have made it an herb of choice for the treatment of gastric ulceration in Germany. Further research in Germany has shown it to have a definite ability to inactivate bacterial toxins. In studies there, both staphyloccal and streptococcal toxins were responsive to extremely low doses of the herb. The antibiotic activity of chamomile has also been shown to be of great benefit in bacterial infections of the upper respiratory tract.[227] Because of its mild yet reliable action in so many areas, chamomile is a tremendously useful herb in any herbal repertory. Its use in beer and ale makes it a good medicinal ale for gastric problems, ulceration, nervousness and tension, and respiratory infections. Both its smell and slight bittering quality enhance ales and beers.

BRACKEN FERN ALE

In Siberia and in Norway, the uncoiled fronds have been employed with about two-thirds of their weight of malt for brewing a kind of beer.

—Maude Grieve, 1931[228]

Bracken ferns are those prehistoric-looking plants you may have seen in movies that grow under old-growth trees in the Washington rainforests. They evoke images of ancient times and dinosaurs. They have also been used as food and as an ingredient in ales for thousands of years.

Bracken Fern Ale

Ingredients

3 pounds malt

2 pounds bracken fern fronds

2 gallons water

yeast

> Boil bracken fern fronds in 2 gallons water for one hour
> and strain liquid. At 170 degrees F, pour liquid onto
> malt and let stand 90 minutes. Drain liquid off malt,
> then sparge malt again, using same liquid. Cool to 70
> degrees F and pour into fermenter. Add yeast and fer-
> ment until done. Prime bottles, fill, and cap. Ready to
> drink in one to two weeks.

ABOUT BRACKEN FERN

Pterdium aquilinum

> *The green leaves eaten, purge the belly, and expel choleric and water-
> ish humours that trouble the stomach.*
>
> —Nicholas Culpepper, 1651[229]

Bracken fern grows throughout the globe and is a typical fern. It is usually
from 2 to 3 feet in height but can reach 8 to 10 feet in rainforests. Its Latin
name, *Pteris*, means "feather," as does the common name, fern, which is
derived from the Anglo-Saxon *fepern*, "a feather." Bracken fern root is 33.5
percent starch, the rest being mostly bitter substances, mucilage, and tannins. It would therefore be effective in ales and beers. The starch would be
converted by the diastase present in the malt, adding more sugar to the ferment. Further, the tannins and bitters would enhance the flavor. The plant is
astringent and anthelmintic (expels worms). It has been used traditionally in
dysentery, diarrhea, and hemorrhages. Topically it has been of use in ulcers
and stubborn wounds, the mucilaginous content and the tannins helping to
soothe and stimulate healing. Its most powerful and consistent effects have
been found in the treatment of dysentery and diarrhea. The young shoots
and root have been used as foods in many countries for millennia.[230]

HYSSOP ALE

*In a fifteenth-century manuscript, it is included among "Herbes
for the Coppe."*

—Margaret Freeman, 1943, citing the
Hortus Sanitatis, or *Gart Der Gesundheit*, 1485[231]

Hyssop has been used in medical herbal practice for at least 3,000 years. It is
a wonderfully aromatic herb, imparting a fresh, vital quality to ale and beer.

Hyssop Ale

Ingredients

> 12 ounces molasses
>
> 8 ounces brown sugar
>
> 1 gallon water
>
> 1/2 ounce dried hyssop herb
>
> yeast

> Boil molasses, water, sugar, and herb for 30 minutes.
> Cool to 70 degrees F and pour into fermenter; add yeast.
> Ferment until complete, approximately one week,
> siphon into bottles primed with 1/2 teaspoon sugar, and
> cap. Ready to drink in 10 days to two weeks.

ABOUT HYSSOP

Hyssopus officinalis

> *Of course there were many kinds of ale that were dependent upon their various ingredients . . . , "Hysope-Ale," "worm-wood ale," "ale of rosemary," and "Bettony." "Heather ale" was of very ancient origin in certain parts of the country and butter ale was most plentiful in the seventeenth century.*
>
> —Edward Emerson, 1908[232]

Hyssop (Hyssopus officinalis)

Hyssop's name was derived from the Hebrew name Esob or Ezeb and is mentioned frequently throughout the Bible as an herb that cleanses and purifies the body. It is a native to Europe and is naturalized throughout the world, including North America. It has a particularly "herb" look, being something of a cross between rosemary and mint, and it grows as a low bush, reaching up to two feet in height. For medicinal use the above-ground plant is usually gathered before it flowers. It contains a strongly aromatic volatile oil that accounts for many of its physical actions. Though rarely used in contemporary standard practice herbalism, it possesses a wide range of actions that make it useful in a number of complaints. Hyssop is antispasmodic, expectorant, diaphoretic, sedative, bitter, and carminative. Its bitterness stimulates gastric secretions, and like most bitters, it is a nice adjunct to ales and beers. Its aromatic oils are quite uplifting to the spirits. Its antispasmodic activity makes it useful in chronic coughs and bronchitis, and its diaphoretic (sweating) action makes it of benefit in colds and flu. These together make it a good herb for any upper respiratory infection. Its sedative action makes it beneficial in anxiety and stress-related conditions. Hyssop contains marrubin, which horehound also possesses. While calming chronic coughing, that constituent also helps break up mucous trapped in the lungs and move it up and out of the system. It is particularly useful in upper respiratory infections as an herbal steam. Some of the compounds in hyssop have shown antiviral activity, thus making it especially useful in treatment of flu and *Herpes sim-plex* virus.[233] One compound in hyssop, MAR-10, has also been found to inhibit the replication of the HIV virus in test tube trials without toxicity to healthy cells. Though research on hyssop is still relatively new, it is consistently showing a range of antiviral activity. Hyssop also stimulates menstruation and is useful for delayed or scanty menstruation. Though several herbal texts suggest caution in its use, clinical trials have shown no known toxicity even in large quantities.[234] Still, it is contraindicated in pregnancy because of its tendency to stimulate menstruation.

RUE BEER

Rue is mentioned in the fifteenth century manuscript among "herbes for the coppe."

—Margaret Freeman, 1943, citing the
Hortus Sanitatis, or Gart Der Gesundheit, 1485[235]

Rue is another herb that was once used a great deal but has now fallen out of favor. Its common European name was "herb of grace" and reflected the esteem in which it was held. It is strongly bitter and should be used with a light hand.

Rue Beer
Ingredients

> 5 pounds malted barley
> *or* 3-pound can malt extract
> 2 pounds brown sugar
> 4 gallons water
> 1 ounce dried rue herb
> yeast

Mash the barley in water at 150 degrees F for 90 minutes. Sparge with boiling water until a total of 4 gallons is drawn off. Boil the 4 gallons water with the herb for one hour. Strain, add 2 pounds sugar, and stir until dissolved. Cool to 70 degrees F and pour into fermenter; add yeast. Ferment until complete, approximately one week, siphon into bottles primed with 1/2 teaspoon sugar, and cap. Ready to drink in 10 days to two weeks.

Alternative Method: Or boil 1 gallon water, add 3-pound can of malt extract and 2 pounds sugar and allow to cool while you are boiling remaining 3 gallons of water with the herb. Cool both to 70 degrees F, strain, and pour both solutions into fermenter and continue as above.

ABOUT RUE
Ruta graveolens

Common rue (Ruta graveolens)

For feebleness of sight put rue in a pot with ale and let the patient to drink of it.
—Banckes Herbal, 1525[236]

Rue's botanical name, *Ruta*, comes from the Greek *reuo*, meaning "to set free." The herb was so named because of its physical and spiritual actions. It was considered a powerful remedy against disease, setting the body free. Additionally, it was considered to bestow second sight and free the spirit from negative and harmful influences. Rue is primarily an herb that strongly stimulates menstruation. In large doses it can cause abortion and should not be used in pregnancy. It also possesses an antispasmodic action that makes it useful in cramping of the intestinal tract, and in chronic coughing. Its aromatic properties give it a place in alleviating tension headaches and anxiety.[237] Its use in beers can be traced to its bittering action and its aromatic properties. It was often used in ancient times as a culinary herb and is still used in Italy for this, being a common additive to salads.

LEMON BALM ALE

Bawme drunke in wine, is good against the biting of venemous beasts,
comforteth the harte, and driueth away all melancholie and sadnesse.
—John Gerarde, 1597[238]

Lemon balm was one of the most widely used herbs in beers and ales of the Middle Ages. I found it referred to time and time again. It is quite a pleasant plant, imparting a good taste and aroma to any preparation. It was traditionally called balm. Here are two recipes.

Lemon Balm Ale—1827

Ingredients

> 10 pounds brown sugar
> 4 gallons water
> 1 1/4 pound fresh lemon balm tops
> yeast

> Boil ten pounds of moist sugar in four gallons water for over an hour, and skim it well. Pour into an earthenware vessel to cool. Bruise a pound and a quarter of balm tops and put them into a small cask with yeast

spread on toast, and when the above liquor is cool, pour it on the balm. Stir them well together, and let the mixture stand for twenty-four hours, stirring it frequently; then close it up, lightly at first and more securely after fermentation has quite ceased. When it has stood six or eight weeks bottle it off, putting a lump of sugar into each bottle. Cork the bottle well.[239]

Lemon Balm Ale — *Another Recipe*
Ingredients

    4 pounds dark brown sugar
    3 gallons water
    1/2 pound dried lemon balm herb
    yeast

Boil 3 gallons water with 8 ounces dried lemon balm herb and 4 pounds sugar for one hour; skim off scum. Let cool and strain into fermenter. Add yeast. Ferment until complete, 7 to 10 days. Prime bottles, fill with beer, and cap. Ready to drink in one to two weeks.

ABOUT LEMON BALM
Melissa officinalis

> 'Tis so friendly and fragrant that it strengthens Nature in all its Faculties. . . . Sage and Balm make a good Tea, so does Balm and Sweet Marjoram.
>
> —*An English Herbal*, 1690[240]

The word *balm* comes from *balsam*, meaning "an aromatic or resinous substance." When crushed, lemon balm gives off a fresh, lemony fragrance. However, one of balm's meanings is that of a substance that heals or soothes. Medicinal plants called balm, of which there are several, such as balm of Gilead or balmony, eventually caused the name to mean simply something that heals or soothes. Lemon balm is carminative, antispasmodic, sedative, antidepressive, diaphoretic, antiviral, immune stimulating, and hypotensive. It is effective in all digestive spasms and flatulence. Its volatile oils relieve anxiety, depression, tension, and stress. It has a tonic effect on the circulatory system and causes vasodilation, lowering blood pressure.[241] Research in Germany has shown that balm acts to protect the brain from excessively powerful stimuli. It thus acts as a gentle herbal tranquilizer. These sedative effects have been verified in a number of clinical studies.[242] Lemon balm has also shown consistent antiviral properties, making it useful in the treatment of any viral infections such as flus and herpes. Clinical trials have shown that lemon balm significantly shortens healing times for both shingles and herpes sores, both caused by viral infection. It has also been shown that constituents in lemon balm strengthen the immune system.[243] Because of its antiviral and immune-stimulating properties, its antidepressive action and its diaphoretic (sweating) properties, it is useful in colds and flus, especially where they are attended with depression. The sedative, tranquilizing, and antidepressive effects combined with the vasodilating properties of the herb act together in fermentations to move the active properties of the herb and the alcohol rapidly into the bloodstream and the brain. It is no wonder the herb found such a prominent place in the brewing of ales and beers.

AVENS ALE

Wine wherein the Root has been infus'd has a fine pleasant Taste and Smell: It chears the Heart and opens Obstructions. The Root infus'd in Beer is excellent for strengthening the Joints and Bowels.

—John Pechet, 1694[244]

Avens was at one time commonly used in beer and supposedly still is in real Augsburg ales. Maude Grieve notes that "The Augsburg Ale is said to owe its peculiar flavour to the addition of a small bag of Avens in each cask. The fresh root imparts a pleasant clove-like flavour to the liquor, preserves it from turning sour, and adds to its wholesome properties."[245]

Avens Ale

Ingredients

> 5 pounds malted barley
> or 3-pound can malt extract
> 2 pounds brown sugar
> 4 gallons water
> 2 ounces dried avens root (or 4 ounces fresh chopped root) in muslin bag
> yeast

Mash the barley in water at 150 degrees F for 90 minutes. Sparge with boiling water until a total of 4 gallons is drawn off. Add 2 pounds sugar and stir until dissolved. Cool to 70 degrees F and pour into fermenter; add yeast. Hang avens bag in fermenter. Ferment until complete, but let herbs infuse at least 10 days; siphon into bottles primed with 1/2 teaspoon sugar, and cap. Ready to drink in 10 days to two weeks.

Alternative Method: Or boil 1 gallon water, take from heat, and add 3-pound can of malt extract and 2 pounds sugar; stir to dissolve. Add rest of water and adjust all to 70 degrees F. Pour into fermenter, hang muslin bag of avens, add yeast and continue as above.

ABOUT AVENS
Geum urbanum

> *The root consists of many brownish strings of fibres, smelling some-*
> *what like unto cloves, especially those which grow in the higher, hot-*
> *ter, and drier grounds, and in free and clear air.*
>
> —Nicholas Culpepper, 1651[246]

European avens is uncommon in the United States, not being indigenous, though there are several American species that are used in much
the same manner. The root of European avens, especially fresh, possesses
a strongly aromatic odor, reminiscent of cloves. Its botanical name,
Geum, comes from the Greek *geno*, "to yield an agreeable fragrance." It is
this clovelike odor that is imparted to ales and beers in which it is used.
The root loses much of its fragrance when dried and should be kept
whole and dried carefully to preserve it as much as possible. The odor is
extremely agreeable and uplifting when encountered. The root (and
herb) are strongly astringent and have been primarily used in herbal
medicine for that property. It is useful in diarrhea and dysentery and any
situation where a stomach tonic is needed. The astringency of the plant
is also useful in treating gum inflammations. It would be of benefit in
external wound powders and salves.[247]

SERVICEBERRY ALE

> *The service tree, the name of which is said to be a corruption of cere-*
> *visia, was so called because in former times a kind of ale was brewed*
> *from its berries. Evelyn said that ale and beer, "brewed with these*
> *berries, being ripe, is an incomparable drink."*
>
> —John Bickerdyke, 1890[248]

The (western) serviceberry is a fairly common shrubby bush kind of thing up to 30 feet tall that grows mostly in the Northwest, though it dips down as far as New Mexico. The berries look sort of like a cross between wild cherries and currants—round, dark, and purplish-red.

Serviceberry Ale

Ingredients

   1 gallon water

   3 cups fresh serviceberries

   2 pounds malt extract

   yeast

> Place serviceberries and 1 quart water in blender and puree. Slow-boil serviceberry puree and remaining water for one hour; cool to handling temperature and strain (and press) through a sieve. Add malt extract. Pour into fermenter and add yeast at 70 degrees F. Ferment until completion. Prime bottles, fill, and cap. Like many beers and wines, serviceberry is felt to attain a better flavor when stored a long time. However, this recipe can be drunk after one to two weeks.

ABOUT SERVICEBERRY
Amelanchier alnifolia

> *[Serviceberries] were by far the most important type of berry to the Okanagans. Along with bitter-root they were considered the most important food, even more important than fish or game because they are available for only a short time during the year. . . . In all, eight different varieties of [serviceberry] were recognized by the*

Okanagans, although botanists delineate only three varieties within
Okanagan territory.

—Nancy Turner, 1975[249]

Serviceberry is a member of the rose family, with typical rose-like leaves. The bush produces clusters of beautiful white flowers that become, when ripe, serviceberries. They were once commonly used in jams, jellies, pies, and fermentation. Like most members of the rose family, the serviceberry is mildly astringent. The bark, leaves, and berries possess this property, and these were traditionally used by indigenous cultures for all complaints for which a gentle astringent is beneficial. The bark or leaf tea or the berries are useful in excessive menstrual bleeding, diarrhea, dysentery, and stomach complaints. A wash of the leaves or bark is helpful in treating external skin problems and wounds.[250] Serviceberries are about the same size as currants and, like currants, are somewhat pulpy. Besides the sweetish pulp, however, the profusion of small serviceberry seeds in the pulp add a wonderful flavor to beers and ales. They possess a strong almond aftertaste that is extremely pleasant. When the berries are pureed in a blender, this flavor results in a uniquely enjoyable beer.

MINT ALE

And also they add great strength and fragrancy, and makes brave,
well tasted Drink, good to prevent and cure all, or most of those
Diseases which the wise Ancients have appropriated that Herb unto.
The like is to be understood of Mint, Tansie, Wormwood,
Broom, Cardis, Centaury, Eye-bright, Betony, Sage,
Dandelion, *and good* Hay; *also many others, according to their*

Natures and Qualities, and for those Diseases to which they are respectively appropriated.

—Thomas Tryon, 1691[251]

Mint is known primarily for its use in candies, iced tea, and that horrible jelly people use on lamb. It has, however, a long tradition of use in beers, primarily on the Russian steppes.

A Rich, Dark Mint Ale

Ingredients

> 4 pounds pale malt extract
>
> 1 1/2 pounds medium-dark dried malt extract
>
> 1/2 pound black malt
>
> 6 ounces dried peppermint herb
>
> 4 gallons water
>
> ale yeast

> Place mint in small muslin bag. Bring 1 gallon water to a boil, take from heat, and add mint bag. Cover and let stand overnight. Remove muslin bag, add remaining water, and heat to 150 degrees F. Add malt and malt extract. Cover and allow to cool naturally to 70 degrees F (several hours). Strain and pour into fermenter. Add yeast and allow to ferment to completion. Prime bottles, fill, and cap. Ready to drink in 7 to 10 days.

Kvass is a traditional Russian tribal beer. In many areas, the beer is allowed to ferment with the solids, then the whole thing consumed as a food/drink. It is very high in nutrients. For this recipe (and for bottling) the solids are removed.

Mint Kvass
Ingredients

    1/2 ounce dried peppermint herb

    12 ounces rye flour

    1 ounce wheat flour

    4 ounces barley malt

    1 gallon water

    yeast

Heat 1/2 the water to 170 degrees F. When hot add malt and flours. Cover and allow to stand 90 minutes. While the malt and flours are standing combine mint and remaining water and bring to a boil then take from heat and cover. Allow to stand until malt and flours have been standing 90 minutes then combine both liquids (with solids) together. Cool to 70 degrees and add yeast. Allow to ferment until complete. Strain liquid from solids, prime bottles, fill and cap. Ready to drink in 7 to 10 days.[252]

ABOUT MINT
Mentha piperita

Two species of mint were used by the ancient Greek physicians . . . [and] there is evidence that M. piperita was cultivated by the Egyptians. It is mentioned in the Icelandic Pharmacopoeias of the thirteenth century.

—Maude Grieve, 1931[253]

Above all, mint is a diaphoretic and soothing stomach remedy. Peppermint is strongly effective as an antinausea herb and can quiet severe indigestion gently and surely. Peppermint's essential oil, of which the plant has an

Peppermint (Mentha piperita)

abundance, is strongly antispasmodic. Medical researchers, trying to find something to quiet the cramping when inserting small optical cameras into the intestine, tried a variety of drugs, all of which proved ineffective or too toxic. A small amount of peppermint oil, coating their instruments, effectively stopped intestinal spasming. (They found the information in an old herbal text.) Pain from duodenal or stomach ulceration is helped almost immediately by peppermint, as is irritable bowel syndrome, stomach cramping, and any kind of nausea, including motion and morning sickness. The pain of gall and kidney stones is often helped by the use of peppermint. In duodenal ulceration and irritable bowel syndrome, peppermint is more effective if a small amount of the oil is mixed with marshmallow or slippery elm root and taken in capsule. This mucilaginous mass sits in the bottom of the stomach, then drops down into the duodenum fairly intact and immediately soothes the affected area. As peppermint is safe for use in pregnancy, it is of tremendous benefit for attendant nausea.

Like other herbs in the mint family (such as lemon balm and rosemary), peppermint contains many antioxidant compounds (see "About Rosemary"). These have shown effectiveness in treating Alzheimer's disease, senility, cancer, and heart disease. Peppermint also contains nine expectorant compounds; they help move mucous up and out of the lungs. Its main constituent, menthol, thins mucous, making the expectoration easier. Peppermint also contains antiseptic, antibacterial, antiviral, and antimicrobial compounds. For this reason, it is used effectively in the treatment of gingivitis, colds and flus, and respiratory infections.[254]

ROSEMARY ALE

Of course there were many kinds of ale that were dependent upon their various ingredients. . . . "Hysope-Ale," "worm-wood ale," "ale of rosemary," and "Bettony." "Heather ale" was of very ancient origin in certain parts of the country and butter ale was most plentiful in the seventeenth century.

—Edward Emerson, 1908[255]

Rosemary, the traditional culinary herb, was often used in ales. Two methods of using rosemary follow. The first is a rosemary ale, the second is an ale flavored with rosemary.

Rosemary Ale

Ingredients

    3-pound can malt extract

    2 pounds brown sugar

    4 gallons water

    3 ounces dried rosemary herb

    yeast

> Boil malt extract, sugar, herb, and water for 30 minutes. Cool to 70 degrees F, strain into fermenter, and add yeast. Ferment until complete, siphon into bottles primed with 1/2 teaspoon sugar, and cap. Ready to drink in 10 days to two weeks.

The following recipe from 1695 was used to impart both medicinal herbs and specific flavors to ales. The nonhopped malt beer, a barley ale, with no herbal additives should be made first. When fermentation is complete, it should be siphoned into bottles, but without priming. Then the second recipe should be used for priming.

Barley Ale

Ingredients

> 5 pounds malted barley
> *or* 3-pound can malt extract
> 2 pounds brown sugar
> 4 gallons water
> yeast

Mash the barley in water at 150 degrees F for 90 minutes. Sparge with boiling water until a total of 4 gallons is drawn off. Cool to 70 degrees F and pour into fermenter, add yeast. Ferment until complete.

Alternative Method: Or boil 1 gallon water, take from heat, and add 3-pound can of malt extract and 2 pounds sugar; stir to dissolve. Add remaining water. Cool all to 70 degrees F. Pour into fermenter, add yeast, and continue as above.

When the beer is ready to be bottled, follow the recipe below. Use 3 to 4 ounces dried rosemary herb for the handful specified. Other herbs can be used instead of rosemary, depending on the taste or medicinal effect desired.

Rosemary Ale—1695

Take a handful of Rosemary and Boyl in a Quart of fair Water skimming it very well, and add thereto half a pound of fine Loaf Sugar, and a few Cloves, and when it is Milk warm put it thereto a spoonful of Barm, and when it begins to work skim off the Barm, and put two spoonfuls of this to one Bottle, and fill the Bottle almost to the neck. Then Cork it very well, your drink must neither be stale nor new.[256]

ABOUT ROSEMARY
Rosmarinus officinalis

If thou set it in thy garden, keep it honestly for it is much profitable.
—*Banckes Herbal,* 1526[257]

Rosemary has been used primarily as an antidepressant and carminative (dispelling gas). It contains a number of volatile oils, tannins, bitter principles, and resins. One compound, cenole, gives rosemary its unique aroma, and has been shown to be a stimulant to the central nervous system. It plays a role in the treatment of depression and is also useful in reviving someone who has fainted. Though known now more for its use as a culinary herb, it has a long tradition of use as a medicinal plant. Modern research is verifying many of the medicinal properties of rosemary. Research suggests that free radical oxygen molecules play an important part in Alzheimer's disease. Rosemary possesses at least 24 antioxidants (among them, the powerful rosmarinic acid), compounds that consume free radicals. It also contains at least six compounds that prevent the breakdown of acetylcholine. Acetylcholine plays a crucial role in the transmission of impulses from one nerve fiber to another across synaptic junctions, making it highly useful in the treatment of Alzheimer's disease, Parkinson's disease, and multiple sclerosis. Rosemary's protection of acetylcholine helps prevent further deterioration of this important chemical in the body and makes it useful in conjunction with nettles and royal jelly (both of which contain large amounts of acetylcholine). Additionally, the frequent use of rosemary helps prevent the development of Alzheimer's, Parkinson's, and multiple sclerosis. Rosemary is historically known as "the herb of remembrance" suggesting its antisenility and memory-enhancing activity.

The antioxidant activity of rosemary prevents spoilage of foods, comparable to the commercial preservatives BHT and BHA. It has long been used by indigenous peoples to preserve food from spoilage. Further, antioxidants have been shown to be effective in the treatment of arthritis. In addition to its multiple antioxidants, rosemary contains a number of antiarthritic compounds. Antioxidants have also been shown to play a role in the prevention and treatment of cataracts, rosemary also contains a number of other compounds that have known anticataract effects. These antioxidants also play a role in preventing heart disease. In addition, rosemary is a vascular and circulatory stimulant. These combined actions of the herb make it useful in the treatment of heart disease. Rosemary's essential oils are antiseptic and also possess antispasmodic and parasiticide actions.[258]

COSTMARY ALE

It was grown especially, however, as an herb "for the Coppe" and was sometimes called "alecost" because of its importance in flavoring ale and beer.

—Margaret Freeman, 1943, citing *Hortus Sanitatis,*
or *Gart Der Gesundheit,* 1485[259]

Costmary is a relative of tansy but is not so bitter. It is not much used now and has probably not been used in ale for many years, at least until now.

Costmary Ale
Ingredients

> 2 pounds brown sugar
>
> 2 1/2 gallons water
>
> 1 ounce dried costmary herb
>
> yeast

Boil herb, sugar, and water, for 30 minutes. Cool to 70 degrees F, strain into fermenter, and add yeast. Ferment until complete, siphon into bottles primed with 1/2 teaspoon sugar, and cap. Ready to drink in 10 days to two weeks.

About Costmary
Tanacetum balsamita

> *The whole of this plant emits a soft balsamic odour—pleasanter and more aromatic than that of Tansy—to which fact it owes its name of balsamita, and we find it referred to by Culpepper and others as the "Balsam Herb.". . . On account of the aroma and taste of its leaves, Costmary was much used to give a spicy flavouring to ale—whence its other name, Alecost. Markham (The Countrie Farmer, 1616) says that "both Costmarie" and Avens "give this savour."*
>
> —Maude Grieve, 1931[260]

Like its relatives, feverfew and tansy, costmary is useful in the treatment of headaches, migraines, and amenorrhea (scanty menstruation). It is a bitter herb and thus stimulates gastric secretions, making it useful in feeble digestion. Costmary contains, as do tansy and feverfew, parthenolides, which have been shown to help in the prevention of migraine headaches. It will stimulate menstruation and thus is contraindicated during pregnancy. It can be used nearly identically to tansy.[261]

GRAINS OF PARADISE ALE

> *This plant is used to give a heating quality to beer, being a wicked adulteration, rendering it to some constitutions highly inflammatory.*
>
> —Whitlaw's New Medical Discoveries, 1829[262]

Grains of paradise continually crop up in older beer recipes. Brewer Randy Mosher came across a book I have not yet seen (which sounds wonderful)—*Mackenzie's 5000 Receipts*, originally published in 1829, the same year as Whitlaw (above). In a 1994 *Zymurgy* magazine article, Mosher offers the original wording from Mackenzie and his modernization of a recipe for Windsor ale, which includes grains of paradise.

Windsor Ale

Mackenzie's comments about the ingredients in Windsor ale: "The drugs [below] mentioned are forbidden, under the penalty of two hundred pounds, and the forfeiture of all utensils; but of course private families are at liberty to use whatever they please. Nothing but malt and hops are permitted to public brewers, except the coloring extract; and the druggists who sell to brewers are subject to a penalty of five hundred pounds." These restrictions are, of course, the result of the so-called beer purity laws, in actuality, the first drug control laws in the world.

The original recipe continues: "Take 5 quarters of the best pale ale malt, Half a cwt. of hops, 8 lbs of honey, 1 lb of coriander seed, half lb of Grains of Paradise, half pound of orange peel, and two-and-a-half pounds of liquorice root . . . six ounces of ground ginger, and six ounces of ground caraway seed."[263]

Ingredients

　　12 pounds pale ale malt (or 9 pounds pale malt extract syrup)

　　1 pound honey

　　3 ounces hops

　　1/4 ounce coriander seed

　　1/8 ounce orange peel

　　1/8 ounce grains of paradise

　　1/2 ounce ground licorice root

1 teaspoon grated ginger

1 teaspoon caraway seed

yeast

Place malt in mash tun and mash with water added at 170 degrees F either two hours or overnight. Sparge grains with 150 degree F water until five gallons total is drawn off and boil hops and wort for 2 hours. Add 1/2 ounce hops for the first 1 1/2 hours and 1 ounce after 1 1/2 hours. After one hour forty minutes add the remainder of the hops and all the spices and herbs. Boil after their addition only 5 to 10 minutes. Take from heat and strain hops and herbs from wort—add honey. Allow to cool to 70 degrees F, pour into fermenter, add yeast and ferment until complete. Siphon into primed bottles, cap and store. To use extract instead of malted grain: add extract to water, bring to boil, stirring frequently to avoid burning and proceed as above.

ABOUT GRAINS OF PARADISE
Amomum Melegueta or Aframomum melegueta

Pungent and aromatic seeds, rivaling pepper in popularity during the Middle Ages. The seeds are used as a substitute or adulterant for black pepper, and to give false strength to wines, beer, spirits, and vinegar.

—Joseph Meyer, 1918[264]

Grains of paradise come from a reedlike plant of the ginger family and are related to cardamom. A strong pepperlike seed, grains of paradise were discovered during the spice trades and were long popular in Europe. Today they may be found in some upscale restaurants that use them as an alternative to pepper. The seeds are brownish and about half the size of peppercorns. Randy Mosher describes the taste as being "an intensely hot white-pepper taste with a spruce-juniper aroma."[265] They are being used again by the more exotic small breweries for some of their beers. Due to their strength, they are used in tiny amounts—7/100 to 1/5 of an ounce per five-gallon batch. They have been difficult to find—exclusive restaurant supply houses sometimes carried them. They are preferred by many African immigrants, and cities with a large African immigrant community, such as New York, have many stores that cater to that group. Many African products, including grains of paradise, may be found at a number of those stores. Recently some homebrew stores have begun carrying them under the Brewers Garden brand name.

Grains of paradise were used like a combination pepper/cardamom in herbal medicine in the Middle Ages specifically to stimulate peripheral circulation and reduce flatulence. However, even by the nineteenth century they were rarely used, having fallen out of favor, though they were still noted as being used in brewing and in veterinary practice.[266]

IRISH MOSS ALE

It is used to some extent in the arts, as sizing for paper and cotton fabrics in calico printing, for filling mattresses, and in this country for making beer.

—Felter and Lloyd, 1895[267]

Commonly called carrageen (Gaelic, meaning "moss of the rock"), Irish moss is often used in beer as a late additive to the boiling wort to encourage solids to precipitate out of solution and fall to the bottom, thus clarifying the beer. Irish moss is thus referred to as copper finings. And no, this does not mean it has copper in it—the kettle in which the wort is boiled is sometimes called a "copper."

The following recipe from 1890 is called "Irish Moss Ale" though the author's commentary at the end of the recipe is enlightening. I am not sure what Spanish Juice is. Alan Eames suggests it might be what is now called Spanish fly, cantharides, which is made from a dried beetle (sometimes called a "fly"), *Cantharis vesicatoria*, also denoted *Lytta vesicatoria*.

Irish Moss Ale—1890

Ingredients

    10 gallons water

    1 ounce Irish moss

    1 ounce hops

    1 ounce grated ginger

    1 ounce Spanish juice

    1 pound sugar

    yeast

> Take one ounce of Irish moss, one ounce of hops, one ounce of ginger, one ounce of Spanish Juice, and one pound of sugar. Ten gallons of water are added, and the mixture is boiled, fermented, and bottled. The consideration of the name of this liquor and the actual constituents may possibly remind readers of the old tale of that very clever person who made soup out of a stone with the assistance of a few such trifles as beef, vegetables, and flavourings.[268]

ABOUT IRISH MOSS

Chondrus crispus

> *It is found attached by its disk to the rocks along the sea, where it is collected in the spring-time, washed, and spread on the sands some distance from the shore-line and allowed to lie in the sun until it*

becomes well bleached and of translucent, horny texture, when it is ready for market.

—Felter and Lloyd, 1895[269]

Irish moss is a seaweed that is common on seashores throughout the North Atlantic, especially throughout Ireland and along the Massachusetts coastline. Now almost exclusively used in beer making, it was once part of standard practice medicine and herbalism. If boiled in water, it will entirely disappear; the water will then form jelly when cold. Irish Moss is 80 percent pectin, the rest being calcium, sulphur, chlorine, bromine, potassium, magnesium, and sodium, and can be used as a natural pectin source for jams and jellies. It is extremely nutritious, easy to digest, and highly mucilaginous. As such, it has been traditionally used as a gruel in enfeebled digestive states and as an added agent in herbal formulas to provide a soothing mucilage to inflamed internal tissues. Specifically, it is good for chronic pulmonary infections, chronic diarrhea and dysentery, and irritations from infection in the kidneys and bladder. Slippery elm bark is used in much the same manner. Given slippery elm's overuse and the damage to the tree population from which it is harvested, Irish moss is an excellent alternative and is available from most homebrew stores and from wholesale herbal suppliers. It has also been found to possess laxative properties, reduce gastric secretions, reduce high blood pressure, and alleviate gastric and duodenal ulcers. It is also an anticoagulant (a blood "thinner").[270]

Spanish fly (if that is in fact what Spanish juice is) is used in standard practice medicine. The dried and powdered beetle is a powerful blistering agent and rubefacient. In moderate doses internally, it is diuretic and stimulant to the urinary and reproductive organs. In any large dose it is poisonous.

Hops are diuretic and antibacterial (see "About Hops"). Ginger is diuretic, antibacterial, and antiviral, and increases peripheral circulation (see "About Ginger"). Thus, this beer recipe would primarily be a low-alcohol beverage for urinary tract problems, the Irish moss soothing the inflamed tissues. I would substitute 1 ounce dried juniper berries, crushed, for the Spanish fly. These would be a decent and tasty substitute, with similar properties (see "About Juniper," in chapter 8).

MUM AND PURL AND MORE

There are innumerable other beers, ales, and meads. I found a few interesting pieces about some of them, some in the form of poems. Those are not very good; there is a reason why their author's work isn't familiar to us. But these pieces do describe what the drinks of the time were like, to some extent.

> *There's an odd sort of liquor*
> *New come from Hamborough,*
> *Twill stick a whole wapentake*
> *Thorough and thorough;*
> *'Tis yellow, and likewise*
> *As bitter as gall,*
> *And as strong as six horses,*
> *Coach and all.*
> *As I told you 'twill make you,*
> *As drunk as a drum;*
> *You'd fain know the name on't,*
> *But for that my friend, mum.*
>
> —Anonymous, ca. 1720[271]

MUM

Mum was quite a famous ale; I would like to taste a traditional recipe, though "bitter as gall" doesn't sound all that exciting. The following recipe is supposedly that of the famous Brunswick mum. It should have a somewhat resinous, flowery flavor, with a fair bitterness, the primary bitterness being from the *Cardus*.

Mum, at least from this recipe, is really more of a barley herbal wine; the oats and beans adding a distinct flavor of their own. A hogshead is generally thought of as being 63 gallons. I haven't yet tried to reformulate this into a recipe for five gallons.

To Brew As Good Mum as Brunswick

To make a Hogshead of Mum, you must use as much water as (when Boyled to the Consumption of one 3d part) may make a Hogshead of Drink, which I believe may be about 100 Gallons: To which you must put 7 Bushels of Wheat Malt, one Bushel of Oat Malt, and one Bushel of ground Beans, being Brewed according to the Method of Beer and Ale; you are to Tun it when it is sufficiently wrought (but not too long) into your Cask, the same being well season'd, and not fill'd too full; put into the Cask when working, the Tops of Fir and Birch, of each one Pound, three handfuls of Cardus Benedictus dry'd, Flowers of Rosa Solis a handful, Bettony, Marjorum, Penny-royal, Flowers of Elder and Thyme, of each a handful, Seeds of Cardamum and Barberries bruised, of each two Ounces. When the Liquor has wrought a while with the Herbs, fill it up with the remaining Liquor, and then put in the Cask a dozen of new laid Eggs, the shells not cracked, then Bong it up close, and keep it for one, two, or three whole years before you use it, for the longer you keep it, the better it is.[272]

John Harrison has a recipe for mum in his, *Old British Beers and How to Make Them* (1991). The ingredients are very similar to those from 1695, and he notes that his recipe is adapted from the late seventeenth century, perhaps from the recipe above.

Mum—1991

Ingredients

    1 gallon water

    1 pound wheat malt

    1 pound pale malt

    1/2 pound rolled oats

    1/2 pound ground beans

    1 gram *Cardus Benedictus*

    1 gram marjoram

    1 gram betony

    1 gram burnet

    1 1/2 gram crushed cardamom seeds

    1/2 gram bruised bayberries

    yeast

> Simmer oats and beans for 20 minutes. Heat water to 170 degrees and pour over wheat and pale malt to make a stiff mash. Add oats and beans and stir all together, adding more water if necessary. Cover and leave three hours. Sparge grains with 170 degree F water until one gallon is obtained. Ferment 3–4 days. Rack from first fermenter into second fermenter, add all herbs at this time. Allow to ferment and infuse for 10 days more. Strain, allow to clear, then bottle as for ale. Mature 8 months.[273]

MOLASSES ALE

Molasses is a thick, dark, honeylike sugar syrup usually made from sorghum or sugar cane. The word *molasses* is from the Latin *mellaceus*, meaning "honeylike." It is used a great deal in England and is there known as treacle. It has traditionally been used much like honey in making beers and ales. It was one of the primary types of "lower" class beers in Colonial America and was available throughout the Colonies.

English Molasses Ale—1692

Ingredients

    100 pounds molasses

    36 gallons water

    3 pounds dried lignum vitae

    1 pound dry lemon balm

    1 1/3 ounce nutmeg

    1 1/3 ounce clove

    1 1/3 ounce cinnamon

    yeast

> Add to every hundred of Molasses thirty six or forty Gallons of Liquor, and stir them well together, until the whole is Dissolved; and then up with it into your Copper, adding thereunto three pounds of *Lignum vite*, one pound of dry *Balm*, and four Ounces of nutmeg, clove, and cinnamon together; clap on its blind Head, and lute fast, and digest twenty four Hours, then let it run into its Receiver; and as it is fit to set to work, put your Yeast in, and let it work sufficiently; then tun it up, and let come by its Age Mellow and Brisk to drink, and you shall have an excellent Drink, very wholsome to Man's Body.[274]

American Molasses Ale—Ca. 1750

Ingredients

    5 pounds molasses

    half pint yeast

1 spoonful powdered gingerroot

15 gallons water

> Take five pounds of molasses, half a pint of yeast, and a
> spoonful of powdered race ginger: put these ingredients
> into your vessel, and pour on them two gallons of scald-
> ing hot, soft and clear water: Shake them well till it fer-
> ments; and add thirteen gallons of the same water cold, to
> fill up the cask: Let the liquor ferment about twelve hours,
> then bottle it off, with a raisen or two in each bottle.[275]

Molasses Ale — *A Modern Recipe*

Ingredients

   1/2 pound golden syrup

   1/2 pound treacle [i.e., molasses]

   1/2 pound Demerara sugar

   1 ounce hops

   1 gallon water

   yeast and nutrient

> Bring water to the boil, add the hops, syrup, treacle and
> sugar, and simmer for 45 minutes. Strain, cool to 70
> degrees F, add yeast and nutrient, and ferment for at least
> a week before bottling in screw stoppered flagons.[276]

PURL

Purl, or purle, was also a famous ale, and many insisted they had the original recipe. This recipe is not as detailed as the last one for mum, but there
is enough here that, with experimentation, a good result could be had.
Like all the herbal beers of the Middle Ages, it would possess strong flavor and medicinal actions.

Purl

> According to one receipt, common Purl contained the
> following ingredients:—Roman Wormwood, gentian
> root, calamus aromaticus, snake root, horse radish,
> dried orange peel, juniper berries, seeds or kernels of
> Seville oranges, all placed in beer and allowed to stand
> for some months.[277]

MOUNTAIN ASH AND SYCAMORE

I didn't seek out more about these particular beers, but they sound wonderful. John Bickerdyke, writing in 1890, noted about them: "In Wales
berries of the Mountain Ash were once used, and were said to greatly
improve the flavour of the beverage. The sap of the sycamore tree is
mentioned by Evelyn as being a most useful adjunct to the brewhouse;
he says that one bushel of malt with sycamore sap makes as good ale as
four bushels with water alone.[278] I found references to these beers in
more than one place. I was surprised to discover that there are scores of
trees that, like maple and birch, posses sweet sap. Most of these, like
sycamore, were made into beers and ales at one time or another.

JOHN TAYLOR'S POETICS ON BEER

Perhaps one of the most famous connoisseurs of ale and beer was John
Taylor, born in Gloucester, England, on August 24, 1580. He was a sailor,
waterman, poet (though not very good), author of satires, epigrams, ana-
grams, odes, elegies, sonnets, and an adventurer, saloon keeper, and publisher. He wrote more than 100 tracts and pamphlets on the virtues of ale
and beer. The one included here speaks of many of the ales common in
England in the early seventeeth century.

SONG OF EIGHT ALES

We went into the house of one John Pinners,
(A man that lives among a crew of sinners)
And there eight several sorts of Ale we had,
All able to make one starke drunke or mad
But I with courage bravely flinched not,
And gave the Towne leave to discharge the shot,
We had at one time set upon the table,
Good Ale of Hisope, 'twas not Esope fable:
Then had we Ale of Sage, and Ale of Malt,
And Ale of Woorme-wood, that could make one halt,
With Ale of Rosemary, and Bettony,
And two Ales more, or else I needs must lye.
But to conclude this drinking Alye tale,
We had a sort of Ale called scurvy Ale.

—John Taylor, *Pennyless Pilgrimage,* ca. 1620[279]

EPILOGUE

In the clash between machine and Earth there is always great loss. Sometimes on the human side, more often on the side of Earth. But for those of us who go to the wildness of the world to heal ourselves with plants, to gather plants to make fermentations, there is this: if we bend close and hold tightly we can hear the heartbeat of ancient peoples no longer with us, the slow steady rhythms of the great trees, and beneath it all the heartbeat of our common mother, the Earth.

There is more to this life than the mind; we are governed by more than reason alone. We know this is true when deep feeling comes upon us, when timeless truths catch us up and carry us along, when we hear in the stories of women brewers in the deep rainforest some echo of our own humanity.

Sipping from the ancient fermentations of our ancestors is also taking a drink from the Well of Remembrance. Afterward, we carry within us echoes of an ancient way of life, another way of seeing the world, something more than reason alone.

It is worth the cost.

For those who brought us the gift of fermentation

THE APPENDICES

Though I have no other Design, in respect of Brewers than only to save them a great deal of Pains, and no small part of their daily Charge, and towards the rest of Mankind, but an honest and most charitable Intention of Advertizing them what may conduce, both to the Health of their Bodies, Tranquility of their Minds, and Advantage to their Estates; yet I am not so Ignorant of the Worlds common usage, as not to expect, that in offering to disswade from certain inveteral (but mischievous) Customs, I am like to meet with no less than Hate or Reproach, or at least Scorn and Contempt, from the greatest part of those, whose welfare I would gladly promote. However, as the Conscience of my own Innocence, and certain Experience and Knowledge of Truth, of what I recommend will be a sufficient Buckler against all the Darts of Envy, Ingratitude, Noise and Folly: So I do not Despair, but this small Treatise may have the happiness to meet with some few, so little wedded to Tradition and their own Humours, as to be willing to hearken to the Dictates of Wisdom, Reason, and Nature, wherever they meet them, or though communicated in a homely manner, by a very weak and imperfect Instrument.

—Thomas Tryon, 1691[1]

APPENDIX ONE

The Ancient Magic of Making Beer

There are many different Opinions concerning Brewing, and particularly in the Boyling of the Liquor of Worts, but I shall not trouble my self here to compose the difference of Men's Opinions therein, but shall treat of what natural Reason and my own Experience (by unwearied Travel and inspection therein) has taught me.

—F. Lighibodt, 1695[1]

Making a fermented beverage, a beer, is fairly straightforward. Many of the newer texts of the homebrewing movement, however, make it seem more complicated and intimidating than it really is. Most of those books are usually authoritarian, handing down the word from some homebrewing god on high, and seem quite complex, making the casual reader feel slow, if not retarded, upon reading them. There is a lot of talk about the necessity for the use of chemicals to keep everything sterile, the need for other chemicals to make the beer work well, the crucial necessity for Teutonic authoritarian temperature controls, and the importance of complex understandings of minuscule differences in grains, malts, hops, and yeasts. Generally, this frightens off a lot of people and takes all the fun out of brewing. It also means very few women are involved in beer making, which, historically, is an aberration—beer making has been the province of women for most of our history on Earth. But it need not be so distressingly complex and joyless. Fermentation in most of the world is done in conditions that most brewing advocates find to be distressingly unsterile and unscientific. Yet they are consistently amazed to find that those beers are of exceptional quality—quite often rivaling the finest beers made in high-technology operations. Having made my peace with being a heretic, I offer here some guidelines for beer making that you will find advocated in few other books. (If you want more high-tech and conventional guidelines, there are many good books on the market. Charlie Papazian's *The New Complete Joy of Home Brewing* [New York: Avon Books, 1983] is one of the best.)

FOUR HERETICAL RULES OF BREWING

RULE NUMBER ONE. Don't get tense, worried, or think you don't know enough. Remember that although you are re-learning an ancient human art and expression of plant medicine, it is important to have fun. If you screw up a batch of beer, it makes great fertilizer for the garden, it's not that expensive, and you can always make more.

RULE NUMBER TWO. Give yourself permission to have fun, make mistakes, and make a mess of the house and kitchen. Brewing is a messy, chaotic, wet, stimulating, and strenuous activity that produces euphoria and health—sort of like sex. If you need motivation to give yourself permission to jump in, just think of yourself as taking back something stolen and perverted by technologists and restoring it to its original form.

RULE NUMBER THREE. Take pride in being brewing-language illiterate and equipment deficient. You only need to know four terms: sugar, water, herb, and yeast. You can use the word *wort* if you really want to. You don't really need a hydrometer or anything else, though a thermometer is helpful (you don't really need that either).

RULE NUMBER FOUR. Figure out what works for you and don't be embarrassed by it.

SIMPLIFIED BEER MAKING BASED ON OTHER HERETICAL NOTIONS

HERESY NUMBER 1. To begin with, you need some source of sugar. It can be anything sweet. Here are some conversion tables for sweet sources that all technological brewers will disagree with. To make 1 gallon of a 5 percent alcohol beer (about what you buy in the store) you need 1 gallon of water, yeast (sometimes included at grocery stores when purchasing malt extract [bread yeast will work but has a stronger taste], or available at homebrew stores), and one of the following: 1.1 pounds malt extract, 1 pound white or brown sugar, 1 3/4 pounds malted grain (usually barley), 1 pound honey, 1 pound maple syrup, 1 cup corn syrup, 1 pound molasses. In these amounts each sugar is about equivalent for the yeast to make a 5 percent alcohol beer.

Be aware, however, that white sugar makes a beer with a "cidery" flavor that takes some getting used to. Some other sugar source combined with table sugar really does taste best (at least to me). The ratio should be two parts other sugar to one part table sugar (at the most). Everything except malted grains (this includes malt extract) is available at most grocery stores. The easiest and best-tasting sugar sources for brewing (that I have found) consist of either canned malt extract, brown sugar or a combination of brown sugar and molasses. For 2 1/2 gallons of water, use 2.2 pounds malt extract and 8 ounces sugar, 2 1/2 pounds brown sugar, *or* 2 pounds brown sugar and 12 ounces molasses.

HERESY NUMBER 2. You don't need *any* hops.

HERESY NUMBER 3. You don't need any chemicals or additives.

HERESY NUMBER 4. Germanic cleanliness is not necessary. Hot water and soap will work fine 99 times out of 100, or else use a strong herbal tea made with antiseptic herbs. As the English brewer, Thomas Tryon, explained in 1691: "Now the best way to prevent this Evil [wort infection] is that your Coolers are still washed well in cold water, wherein some bitter Herbs or Seeds are infused 24 hours, as *Wormwood* gathered and dried."[2]

HERESY NUMBER 5. Once you make a beer you like, you can use the excess yeast over and over again like a sourdough starter. You never need to buy any more.

HERESY NUMBER 6. To begin making beer, it is better to start in one-gallon batches, which will make the equivalent of two to three six-packs. When you get the hang of it and find a recipe you like, you can increase the amount brewed. (Not really heretical, but you won't be told this when you go to buy your equipment in most homebrewing stores.)

EQUIPMENT NEEDED

- 2 1/2-gallon pot (kitchen supply store)
- Thermometer if you want (candy thermometer or brew thermometer)
- Plastic trash can (discount store) or glass carboy (homebrew store in 2 1/2- or 5-gallon sizes)
- Airlock (if using glass carboy—available from homebrew stores)
- Sheet of plastic (if not using glass carboy)
- Bottles (recycling stores, save your own, or homebrew stores)
- Bottle caps (homebrew stores)
- Bottle capper (homebrew stores)
- Clear plastic hose (aquarium supply or homebrew store)

(NOTE: If going to a homebrew supply store, admit your ignorance immediately and cast yourself on their mercy. They are a lot more helpful if they know you know you don't know anything. If you get talked into buying a few things you don't really need, and out of a few things you do really need, you have had a normal experience.)

DOING IT

A SAMPLE RECIPE

Clean your fermenter of choice with hot water and soap. Some people use chlorox (it smells and feels bad) to ensure sterility, but if you do, your fermenter will need to be rinsed well (at least three times). You can also use antiseptic herbal infusions such as sage, juniper, wormwood, or hop tea as a cleanser (it smells and feels good). Also clean your plastic sheet or airlock with whatever solution you use. (An airlock allows the carbon dioxide gas the yeast makes to get out of the fermenter but nothing else to get in.)

Bring 1 gallon water to a boil in your cooking pot. If adding an herb—say, sage—add 1/2 ounce sage. (See specific recipes for amounts of herbs used.) Add sugar source, for example, 12 ounces molasses and 8 ounces brown sugar. Boil 15 to 60 minutes, turn off heat, let cool enough to strain, and strain out the herb. (You can avoid the straining problem by putting the herb in a muslin bag and boiling *that*, in essence making a huge tea bag.) Let cool to 70 degrees F (if using thermometer) or slightly warm to the back of your hand.

Pour the herbed sugar water (the "wort") into your cleaned fermenter of choice. Add yeast. Cover with plastic sheet or insert airlock. The yeast will take awhile to wake up and begin working. When it does, a thick froth will form on the top of the liquid in your fermenter. After six or seven days of active working, this will taper off, leaving only a few floating specks of foam on the top of the wort. At this time, clean your bottles and caps and plastic hose. Siphon the beer from the fermenter into the bottles until they are filled about like the beers you get in a store. Before siphoning, put 1/2 teaspoon of sugar in each bottle—this allows the yeast still floating in the liquid (even though it looks clear) to create carbon dioxide and give you a carbonated beer. Crimp the caps with your bottle capper. If you want to avoid bottle capping, you can buy beer brands (save the bottles) or bottles that have an attached porcelain cap and rubber washer. After the beer stands one to two weeks in a darkish, cool place, the yeast will have eaten the new sugar and carbonated your beer. It is now ready for drinking. *All beer making is some variation of this process.*

USING MALTED GRAINS

As you can tell from what I have said about malted grains, this process is somewhat more complicated than using a sugar source like molasses or brown sugar, but not really as much as it is made to seem in most beer books. Basically, all you need to know is that you need malted grains, hot water, and time. It is easiest to buy a malter/sparger from a homebrew supply if you want to pursue this kind of brewing (though I have been unable to find *any* indigenous cultures that use one. The rural Norwegians come the closest; they make their own unique sparger). Basically this is a container (usually made from an Igloo®-brand water cooler) with a spigot at the bottom. A screen is placed in the bottom of the cooler, malted grain that has first been coarsely crushed is placed on top of the screen, and enough hot water (at 170 degrees F) is poured on the grain to cover it and make a stiff oatmeal-like mush. It is covered and allowed to stand a minimum of one hour (some people think up to eight hours is better).

After one hour, open the spigot and allow the liquid to really, really slowly drain off. Take that liquid and add enough more hot water to make up the total amount of liquid you want and pour it slowly over the wet malt while allowing it to (again) really, really slowly trickle out of the spigot. Do not press the grains to remove all liquid—it adds a strong taste. Give the spent malt to the chickens, horses, or cows, or compost it. It is very nutritious. Check your liquid for quantity, add more hot water if necessary, and then use as in the recipe above. Because there is an excess of the enzyme that converts starch to sugar in barley malt, you can add other, unmalted grains in this process. Take the grain (wheat, rice, rye, oats, etc.), boil it with water for half an hour, and add it to the malt after the malt has had the first load of hot water added, still keeping it an oatmeal-like consistency. Then let the mixture sit for one to eight hours for conversion to sugar. Proceed as above.

To Wake Up the Yeast

You can take 2 cups cold water, boil it for 15 minutes, let it cool to slightly warm, add 1/2 cup white sugar and stir until dissolved, add yeast and cover it loosely with a plastic sheet or fit with an airlock. Let the solution sit until the yeast is exceptionally active, then make the wort as above and add this active yeast to it.

Usually the yeast needs to sit overnight. However I am happiest with the use of a Danstar brand Windsor yeast. It is dry and is prepared by mixing it in 8 ounces of slightly warm water, letting it sit for 30 minutes or so, mixing it well again and then adding it to the fermenter and the sweet wort. It begins working almost immediately and is exceptionally reliable. Yeast that I save from previously made beer seems to like to "wake up" overnight. At the end of each batch of beer there will be a lot of yeast left in the bottom of the fermenter. You can bottle this and when desiring to make more beer simply open the bottle, pour it into a clean container and add sugar. By the next day it will, usually, be quite active. When using these yeasts I prepare them the night before for use during brewing the next day.

A Note on Water

Tap water has chlorine and fluoride in it (among other things). If you do not drink it all the time, it does taste funny when you do. Either boil the water one hour to remove the chemicals, use store-bought spring water, or move to the country and get a well.

IMPARTING FLAVOR TO BEERS

Each sugar source has a different taste to it, as does each herb used in beers. Making beers and exploring the taste of each additive is the best way to get an idea of the tastes being created. It's like cooking. As Dr. W. P. Worth noted in 1692:

> How many different Savors may be impregnated in the Wort, from whence different Relishes to Beer or Ale proceeds: For if we add but a few Coriander-Seeds, gently infused in a small quantity of Wort, and afterward wrought in the whole, it will make a drink like Chinay-Ale; and so if you add an Ounce of the Powder of Orrice into a Quart of new Drink, gently infused, and then add that to a Barrel, it gives it the Relish of Rasberry, adding vertue thereunto; for this Reason do we advise to add six or eight Ounces of Ginger, and as much Orrice to an Hogshead of Strong Wormwood; and then you will enrich it so, as two or three spoonfuls will be sufficient for a Quart of clear Drink, having Vertues also equal with the smallness of its Dose. Likewise Black-cherries, Elder-berries, Rasberries, &c. being added, make excellent and vertuous Drinks; nay how many Physical Ales may be made by Simple and Compound Infusions; but seeing this is so obvious to all, that impregnation of different Idea's gives a different Alteration of Vertue, according as they proceed from a pure Root, but the contrary if they proceed from an impure one, as is manifested by daily Experience.[3]

Generally, beers are more tasty if some source of tannins and some source of bitterness is used in the brewing. The easiest source of tannin is black tea, and it is an excellent additive to beers (about 1/2 cup per gallon of beer).

A bitter taste in beer or ale blends well with the sweetness of the sugars (not all of which are converted to alcohol) and balances them out. Many herbs have a bitter principle in them and will work as well as hops. Experience in their use is the best way to find out how much of which to use, though I have given guidelines throughout the text for most of them. Here is what Thomas Tryon had to say about it in 1691. It's still true after 300 years. (In brief, use a little for not too long.)

> When you infuse in your Beer or Ale *Wormwood, Broom, Tansey, Cardis,* or any other herb which exceeds in bitterness, you ought not to let them lye in your Wort above half an hour, or if you put in a good quantity, a quarter of an hour will be enough, for in all such bitter Herbs the Martial and Saturnine harsh Properties are near at hand, and the warm Wort will quickly stir up and awaken their harsh, bitter, strong, astringent qualities which will presently devour, suffocate, and destroy the fine spirituous Virtues and opening cleansing Properties; and then such Drinks become of an hard, harsh, constringent Nature, and are apt to obstruct the Stomach, and send Fumes into the Head, heating the body and blood too violently; therefore all, or most Infusions of Herbs, made after this common way, more especially of bitter Herbs, are naughty and injurious to Health. As for Example; They put a quantity of *Wormwood,* or some other bitter Herb, into their Beer or Ale, at or after it hath done working, and there let it lye infusing (or rather rotting) two, three, four, five, or six Weeks, and in Ale-houses so many months, until the Cask be out, whereby all the good, opening, penetrating,

brisk Spirits, and fine Vertues of such Herbs are totally
destroyed, and instead thereof the Drink impregnated
with their contraries, (*viz.*) with the harsh, bitter, churl-
ish, inimical Properties, especially when such Infusions
are made of *Wormwood;* for this reason common
Wormwood Beer and Ale does not only hurt, but by
degrees weaken the natural heat of the Stomach, but
sends dulling Fumes and Vapours into the Head, and
does prejudice the Eyes. 'Tis certain, Infusion of Herbs,
if due order be observed, is the best and most profitable
way yet found to obtain their Vertues, both for common
life and Physick, far beyond Waters and Spirits drawn
from them by Distillation, for thereby a burning, fierce,
brimsony Spirit is extracted, void of all the mild, cleaning, opening Qualities or mild Virtues.[4]

BOTTLING BEER AND ALE

Though most brewers simply put a bit of sugar in their bottles now to carbonate the beer, in the old days there was a lot of fussing about with this
stage of the process. It was considered an art in its own right. Many brewers in the Middle Ages made a strong tea (infusion) from an herb and
added sugar to it. This flavored liquid was then used to prime the bottles
for carbonation. Many of the older brewers would add yeast (they called
it *barm*) to this, allow it to begin fermenting, and then add a spoonful or
three of that fermenting liquid to their bottles. Dr. W. P. Worth shares
his perspective from 1692.

A good way for the Bottling Beer
In the first place take a little clear Water, or else such as
is truly impregnated with the Essence of any Herb, and
to every Quart thereof add half a pound of *Mevis Sugar,*

and having very gently boyled and scumed the same, adding thereunto a few *Cloves*, let it cool, fit to put Barm thereto; and being brought to work, scum off the same again, and while it is in a smiling condition put three spoonfuls thereof to each Bottle, and then filling up the same, cork fast down. A few *christals of Tartar* also do well in Bottling Beer, adding a few Drops of the *Essence of Barley, Essence of Wine,* or some other *Essential Spirits*.[5]

I love that expression, "a smiling condition." It means when the yeast is eating the sugar, the whole solution is active, and the yeast happy in its work.

STORING YOUR BEER

The brewing of ales was important, and nearly every home had a brewery. Mostly it was the housewife's domain, a part of cooking. During the Middle Ages, most beers and ales were kept in wooden kegs in root cellars along with jams, jellies, pickles, and sauerkraut. Herbal beers, like herbal tinctures and herbs in general, like to be in cool, dark places. They last longer, age nicely, and taste better. After bottles became cheap enough to afford, they were stoppered with wired-down corks, like champagne. Many of the old recipes recommend storing bottles in the basement or root cellar, partly buried in sand. It is pleasant to keep a few bottles from each batch for a year or longer to gain an idea of how they age. Not many people now have the time or inclination to really develop fermentation as an art, but it does pay off, especially with meads.

Maude Grieve comments about this rich history of herbal healing:

Formerly every farmhouse inn had a brewing plant, and brewhouse attached to the buildings, and all brewed their own beer till the large breweries were established and supplanted home-brewed beers. Many of these farmhouses then began to brew their own "stingo" from wayside herbs, employing old rustic recipes that had been carried down from generation to generation. The true value of vegetable bitters and herb beers have yet to be recognized by all sections of the community.[6]

Will they ever be? I wonder.

Some Meads of the Middle Ages

Because mead was still especially esteemed throughout Europe at the development of printing, many ancient European recipes survive. Many of these meads were enhanced by the addition of herbs, spices, and fruits. Meads with only honey, water, and yeast are now often referred to as hydromels (literally "water-honey"), or just plain mead. With the addition of herbs it becomes metheglin. Adding grape juice makes it pyment, with apple juice it becomes cyser, and adding other fruit juices make it melomel. I think of them all as meads. Generally, a mead without the addition of tannin is not thought to develop a full body and flavor. Many of the traditional meads that used herbal additives usually included one herb specifically designed to impart tannins to the mead. Quite often this was sweetbrier (wild rose) leaves. Tannin can be bought and added to simple meads, generally 1/15 ounce (about 1/2 teaspoon) per gallon of mead being made, though black tea works just as well and is cheaper.

Though mead has not yet begun to be commercially brewed there is a surprisingly strong underground renaissance occurring in mead making in the United States. Many of the meads being brewed are truly amazing in their range of flavors. Part of the current trend recognizes the wonderful aromatic plant compounds in honey thus many mead makers no longer boil the honey. Boiling any aromatic herb causes the aromatic oils to boil off. Simply heating the honey (or aromatic herb) to 160 degrees F or so is enough.

The properties and history of some of the herbs used in the following recipes are covered in chapter 9 (see appendix 3 for those that were not covered).

A Basic Honey Mead
Ingredients

> 1 quart honey
>
> 3 quarts water
>
> yeast

> Boil water and honey together for 30 minutes. Cool to 70 degrees F and add yeast. Ferment until complete, 16 to 26 days. Prime bottles if carbonated mead is desired, siphon the mead into bottles, cap and store. Ready to drink in two weeks to one year depending on how long you wish it to age. The longer the better.

Ethiopian Tej

Tej is a traditional mead of Ethiopia. Generally it was made from one part honey to four parts water. A little tree bark and roasted barley were added as an inoculum, and it was allowed to ferment for five or six days. Over time this has changed. What follows is how they make it now.

Ingredients

> 4 pounds of honey in the comb
>
> 12 gallons water
>
> 3 ounces hops and 1 more gallon water
>
> olive wood and hops stems

> Add four pounds honey in the comb to 12 gallons water in a large cooking vessel. Place it over a fire of olive

wood and hops stems (this imparts a smokey flavor to the tei). After it comes to a boil, cook it for three hours. Remove from the fire, let cool slightly, and cover with cloths. Keep warm for two or three days. Remove the cloth and remove wax and scum. Add 3 ounces hops boiled in one gallon of water, stir and re-cover. (At this point add yeast and nutrient if you do not want a naturally fermented tej.) Leave covered to ferment for 8 to 20 days. Strain and drink or bottle.

Cyser

Ingredients

> 1 gallon fresh apple juice
> 3 pounds honey
> yeast

Heat apple juice until the honey will dissolve. Take from the fire and cool to 70 degrees F. Pour into fermenter, add yeast, and ferment until complete. Bottle as you will, either with priming or not.

Pyment

Ingredients

> 2 1/2 gallons grape juice (without preservatives)
> 2 gallons water
> 7 pounds honey
> yeast

Combine grape juice and water. Heat just until the honey will dissolve. Do not boil as the pectins in the grape juice will set. (A number of brewers feel that heating the honey in the water alone is more effective.

When the liquid has cooled to 70 degrees F the grape juice is added.) Remove from fire and cool. Pour into fermenter and add yeast. Ferment until complete, and bottle as desired.

Melomel

Ingredients

4 pounds crushed black currents

1/2 pint red grape concentrate

2 pounds honey

3 quarts water

yeast starter (an already active yeast solution)

Warm two quarts water and dissolve honey therein. When dissolved add the black currents and the rest of the water. Let stand 24 hours covered. Add yeast starter and allow to ferment on the pulp for 3 days. After three days, strain and press the pulp, combine with grape juice concentrate, and add water to make one gallon. Pour the liquid into a one gallon fermenter with air lock and ferment until complete. Bottle as desired.[1]

TRADITIONAL HERBAL MEAD RECIPES

Basically, mead is honey and water with wild yeast providing fermentation. It is allowed to ferment to completion and then kept as long as possible to allow it to age. All mead makers throughout history who kept records noted that the longer it aged, the better, as with wines. But during the Middle Ages and throughout history, a great many herbs were added to fermenting honey beverages. In many instances, this was for taste, but often it was for the medicinal effects of the herbs. Most of the following recipes are herbal meads intended for medicinal use. In all recipes I am assuming the use of a wildflower honey.

Pliny's Mead—A.D. 77

The most basic mead recipe, and the oldest written account, is from Pliny the Elder, who wrote this about A.D. 77.

Ingredients

> 3 parts rainwater
> 1 part honey

> A wine is also made of only water and honey. For this it is recommended that rain water should be stored for five years. Some who are more expert use rain-water as soon as it has fallen, boiling it down to a third of the quantity and adding one part of old honey to three parts of water, and then keeping the mixture in the sun for 40 days after the rising of the Dog-star. Others pour it off after nine days and then cork it up. This beverage in Greek is called "water-honey"; with age it attains the flavour of wine.[2]

Martha Washington's Recipe—Ca. 1600

Ingredients

> 1 quart honey
> 7 quarts water
> 1 sprig bay
> 1 sprig hyssop
> 1 sprig rosemary
> yeast

Take a quart of honey & 7 quarts of water; of bay, rosemary, & hyssope, of each a sprigg. mix them together &
boyle them halfe an houre, & then let it stand till it be
clear. then put it up in a pot with a tap, & set new yeast on
it, & let it worke untill it be clear, then bottle it up & let it
be two moneths ould before you drink it. it may be drunk
before, but ye keeping it soe long makes it brisker.[3]

Two Mead Recipes from 1695

Ingredients

    20 gallons water

    60 pounds honey (about 5 gallons)

    40 spoonfuls ale yeast

    10 ounces powdered nutmeg

    10 ounces powdered mace

    10 ounces powdered cinnamon

To Make Mead

Take Twenty Gallons of the best Spring-water can be
gotten and put it over the Fire, and let it stand for two or
three Hours, but suffer it not to boil; and to every Gallon
of Water add three Pound of Virgins Honey, and let it
gently boil an Hour or more, and take off the Scum in the
boiling; and when it is almost cold, add two spoonfuls of
Ale-yeast to every gallon, and so let it work two Days;
then Barrel it up, and add to every Gallon of Liquor,
Nutmegs, Mace, Cinnamon in powder, each half an
Ounce, tye it up in a Bag, and cast it into the Liquor, then
stop it close for a Month, two or three, the longer the
better; draw it out and bottle it, and a bit of Loaf-Sugar.[4]

Ingredients

 20 gallons water

 40 pounds honey (about 3 1/2 gallons)

 3 ounces dried marjoram

 3 ounces dried lemon balm herb

 3 ounces dried rosemary

 1/2 ounce powdered nutmeg

 1/2 ounce powdered mace

 1/2 ounce powdered cinnamon

 1/2 ounce powdered ginger root

 1/2 ounce powdered orris root

 3–4 Lent figs

 40 spoonfuls ale yeast

Another Highly Esteem'd of

Take to every Gallon of cold Distilled Water of
Cowslips, or Spring Water, two Pounds of the best
Virgins Honey, and to every twenty Gallons, add in the
boiling a good handful of Marjorum, Balm and
Rosemary each together, and before it be quite cold
strain it through a Sieve, and Ferment it as before is said;
then add in the Barrel Cinnamon, Nutmegs, Mace,
Ginger, Orice-roots half an Ounce, and three or four
Lent-figs, then stop it close for a Month, two or three,
the longer the better; draw it out and bottle it, and a bit
of Loaf-Sugar.[5]

To make cowslip water: take 20 gallons warm water and two pounds
fresh cowslip flowers, mix, cover, and let stand 24 hours, then strain and
use as above.

SOME MEAD RECIPES
FROM SIR KENELME DIGBY—1669

Sir Kenelme Digby's book, *The Closet of the Eminently Learned Sir Kenelme Digby Kt. Opened: Whereby is Discovered Several ways for making of Metheglin, Sider, Cherry-Wine, &c. Together with Excellent Directions for Cookery: As Also for Preserving, Conserving, Candying, &c.*, published in 1669, contained some 100 recipes for meads of his day along with cooking tips of all sorts. Long out of print, it has just been reissued by the English publisher Prospect, in a hard-cover edition. The first 90 pages of the book contain Sir Kenelme's recipes for medicinal and herbal meads and ales, a truly remarkable collection of healing drinks from the late seventeenth century. Many of the recipes are included in Cindy Renfrow's *A Sip Through Time* (n.p.: Renfrow Press, 1995), an excellent and more easily found compilation and historical record of fermented beverages. (However, her herbal information is curious, extremely conservative, and sometimes highly inaccurate.)

I have added measurements for the herbs used in the meads if they were missing; it is, however, a matter of preference. Most of the older recipes used the term *handful* as a term of measurement. Most of my herbs are dried, herb industry standard cut-and-sifted density (somewhat larger pieces than those of culinary spices, such as oregano, found in stores). The herbs I harvest myself and dry are in pieces a bit larger than that. My "handful" is about 3 ounces of dried herb. Though this can vary significantly from herb to herb, most of the herbs run about the same. For those that do not, such as horehound, which is much lighter and fluffier than most of the herbs in these recipes, I have adjusted the amount accordingly. I have also added information at the end of Sir Kenelme's instructions. Most of these recipes I made as ales, not wines, and there were other changes I made to enable a somewhat easier process. Sir Kenelme adds honey until an egg will float, one end sticking up the width of a groat—an English coin of that time. I instead used a water/honey mixture in proportion of either four to one or three to one.

A Receipt for Making of Meath
====

Ingredients

- 1 quart honey
- 1 gallon water
- 6 cloves
- 2 egg whites
- 1 1/2 ounces strawberry leaves
- 1 1/2 ounces violet leaves
- 2 sprigs spike lavender
- 1 sprig rosemary
- 1 teaspoon powdered nutmeg
- 2 teaspoon powdered ginger
- 1 cinnamon stick
- 6 cloves
- ale yeast

Take a quart of honey, and mix it with a Gallon of Fountain-water, and work it well four days together, four times a day; the fifth day put it over the fire, and let it boil an hour, and scum it well. Then take the whites of two Eggs, and beat them to a froth, and put it into the Liquor; stirring it well, till the whites of Eggs have raised a froth of Scum; then take it off, scumming the liquor clean. Then take a handful of Strawberry-leaves and Violet-leaves together, with a little sprig of Rosemary, and two or three little Sprigs of Spike; and so boil it again (with these herbs in it) a quarter of an hour. Then take it off the fire, and when it is cold, put it into a little barrel, and put into it half a spoonful of Ale-yest, and let it work; which done, take one Nutmeg sliced, and twice as much Ginger sliced, six Cloves bruised, and a little stick of Cinnamon, and sow these Spices in a little bag, and stop it well, and it will be fit for use within a fort-night, and will last half a year.[7]

Skip the first part of this recipe and begin with boiling the honey and water. Add ginger, nutmeg, cinnamon, and cloves to the fermenter when it is working. When done, prime the bottles, fill, and cap. Drink in a month.

Another Way of Making Meath

Ingredients

> 4 gallons water
> 1 gallon honey
> ale yeast
> 2 ounces sweetbrier
> 1/2 ounce mace
> 1 ounce lemon peel
> 1/2 ounce sweet marjoram
> 10 cloves
> raisins

Boil Sweet Bryar, Sweet Marjoram, Cloves and Mace in Spring-water, till the water taste of them. To four Gallons of water put one Gallon of honey, and boil it a little to skim and clarifie it. When you are ready to take it from the fire, put in a little Limon-peel, and pour it into a Woodden vessel, and let it stand till it is almost cold. Then put in some Ale-yest, and stir it together. So let it stand till next day. Then put a few stoned Raisins of the Sun into every bottle, and pour the Meath upon them. Stop the bottles close, and in a week the Meath will be ready to drink.[8]

Sweetbrier leaves are from a species of wild rose. They are not commercially available, as far as I know, but any wild rose leaf is a good substitute and will offer a similar flavor. Sweetbrier seems to be less astringent than the other wild rose species and somewhat sweeter (as the name indicates). I have added estimated amounts to this recipe. Instead of bottling so close to yeast addition, let it ferment until complete, then bottle with 3 raisins in each bottle.

My Lady Morices Meath

Ingredients

> 3 gallons water
>
> 1 gallon honey
>
> 1 ounce angelica herb (dried)
>
> 1 ounce lemon balm (dried)
>
> 1 ounce borage herb (dried)
>
> 1/2 ounce rosemary herb (dried)
>
> 1 ounce sliced fresh gingerroot
>
> 8 cloves
>
> ale yeast

> Boil first your water with your herbs. Those she likes best, are, Angelica, Balm, Borage, and a little Rosemary (not half so much as of any of the rest) a handful of all together, to two or three Gallons of water. After about half an hours boiling, let the water run through a strainer (to sever the herbs from it) into Woodden or earthen vessels, and let it cool and settle. To three parts of the clear, put one or more of honey, and boil it till it bear an Egge, leaving as broad as a shilling our of the water, skimming it very well. Then power it our into vessels, as before; and next day, when it is almost quite cold, power it into a

Sack-cask, wherein you have first put a little fresh Ale-
yest, about two spoonfuls to ten Gallons. Hang in it a bag
with a little sliced Ginger, but almost a Porengerfull
[about 1/2 cup] of Cloves. Cover the bung lightly, till it
have done working; then stop it up close. You may tap
and draw it a year or two after. It is excellent good.[9]

Place the mead in a fermenter at 70 degrees F with the cloves and
ginger either in a weighted muslin bag or not. Add ale yeast and ferment
until completion. Prime bottles, fill, and cap. Ready to drink in a month.
NOTE: The amount of cloves used (1/2 cup) is a bit intense for me. I
would recommend about 8 cloves total.

A Receipt for Meathe

Ingredients

7 quarts water

2 quarts honey

3 or 4 fresh parsley roots

3 or 4 fresh fennel roots

3 cloves

ale yeast

To seven quarts of water, take two quarts of honey, and
mix it well together; then set it on the fire to boil, and
take three or four Parsley-roots, and as many Fennel-
roots, and shave them clean, and slice them, and put
them into the Liquor, and boil altogether, and skim it
very well all the while it is boyling; and when there will
no more scum rise, then it is boiled enough: but be care-
ful that none of the scum boil into it. Then take it off,
and let it cool till the next day. Then put it up into a
close vessel, and put thereto half a pint of new good

barm, and a very few Cloves pounded and put in a
Linnen-cloth, and tie it in the vessel, and stop it up
close; and within a fortnight, it will be ready to drink,
but if it stay longer, it will be the better.[10]

Another Pleasant Meathe of Sir William Paston's

Ingredients

    1 gallon water

    1 quart honey

    10 sprigs sweet marjoram

    5 bay leaves

    ale yeast

To a Gallon of water put a quart of honey, about ten
sprigs of Sweet-marjoram; half so many tops of Bays.
Boil these very well together, and when it is cold, bottle
it up. It will be ten days before it be ready to drink.[11]

As made, this is really a honey drink, not a mead. After boiling, cool
it to 70 degrees F, pour it in the fermenter, add ale yeast, then allow it to
work until completion. Prime the bottles, fill, and cap. And keep it a
month before drinking.

A Very Strong Meathe

Ingredients

    10 gallons water

    4 gallons honey

    6 cloves

    1 ounce ginger

    1 ounce lemon peel

    2 ounces dried or 4 ounces fresh elderflowers or 1 ounce dried orris root; or

        4 ounces fresh hypericum (St.-John's-wort), fresh flowering tops; or 1

ounce rosemary, 1 ounce betony, 1 ounce eyebright, 1 ounce wood
sorrel—all dried herb.

ale yeast

> Take ten Gallons of water, and four of Honey. Boil
> nothing in it. Barrel it when cold, without yest. Hang in
> it a bag of Cloves, Elder-flowers, a little ginger and
> Limon peel; which throw away, when it has done work-
> ing, and stop it close. You may make also strong and
> small [mead] by putting into it Orris-roots; or with
> Rose-mary, Betony, Eyebright and Wood-sorrel; or by
> adding to it the tops of Hypericon with the flowers of it'
> Sweet-bryar, Lilly of the valley.[12]

In this recipe, he is allowing it to work with a wild yeast. I skipped
that and used an ale yeast. I see it as four recipes: elderflower—dried and
fresh, the fresh has a much better flavor; orris root; St.-John's-wort; and the
four-herb combination. Work it as an ale, bottle and prime when done.

Another Very Good White Meath—1

Ingredients

    1 gallon water
    1 quart honey
    1/4 teaspoon rosemary
    1/4 teaspoon sweet marjoram
    3 ounces sweetbrier leaves
    1 ounce powdered ginger
    ale yeast

> Take to every Gallon of water a quart of Honey boil in
> it a little Rosemary and Sweet-marjoram: but a large

quantity of Sweet-bryar-leaves, and a reasonable proportion of Ginger: boil these in the Liquor, when it is
skimed; and work it in due time with a little barm. Then
tun it in a vessel; and draw it into bottles, after it is sufficiently settled. Whites of Eggs with the shells beaten
together, do clarifie Meath best. . . . Tartar makes it
work well.[13]

I work this one as a standard ale: After boiling the herbs, let them
stand overnight, strain into the fermenter, add ale yeast, and let work
until completion. Then bottle.

Another Very Good White Meath—2

Ingredients

    1 gallon water

    1 quart honey

    1/4 teaspoon rosemary

    1/4 teaspoon sweet marjoram

    1 ounce powdered ginger

    1 1/2 ounces dried borage herb

    1 1/2 ounces dried bugloss herb

    ale yeast

[The recipe above continues with] If you will have your
Meath cooling, use Violet and Straw-berry-leaves,
Agrimony, Eglantine [sweetbrier] and the like: Adding
Borage and Bugloss, and a little Rosemary and Sweet-
Marjoram to give it Vigor.[14]

As violet and strawberry leaves were used in a prior recipe, I use the
bugloss and borage here and work it as I do the previous recipe.

White Metheglin of My Lady Hungerford
Which is Exceedingly Praised
Ingredients

6 gallons water

1 gallon honey

1 1/2 ounces dried violet leaves

1 ounce dried wood sorrel herb

3 ounces dried strawberry leaves

3 ounces dried hart's tongue herb

3 ounces dried liverwort herb

12 sprigs rosemary

5 sprigs dried lemon balm herb

1 ounce dried red sage herb

1/2 ounce thyme

1/2 ounce cloves

1/2 ounce nutmeg

4 ounces gingerroot

yeast

Take your honey, and mix it with fair water, until the Honey be quite dissolved. If it will bear an Egge to be above the liquor, the breadth of a groat, it is strong enough; if not, put more Honey to it, till it be so strong; Then boil it, till it be clearly and well skimmed; Then put in one good handful of Straw-berry leaves, and half a handful of Violet leaves; and half as much Sorrel: a Douzen of Rosemary; four or five tops of Baulme-leaves: a handful of Hart's-tongue, and a handful of Liver-worth; a little Thyme, and a little Red-sage; Let it boil about an hour; then put it into a Woodden Vessel, where let it stand until quite cold; Then put it into the Barrel; Then take half an Ounce of Cloves, as much

Nutmeg; four or five Races of Ginger; bruise it, and put
it into a fine bag, with a stone to make it sink, that it
may hang below the middle: Then stop it very close.[15]

The recipe continues with an addendum: the dried herbs are to be
infused in hot water until it is strong—by this absorbing some of the
water—then the infusion is strained and the water increased back to 6
gallons by the addition of more water. Then the honey is added, the
whole boiled and scummed. The original recipe did not call for the addition of yeast—it was fermented with a wild yeast. Use yeast and bottle it
when done working, some as wine, some as a carbonated mead.

Another Metheglin

Ingredients

   3 gallons water

   1 gallon honey

   6 ounces fresh cowslip flowers

   1 1/2 ounces rosemary

   1 1/2 ounces liverwort, dried herb

   1 1/2 ounces lemon balm, dried herb

   6 ounces dried sweetbrier leaves

   3 ounces dried betony herb

   1 pint ale yeast

In every three Gallons of water, boil Rosemary,
Liverwort, balm, ana, half a handful, and Cowslips two
handfuls. When the water hath sufficiently drawn out
the vertue of the herbs, pour all into a Tub, and let it
stand all night. Then strain it. And to every three gallons of the clear Liquor (or 2 1/2, if you will have your
drink stronger) put one Gallon of honey, and boil it, till
it bear an Egge, scuming it till no more scum will rise:

which to make rise the better, put in now and then a
Porrenger full of cold water. Then pour it into a Tub,
and let it stand to cool, till it be blood warm, and then
put by degrees a Pint of Ale-yest to it, to make it work.
So let it stand three days very close covered. Then skim
off the yest, and put it into a seasoned barrel; but stop it
not up close, till it have done hissing. Then either stop it
very close, if you will keep it in the barrel, or draw it
into bottles. Put into this proportion, Ginger sliced,
Nutmegs broken, ana, one ounce, Cinamon bruised half
an ounce in a bag, which hang in the bung with a stone
to make it sink. You may add, if you please, to this proportion of water, or one Gallon more, two handfuls of
Sweet-bryar-leaves, and one of Betony.[16]

Since I bottle mead, I skipped the ginger, nutmeg, and cinnamon.

To Make White Metheglin

Ingredients

    5 gallons water
    1 1/2 gallons honey
    1 ounce propolis
    1 ounce bee pollen
    1 ounce royal jelly
    6 ounces angelica herb, dried
    1/2 ounce marshmallow root, dried
    1 ounce parsley root, dried
    1/2 ounce fennel root, dried
    1 1/2 ounces rosemary
    1 1/2 ounces borage herb, dried
    1 1/2 ounces maidenhair fern herb, dried
    1 1/2 ounces pennyroyal herb, dried

1 1/2 ounces hart's tongue herb, dried

1 1/2 ounces liverwort herb, dried

1 1/2 ounces fresh watercress

1 1/2 ounces scurvy grass herb, dried

ale yeast

> Take the Honey-combs, that the Honey is run out from them, and lay them in water overnight; next day strain them, and put the Liquor a boiling; Then take the whites of two or three Eggs, and clarifie the Liquor. When you have so done, skim it clean. Then take a handful of Peny-royal, four handfuls of Angelica; a handful of Rosemary; a handful of Borrage; a handful of Maidenhair, a handful of Hart's-tongue; of Liverwort, or Water-cresses, of Scurvy-grass, ana, a handful; of the roots of Marshmallows, Parsley, Fennel, ana, one Ounce. Let all these boil together in the Liquor, the space of a quarter of an hour. Then strain the Liquor from them, and let it cool, till it be Blood-warm. Put in so much honey, until an Egge swim on it; and when your honey is melted, then put it into the Barrel. When it is almost cold, put a little Ale barm to it; And when it hath done working, put into your barrel a bag of Spice of Nutmegs, Ginger, Cloves and Mace, and grains good store [grains of paradise]; and if you will, put into a lawn-bag two grains of Amber-greece and two grains of Musk, and fasten it in the mouth of your barel, and so let it hang in the Liquor.[17]

There is no amount of water stated for this recipe. That is meant to be determined from the size of the honeycomb from a harvested hive—enough to cover it, I imagine. In doing this, the content of the hive would become part of the wort: propolis, royal jelly, bee pollen. So I substituted them in the recipe and set the water amount at 5 gallons. I guesstimated that 10 gallons was an amount to easily cover a comb and reduced the herb proportions for 5 gallons.

An Excellent Metheglin

Ingredients

    1 gallon water

    1 quart honey

    1/2 ounce rosemary

    1/2 ounce dried sage

    1/2 ounce sweet marjoram

    1/2 ounce lemon balm herb, dried

    1/2 ounce sassafras root bark, dried

    yeast

> Take Spring-water, and boil it with Rose-mary, Sage, Sweet Marjoram, Balm and Sassafras, until it hath boiled three or four hours: The quantity of Herbs is a handful of them all, of each a like proportion, to a Gallon of water. And when it is boiled, set it to cool and settle until the next day: Then strain your water, and mix it with honey, until it will bear an Egg the breadth of a Groat. Then set it over the fire to boil. Take the whites of twenty or thirty Eggs, and beat them mightily, and when it boileth, pour them in at twice; stir it well together, and then let it stand, until it boileth a pace before you scum it, and then scum it well. Then take it off the fire, and pour it in earthen things to cool: and when it is cold, put to it five or six spoonfuls of the best yest of Ale you can get: stir it together, and then every day scum it with a bundle of Feathers til it hath done

working: Then tun it up in a Sack-cask and to every six gallons of metheglin put one pint of Aquavitae, or a quart of Sack; and a quarter of a pound of Ginger sliced, with the Pills of two or three Limons and Orenges in a bag to hang in it. The Whites of Eggs above named, is a fit proportion for 10 or 12 Gallons of the Liquor.[18]

I expect this would be bottled, not casked, and so skipping the spices is a good idea. I personally would skip the sack and aqua vitae.

To Make Another White Metheglin

Ingredients

8 gallons water

2 gallons honey

2 teaspoonfuls caraway seed

2 teaspoonfuls coriander seed

2 teaspoonfuls fennel seed

3 ounces sweet marjoram

4 ounces sweetbrier hips, dried

3 ounces violet leaves, dried

3 ounces violet flowers, dried

3 ounces strawberry leaves, dried

1 1/2 ounces thyme

1 1/2 ounces dried borage herb

1 1/2 ounces agrimony herb, dried

3 or 4 blades of mace

2 sprigs rosemary

yeast

Take Sweet-marjoram, Sweet-bryar-buds, Violet-leaves, Strawberry-leaves, of each one handful, and a good handful of Violet flowers (the dubble ones are the best) broad Thyme, Borrage, Agrimony, of each half a handful, and two or three branches of Rosemary, The seeds of Carvi, Coriander, and Fennel, of each two spoonfuls, and three or four blades of large-mace. Boil all these in eight Gallons of running-water, three quarters of an hour. Then strain it, and when it is but blood-warm, put in as much of the best honey, as will make the Liquor bear an Egg the breadth of six pence above the water. Then boil it again as long as any scum will rise. Then set it abroad a cooling; and when it is almost cold, put in a half a pint of good Ale-barm; and when it hath wrought, till you perceive the barm to fall, then Tun it, and let it work in the barrel, till you stop it up, put in a bag with one Nutmeg sliced, a little whole Cloves and Mace, a stick of Cinnamon broken in pieces, and a grain of good Musk. You may make this a little before Michaelmas, and it will be fit to drink at Lent. This is Sir Edward Bainton's Receipt, Which my Lord of Portland (who gave it me) saith, was the best he ever drunk.[19]

A Receipt for Metheglin of My Lady Windebanke

Ingredients

- 4 gallons water
- 1 gallon honey
- 5 eringo roots
- 3 parsley roots
- 2 red nettle roots
- 1 fennel root
- 1 ounce pellitory of the wall herb, dried
- 1 ounce sage, dried

1 ounce thyme

1 ounce clove gillyflowers, dried

1/2 ounce borage herb, dried

1/2 ounce bugloss flowers, dried

1/2 ounce hart's tongue herb, dried

1 sprig hyssop

> Take four Gallons of water; add to it these herbs and Spices following. Pellitory of the Wall, Thyme, of each a quarter of a handful, as much Clove gilly-flowers, with half as much Borage and Bugloss flowers, a little Hyssop, Five or six Eringo-roots, three or four Parsley-roots: One Fennel-root, the pith taken out, a few Red-nettle-roots, and a little Harts-tongue. Boil these Roots and Herbs half an hour; Then take our the Roots and Herbs, and put in the Spices grosly beaten in a Canvass-bag, viz. Cloves, Mace, of each half an ounce, and as much Cinnamon, of Nutmeg an Ounce, with two Ounces of Ginger, and a Gallon of Honey: Boil all these together half an hour longer, but do not skim it at all: let it boil in, and set it a cooling after you have taken it off the fire. When it is cold, put six spoonfuls of barm to it, and let it work twelve hours at least; then Tun it, and put a little Limon-peel into it: and then you may bottle it, if you please.[20]

A Metheglin for the Colick and Stone *of [Lady Stuart]*

Ingredients

7 gallons water

1 gallon honey

3 ounces pellitory of the wall, dried herb

3 ounces saxifrage [lesser burnet], dried herb

3 ounces betony, dried herb

3 ounces dried parsley flakes

3 ounces groundsel [life root], dried herb

2 ounces parsley seeds

2 ounces nettle seeds

2 ounces fennel seeds

2 ounces caraway seeds

2 ounces aniseed

2 ounces gromwell [*Lithospermum officinale*] seeds

2 ounces parsley root, dried

2 ounces alexander root, dried

2 ounces fennel root, dried

2 ounces mallow root, dried

yeast

Take one Gallon of Honey to seven Gallons of water;
boil it together, and skim it well; then take Pellitory of
the Wall, Saxifrage, Betony, Parsley, Groundsel, of
each a handful, of the seeds of Parsley, of Nettles,
Fennel and Carraway-seeds, Anise-seeds and
Grumelseeds, of each two Ounces. The roots of parsley, of Alexander, of Fennel and Mallows of each two
Ounces, being small cut; let all boil, till near three
Gallons of the Liquor is wasted: Then take it off the
fire, and let it stand till it be cold; then cleanse it from
the drugs, and let it be put into a clean vessel well
stoppered, taking four Nutmegs, one Ounce and a half
of Ginger, half an Ounce of Cinnamon, twelve
Cloves; cut all these small, and hang them in a bag
into the vessel, when you stop it up. When it is a

fortnight old, you may begin to drink of it; every morning a good draught.[21]

This particular recipe was not originally designed to "work," that is, ferment. It is, actually, a highly concentrated herbal infusion with honey added. And, indeed, it would be good for "the colick and stone." I added yeast to the recipe and would also bottle it.

Sir Thomas Gower's Metheglin for Health

Ingredients

12 gallons water

2 gallons honey

18 ounces dried sweetbrier leaves

3 ounces sweet marjoram

3 ounces rosemary

3 ounces thyme

6 ounces dried marigold flowers [*Calendula*]

6 ounces dried borage herb

6 ounces dried bugloss herb

6 ounces dried sage

yeast

First boil the water and scum it. Then to 12 gallons put 6 handfuls of Sweet-bryar-leaves, of Sweet-marjoram, Rosemary, Thyme, of each a handful: Flowers of Marigold, Borrage, Bugloss, Sage, each two handfuls. Boil all together very gently, till a third waste. To eight gallons of this put two gallons of pure honey, and boil them till the Liquor bear an Egge, the breadth of three-pence or a Groat, together with such spices as you like (bruised, but not beaten) an ounce of all is sufficient.

You must observe carefully. 1. Before you set the Liquor to boil, to cause a lusty Servant (his Arms well washed) to mix the honey and water together, labouring it with his hands an hour without intermission. 2. That when it begins to boil fast, you take away part of the fire, so as it may boil more slowly, and the scum and dross go all to one with the dross. 3. When you take it from the fire, let it settle well, before it be tunned into the vessel, wherein you mean to keep it: and when it comes near the bottom, let it be taken carefully from the sediment, with a thin Dish, so as nothing be put into the vessel, but what is clear. 4. Stop it very close (when it is set in place, where it must remain) cover it with a cloth, upon which some handfuls of Bay-salt and Saltpeter is laid, and over that lay clay, and a Turf. 5. Put into it, when you stop it, some New-laid-eggs in number proportionable to the bigness of the vessel, Shell's unbroken. Six Eggs to about sixteen Gallons. The whole Egg-shell and all will be entirely consumed.[22]

Again, this recipe was wild yeast fermented. I would skip the storage instructions and the eggs and ferment it in a standard 5 gallon carboy fermenter—decreasing the recipe by half—and use ale yeast. A *very* strong herbal-tasting mead.

To Make a Meath Good for the Liver and Lungs

Ingredients

    5 gallons water

    5 pints honey

    4 ounces coltsfoot root, dried

4 ounces fennel root, dried

4 ounces licorice root, dried

4 ounces bracken fern, dried

2 ounces succory [chicory root], dried

2 ounces wood sorrel root, dried

2 ounces strawberry root, dried

2 ounces bittersweet root [*Solanum dulcamara*], dried

1 1/2 ounces scabious root, dried

1 1/2 ounces elecampane root, dried

6 ounces ground ivy herb, dried

3 ounces horehound herb, dried

6 ounces oak of Jerusalem

6 ounces lungwort, dried lichen

6 ounces liverwort herb, dried

6 ounces maidenhair fern, dried

6 ounces hart's tongue herb, dried

2 ounces jujubes

2 ounces raisins

2 ounces currants

1 teaspoon coriander seeds

1 teaspoon cinnamon

Take of the Roots of Colts-foot, Fennel and Fearn each four Ounces. of Succory roots, Sorrel-roots, Strawberry-roots, Bitter-sweet roots, each two Ounces, of Scabious-roots and Elecampane-roots each an Ounce and a half. Ground-ivy, Horehound, Oak of Jerusalem, Lung-wort, Liver-wort, Maiden-hair, Hart's-tongue of each two good handfulls. Licorish four Ounces. Jujubes, Raisins of the Sun and Currents, of each two Ounces; let the roots be sliced, and the herbs be broken a little with your hands; and boil all these in twenty quarts of fair running water, or, if you have it, in Rain water, with five Pints of good white honey, until one third part be boiled away; then pour the liquor through a jelly bag often upon a little Coriander-seeds, and Cinnamon; and when it runneth very clear, put it into Bottles well stopped, and set it cool for your use, and drink every morning a good draught of it, and at five in the afternoone.[23]

This, again, is not primarily a fermented mead but a medicinal honey-water and herb infusion. It is not one I have made.

APPENDIX THREE

Herbs Used in Meads of the Middle Ages
A Brief Compendium

We see that Beer made from Cypress, Cedar, Sassafrax, Wormwood, Scurveygrass, Elder, Mint, Balm, &c. *are highly esteemed, especially* Purle *and* Scurveygrass, *here in* England: *but here is one thing I cannot omit, which is this, they take the Herbs at any Season, with the Gross and more Vertuous part together; and put these into Low, Weak, Sick, Defective or Prick'd Beers, and so the Tast of the Herb overpowering the same, they think it sufficient, the Pallats of the Drinkers being pleased, not minding whether they answer the End desired. . . . [Therefore] we shall recommend three things to the Consideration of every Honest Brewer, whereby this Defect may in great Measure be Repaired and Supplyed: The first is this, if you design to make any sort of Physical Beer, let your Wort have a Sound Body, well wrought, and settle three Days, and while it hath yet a more Invisible and Secret Fermentation. Secondly, that you only add in the Tops and choice parts of such Herbs as are design'd for the same. And thirdly, That those Herbs lie not so long therein, as that their Spiritual Qualities may be so much exhausted, that their Terrene ones by the Beer or Liquor should be extracted; therefore they ought to be well pounded and macerated, and in a small Bag put into the Cask, that so after their due Time, which may be at the most twenty Days, they may be taken out again. These being observed, you may make excellent Beer or Drinks, fully*

*answering the End of their Preparation. Also instead of such Herbs
as are naturally juicy, you may add in the Juice thereof; if Elder, let
it be about two Gallons to a Barrel of Strong Beer; but if the Juices
are Stiptick, Bitter or Astringent, then will a smaller Quantity serve.
. . . Now if you have a mind to have any other Variations, in making divers Physical Ales, then proceed thus; Make a Syrrup of the
Herb, and put two or three Spoonfuls thereof into the Ale or Beer in
Bottleing, and in a Spoonful or two of the Essence, whether it be*
Oranges, Lemons, or Scurvygrass, Cypress, Wormwood,
Mint, Balm *or the like: And if the practice this, your Experience will
prompt you beyond Words.*

—Dr. W. P. Worth, 1692[1]

agrimony herb. *Agrimonia eupatoria*—Astringent bitter. Used for digestive
problems, diarrhea, and wound healing.

alexander root. *Smyrnium Olisatrum*—Black lovage. Emmenagogue,
carminative, diuretic. It is now rarely used in herbal medicine.

angelica herb and root. *Angelica archangelica*—A remarkable herb and
one of my closest plant allies. The woman's spirit herb. Expectorant, antiseptic, antibacterial, antiviral, hormonal normalizer, anti-inflammatory,
antispasmodic. Used for restoring uterine and female reproductive balance, griping pains (both uterine and intestinal), rheumatic inflammations, bronchitis, coughs, and colds. (Most herbalists will want to narrow
my range of actions and limit *Angelica* to antispasmodic and expectorant
properties. I have found it of use across a broader spectrum.)

aniseed. *Pimpinella anisum*—Antispasmodic, expectorant, antiseptic. Used
in griping pains of the stomach, bronchitis, and persistent coughing.

bay leaves. *Laurus nobilis*—The well-known culinary herb, bay is aromatic, astringent, stomachic, and carminative. It tones and strengthens the function of the stomach, relieves flatulence and griping pains, and shrinks inflamed tissues. It is rarely used in medicinal practice.

bittersweet root and herb. *Solanum dulcamara*—An herb that due to its membership in the deadly nightshade family is usually warned against in shrill tones. However, it is much milder than many nightshade plants and is a reliable herb when used with intelligent intention. It is toxic in large doses. Diuretic, antirheumatic, expectorant, narcotic, sedative. Used internally to increase urine flow, to relieve rheumatic and arthritic inflammations, and as a relaxing sedative. It is a beautiful plant and wonderful herb.

bugloss herb. *Lycopsis arvensis*—A member of the borage family, bugloss is a native of Europe now naturalized in the United States. The flowers look somewhat like those of borage and comfrey, but the leaves are much smaller; they are rough-bristly and somewhat pointed, looking like a wolf's ear, hence the name of the plant—*lycos*, "wolf," and *opsis*, "appearance." The plant has been historically used somewhat like both borage (see "About Borage" in chapter 9) and comfrey. It possesses mild nervine properties, soothes inflammations, and is useful internally as an antiscorbutic and tonic. It is mucilaginous, expectorant, calmative, diuretic, and anti-inflammatory. It is rarely used in contemporary herbal medicine, and much confusion surrounds the herb itself. Some authors insist it is borage, others alkanet (*Anchusa officinalis*). It is, however, a distinct, separate plant, once used extensively in herbal practice.

chicory root and herb. *Cichoriem intybus*—Formerly known as succory. Identical, though weaker, in medicinal use to dandelion.

cinnamon. *Cinnamomum zeylanicum*—Astringent, carminative, stimulant, aromatic. Used to stop or slow bleeding in the lungs, and in the treatment of diarrhea. It also relieves stomach and intestinal cramping.

clove. *Eugenia caryophyllus*—Antiseptic, analgesic, carminative, aromatic. Powerful local anesthetic used mostly to relieve toothache pain. It also possesses antiseptic properties to fight local infection and is carminative, relieving gas, cramping, and nausea.

clove gillyflower. *Cherranthus cheiri*—Another herb about which there is some confusion. The gillyflower or wallflower was a major ceremonial and medicinal herb throughout the Middle Ages. Its scent is reminiscent of a cross between violets and cloves. It is a nervine, muscle relaxant, mild cardiac stimulant, and diuretic. Some authors think clove gillyflowers to be the flower of *Dianthus caryophyllus*—known as clove pink—at one time used to color and flavor syrups in Europe.

coltsfoot root and herb. *Tussilago farfara*—Expectorant, antitussive, demulcent, anticatarrhal, diuretic. Relieves coughing while helping mucous trapped in the lungs come up and out. It is especially useful in upper respiratory infections such as colds, flu, and bronchitis. In Yorkshire, England, coltsfoot is traditionally used in the making of Cleats Beer.

eringo roots. *Eryngium maritimum*—Also called sea holly. Diaphoretic, diuretic, aromatic, stimulant, expectorant. Used for upper respiratory infections, to increase sweating, and to move mucous up and out of the lungs.

fennel seed and root. *Foeniculum vulgare*—Carminative, antispasmodic, expectorant, antiseptic, antibacterial. After mint, one of the most reliable antinausea and anticramping herbs; it helps soothe the stomach. It is useful in upper respiratory infections to help mucous move out of the lungs.

gromwell herb and seeds. *Lithospermum officinale*—Diuretic, anti-inflammatory, astringent, vulnerary. Used in cystitis, urinary tract infections, and for external wound healing.

groundsel herb. *Senecio vulgaris*—Diaphoretic, antiscorbutic, purgative, diuretic. Generally used to gently stimulate vomiting. John Pechet (1694) observes: "The Juice of the herb taken in Beer, or a Decoction of it with Hony, vomits gently."[2] The herb was formerly used as the most gentle herb to induce vomiting and it had a reputation for only inducing vomiting if stomach illness was present. But as someone who will let the most awful food work its way (day by painful day) through my intestines rather than vomit early on, I admit Pechet's description doesn't entice me.

hart's tongue. *Scolopendrium officinarium* or *Asplenium Scolopendrium*—A fern indigenous to Europe and the Americas. Its leaves impart a somewhat sweetish taste, making it a useful addition to cough syrups and formulations. Its astringent qualities make it useful for dysentery and diarrhea. Historically, other actions were attributed to its ingestion. John Pechet (1694) observes: "The Powder of it is of excellent use for the Palpitation of the Heart, for Mother-fits, and Convulsions, being taken in Small Beer, and Posset-drink."[3] Its use in herbal medicine is now somewhat uncommon.

jujubes. *Ziziphus vulgaris*—A fruit, not a rubberoid candy. Much in the same vein as raisins, dates, and figs. Antiscorbutic, nutritive, demulcent, pectoral. Used mostly for upper respiratory infections, bronchial and throat irritations. Basically a demulcent pectoral useful in cough syrups for its actions, coloring, and flavor.

lavender herb. *Lavandula officinalis*—Carminative, antispasmodic, antidepressant. Especially useful for depression, nervous headaches, debility, and exhaustion. Adds quite a unique flavor and taste to fermentation.

liverwort herb. One of two herbs: *Hepatica americana*, an American plant, or *Peltigera Canina*, a European lichen. Both used in similar manners to tonify, cleanse, and enhance the function of the liver.

lungwort lichen. *Lobaria pulmonaria*—A dried lichen, it has been used for centuries for healing. John Pechet noted in 1694 that "It grows on old Oaks and Beeches in dark, shady old Woods. That which grows on an Oak is excellent in curing the Jaundice: Take one Handful of it, and boyl it in a Pint of Small Beer, in a Pot well stoppered, till half is consum'd: Take thirteen Spoonfuls of it warm, Morning and Evening."[4] Lungwort is a good and gentle expectorant and soother of inflamed bronchial tissues. It is used primarily in upper respiratory infections, coughs, colds, and bronchitis.

mace. *Myristica fragrans*—Mace and nutmeg both come from this plant. Mace is the inner covering of the nut or fruit of *Myristica*. The outer covering is thrown away or made into a preserve, and this inner covering is compressed, dried in the sun, and then mixed with saltwater to preserve it. Generally used as a spice, it has the same medicinal action as nutmeg. It is antipyretic, astringent, stimulant, carminative, and antinausea. Traditionally it has been used in intermittent fevers, diarrhea, flatulence, and nausea.

maidenhair fern herb. *Adiantum* spp.—Emmenagogue, pectoral tonic, and expectorant. Generally used to stimulate menstruation, to help in healing upper respiratory infections, and, most often, in cough syrups to promote expectoration, ease coughing, and soothe inflamed membranes.

marjoram. *Origanum vulgare*—Diaphoretic, antiseptic, expectorant, and emmenagogue. Stimulates menstruation. Used in colds, flu, and upper respiratory infections to promote expression of mucous and alleviate coughing. Its antibacterial properties make it useful here as well, helping combat infection.

marshmallow root. *Althea officinalis*— Primarily demulcent and expectorant. Helps move trapped mucous out of the lungs and soothe inflamed bronchial tissue. Useful in all other conditions where there is inflammation, such as cystitis and external wounds.

orris roots. Orris is made from the roots of any of three iris species: *Iris germanica, Iris florentina,* or *Iris pallida.* The fresh roots, as with so many iris family members, are actively irritant. Upon drying, this quality is lost, and the roots of iris species are used in herbal medicine in much the same way. Primarily, they are a gastric, bile, and pancreatic enzyme stimulant. They also possess diuretic and expectorant qualities. Strong in their action, they are usually used with other herbs that soften their impact on the system. Orris roots, possessing a wonderful fragrance, are now most commonly used as an additive in perfumes and bath salts. The primary iris used in herbal medicine is the American blue flag, or wild, iris, *Iris missouriensis.*

parsley herb and root and seed. *Petroselinum crispum*—Antiscorbutic, diuretic, emmenagogue, carminative. One of the richest sources of vitamin C, parsley is a scurvy alleviator and preventative; it is a reliable diuretic, increasing the flow of urine; it also stimulates suppressed menstruation and eases flatulence and griping intestinal pains.

pellitory of the wall herb. *Parietaria diffusa*—Diuretic, demulcent. Especially useful in any infection or inflammation of the urinary tract. It helps increase flow of urine and coats and soothes inflamed urethral tissue. Useful in cystitis and for treatment of kidney stones.

scabious root. *Scabious succisa*—Once a common medicinal herb in England and to some extent in the United States, it has fallen out of use almost entirely. Demulcent, diaphoretic, and febrifuge. Used in colds, flu, and upper respiratory infections with attendant coughing. Lowers fevers; coats and soothes inflamed tissues. Its relative, *Scabiosa arvensis* (blue buttons), was used somewhat similarly, though the flowers were usually used instead of the root.

strawberry leaves. *Fragaria* spp.—A *mild* astringent, diuretic, and pleasant-tasting tea. It can be reliably used for diarrhea, urinary tract infections, stomach sensitivity, dysentery, gum inflammation, and hematuria and excessive menstrual bleeding.

sweetbrier (wild rose) leaves and rose hips. *Rosa* spp.—Above all a safe and reliable tonic astringent. Useful in all conditions where astringent action is indicated, much like strawberry leaves but stronger in their action. In general, it strengthens and tones the stomach and bowels. Rose hips are well known as one of the best sources of vitamin C and pectin. They are antiscorbutic and astringent.

violet leaves. *Viola odorata*—A mild pectoral sedative, expectorant, and mild laxative. Possessing a wonderful taste, it is most often used in cough syrups to ease coughing and promote expectoration. The leaves are best used fresh to preserve the flavor they impart in solution.

watercress herb. *Nasturtium officinale*—Antiscorbutic and metabolic stimulant. Long used as a spring tonic herb, to prevent scurvy, and to throw off the metabolic sluggishness of winter. Best if used fresh. Not to be confused with brooklime, also called for in many herbal beer recipes. Brooklime is *Veronica Beccabunga*, a relative of speedwell (*Veronica officinalis*). Also growing in streams, it was used somewhat similarly to watercress: as antiscorbutic, diuretic, febrifuge, and emmenagogue.

wood sorrel herb and root. *Oxalis Acetosella*—Refrigerant (i.e., cools fevers), antiseptic, diuretic, and antiscorbutic. It should be used fresh if at all possible. Used for treatment and prevention of scurvy and as a pot herb, it also has a long history of use for mouth sores, fevers, sore throats, and nausea. It has an even longer history of use among folk and indigenous peoples in the treatment of cancer, usually skin cancers. Its relative, sheep sorrel, is one of the ingredients in *Essiac*, the popular Canadian herbal cancer treatment. The fresh juice can be used in a poultice. It contains oxalic acid, and internal use of large quantities can lead to oxalate poisoning. The plant, like all the sorrels, has a pleasantly sour taste. The cold tea tastes somewhat like lemonade.

APPENDIX FOUR

Sources of Supply and Useful Books

ON BREWING, ALCOHOL, AND INTOXICATION

1. Robert Gayre, *Brewing Mead* (Boulder, CO: Brewers Publications, 1986). The best book on the history, meaning, and effects of mead.

2. Charlie Papazian, *The New Complete Joy of Home Brewing* (New York: Avon Books, 1983). The best overall book on home brewing.

3. Odd Nordland, *Brewing and Beer Traditions in Norway* (Norway: The Norwegian Research Council for Science and the Humanities, 1969). The best study of the essence of folk brewing, its beliefs, history, and religious perspectives. The *only* real look at what ancient European brewing was in all probability like. Unfortunately, out of print.

4. Mikal Aasved, *Alcohol, Drinking, and Intoxication in Preindustrial Society: Theoretical, Nutritional, and Religious Considerations*, 2 vols., University of California, Santa Barbara, Ph.D. diss., 1988. Available from UMI Dissertation Services (1-800-521-0600) for about $35 with a credit card. You have to tell them you are a student or teacher. The best (and really only) exploration of the *meaning* of indigenous brewing.

5. Dale Pendell, *Pharmako/poeia* (San Francisco: Mercury House, 1995). The best look at the effects of mood-altering substances on human consciousness from a poetic perspective. The book has a lot of material on alcohol and fermentations.

HERBALISM

1. Stephen Buhner, *Sacred Plant Medicine* (Boulder, CO: Roberts Rinehart Publishing, 1996). The most extensive look at the *meaning* and practice of indigenous herbalism for the nonindigenous reader.

2. James Green, *The Herbal Medicine Maker's Handbook* (Forestville, CA: Wildlife and Green Publications, 1990). Phone: 1-707-887-2012. The best work on the practical aspects of herbal medicine making from an Earth-spirituality perspective.

3. David Hoffmann, *The New Holistic Herbal* (Rockport: Element, 1993). The best overall herbal on the market. The new illustrated version is quite nice.

4. Any of Michael Moore's books on herbalism—see your local bookstore. *The* elder of American herbalism.

5. Maude Grieve, *A Modern Herbal* (1931; reprint, New York: Dover, 1971). Always in print. The best comprehensive book on European history and use of herbs and medicinal actions up to 1931. Though a lot of her information came from John Uri Lloyd and Harvey Felter's *King's American Dispensatory*, Felter and Lloyd's book is $250; hers has more history and interesting anecdotes, and is more fun to read.

HERBAL SOURCES

1. Trinity Herbs, P.O. Box 1001, Graton, CA 95444, 1-707-824-2040. They will carry most of the herbs used in these recipes. A number of them, however, are difficult to come by.

2. Horizon Herbs, P.O. Box 69, Williams, OR 97544, 1-541-846-6704. They carry a wide variety of herb seeds in stock, many of which are endangered or so rare as to never be found elsewhere.

SOURCES FOR
HONEY AND HIVE PRODUCTS

1. Glorybee bee products, 1-800-456-7923. Visa and Mastercard accepted. A very good and price-competitive source of all bee products in bulk form.
2. CC Pollen Company, 3627 East Indian School Road, Suite 209, Phoenix, AZ 85018, 1-800-875-0096. A good source for bee products in capsule form for personal and medicinal use.

SOURCE FOR AGAVE NECTAR

Stein Fillers, Inc.
4180 Viking Way
Long Beach, CA 90808
1-562-425-0588

WORKSHOPS AND PROGRAMS ON ANCIENT
FERMENTATION AND SACRED PLANT MEDICINE

Stephen Harrod Buhner
PO Box 1147
Tum Tum, WA 99034
1-509-258-9148

CHAPTER REFERENCES

PROLOGUE

1. Alan Eames, *The Secret Life of Beer* (Pownal, VT: Storey Communications), 1995, 14–16.
2. Quoted in Dale Pendell, *Pharmako/poeia* (San Francisco: Mercury House, 1995), 73.
3. Quoted in ibid., 52.

CHAPTER ONE

1. Peter Farb, *Man's Rise to Civilization (As Shown by the Indians of North America from Primeval Times to the Coming of the Industrial State)* (New York: E. P. Dutton, 1968), 47–48.
2. Ibid., 129–131.
3. Mikal Aasved, "Alcohol, Drinking, and Intoxication in Preindustrial Society: Theoretical, Nutritional, and Religious Considerations" (Ph.D. diss., University of California, Santa Barbara, 1988), 5.
4. Ibid., 248–249.
5. Frances Densmore, *Teton Sioux Music* (Washington: Smithsonian Institution, Bureau of American Ethnology, Bulletin 61, 1918), 173.
6. Ken Wilbur, *A Brief History of Everything* (Boston: Shambhala, 1996), 173.
7. Aasved, "Alcohol," 1235.
8. Ibid., 125.
9. Ibid., 1236.
10. Ibid., 1236–1237.
11. Vaclav Havel, address of the president of the Czech Republic, on the occasion of receiving the Liberty Medal in Philadelphia, PA, July 4, 1994.
12. Norbert Mayer, "The New Berserkers," in Ralph Metzner, *The Well of Remembrance* (Boston: Shambhala Press, 1994), 135.
13. Walt Whitman, *Leaves of Grass* (New York: Penguin Books, 1978), 55.

CHAPTER TWO

1. Mikal Aasved, "Alcohol, Drinking, and Intoxication in Preindustrial Society: Theoretical, Nutritional, and Religious Considerations" (Ph.D. diss., University of California, Santa Barbara, 1988), 410–411.
2. Robert Gayre, *Brewing Mead* (Boulder, CO: Brewers Publications, 1986).
3. Ibid., 27.
4. Retold by the author from the ancient Norse *Edda* (Icelandic for "great-grandmother"), first written from ancient oral versions in the sixth century A.D.
5. Quoted in Gayre, *Brewing Mead*, 26.
6. Quoted in Pendell, *Pharmako/poeia* (San Francisco: Mercury House, 1995), 96.
7. Quoted in John Bickerdyke, *The Curiosities of Ale and Beer* (London: Leadenhall Press, ca. 1890), 158.
8. Gayre, *Brewing Mead*.
9. Aasved, "Alcohol," 410–416; see also Robert Gayre, *Brewing Mead*.
10. Dr. W. P. Worth, *On the New and True Art of Brewing* (London: 1692), 65.
11. Quoted in John Arnold, *Origin and History of Beer and Brewing* (Chicago: Alumni Association of the Wahl-Henius Institute of Fermentology, 1911), 370.
12. Ibid.
13. W. T. Marchant, *In Praise of Ale: or Songs, Ballads, Epigrams, and Anecdotes Relating to Beer, Malt, and Hops* (London: Redway, 1888), 46.
14. Odd Nordland, *Brewing and Beer Traditions in Norway* (Norway: the Norwegian Research Council for Science and the Humanities, 1969), 219.
15. Adapted from Bruce Williams, "Leann Fraoch—Scottish Heather Ale" *Zymurgy* 17, no. 4 (Special 1994): 25.
16. Marchant, *In Praise of Ale*, 46.
17. Williams, "Leann Fraoch," 24.
18. Quoted in Alan Eames, *The Secret Life of Beer* (Pownal, VT: Storey Communications, 1995), 52–54.
19. Charles Millspaugh, *American Medicinal Plants* (Philadelphia: Yorston, 1892; reprint, New York: Dover, 1974), 392.
20. Alan Eames, personal communication, November 1997.
21. Quoted in Williams, "Leann Fraoch," 24.
22. Carol Henderson, "Some Unusual Properties of Honey: Thixotropy and Dilatancy," *American Bee Journal* 124, no. 8 (August 1984): 600.
23. Gayre, *Brewing Mead*.

24. Williams, "Leann Fraoch," 24.

25. Gayre, *Brewing Mead*, 18.

26. Ibid., 22.

27. Patrick Quillin, *Honey, Garlic, and Vinegar* (North Canton, OH: The Leader Company, 1996), 15.

28. Ibid., 17.

29. Rita Elkins, *Bee Pollen, Royal Jelly, Propolis, and Honey* (Pleasant Grove, UT: Woodland Publishing, 1996), 49.

30. Ibid., 48.

31. Robert and Michele Root-Bernstein, *Honey, Mud, and Maggots* (Boston: Houghton Mifflin, 1997), 41.

32. Elkins, *Bee Pollen*, 48.

33. Root-Bernstein, *Honey, Mud, and Maggots*, 41.

34. N. al Somal, et al., *JR Society of Medicine* 87, no. 1 (January 1994): 9, and T. Postmes, et al., *Lancet* 341 (March 20, 1993): 756 [*see also* 341 (January 9, 1993): 90]. Quoted in Patrick Quillin, *Honey, Garlic, and Vinegar* (North Canton, OH: The Leader Company, 1996), 26.

35. A. T. Ali and M. N. Chowdhury, et al., "Inhibitory effect of natural honey on *Helicobacter pylori*," *Trop-Gastroenterology* 12, no. 3 (July–September 1991): 139–143. Cited in Elkins, *Bee Pollen*, 51.

36. M. Subrahmanyam, *British Journal of Plastic Surgery* 46, no. 4 (June 1993): 322. Cited in Quillin, *Honey, Garlic, and Vinegar*, 27.

37. W. Phuapradit, et al., *Australia and New Zealand Journal of Obstetrics and Gynecology* 32, no. 4 (November 1992): 381, and S.E. Efem, *Surgery* 113, no. 2 (February 1993): 200. Cited in Quillan, *Honey, Garlic, and Vinegar*, 27.

38. E. F. Elbagoury and S. Rasmy, "Antibacterial action of natural honey on anaerobic bacteroides," *Journal of Egyptian Dentistry* 39, no. 1 (January 1993): 381–86, and G. Ndayisaba, L. Bazira, and E. Haboniman, "Treatment of Wounds with Honey," *Presse-Med.* 3:21, no. 32 (October 1992): 1516–8. Cited in Elkins, *Bee Pollen*, 51.

39. J. H. Dustmann, "Bee Products for Human Health," *American Bee Journal* 136, no. 4 (April 1996): 275.

40. Root-Bernstein, *Honey, Mud, and Maggots*, 32.

41. Ibid., 35.

42. Ibid., 36. Citing Postumes, van den Bogaard and Hazen, "Honey for Wounds, Ulcers, and Skin Graft Preservation," *Lancet* 341 (1993): 756–757.

43. Elkins, *Bee Pollen*, 51.

44. Ibid., 52.

45. Ibid., 47.

46. Bodog Beck and Doree Smedley, *Honey and Your Health* (New York: Robert McBride, 1944), 35.

47. Aasved, "Alcohol," 414.

48. Ann Harmon, "Hive Products for Therapeutic Use," *American Bee Journal* 123, no. 1 (January 1983): 42.

49. G. W. Hayes, "Supplemental Feeding of Honey Bees," *American Bee Journal* 124, no. 1 (January 1984): 35.

50. Elkins, *Bee Pollen*, 24.

51. Gyorgy Toth, "What's New in Pollen Research," *American Bee Journal* 123, no. 7 (July 1983): 522.

52. Gerald Loper and Allen Cohen, "The Caloric Content of Bee-Gathered Pollen," *American Bee Journal* 122, no. 10 (October 1982): 709.

53. Elkins, *Bee Pollen*, 25.

54. Ibid., 26.

55. Toth, "What's New in Pollen Research," 522–524.

56. Elkins, *Bee Pollen*, 22.

57. Toth, "What's New in Pollen Research," 522.

58. Melvyn Werbach and Michael Murray, *Botanical Influences on Illness* (Tarzana, CA: Third Line Press, 1994), 79.

59. Ibid., 286.

60. Toth, "What's New in Pollen Research," 524.

61. Ibid., 522.

62. Elkins, *Bee Pollen*, 29.

63. Werbach and Murray, *Botanical Influences on Illness*, 212–213.

64. Elkins, *Bee Pollen*, 28.

65. Toth, "What's New in Pollen Research," 525.

66. J. Iannuzzi, "Propolis: The Most Mysterious Hive Element," part 1, *American Bee Journal* 123, no. 8 (August 1983): 573–574.

67. Maung Maung Nyein "The Use of Asphalt as a Propolis Substitute," *American Bee Journal* 123, no. 10 (October 1983): 732.

68. Elkins, *Bee Pollen*, 34.

69. Ibid., 34, and Harmon, "Hive Products for Therapeutic Use," 41–42.

70. J. Iannuzzi, "Propolis:The Most Mysterious Hive Element," part 2, *American Bee Journal* 123, no. 9 (September 1983): 631–633.

71. Justin Schmidt, "Apitherapy Meeting Held in the Land of Milk and Honey," *American Bee Journal* 136, no. 10 (October 1996): 722.

72. Galina Kotova, "Apiary Products Are Important in Soviet Medicine," *American Bee Journal* 121, no. 12 (December 1981): 850.

73. V. P. Kivalkina. *Propolis: Its Antibacterial and Therapeutic Properties* (Russia: Kasan Publishing, 1978). Cited in Elkins, *Bee Pollen*, 39.

74. Connie and Arnold Krochmal, "Apitherapy in Romania," *American Bee Journal* 121, no. 11 (November 1981): 786.

75. J. H. Dustmann, "Bee Products for Human Health," 275.

76. Elkins, *Bee Pollen*, 38.

77. G. F. Zabelina, "Propolis" (thesis delivered at Rachfuss Children's Hospital, Russia). Cited in Elkins, *Bee Pollen*, 41.

78. Schmidt, "Apitherapy Meeting Held in the Land of Milk and Honey," 722.

79. Elkins, *Bee Pollen*, 37.

80. C. V. Rao, et al., "Effect of caffeic acid esters on carcinogen-induced mutagenicity and human colon adenocarcinoma cell growth," *Chemical-Biological Interaction* 84, no. 3 (November 16, 1992): 277–290. Quoted in ibid., 42.

81. Elkins, *Bee Pollen*, and Royden Brown, *Royden Brown's Bee Hive Product Bible* (Garden City: Avery Publishing, 1993).

82. Harmon, "Hive Products for Therapeutic Use."

83. Brown, *Bee Hive Product Bible*; Elkins, *Bee Pollen*.

84. Royden Brown, citing Albert Saenz, "Biology, Biochemistry, and the Therapeutic Effects of Royal Jelly in Human Pathology," Pasteur Institute of Paris, 1984.

85. Quoted in ibid., 110.

86. Brown, *Bee Hive Product Bible*; Elkins, *Bee Pollen*.

87. Royden Brown, citing B. Filipic and M. Likvar, "Clinical Value of Royal Jelly and Propolis Against Viral Infections," University of Sarajevo, n.d., in Brown, *Bee Hive Product Bible*.

88. Quoted in Ibid., 119.

89. Harvey Felter and John Uri Lloyd, *King's American Dispensatory* (Cincinnati: Eclectic Publications, 1895), 225.

90. Schmidt, "Apitherapy Meeting Held in the Land of Milk and Honey."

91. Kotova, "Apiary Products Are Important in Soviet Medicine."

92. Charles Mraz, "Bee Venom for Arthritis—An Update," *American Bee Journal* 122, no. 2 (February 1982).

93. North American Apitherapy Abstracts, *American Bee Journal* 123, no. 2 (February 1983).

94. Anne Robinson and Gard Otis, "Bee Venom: Concerns About Variability," *American Bee Journal* 136, no. 8 (August 1996).

95. James Duke, *The Green Pharmacy* (New York: Rodale Press, 1997).

96. Beck and Smedley, *Honey and Your Health*, 27.

97. Ibid., 28.
98. Ibid.
99. Quoted in Gayre, *Brewing Mead*, 23.

CHAPTER THREE

1. Odd Nordland, *Brewing and Beer Traditions in Norway* (Norway: The Norwegian Research Council for Science and the Humanities, 1969).
2. Dale Pendell, *Pharmako/poeia* (San Francisco: Mercury House, 1995), 55.
3. Quoted in ibid., 54.
4. Ibid., 53.
5. Nordland, *Brewing and Beer Traditions in Norway*, 242.
6. Quoted in ibid., 256.
7. Ibid., 264.
8. Ibid., 267.
9. Ibid., 267.
10. Mikal Aasved, "Alcohol, Drinking, and Intoxication in Preindustrial Society: Theoretical, Nutritional, and Religious Considerations" (Ph.D. diss., University of California, Santa Barbara, 1988).
11. Aasved "Alcohol"; *Dorland's Illustrated Medical Dictionary*, 24th Edition (Philadelphia: W. B. Saunders Company, 1965); *Funk and Wagnalls New Encyclopedia* (New York: Funk and Wagnalls, 1983); Harvey Felter and John Uri Lloyd, *King's American Dispensatory* (Cincinnati: Eclectic Publications, 1895).
12. Clifford Gastanieu, et al., *Fermented Food Beverages in Nutrition* (New York: Academic Press, 1979); Aasved, "Alcohol."
13. Ibid., Gastanieu.
14. Aasved, "Alcohol," 757.
15. Ibid.
16. Ibid., 734.
17. Ibid.
18. Ibid., 775.
19. Ibid., 775.
20. Quoted in Ruth Underhill, *Singing For Power* (Berkeley: University of California Press, 1938), 32–33.

CHAPTER FOUR

1. Mikal Aasved, "Alcohol, Drinking, and Intoxication in Preindustrial Society: Theoretical, Nutritional, and Religious Considerations" (Ph.D. diss., University of California, Santa Barbara, 1988), 781–782.

2. Frank Crosswhite, "The Annual Saguaro Harvest and Crop Cycle of the Papago," *Desert Plants* 2, no. 1 (spring 1980), University of Arizona: 7.

3. Quoted in Ruth Underhill, *Singing for Power* (Berkeley, CA: University of California Press, 1938), 40.

4. Ibid., 35.

5. Ibid., 34.

6. Ibid.

7. Frances Densmore, *Papago Music*, Smithsonian Institution, Bureau of American Ethnology, Bulletin 90 (Washington, D.C.: United States Government Printing Office, 1929), 150.

8. Crosswhite, "The Annual Saguaro Harvest," 36.

9. Retold by the author from traditional stories of the coming of the sacred saguaro.

10. Densmore, *Papago Music*, 153.

11. Ruth Underhill, *Autobiography of a Papago Woman*, Memoirs of the American Anthropological Assoc., no. 46 (Mehasha, WI: American Anthropological Association, 1936), 45.

12. Carl Lumholtz, *New Trails in Mexico* (London: Unwin, 1912), 123.

13. Underhill, *Singing for Power*, 22.

14. Kathleen Harrison, in Stephen Buhner, *Sacred Plant Medicine* (Boulder, CO: Roberts Rinehart Publishers, 1996), 41.

15. Underhill, *Singing for Power*, 5–6. Quoted in Aasved, "Alcohol," 730.

16. Lumholtz, *New Trails in Mexico*, 121.

17. L. S. M. Curtain, *By the Prophet of the Earth* (Sante Fe: Vincente Foundation, 1949).

18. Richard Felger and Mary Beck Moser, in *Economic Botany* 28, no. 4 (1974).

19. Elizabeth Hart, "Native foodstuffs as a supplement to the food budget of Arizona Desert Indians," *Indians At Work* 5, no. 3 (November 1937): 14.

20. Crosswhite, "The Annual Saguaro Harvest," 7, 42.

21. Valery Harvard, "Drink plants of the North American Indians," *Bulletin of the Torrey Botanical Club* 23, no. 2 (February 1896).

22. Aasved, "Alcohol," 782.

23. Ibid., 733.

24. Ibid.

25. William Merrill, "Thinking and Drinking: A Raramuri Interpretation," in Richard Ford, editor, *The Nature and Status of Ethnobotany* (Ann Arbor, MI: Museum of Anthropology, anthropological paper no. 67, 1978).

26. Michael Moore, *Medicinal Plants of the Desert and Canyon West* (Sante Fe: Museum of New Mexico Press, 1989); Rosita Arvigo and Michael Balick, *Rainforest Remedies* (Twin Lakes, WI: Lotus Press, 1993).

27. Marilou Awiakta, *Selu: Seeking the Corn Mother's Wisdom* (Golden, CO: Fulcrum Publishing, 1993), 9.

28. Virgil Vogel, *American Indian Medicine* (Norman: University of Oklahoma Press, 1970); Awiakta, *Selu;* Gastineau, *Fermented Food Beverages in Nutrition* (New York: Academic Press, 1979).

29. Hugh Cutler and Martin Cardenas, "Chicha, a Native South American Beer," Cambridge: Botanical Museum Leaflets 13, no. 3 (December 19, 1947).

30. Aasved, "Alcohol," 784.

31. John Kennedy, *The Tarahumara of the Sierra Madre* (Arlington Heights, IL: AHM Publishing Corp., 1978), 115.

32. Aasved, "Alcohol," 359–360.

33. Wendy Aaronson and Bill Ridgely, "Adventures in Chicha and Chang," *Zymurgy* 17, no. 1 (Spring 1994): 34–36. Recipe adapted by them from Felipe Rojas-Lombardi, *The Art of South American Cooking* (New York: Harper Collins, 1991).

34. Quoted in Sanborn Brown, *Wines and Beers of Old New England* (Hanover, MA: University Press of New England, 1976), 42.

35. Quoted in ibid., 44–45.

36. Adapted from ibid.

37. Ernest Cherrington, ed., *Standard Encyclopedia of the Alcohol Problem* (Westerville, OH: American Issue Publishing, 1925). From a xerox, no page number present.

38. Quoted in Awiakta, *Selu*, 302.

39. Compiled and retold by the author from traditional stories.

40. Evelyn Fox Keller, *A Feeling for the Organism: The Life and Work of Barbara McClintock* (New York: W. H. Freeman, 1983), xix.

41. Ibid.

42. Keller, *A Feeling for the Organism*, cited in Awiakta, *Selu*, 324–325.

43. Cited in Vogel, *American Indian Medicine*, 292.

44. Ibid.; Michael Moore, *Medicinal Plants of the Mountain West* (Santa Fe: Museum of New Mexico Press, 1979); Harvey Felter and John Uri Lloyd, *King's American Dispensatory* (Cincinnati: Eclectic Publication, 1895).

45. Aasved, "Alcohol," 735.

46. Jean de Lery, *History of a Voyage to the Land of Brazil, Otherwise Called America,* 1578. This excerpt is from a photocopy of a translation of de Lery's book by Janet Whatley, Latin American Literature and Culture Series, ed. Roberto Echevarria, vol. 6, 73. Regrettably the photocopier did not include further publishing data in the material I have.

47. Aasved, "Alcohol," 736.

48. Retold by the author from the traditional stories.

49. Aasved, "Alcohol," 741.

50. Ibid.

51. Ibid., 749–750.

52. Gloria Levitas, "Saturday Staple in Brazil: Manioc," *New York Times* (December 11, 1988): 6.

53. Felter and Lloyd, *King's American Dispensatory.*

54. Levitas, "Saturday Staple in Brazil," 6; Aasved, "Alcohol"; Gertrude Dole, "Manioc and the Kuikuru" in Richard Ford, ed., *The Nature and Status of Ethnobotany* (Ann Arbor, MI: Museum of Anthropology, anthropological paper no. 67, 1978).

55. Aaronson and Ridgely, "Adventures in Chicha and Chang," 32.

56. Ibid.

57. Ibid., 33.

58. de Lery, *History of a Voyage to Brazil,* 74.

59. Aasved, "Alcohol," 871.

60. Ibid., 798.

61. Adapted from Bertrand Remi, *Home Brew* (Katmandu, Nepal: Sahayogi Press, 1976), 29.

62. Cherrington, *Standard Encyclopedia of the Alcohol Problem.*

63. Aasved, "Alcohol," 771.

64. Ibid., 766.

65. Adapted from Remi, *Home Brew,* 31.

66. Aasved, "Alcohol," 859.

67. Felter and Lloyd, *King's American Dispensatory;* Maude Grieve, *A Modern Herbal* (New York: Dover, 1971).

68. Quoted in Aasved, "Alcohol," 784.

69. Adapted from Remi, *Home Brew,* 18.

70.   Trilock Majupuria and D. P. Joshi, *Religious and Useful Plants of Nepal and India* (Lalitpur Colony, India: Craftsman Press, 1989), 115.

71.   Arvigo and Balick, *Rainforest Remedies*.

72.   Majupuria and Joshi, *Plants of Nepal*.

73.   Aasved, "Alcohol," 768.

74.   Retold from the traditional story by the author.

75.   Ibid.

76.   Alan Eames, "Drinking with the Dead," *Beer, the Magazine*. Xerox of the article, no publication information present.

77.   Emmanuel Kwaku Akyeampong, *Drink, Power, and Cultural Change: A Social History of Alcohol in Ghana c. 1800 to Recent times* (Portsmouth, NH: Heinemann, 1996), 27.

78.   Ibid.; Harry Wolcott, *The African Beer Gardens of Bulwayo* (New Brunswick, NJ: Publications Division Rutgers Center of Alcohol Studies, 1974); Elizabeth Colson and Thayer Scudder, *For Prayer and Profit: The Ritual, Economic, and Social Importance of Beer in Gwembe District, Zambia, 1950-1982* (Stanford, CA: Stanford University Press, 1988); Aasved, "Alcohol."

79.   Aasved, "Alcohol."

80.   Arvigo and Balick, *Rainforest Remedies*; Majupuria and Joshi, *Plants of Nepal*.

81.   Majupuria and Joshi, *Plants of Nepal*.

82.   Akyeampong, *Drink, Power, and Cultural Change*; Colson and Scudder, *For Prayer and Profit*; Aasved, "Alcohol."

CHAPTER FIVE

1.   Quoted in Dale Pendell, *Pharmako/poeia* (San Francisco: Mercury House, 1995), 79.

2.   John Bickerdyke, *The Curiosities of Ale and Beer* (London: Leadenhall Press, ca. 1890), 408.

3.   Quoted in Ruth Underhill, *Singing for Power* (Berkeley: University of California Press, 1938), 40–41.

4.   Mikal Aasved, "Alcohol, Drinking, and Intoxication in Preindustrial Society: Theoretical, Nutritional, and Religious Consideration" (Ph. D. diss., University of California, Santa Barbara, 1988), 321.

5.   E. A. Speiser translation, quoted in Herbert Mason, *Gilgamesh* (New York: NAL, 1970), 123.

6.   Kenneth Pelletier, *Toward a Science of Consciousness* (New York: Delta, 1978), 66.

      Kenneth Pelletier touches on the reason for this capacity in nonindustrial cultures and why science has misunderstood it. In his *Toward a Science of Consciousness*, he observes that the mind is capable of much finer discrimination than scientific instrumentation can be. He notes that understanding of deep truths about the interactions of the universe is and has always been available to human beings because all human beings, irrespective of culture and era, have had access to "the finest probe ever conceived—the trained and focused attention of consciousness itself." Many non-Western cultures and religions have used their understanding of this capacity to develop fairly subtle and refined expressions of what can be called sacred science. Western scientists, in relying on external (and fairly gross) probes, have only been able to perceive rather gross truths and elements of the universe. In developing this capacity of perception, one is training, as Kenneth Pelletier said, "the finest probe ever conceived."

7. Quoted in Pendell, *Pharmako/poeig*, 97.
8. Aasved, "Alcohol," 1105.
9. Harvey Felter and John Uni Lloyd, *King's American Dispensatory* (Cincinnati: Eclectic Publications, 1895), 136.
10. David Hoffmann, *Therapeutic Herbalism: A Correspondence Course in Phytotherapy* (n.p., n.d.), 2–19.
11. Aasved, "Alcohol," 761.
12. Quoted in Pendell, *Pharmako/poeia*, 62.

CHAPTER SIX

1. Quoted in Solomon Katz and Fritz Maytag, "Brewing and Ancient Beer," *Archaeology* (July/August 1991): 109.
2. Masanobu Fukuoka, *The Natural Way of Farming* (New York: Japan Publications, 1985).
3. Delores LaChappelle, *Sacred Land, Sacred Sex, Rapture of the Deep* (Silverton, CO: Finn Hill Arts, 1988).
4. Alan Eames, personal communication, 1997.
5. Katz and Maytag, "Brewing and Ancient Beer."
6. Mikal Aasved, "Alcohol, Drinking, and Intoxication in Preindustrial Society: Theoretical, Nutritional, and Religious Consideration" (Ph.D. diss., University of California, Santa Barbara, 1988), 333.
7. From the Peter Borne Missza 1578 edition, quoted in John Arnold, *Origin and History of Beer and Brewing* (Chicago: Alumni Association of the Wahl-Henius Institute of Fermentology, 1911), 255–258.
8. Aasved, "Alcohol," 763.

9. Retold from traditional tales by the author.

10. Retold from traditional tales by the author.

11. Dale Pendell, *Pharmako/poeia* (San Francisco: Mercury House, 1995), 214.

12. Anne Baring and Jules Cashford, *Myth of the Goddess* (New York: Viking, 1991), 389.

13. Quoted in ibid.

14. Ibid.; Aasved, "Alcohol," 1115.

15. Frazier, *The Golden Bough* (1959). Quoted in Aasved, "Alcohol," 783.

16. Ibid., 783–784.

17. Ibid.

18. Ibid., 327.

19. Harvey Felter and John Uri Lloyd, *King's American Dispensatory* (Cincinnati: Eclectic Publications, 1895), 808.

20. Ibid.

21. Aasved, "Alcohol," 1286.

CHAPTER SEVEN

1. Christian Ratsch, "The Mead of Inspiration," in Ralph Metzner, *The Well of Remembrance* (Boston: Shambhala Press, 1994), 280.

2. W. T. Marchant, *In Praise of Ale* (London: George Redway, 1888), 39.

3. Quoted in Dale Pendell, *Pharmako/poeia* (San Francisco: Mercury House, 1995), 213.

4. R. Bruce Lamb, *Wizard of the Upper Amazon* (Boston: Houghton Mifflin, 1974), 89.

5. John Arnold, *Origin and History of Beer and Brewing* (Chicago: Alumni Association of the Wahl-Henius Institute of Fermentology, 1911), 239, 241.

6. Maude Grieve, *A Modern Herbal* (1931; New York: Dover, 1971), 411.

7. Arnold, *Origin and History of Beer and Brewing*, 375.

8. Ibid., 235.

9. Ibid., 237.

10. Odd Nordland, *Brewing and Beer Traditions in Norway* (Norway: The Norwegian Research Council for Science and the Humanities, 1969), 221.

11. Ibid., 238.

12. Ernest Cherrington, *Standard Encyclopedia of the Alcohol Problem* (Westerville, OH: American Issue Publishing, 1925), 406.

13. Nordland, *Brewing and Beer Traditions in Norway*.

14. Adapted from Dr. John Harrison (and members of the Durden Park Beer Circle), *Old British Beers and How to Make Them* (London: Durden Park Beer Circle, 1991), 21.

15. Nordland, *Brewing and Beer Traditions in Norway*, 216.

16. Ibid.

17. Ibid., 220.

18. Ibid.

19. Ibid., 221.

20. Charles Millspaugh, *American Medicinal Plants* (Philadelphia: Yorston, 1892; reprint, New York: Dover, 1974), 642.

21. Grieve, *A Modern Herbal*, 341.

22. Nordland, *Brewing and Beer Traditions in Norway*, 216.

23. Charlotte Erichsen-Brown, *Medicinal and Other Uses of American Plants* (New York: Dover, 1979), 192–193.

24. Harvey Felter and John Uri Lloyd, *King's American Dispensatory* (Cincinnati: Eclectic Publications, 1895), 1203–1204.

25. Ibid.; Michael Moore, *Medicinal Plants of the Pacific West* (Sante Fe: Red Crane, 1993); David Hoffmann, *The New Holistic Herbal* (Rockport, MA: Element, 1990).

26. Arnold, *Origin and History of Beer and Brewing*, 240.

27. Grieve, *A Modern Herbal*, 460.

28. Charles Millspaugh, *American Medicinal Plants*, 392. Note: He incorrectly refers to this plant as *Ledum latifolium* in the text and to Labrador tea as *Ledum Palustre*. From his reference to this plant as marsh tea (a common name for wild rosemary) and to the other plant as Labrador tea, it is almost certain that there was an error, uncaught, in the original text.

29. Ratsch, "The Mead of Inspiration," 291.

30. Moore, *Medicinal Plants of the Pacific West*, 161.

31. Erichsen-Brown, *Medicinal and Other Uses of American Plants*, 195.

32. Ibid., 196.

33. Felter and Lloyd, *King's American Dispensatory*, 1124–1125.

34. Grieve, *A Modern Herbal*.

35. Daniel Moerman, *Medicinal Plants of Native America* (Ann Arbor: University of Michigan Museum of Anthropology, Technical Reports, no. 19, 1986), 256–257.

36. Felter and Lloyd, *King's American Dispensatory*, 1125.

37. Nordland, *Brewing and Beer Traditions in Norway*, 223.

38. Ibid.

39. Grieve, *A Modern Herbal*, 864.

40. *Protocol Journal of Botanical Medicine* 1, no. 1 (summer 1995).

41. Moore, *Medicinal Plants of the Pacific West*.

42. Erichsen-Brown, *Medicinal and Other Uses of American Plants*, 401.

43. Ibid., 400.

44. Ibid., 401.

45. Kelly Kindscher, *Medicinal Wild Plants of the Prairie* (Lawrence: University press of Kansas, 1992), 52. Quoting Duke.

46. Dr. W. P. Worth, *On the New and True Art of Brewing* (London: 1692), 66–67.

47. Nordland, *Brewing and Beer Traditions in Norway*.

48. Charles Millspaugh, *American Medicinal Plants*, 349.

49. Felter and Lloyd, *King's American Dispensatory*, 5.

50. John Bickerdyke, *The Curiosities of Ale and Beer* (London: Leadenhall Press, ca. 1890), 409.

51. John Pechet, *The Compleat Herbal of Physical Plants* (London: 1694), 194.

52. Quoted in Grieve, *A Modern Herbal*, 858.

53. Delores LaChappelle, *Sacred Land, Sacred Sex, Rapture of the Deep* (Silverton, CO: Finn Hill Arts, 1988), 272.

54. Rob Talbot and Robin Whiteman, *Brother Cadfael's Herb Garden* (Boston: Little Brown, 1997), 194.

55. Trilock Majupuria and D. P. Joshi, *Religious and Useful Plants of Nepal and India* (Lalitpur Colony, India: Craftsman Press, 1989), 239.

56. Quoted in Kindscher, *Medicinal Wild Plants of the Prairie*, 51.

57. Felter and Lloyd, *King's American Dispensatory*, 5.

58. NAPRALERT database as of February 14, 1996.

59. Parkinson (1629), 478. Quoted in Cindy Renfrow, *A Sip Through Time* (n.p.: Renfrow, 1995), 8.

60. Gerarde (1597), 624. Quoted in Grieve, *A Modern Herbal*, 702; also quoted in Renfrow, *A Sip Through Time*, 8.

61. *The Universal Herbal* (1820). Quoted in Joseph Meyer, *The Herbalist* (Glenwood, IL: Meyer Books, 1918; revised edition, 1986), 192.

62. Mrs. Cornelius, *The Young Housekeeper's Friend* (1846). Quoted in Renfrow, *A Sip Through Time*, 23.

63. Thomas Newington (1719). Quoted in Renfrow, *A Sip Through Time*, 179.

64. Margaret Freeman, *Herbs for the Medieval Household for Cooking, Healing, and Divers Uses* (New York: Metropolitan Museum of Art, 1943), 6. Quoting the *Hortus Sanitatis, or Gart Der Gesundheit* (Mainz: Peter Schoeffer, 1485).

65. John Murrell (1612). Quoted in Renfrow, *A Sip Through Time*, 139.

66. Maude Grieve, *A Modern Herbal*, 204.

67. *Protocol Journal of Botanical Medicine* 2, no. 2 (1997).

68. Richard Mabey, *The New Age Herbalist* (New York: Simon and Schuster, 1988); James Duke, *The Green Pharmacy* (New York: Rodale Press, 1997); *Protocol Journal of Botanical Medicine* 1, no. 1 (summer 1995); Michael Moore, *Medicinal Plants of the Mountain West* (Sante Fe: Museum of New Mexico Press, 1979).

69. Duke, *The Green Pharmacy*; *Protocol Journal of Botanical Medicine* 1, no. 1 (summer 1995), and 2, no. 2 (1997).

70. Mabey, *The New Age Herbalist*.

71. Grieve, *A Modern Herbal*, 126.

72. F. Lighibodt, *Every Man His Own Gauger* (London: 1695), 60–61.

73. Grieve, *A Modern Herbal*, 127.

74. Ibid.; Felter and Lloyd, *King's American Dispensatory*; Hoffmann, *The New Holistic Herbal*.

75. Nordland, *Brewing and Beer Traditions in Norway*, 221.

76. Ratsch, "The Mead of Inspiration," 285.

77. Gustav Schenk, *The Book of Poisons* (New York: Rinehart and Company, 1955), 49.

78. Ibid., 53.

79. Felter and Lloyd, *King's American Dispensatory*; Grieve, *A Modern Herbal*; Mark Evans, *Herbal Plants* (London: Studio Editions, 1991); Talbot and Whiteman, *Brother Cadfael's Herb Garden*.

80. Talbot and Whiteman, *Brother Cadfael's Herb Garden*.

81. Ibid.; Felter and Lloyd, *King's American Dispensatory*; Grieve, *A Modern Herbal*; Evans, *Herbal Plants*; Christian Ratsch, *Plants of Love* (Berkeley: Ten Speed Press, 1997).

82. Quoted in Grieve, *A Modern Herbal*, 372.

83. Ibid., 372.

84. Ibid.

85. Ibid.; Felter and Lloyd, *King's American Dispensatory*.

86. J. Johnston, *The Chemistry of Common Life* (1879). Quoted in Meyer, *The Herbalist*, 191.

87. Grieve, *A Modern Herbal*; Felter and Lloyd, *King's American Dispensatory*; Majupuria and Joshi, *Plants of Nepal*; Ratsch, *Plants of Love*, 54.

88. Michael Moore, *Medicinal Plants of the Desert and Canyon West* (Sante Fe, NM: Museum of New Mexico Press, 1989), 129.

89. Ibid.; Felter and Lloyd, *King's American Dispensatory*; Grieve, *A Modern Herbal*; Ratsch, *Plants of Love*.

CHAPTER EIGHT

1. Quoted in Moyra Caldecott, *Myths of the Sacred Tree* (Rochester, VT: Destiny Books, 1993), 3.
2. Ibid., 2.
3. Maude Grieve, *A Modern Herbal* (New York: Dover, 1971), 452.
4. Odd Nordland, *Brewing and Beer Traditions in Norway* (Norway: Norwegian Research Council for Science and the Humanities), 173.
5. Ibid., 180.
6. Ibid., 181.
7. Ibid., 182.
8. Ibid., 190.
9. Ibid., 190–191.
10. Mike Schaefer, "Sahti: A Traditional Finnish Brew," *Zymurgy* 17, no. 4 (Special Issue 1994): 8.
11. Ibid.
12. Ibid.
13. Ibid.
14. Michael Moore, *Medicinal Plants of the Mountain West* (Sante Fe: Museum of New Mexico Press, 1979), 94.
15. Daniel Moerman, *Medicinal Plants of Native America* (Ann Arbor: University of Michigan Museum of Anthropology, Technical Reports, no. 19, 1986).
16. Melvin Gilmore, *The Uses of Plants by the Indians of the Missouri River Region* (1919; Lincoln: University of Nebraska Press, 1977), 12.
17. Joseph Bruchac, *Native Plant Stories* (Golden, CO: Fulcrum Publishing, 1995), 85.
18. Lesley Gordon, *The Mystery and Magic of Trees and Flowers* (London: Grange Books, 1993); Caldecott, *Myths of the Sacred Tree*.
19. Gilmore, *Uses of Plants*, 5.
20. Quoted in Kelly Kindscher, *Medicinal Wild Plants of the Prairie* (Lawrence: University Press of Kansas), 133.
21. Moerman, *Medicinal Plants of Native America*.
22. W. C. Evans, *Trease and Evans Pharmacognosy*, 13th edition (Philadelphia: Bailliere Tindall [The Curtis Center], 1989), 445. Quoted in *The Protocol Journal of Botanical Medicine* 1, no. 1 (1995).

23. Wade Boyle, "Juniper Berries," in Paul Bergner, ed., *Medical Herbalism* 4, no. 4 (winter 1992): 10.

24. Daniel Mowrey, *The Scientific Validation of Herbal Medicine* (New Canaan, CT: Keats, 1986).

25. Moerman, *Medicinal Plants of Native America*.

26. Harvey Felter and John Uni Lloyd, *King's American Dispensatory*, (Cincinnati: Eclectic Publications, 1895), 1092.

27. Ibid.

28. Ibid., 1092, 1361, 1691.

29. Chancel Cabrera, "Urinary Tract Infections," in Paul Bergner, ed., *Medical Herbalism* 3, no. 4 (fall 1991): 9.

30. Boyle, "Juniper Berries."

31. Ibid.

32. Michael Moore, *Herbal Tinctures in Clinical Practice* (Albuquerque: Southwest School of Botanical Medicine, 1994).

33. Nordland, *Brewing and Beer Traditions in Norway*, 181.

34. Ibid., 185.

35. Felter and Lloyd, *King's American Dispensatory*.

36. Michael Moore, *Medicinal Plants of the Pacific West* (Santa Fe: Red Crane, 1993); Virgil Vogel, *American Indian Medicine* (Norman: University of Oklahoma Press, 1970); Felter and Lloyd, *King's American Dispensatory*.

37. C. S. Rafinesque, *Medical Flora or Manual of Medical Botany of the United States*, vol. 1 (Philadelphia: Atkinson and Alexander, 1828). Quoted in Charlotte Erichsen-Brown, *Medicinal and Other Uses of North American Plants* (New York: Dover, 1979), 46.

38. Grieve, *A Modern Herbal*, 103.

39. Sanborn Brown, *Beers and Wines of Old New England*, 41.

40. Samuel Moorewood, *An Essay on the Inventions and Customs of Both Ancients and Moderns in the Use of Inebriating Liquors* (London: Longman, Hurst, Rees, Orme, Brown, and Green, 1824), 240–241.

41. *Martha Washington's Book of Cookery* (ca. 1550–1625). Quoted in Cindy Renfrow, *A Sip Through Time* (n.p.: Renfrow, 1995), 128.

42. John Pechet, *The Compleat Herbal of Physical Plants* (London: 1694), 20.

43. Moore, *Medicinal Plants of the Pacific West*; Felter and Lloyd, *King's American Dispensatory*; Vogel, *American Indian Medicine*.

44. Quoted in Erichsen-Brown, *Medicinal and Other Uses of American Plants*, 79.

45. Mrs. Cornelius, *The Young Housekeeper's Friend* (1846). Quoted in Renfrow, *A Sip Through Time*, 29.

46. Quoted in Erichsen-Brown, *Medicinal and Other Uses of American Plants*, 82.

47.   Ibid.; Moerman, *Medicinal Plants of Native America*; Vogel, *American Indian Medicine*.

48.   Nordland, *Brewing and Beer Traditions in Norway*, 218.

49.   Charles Millspaugh, *American Medicinal Plants* (Philadelphia: Yorston, 1892; reprint New York: Dover, 1974), 655.

50.   Felter and Lloyd, *King's American Dispensatory*, 2.

51.   Ameila Simmons, *The First American Cookbook, A Facsimile of "American Cookery"* (1796), 47. Quoted in Renfrow, *A Sip Through Time*, 25.

52.   Vogel, *American Indian Medicine*, 249.

53.   Felter and Lloyd, *King's American Dispensatory*, 2.

54.   Charles Millspaugh, *American Medicinal Plants*; Steven Foster and James Duke, *Peterson's Field Guide to Eastern/Central Medicinal Plants* (Boston: Houghton Mifflin, 1990); Erichsen-Brown, *Medicinal and Other Uses of American Plants*; Felter and Lloyd, *King's American Dispensatory*.

55.   Pechet, *The Compleat Herbal of Physical Plants*, 149.

56.   Nordland, *Brewing and Beer Traditions in Norway*, 218.

57.   Ibid.

58.   Adapted from Renfrow, *A Sip Through Time*, 303–304.

59.   Pechet, *The Compleat Herbal of Physical Plants*, 149.

60.   Quoted in Mikal Aasved, "Alcohol, Drinking, and Intoxication in Preindustrial Society: Theoretical, Nutritional, and Religious Considerations" (Ph.D. diss., University of California, Santa Barbara, 1988), 719.

61.   Retold by the author from the original tale.

62.   Moore, *Medicinal Plants of the Mountain West*; Vogel, *American Indian Medicine*; David Hoffmann, *The New Holistic Herbal* (Rockport, MA: Element, 1990).

63.   Pechet, *The Compleat Herbal of Physical Plants*, 84.

64.   John Arnold, *Origin and History of Beer and Brewing* (Chicago: Alumni Association of the Wahl-Henius Institute of Fermentology, 1911), 396.

65.   Peter Kalm, *Travels in North America, 1748–1751*. Quoted in Erichsen-Brown, *Medicinal and Other Uses of American Plants*, 11.

66.   Nancy Turner, *The Ethnobotany of the Okanagan Indians of British Columbia and Washington State* (n.p.: The British Columbia Indian Language Project, 1975). Xeroxed manuscript.

67.   Foster and Duke, *Peterson's Field Guide*; Erichsen-Brown, *Medicinal and Other Uses of American Plants*.

68.   John Bickerdyke, *The Curiosities of Ale and Beer* (London: Leadenhall Press, ca. 1890), 409.

69.   Pechet, *The Compleat Herbal of Physical Plants*, 140.

70.   Caldecott, *Myths of the Sacred Tree*, 113–114.

71. Ibid.; Anonymous, "A Druidess With the Mistletoe," *Frank Leslie's Sunday Magazine* XV, no. 85 (January 1884); Moore, *Medicinal Plants of the Mountain West*; Felter and Lloyd, *King's American Dispensatory*; Grieve, *A Modern Herbal*.

CHAPTER NINE

1. Thomas Tryon, *The Art of Brewing Beer, Ale, and other sorts of Liquors* (London: 1691), 38–40.
2. Quoted in John Arnold, *Origin and History of Beer and Brewing* (Chicago: Alumni Association of the Wahl-Henius Institute of Fermentology, 1911), 387–388.
3. Susun Weed, *Healing Wise* (Woodstock, NY: Ash Tree Publishing, 1989), 189.
4. Quoted in Cindy Renfrow, *A Sip Through Time* (n.p.: Renfrow, 1995), 29.
5. Gabrielle Hatfield, *Country Remedies: Traditional East Anglian Plant Remedies in the Twentieth Century* (Woodbridge, Suffolk, U.K.: The Boydell Press, 1994), 16.
6. Ibid., 56.
7. Maude Grieve, *A Modern Herbal* (1931; New York: Dover, 1971), 577.
8. C. J. J. Berry, *Home Brewed Beers and Stouts* (Andover, Hampshire, U.K.: Amateur Winemaker, 1963), 102–103.
9. Richard Mabey, *The New Age Herbalist* (New York: Simon and Schuster, 1988), 183.
10. Weed, *Healing Wise*, 189.
11. Ibid.
12. Ibid., 172.
13. Quoted in Charlotte Erichsen-Brown, *Medicinal and Other Uses of North American Plants* (New York: Dover, 1979), 445.
14. Daniel Moerman, *Medicinal Plants of Native America* (Ann Arbor: University of Michigan Museum of Anthropology, Technical Reports, no. 19, 1986); Michael Moore, *Medicinal Plants of the Mountain West* (Santa Fe: Museum of New Mexico Press, 1979); Weed, *Healing Wise*; James Duke, *The Green Pharmacy* (New York: Rodale Press, 1997); David Hoffmann, *The New Holistic Herbal* (Rockport, MA: Element, 1990).
15. "North American Apitherapy Symposium Abstracts," *American Bee Journal* 123, no. 2 (February 1983).
16. Duke, *The Green Pharmacy*, 65.
17. Ibid., 84.
18. Weed, *Healing Wise*, 172.
19. Ibid.
20. Duke, *The Green Pharmacy*, 58–59.

21. John Pechet, *The Compleat Herbal of Physical Plants* (London: 1694), 31.
22. Daniel Mowrey, *The Scientific Validation of Herbal Medicine* (New Canaan, CT: Keats), 1986.
23. *The Protocol Journal of Botanical Medicine* 1, no. 1 (1995).
24. Melvyn Werback and Michael Murray, *Botanical Influences on Illness* (Tarzana, CA: Third Line Press, 1994).
25. Hoffmann, *The New Holistic Herbal*.
26. Duke, *The Green Pharmacy*.
27. Moerman, *Medicinal Plants of Native America*.
28. Grieve, *A Modern Herbal*, 251.
29. Moerman, *Medicinal Plants of Native America*.
30. Grieve, *A Modern Herbal*, 414.
31. Berry, *Home Brewed Beers and Stouts*, 99–100.
32. Weed, *Healing Wise*, 152.
33. Nicholas Culpepper, *Culpepper's Complete Herbal* (1651 reprint, London: Foulsham, n.d.), 113.
34. Mowrey, *The Scientific Validation of Herbal Medicine*, 18.
35. Ibid.
36. Duke, *The Green Pharmacy*.
37. Weed, *Healing Wise*.
38. Michael Moore, *Herbal Tinctures in Clinical Practice* (Albuquerque: Southwest School of Botanical Medicine, 1994).
39. Paul Bergner, ed., *Medical Herbalism* 3, no. 1 (January/February 1991).
40. Weed, *Healing Wise*.
41. Duke, *The Green Pharmacy*.
42. John Bickerdyke, *The Curiosities of Ale and Beer* (London: Leadenhall Press, ca. 1890), 386.
43. Quoted in Christopher Hobbs, "Sarsaparilla: A Literature Review," *Herbalgram*, no. 17 (summer 1988): 11.
44. Ibid., 28.
45. Mowrey, *The Scientific Validation of Herbal Medicine*.
46. Moerman, *Medicinal Plants of Native America*.
47. Quoted in Hobbs, "Sarsaparilla," 13.
48. C. S. Rafinesque, *Medical Flora or Manual of Medical Botany of the United States*, vol. 1 (Philadelphia: Atkinson and Alexander, 1828). Quoted in Erichsen-Brown, *Medicinal and Other Uses of American Plants*, 352.
49. The original recipe did not call for fermentation but added the sugar and honey in the soda fountain with tincture of ginger (4 ozs.) and solution of citric acid (4 ozs.). Shuttleworth, ed., *Canadian Pharmaceutical Journal*, no. 13 (1876). Quoted in ibid., Erichsen-Brown 352.

50. Frank Speck, "Medicine Practices of the Northeastern Algonquins," *Proceedings International Congress of Americanists* xix (Washington Pub, 1917), 303–332. Quoted in ibid., 352.

51. Michael Moore, *Medicinal Plants of the Mountain West* (Santa Fe: Museum of New Mexico Press, 1979); Harvey Felter and John Uri Lloyd, *King's American Dispensatory* (Cincinnati: Eclectic Publications, 1895); Steven Foster and James Duke, *Peterson's Field Guide to Eastern/Central Medicinal Plants* (Boston: Houghton-Mifflin, 1990).

52. Sanborn Brown, *Wines and Beers of Old New England* (Hanover, NH: University Press of New England, 1978), 70.

53. Renfrow, *A Sip Through Time*, 26.

54. Ibid.

55. Ibid., 27.

56. Ibid.

57. Felter and Lloyd, *King's American Dispensatory*, 2111.

58. Berry, *Home Brewed Beers and Stouts*, 100.

59. Bertrand Remi, *Home Brew* (Katmandu, Nepal: Sahayogi Press, 1976), 23.

60. Brown, *Beers and Wines of Old New England*.

61. Rob Talbot and Robin Whiteman, *Brother Cadfael's Herb Garden* (Boston: Little Brown, 1997), 108.

62. Stephen Fulder, *The Ginger Book* (New York: Avery Publishing, 1996), 81.

63. Rafinesque, *Medical Flora*. Quoted in Erichsen-Brown, *Medicinal and Other Uses of American Plants*, 310.

64. Quoted from Stephen Buhner, *Sacred Plant Medicine* (Boulder, CO: Roberts Rinehart Publishers, 1996). From Earl Pliny Goddard, *Hupa Texts*, University of California Publications, American Archaeology and Ethnology, vols. 1 and 2 (Berkeley: University of California Press, 1903), 286–287.

65. Fulder, *The Ginger Book*; Hoffmann, *The New Holistic Herbal*.

66. *Herbalgram* 17 (summer 1988); *Protocol Journal of Botanical Medicine* 1, no. 2 (1995).

67. Duke, *The Green Pharmacy*.

68. Dr. W. P. Worth, *On the New and True Art of Brewing* (London: 1692), 121.

69. Mabey, *The New Age Herbalist*.

70. Ibid.; Hoffmann, *The New Holistic Herbal*; *Protocol Journal of Botanical Medicine* 2, no. 1 (1996).

71. Rafinesque, *Medical Flora*. Quoted in Erichsen-Brown, *Medicinal and Other Uses of American Plants*, 105.

72. Quoted in Arnold, *Origin and History of Beer and Brewing*, 393.

73. Mrs. Cornelius, *The Young Housekeeper's Friend* (1846). Quoted in Renfrow, *A Sip Through Time*, 23.

74. Adapted from Catherine Ferns, *The Kitchen Guide* (1925). Quoted in ibid., Refrow 74.

75. Quoted in Erichsen-Brown, *Medicinal and Other Uses of American Plants*, 103.

76. Foster and Duke, *Peterson's Field Guide*, 278. At least half the plants they discuss are listed as dangerous one way or another—I couldn't take it very seriously after their toxic warnings about oak, cedar, hops, and yucca. Yucca (with a big exclamation point next to it in their text), a traditional plant used for thousands of years and found effective in a number of clinical trials, is noted as being toxic to lower life forms. I couldn't help but wonder if they meant FDA researchers.

77. Felter and Lloyd, *King's American Dispensatory*; Hoffmann, *The New Holistic Herbal*.

78. J. Carver, *Travels Through the Interior Parts of North America, in the years 1766, 1767, 1768* (1779). Quoted in Joseph Meyer, *The Herbalist* (Glenwood, IL: Meyerbooks, 1986), 177.

79. Shuttleworth, ed., *Canadian Pharmaceutical Journal*, no. 13 (1876). Quoted in Erichsen-Brown, *Medicinal and Other Uses of American Plants*, 311.

80. Rafinesque, *Medical Flora*. Quoted in ibid., 310.

81. Felter and Lloyd, *King's American Dispensatory*; Hoffmann, *The New Holistic Herbal*; Foster and Duke, *Peterson's Field Guide*.

82. Grieve, *A Modern Herbal*, 487.

83. Ibid., 492.

84. Culpepper, *Culpepper's Complete Herbal*, 216.

85. Felter and Lloyd, *King's American Dispensatory*.

86. Hoffmann, *The New Holistic Herbal*.

87. Werbach and Murray, *Botanical Influences on Illness*.

88. Selena Heron, "Botanical Treatment of Chronic Gynecological Conditions: Infertility, Endometriosis, and Symptoms of Menopause," in Michael Tierra, ed., *American Herbalism* (Freedom, CA: Crossing Press, 1992).

89. Daniel Mowrey, *The Scientific Validation of Herbal Medicine*.

90. Odd Nordland, *Brewing and Beer Traditions in Norway* (Norway: The Norwegian Research Council for Science and the Humanities), 217.

91. Ibid.

92. Anonymous, *An English Herbal* (London: ca. 1690), 39.

93. Lesley Gordon, *The Mystery and Magic of Trees and Flowers* (London: Grange, 1993), 60.

94. Christopher Hobbs, "St. John's Wort," *Herbalgram*, nos. 18/19 (fall 1988/winter 1989).

95. Ibid., 29.
96. Moore, *Medicinal Plants of the Mountain West*; Duke, *The Green Pharmacy*; Hoffmann, *The New Holistic Herbal*.
97. A. H. Church, *The Chemistry of Common Life* (1879). Quoted in Meyer, *The Herbalist*, 191.
98. Lewis Sturtevant, *Sturtevant's Notes on Edible Plants* (Lyon Albany, 1919). Quoted in Erichsen-Brown, *Medicinal and Other Uses of American Plants*, 231.
99. Moore, *Medicinal Plants of the Pacific West*.
100. Erichsen-Brown, *Medicinal and Other Uses of American Plants*, 233.
101. Hoffmann, *The New Holistic Herbal*; Felter and Lloyd, *King's American Dispensatory*; Grieve, *A Modern Herbal*.
102. Grieve, *A Modern Herbal*, 414.
103. Ibid., 524.
104. Ibid., 415.
105. Quoted in ibid., 524.
106. Ibid.; Hoffmann, *The New Holistic Herbal*; Felter and Lloyd, *King's American Dispensatory*.
107. Bickerdyke, *The Curiosities of Ale and Beer*, 390–391.
108. Quoted in Grieve, *A Modern Herbal*, 120.
109. Heron, "Botanical Treatment of Chronic Gynecological Conditions."
110. *Protocol Journal of Botanical Medicine*, 2, no. 1 (1996).
111. Hatfield, *Country Remedies*, 126.
112. Berry, *Home Brewed Beers and Stouts*, 102.
113. Pechet, *The Compleat Herbal of Physical Plants*, 104.
114. Felter and Lloyd, *King's American Dispensatory*, 1241.
115. Ibid.; Grieve, *A Modern Herbal*; Hoffmann, *The New Holistic Herbal*.
116. Quoted in Grieve, *A Modern Herbal*, 517.
117. Adapted from Renfrow, *A Sip Through Time*, 140.
118. Quoted in Grieve, *A Modern Herbal*, 517.
119. *Protocol Journal of Botanical Medicine* 2, no. 2 (1997).
120. Hoffmann, *The New Holistic Herbal*; Duke, *The Green Pharmacy*.
121. Gordon, *The Myth and Magic of Trees and Flowers*, 44.
122. John Evelyn, 1664. Quoted in Grieve, *A Modern Herbal*, 269.
123. Grieve, *A Modern Herbal*, 274.
124. Gordon, *The Myth and Magic of Trees and Flowers*, 44.
125. Berry, *Home Brewed Beers and Stouts*, 100.
126. Bickerdyke, *The Curiosities of Ale and Beer*, 386.
127. Originally considered a "wine" recipe. Quoted in Grieve, *A Modern Herbal*, 274.

128. John Harrison, *Old British Beers and How to Make Them* (London: Durden Park Beer Club, 1991), 24.

129. Pechet, *The Compleat Herbal of Physical Plants*, 72.

130. Hoffmann, *The New Holistic Herbal;* Moore, *Medicinal Plants of the Mountain West;* NAPRALERT database as of February 14, 1996.

131. Pechet, *The Compleat Herbal of Physical Plants*, 167.

132. Richard Elkes, *Approved Medicines of Little Cost to Preserve Health and Also to Cure Those That are Sick* (London:1651), 20–21.

133. Worth, *On the New and True Art of Brewing*, 115.

134. F. Lighibodt, *Every Man His Own Gauger* (London: 1695), 45.

135. Ibid., 61.

136. *Dorland's Illustrated Medical Dictionary* (Philadelphia: W. B. Saunders Company, 1964), 1357.

137. Pechet, *The Compleat Herbal of Physical Plants*, 167.

138. Felter and Lloyd, *King's American Dispensatory*, 433.

139. Quoted in Grieve, *A Modern Herbal*, 443.

140. Culpepper, *Culpepper's Complete Herbal*, 21.

141. Grieve, *A Modern Herbal*, 442.

142. Culpepper, *Culpepper's Complete Herbal*, 21.

143. Felter and Lloyd, *King's American Dispensatory*, 933.

144. Grieve, *A Modern Herbal;* Hoffmann, *The New Holistic Herbal.*

145. Nordland, *Brewing and Beer Traditions in Norway*, 219.

146. Pechet, *The Compleat Herbal of Physical Plants*, 38.

147. *Protocol Journal of Botanical Medicine* 1, no. 1 (summer 1995); Mabey, *The New Age Herbalist;* Hoffmann, *The New Holistic Herbal.*

148. Pechet, *The Compleat Herbal of Physical Plants*, 39.

149. Grieve, *A Modern Herbal*, 165–166.

150. *London and Country Brewer* (1744). Quoted in Bickerdyke, *The Curiosities of Ale and Beer*, 387.

151. Pechet, *The Compleat Herbal of Physical Plants*, 39.

152. Hoffmann, *The New Holistic Herbal.*

153. James Duke, *The Green Pharmacy.*

154. Pechet, *The Compleat Herbal of Physical Plants*, 66.

155. Ibid., 66–67.

156. Quoted in Erichsen-Brown, *Medicinal and Other Uses of American Plants*, 223.

157. Mowrey, *The Scientific Validation of Herbal Medicine.*

158. *Protocol Journal of Botanical Medicine* 1, no. 1 (summer 1995).

159. Bickerdyke, *The Curiosities of Ale and Beer*, 386.

160. *Penn Family Recipes* (1674). Quoted in Renfrow, *A Sip Through Time*, 141.

161. Lighibodt, *Every Man His Own Gauger*, 52–53.

162. Bickerdyke, *The Curiosities of Ale and Beer*, 386.

163. E. G. Hayden (ca. 1900). Quoted in Renfrow, *A Sip Through Time*, 143.

164. Felter and Lloyd, *King's American Dispensatory*, 1581.

165. Hoffmann, *The New Holistic Herbal*; Grieve, *A Modern Herbal*.

166. Tryon, *The Art of Brewing Beer*, 38–40.

167. Culpepper, *Culpepper's Complete Herbal*, 265.

168. Felter and Lloyd, *King's American Dispensatory*; Hoffmann, *The New Holistic Herbal*.

169. Tryon, *The Art of Brewing Beer*, 38–40.

170. Pechet, *The Compleat Herbal of Physical Plants*, 18.

171. Moore, *Medicinal Plants of the Mountain West*; Hoffmann, *The New Holistic Herbal*; Grieve, *A Modern Herbal*; Felter and Lloyd, *King's American Dispensatory*.

172. Hatfield, *Country Remedies*, 15.

173. Anonymous, *An English Herbal*, 47.

174. Duke, *The Green Pharmacy*.

175. Felter and Lloyd, *King's American Dispensatory*, 1925.

176. Pechet, *The Compleat Herbal of Physical Plants*, 97.

177. Culpepper, *Culpepper's Complete Herbal*, 172.

178. Grieve, *A Modern Herbal*.

179. Pechet, *The Compleat Herbal of Physical Plants*, 103.

180. John Gerarde, *The Herball or General History of Plants Gathered by John Gerarde of London* (London: Norton and Whitakers, 1633).

181. Quoted in Grieve, *A Modern Herbal*, 412.

182. Berry, *Home Brewed Beers and Stouts*, 102.

183. Harrison, *Old British Beers and How to Make Them*.

184. Tryon, *The Art of Brewing Beer*, 30–32.

185. Duke, *The Green Pharmacy*; Hoffmann, *The New Holistic Herbal*; Felter and Lloyd, *King's American Dispensatory*; Fritz Weiss, *Herbal Medicine* (Beaconsfield, England: Beaconsfield Publishers, 1988).

186. Charles Millspaugh, *American Medicinal Plants* (Philadelphia: Yorston, 1892; reprint, New York: Dover, 1974), 515.

187. William Lewis, *An Experimental History of the Materia Medica*, 4th edition (1791). Quoted in Erichsen-Brown, *Medicinal and Other Uses of American Plants*, 205.

188. Hoffmann, *The New Holistic Herbal*; Felter and Lloyd, *King's American Dispensatory*; Grieve, *A Modern Herbal*.

189. Culpepper, *Culpepper's Complete Herbal*, 361.

190. Hoffmann, *The New Holistic Herbal;* Mabey, *The New Age Herbalist;* Grieve, *A Modern Herbal;* Duke, *The Green Pharmacy.*

191. Quoted in Meyer, *The Herbalist,* 191.

192. Grieve, *A Modern Herbal,* 159.

193. *Protocol Journal of Botanical Medicine* 1, no. 1 (summer 1995).

194. Hoffmann, *The New Holistic Herbal;* Mabey, *The New Age Herbalist;* Felter and Lloyd, *King's American Dispensatory.*

195. Gerarde, *The Herball or General History of Plants.* Quoted in Erichsen-Brown, *Medicinal and Other Uses of American Plants,* 260.

196. Culpepper, *Culpepper's Complete Herbal,* 260.

197. Nancy Turner, *The Ethnobotany of the Okanagan Indians of British Columbia and Washington State* (The British Columbia Indian Language Project, n.p.: 1975). Xeroxed manuscript; Moore, *Medicinal Plants of the Mountain West.*

198. Grieve, *A Modern Herbal,* 536.

199. Culpepper, *Culpepper's Complete Herbal,* 240.

200. NAPRALERT database as of February 14, 1996.

201. Hoffmann, *The New Holistic Herbal;* NAPRALERT database as of February 2, 1996.

202. Grieve, *A Modern Herbal,* 347.

203. M. Dods (1829). Quoted in Renfrow, *A Sip Through Time,* 20.

204. Culpepper, *Culpepper's Complete Herbal,* 161.

205. Moore, *Medicinal Plants of the Mountain West;* Hoffmann, *The New Holistic Herbal;* Felter and Lloyd, *King's American Dispensatory;* Michael Cottingham, personal communication.

206. Gerarde, *The Herball or General History of Plants.* Quoted in Grieve, *A Modern Herbal,* 147.

207. Grieve, *A Modern Herbal,* 147.

208. Felter and Lloyd, *King's American Dispensatory,* 268.

209. Ibid.; Grieve, *A Modern Herbal.*

210. Quoted in Grieve, *A Modern Herbal,* 281.

211. Pechet, *The Compleat Herbal of Physical Plants,* 73.

212. Hoffmann, *The New Holistic Herbal.*

213. *Protocol Journal of Botanical Medicine* 2, no. 2 (1997).

214. Mabey, *The New Age Herbalist.*

215. Ibid.; Hoffmann, *The New Holistic Herbal;* Grieve, *A Modern Herbal.*

216. Duke, *The Green Pharmacy.*

217. Werbach and Murray, *Botanical Influences on Illness.*

218. Gerarde, *The Herball or General History of Plants.* Quoted in Grieve, *A Modern Herbal,* 293.

219. Grieve, *A Modern Herbal*, 291.

220. Hoffmann, *The New Holistic Herbal;* Felter and Lloyd, *King's American Dispensatory;* Mowrey, *The Scientific Validation of Herbal Medicine.*

221. Grieve, *A Modern Herbal*, 186.

222. Anonymous, *An English Herbal*, 17.

223. Hoffmann, *The New Holistic Herbal.*

224. *Protocol Journal of Botanical Medicine* 1, no. 1 (summer 1995).

225. Werbach and Murray, *Botanical Influences on Illness.*

226. Ibid.

227. Weiss, *Herbal Medicine;* Mowrey, *The Scientific Validation of Herbal Medicine.*

228. Grieve, *A Modern Herbal*, 306.

229. Culpepper, *Culpepper's Complete Herbal*, 138.

230. Felter and Lloyd, *King's American Dispensatory;* Grieve, *A Modern Herbal.*

231. Margaret Freeman, *Herbs for the Medieval Household for Cooking, Healing and Divers Uses* (New York: Metropolitan Museum of Art, 1943), 9. Quoting the *Hortus Sanitatis, or Gart Der Gesundheit* (Mainz: Peter Schoeffer, 1485).

232. Edward Emerson, *Beverages Past and Present*, vol. 2 (New York: Putnam, 1908), 248.

233. Hoffmann, *The New Holistic Herbal;* Mabey, *The New Age Herbalist.*

234. Duke, *The Green Pharmacy;* *Protocol Journal of Botanical Medicine* 1, no. 1 (summer 1995).

235. Freeman, *Herbs for the Medieval Household*, 12. Quoting the *Hortus Sanitatis, or Gart Der Gesundheit.*

236. *Banckes Herbal* (1525). Quoted in Freeman, *Herbs for the Medieval Household*, 12.

237. Hoffmann, *The New Holistic Herbal;* Weiss, *Herbal Medicine;* Grieve, *A Modern Herbal;* Mabey, *The New Age Herbalist.*

238. Quoted in Renfrow, *A Sip Through Time*, 268.

239. Dr. Fernie, *Herbal Simples* (1897). Quoted in Renfrow, *A Sip Through Time*, 127.

240. Anonymous, *An English Herbal*, 8.

241. Hoffmann, *The New Holistic Herbal.*

242. Weiss, *Herbal Medicine.*

243. Duke, *The Green Pharmacy.*

244. Pechet, *The Compleat Herbal of Physical Plants*, 13.

245. Grieve, *A Modern Herbal*, 74.

246. Culpepper, *Culpepper's Complete Herbal*, 35.

247. Hoffmann, *The New Holistic Herbal;* Grieve, *A Modern Herbal.*

248. Bickerdyke, *The Curiosities of Ale and Beer*, 176–177.

249. Turner, *The Ethnobotany of the Okanagan Indians.*

250. Ibid.; Moerman, *Medicinal Plants of Native America.*

251. Tryon, *The Art of Brewing Beer*, 38–40.
252. Adapted from Remi, *Home Brew*, 49.
253. Grieve, *A Modern Herbal*, 542.
254. Duke, *The Green Pharmacy*; Hoffmann, *The New Holistic Herbal*; *Protocol Journal of Botanical Medicine* 2, no. 1 (1996).
255. Edward Emerson, *Beverages Past and Present*, 248.
256. Lighibodt, *Every Man His Own Gauger*, 45.
257. *Banckes Herbal*. Quoted in Freeman, *Herbs for the Medieval Household*, 40.
258. Duke, *The Green Pharmacy*; Hoffmann, *The New Holistic Herbal*; *Protocol Journal of Botanical Medicine* 2, no. 1 (1996).
259. Freeman, *Herbs for the Medieval Household*, 39. Quoting the *Hortus Sanitatis, or Gart Der Gesundheit*.
260. Grieve, *A Modern herbal*, 226.
261. Ibid.; Mabey, *The New Age Herbalist*.
262. Quoted in Meyer, *The Herbalist*, 192.
263. Quoted in Randy Mosher, "Grains of Paradise—Put a Little Paradise in Your Beer," in *Zymurgy* 17, no. 4 (Special Issue 1994), 50.
264. Meyer, *The Herbalist*, 182.
265. Mosher, "Grains of Paradise," 50.
266. Ibid.; Felter and Lloyd, *King's American Dispensatory*.
267. Felter and Lloyd, *King's American Dispensatory*, 525.
268. Bickerdyke, *The Curiosities of Ale and Beer*, 176.
269. Felter and Lloyd, *King's American Dispensatory*, 525.
270. Mowrey, *The Scientific Validation of Herbal Medicine*; Felter and Lloyd, *King's American Dispensatory*; Hoffmann, *The New Holistic Herbal*; Grieve, *A Modern Herbal*.
271. Lightbodt (1695). From an early eighteenth-century source, quoted in Bickerdyke, *The Curiosities of Ale and Beer*, 174.
272. Lighibodt, *Every Man His Own Gauger*, 45–46.
273. Adapted from Harrison *Old British Beers and How to Make Them*, 21.
274. Dr. W. P. Worth, *On the New and True Art of Brewing*, 62.
275. Colonial American recipe (ca. 1750). Quoted in Arnold, *Origin and History of Beer and Brewing*, 404.
276. Berry, *Home Brewed Beers and Stouts*, 104.
277. Bickerdyke, *The Curiosities of Ale and Beer*, 387.
278. Ibid., 176.
279. John Taylor, *Pennyless Pilgrimmage*, quoted in ibid., 162–163.

THE APPENDICES

1. Thomas Tryon, *The Art of Brewing Beer, Ale, and other sorts of Liquors* (London: 1691), 1–2.

APPENDIX ONE

1. F. Lighibodt, *Every Man His Own Gauger* (London: 1695), 42.
2. Thomas Tryon, *The Art of Brewing Beer, Ale, and other sorts of Liquors* (London: 1691), 24.
3. Dr. W. P. Worth, *On the New and True Art of Brewing* (London: 1692), 121.
4. Tryon, *The Art of Brewing Beer*, 40–42.
5. Worth, *On the New and True Art of Brewing*, 115.
6. Maude Grieve, *A Modern Herbal* (1931; New York: Dover, 1971), 414.

APPENDIX TWO

1. All the above recipes adapted from Bryan Acton and Peter Duncan, *Making Mead* (Ann Arbor, MI: Amateur Winemaker, 1994), 38.
2. Cindy Renfrow, *A Sip Through Time* (n.p.: Renfrow, 1995), 75.
3. Ibid., 33.
4. F. Lighibodt, *Every Man His Own Gauger*, 53–54.
5. Ibid., 54.
7. Renfrow, *A Sip Through Time*, 43.
8. Ibid., 45.
9. Ibid., 44.
10. Ibid., 42.
11. Ibid., 43.
12. Ibid., 52.
13. Ibid., 59.
14. Ibid., 59.
15. Ibid., 84.
16. Ibid., 97.
17. Ibid., 105.
18. Ibid., 112.
19. Ibid., 119.
20. Ibid., 121.

21.   Ibid., 120.
22.   Ibid., 89.
23.   Ibid., 54.

APPENDIX THREE

1.   Dr. W. P. Worth, *On the New and True Art of Brewing* (London: 1692), 111–114.
2.   John Pechet, *The Compleat Herbal of Physical Plants* (London: 1694), 98.
3.   Ibid.
4.   Ibid., 120.

INDEX

Aaronson, Wendy, 122; on chang, 118, 119; chicha and, 97, 98

Aasved, Mikal, 19, 479; on alcohol, 136; on chi, 121; on fermented beverages, 10–11, 79; on Jivaro, 114; on Kungi diet, 13; on manioc, 109; on palm beer, 129; on pulque, 90; on rice wine, 125; on sangucha shiki, 115–16; on Tarahumara/tesguino, 96; on Tepehuane/agave, 91

Abbey, Edward, 16

Absinthe, 188, 194, 195

Absinthin, 196

Account of Two Voyages to New England Made During the Years 1638, 1663, An (Josselyn), 308

Acetaria (Evelyn), 323

Acetylcholine, rosemary and, 409

Achillea millefolium, 185

Active constituents, 142

ADD. *See* Attention deficit disorder

Additives, 366, 431

"Adventures in Chicha and Chang: Indigenous Beers of the East and West" (Aaronson and Ridgely), 119

Aeonia, Great Teacher, Creator, 121

Aesir, 21, 23

Afagddu, 156, 157

Agave (*Agave* spp.), 81, 90; medicinal uses for, 91–93

Agave virginica, 93

Agrimony herb (*Agrimonia eupatoria*), described, 470

Aguamiel, 90

AIDS, St.-John's-wort and, 316

Ainu: fermentation and, 75, 80; millet beverage of, 121

Aipim (Manihot Aipi), 117

Akan, 132

Akerhumle, 183

Alcohol: cultural collapse and, 11; liver/brain and, 143; medicinal uses for, 142–43; negative effects of, 143–44; restrictions on, xvi, 137; sacredness of, 137–38

Alcohol, Drinking, and Intoxication in Preindustrial Society: Theoretical, Nutritional, and Religious Considerations (Aasved), 479

Alder (*Alnus* spp.), 226; medicinal uses for, 244

Ale: hopped, 172; raw, 232–33; strong, 230, 232; weak, 232

Alexander root (*Smyrnium Olisatrum*), described, 470

Algonquins, nettles and, 273

Alkanet (*Anchusa officinalis*), 471

Allende, Isabel: quote of, 1

Alzheimer's disease, rosemary and, 409

Amahuaca prayer, quote from, 166

Amazon, beer in, 2–3

Ambrosia (*Ambrosia artemisiifolia*), eyebright and, 388

American Frugal Housewife, The, 289

American ginseng, 215

American Molasses Ale (ca. 1750),
recipe for, 420–21

American rosebay (*Rhododendron
maximum*), 31

Ameta, 154, 155

Anacreon, honey/hive products and, 57

Angel's trumpet (*Brugmansia* sp.), 165

Angelica herb and root (*Angelica
archangelica*), 195; described, 470

Anise, 195

Aniseed (*Pimpinella anisum*), described,
470

Another Metheglin, recipe for, 457–58

Another Pleasant Meathe of Sir William
Paston's, recipe for, 453

Another Very Good White Meath—1,
recipe for, 454–55

Another Very Good White Meath—2,
recipe for, 455

Another Way of Making Meath, recipe
for, 450–51

Another Wintergreen Ale, recipe for,
305–6

Ansa, 131; palm sap and, 130

Anxiety theory, 10, 11

Apai, 115, 116

Apis, 54–55, 56

Apollonius, bee products and, 56

Aquavit, 141

Arnold, John: on hopped beers, 171; on
wild rosemary, 179

Arnoldus, quote of, x

Artemisia spp., 75, 76, 192, 194, 201, 380

Artemisia absinthium, 189, 194, 196

Artemisia annua, 196

Artemisias, 191, 192, 196, 199, 239; use
of, 193–94

*Art of Brewing Beer and Other Sorts of Liquors,
The* (Tryon), 373

Asarum canadense, 294

Asgard, 22

Aspergillus fungi, 118, 119, 297

Atharva Veda, quote of, x

Atropos, 212, 222

Attention deficit disorder (ADD), borage and, 325

Attested Communications of Scientific Friends,
288

Avati, 120

Avens (*Geum urbanum*), medicinal uses
for, 401

Avens ale, 399–400; recipe for, 400

Awiakta, Marilou, 103, 108; on
corn/indigenous peoples, 93

Azalea pontica, honey from, 38

Aztecs: distillation and, 141; fermentation and, 94

Bacillus coagulans, banana and, 128

Bacillus stereothermophilus, banana and, 128

Backhumle, 183

Balm, 265, 398

Balm of Gilead. *See* Propolis

Banana (*Musa acuminata*), medicinal uses
for, 127–28

Banana beer, 126–27; recipe for, 127

Banckes Herbal: on rosemary, 409; on rue,
396

Barley: medicinal uses for, 162; nutritional value of, 162

Barley ale: discovery of, 152; recipe for,
408

Barleycorn, John, 158

Barley Water, recipe for, 162

Barm, 438, 439

Basic Honey Mead, A: recipe for, 442

Baskets, described, 42, 44, 48

Batara Guru, rice and, 124

Baudelaire, on fermentation, 144

Bayberry (*Myrica cerifera*), 177, 178

Bay leaves (*Laurus nobilis*), described, 471

Bee pollen, 35, 36; medicinal uses for, 42, 44–47

Bee Pollen, Royal Jelly, Propolis, and Honey (Elkins), 44

Beer: ancient, 3–4; gift of, xiii; sacred, 80–81

Beer purity laws, 366

Bee venom, 35; medicinal uses for, 54–56

Belgian White Ale, 298

Bell heather (*Erica tetralix*), brewing with, 35

Bennet, J. Risdon: quote of, 135

Berm, 64

Berry, C. J. J., 325; dandelion beer by, 279; ginger beer by, 291–92; nettle beer by, 269–70

Berry, Wendell, 16

Bertrand Remi's Ginger Beer (1976), recipe for, 292

Betony (*Pedicularis* spp., *Betonica officinalis*), 265; medicinal uses for, 361

Betony ale, recipe for, 360–61

Beverly, Roger: quote of, 266

Bickerdyke, John: on borage, 323; on China ale, 282; on cowslip ale, 354; on elderberries, 332; on mountain ash, 422; on oak bark, 262; on serviceberry, 401; on wormwood ale, 191

Bilsa, 206

Bilsenkraut, 206

Biological ennoblement, 71

"Biology, Biochemistry, and the

Therapeutic Effects of Royal Jelly in Human Pathology" (Saenz), 52

Birch (*Betula fontinalis*): illustration of, 248; medicinal uses for, 249–50

Birch beer, 245–49

Birch Beer (ca. 1600), recipe for, 247–48

Birch Beer (1824), recipe for, 247

Birch Beer (1, 1978), recipe for, 246

Birch Beer (2, 1978), recipe for, 246–47

Birch sap, 81, 245–46, 249

Bittersweet root and herb (*Solanum dulcamara*), 208, 212; described, 471

Black elder, 337

Black Elk, 68

Bloodroot (*Sanguinaria canadensis*), 316

Blue Moon Brewery, 298

Bogbean (*Menyanthes trifoliata*): illustration of, 372; medicinal uses for, 372

Bogbean ale, recipe for, 371–72

Borage (*Borago officinalis*), 323; illustration of, 323; medicinal uses for, 324–25

Borage ale, 323–24; recipe for, 324

Botanical Influences on Illness (Werbach and Murray), 284

Bottle gourd (*Lagenaria siceraria*), 147

Bottling, thoughts on, 438–39

Boyle, Wade, 242; on juniper berries, 241, 243

Bracken fern (*Pterdium aquilinum*), medicinal uses for, 392

Bracken fern ale, recipe for, 391–92

Brain, alcohol and, 143

Brettanomyces bruxellensis, 70

Brettanomyces lambicus, 70

Brewer mountain heather (*Phyllodoce breweri*), 34–35

Brewer's Droop, 370

Brewers Garden, 175, 414

Brewing: ceremonial, 69; heretical rules for, 430

Brewing and Beer Traditions in Norway (Nordland), 225, 479

Brewing Mead (Gayre), 479

Britannean Magazine of Wines, 189

British Journal of Plastic Surgery, The, 39

Brooklime (*Veronica Beccabunga*), described, 476

Broom (*Cytisus scoparius, Sarothamnus scoparius*), 170, 265; infusing, 437; medicinal uses for, 205–6

Broom ale, recipe for, 203–4

Broom Ale for Dropsy (1695), recipe for, 204

Broom heather (*Erica vulgaris, Calluna vulgaris*), 25, 34

Brown, Sanborn, 287; ginger beer by, 283

Brygger, 183

Bryggjemann, 65, 66, 67, 76

Buckbean (*Menyanthes trifoliata*), 170; illustration of, 372; medicinal uses for, 372

Buckbean ale, recipe for, 371–72

Buffalo gourd (*Curcurbita foetidissima*), 212, 213

Bugloss herb (*Lycopsis arvensis*), described, 471

Burdock (*Arctium lappa*): illustration of, 277; medicinal uses for, 276–77

Burnet (*Pimpinella saxifraga*), medicinal uses for, 384–85

Butler's Ale, recipe for, 342–43

Bykhovsky, Rita: birch beer and, 248–49

Cabrera, Chancel: juniper and, 242

Calamus ale, 317–18

Caldecott, Moyra: on oak, 264; quote of, 223–24

Calendula (*Calendula officinalis*), medicinal uses for, 329–30

Calendula ale, 328–29

Calendula Ale (17th cent.), recipe for, 328–29

Calumba (*Jateorhiza calumba*), 325

Canadian Pharmaceutical Journal, recipe from, 285

Candida albicans: caraway and, 349; cardamom and, 376; sage and, 202; yarrow and, 187

Caouin, 110, 114

Caraway (*Carum carvi*): illustration of, 347; medicinal uses for, 348–49

Caraway ale, 347–48; recipe for, 348

Cardamom (*Elettaria cardamomum*), medicinal uses for, 375–76

Cardamom seed ale, recipe for, 375

Cardis, 265, 437

Cardus, 418

Carrageen, 414, 415–17

Carter, Landon: on stalks, 100

Carver, J.: on wintergreen, 304

Cassava, 71, 110

Catherine Fern's Nettle Beer (1925), recipe for, 267–68

CC Pollen Company, 481

Cebadilla (*Swertia radiata*), 382

Cedar, 261; cleansing properties of, 241; legends about, 239–40

Celts: fermentation and, 167; heather and, 33; henbane and, 210; oak and, 263; sacred beverages of, 28

Centuary, 265

Cerridwen, 23, 157; fermentation and, 155–56

Chagga, 147

Chamomile (*Matricaria chamomilla*), 195, 196; illustration of, 389; medicinal uses for, 390

Chamomile Ale (17th cent.), recipe for, 389

Chang, 118–20, 125; recipe for, 119–20

Charlie Millspaugh's Spruce Beer (1892), recipe for, 253–54

Charoti, 143; fermentation and, 73, 74, 76

Chemicals, 431; removing, 435

Cherrington, Ernest: on chiacoar, 101; on rice beer, 123

Chiacoar, 101–2

Chicha, 93–95, 165; indigenous, 98; Quecha Indians and, 94–95; recipe for, 95–96; Tesguino and, 96

Chicha from Germinated Corn, recipe for, 98–99

Chicory root and herb (*Cichoriem intybus*), described, 471

China root (*Smilax* spp.), described, 283–85

China root ale, recipe for, 282–83

Christals of Tartar, 439

Chung, 118–20

Church, A. H.: on calamus, 317

Cinnamon (*Cinnamomum zeylanicum*), described, 472

C. J. J. Berry's Dandelion Beer (1963), recipe for, 279

C. J. J. Berry's Nettle Beer (1963), recipe for, 269–70

C. J. J Berry's Ginger Beer (1963), recipe for, 291–92

Clary (*Salvia scalarea*), 217

Clary ale, 199–201

Clary Ale (17th cent.), recipe for, 200

Clary Ale (modern), recipe for, 200–201

Cleats Beer, 472

Closet of the Eminently Learned Sir Kenelme Digby Kt. Opened: Whereby is Discovered Several ways for making of Metheglin Sider, Cherry-Wine, &c. Together with Excellent Directions for Cookery: As Also for Preserving, Conserving, Candying, &c. (Digby), 448

Clostridium sporogenes, banana and, 128

Clove (*Eugenica caryophyllus*), 439; described, 472

Clove gillyflower (*Cherranthus cheiri*), described, 472

Clove pink (*Dianthus caryophyllus*), 472

Coca leaves (*Erythroxylon coca*), 165

Coconut oil, 134

Coit, 26

Colerus, pine ale and, 257

Coltsfoot root and herb (*Tussilago farfara*), described, 472

Comfrey (*Symphytum officinale*), 324

Complete Hive Mead, A: recipe for, 58–59

Consist, Francis: longevity of, 57

Cook, Roger: quote of, 223

Coriander (*Coriandrum sativum*), 195; medicinal uses for, 299

Coriander ale, recipe for, 298

Corn (*Zea Mays*), 102–9, 156; germination of, 97, 98; medicinal uses for, 108, 109; sacredness of, 102–3

Corn beer, 93–95, 97, 101–2; Cornish heather (*Erica vagans*), 34

Cornmeal, 109

Corn Mother, 94, 102, 103–4; wisdom of, 106

Corn plant ale, 99–100

Cornstalk beer, recipe for, 100–101

Costmary (*Tanacetum balsamita*), 410;

medicinal uses for, 411

Costmary Ale, recipe for, 410–11

Countrie Farmer, The (Markham), 411

Cow parsnip (*Heracleum lanatum*), medicinal uses for, 377–78

Cow parsnip ale, 376–77; recipe for, 377

Cowslip (*Primula veris*); illustration of, 357; medicinal uses for, 357–58

Cowslip Ale (1674), recipe for, 354–55

Cowslip Ale (1695), recipe for, 355–56

Cowslip Ale (1744), recipe for, 356

Cowslip Ale (ca. 1900), recipe for, 356–57

Cream mountain heather (*Phyllodoce glandulifera*), 34

Crearwy, 156

Creator, 103, 132; manioc and, 113

Creator Breathmaker, 92

Cree, sweet flag and, 320

Cross-leaved heather (*Erica tetralix*), 34

Cross-pollination, 42, 62

Crosswhite, Frank: on saguaros, 81

Culinary sage (*Salvia officinalis*), 201

Culli, 94

Culpepper, Nicholas, 385, 411; on avens, 401; on bracken fern, 392; on China root, 283; on cow parsnip, 377; on dandelion, 280; on gentian, 382; on ground ivy, 345, 346; on ground pine, 364; on licorice, 310; on mugwort, 379; on nettles, 275; on pennyroyal, 359; on propolis, 48; on tansy, 374

cummings, e. e., 1, 16

Cyanide, 110, 117

Cyser, recipe for, 443

Dandelion (*Taraxacum officinale*), 265;

illustration of, 281; medicinal uses for, 280–82; nutritive value of, 282

Dandelion beer, 278–80

Danstar brand Windsor yeast, 435

Darne, 217

Darnel (*Lolium temulentum*), 165, 166, 215; medicinal uses for, 216–17

Darnel beer, 215–16; recipe for, 216

Date palm, 134

De la Vega, Garcilaso: on corn beers, 108–9

Democritus, honey/hive products and, 57

Diana, 191

Diastase, 161–62

Digby, Kenelm: on longevity, 57–58; mead recipes by, 448–68

Dionysus, 159; pine ale and, 257

Distillation: ancient, 141; fermentation and, 142

Dock (*Rumex acetus*), medicinal uses for, 353–54

Dock Ale (1694), recipe for, 352–53

Dodoens-Lyte, on calendula, 328

Dorland's Illustrated Medical Dictionary, on scurvy grass, 344

Dossey, Larry, 74

Druids: fermentation and, 28, 167; mandrake and, 210; meadowsweet and, 323; oak and, 263

Duke, James: mustard and, 363; on nettles, 276; on sassafras, 303

Durden Park Beer Club: ebulon by, 334; gruit ale by, 175

Eames, Alan: in Amazon, 2–3; quote of, xiii–xiv; on Spanish Fly, 415; Earth Mother, 124; manioc and, 112, 113–14; pulque and, 90

Eau de vie, 141

Ebulis, 335

Ebulon, 332

Echinacea, 286; licorice and, 312

Elder (*Sambucus* spp.), medicinal uses for, 334–39

Elder Ale, 330–31

Elderberries, 332

Elderberry ale, recipe for, 332–33

Elder Edda, 20, 25; Well of Remembrance and, 15–16

Elderflower champagne, 331–32

Elderflowers, 330–31, 338

Elder Mother, 336

Elecampane (*Inula helenium*): illustration of, 385; medicinal uses for, 386

Elecampane Ale, recipe for, 385

Elkins, Rita, 44

Ellis, William: longevity of, 57

Elphin, 157

Emerson, Edward: on hyssop, 393; on rosemary, 407

Emerson, Ralph Waldo: quote of, 23–24; on yeast, 61

Endomycopsis, 70

English Herbal, An, 390; on lemon balm, 398

English Molasses Ale (1692), recipe for, 420

Enkidu, 138; fermentation and, 139

Ephedra (*Ephedra vulgaris*), eyebright and, 388

Equipment, list of, 432

Eringo roots (*Eryngium maritimum*), described, 472

Erthopfe, 313

Escherichia coli, 349; cardamom and, 376; mugwort and, 380; sage and, 202; yarrow and, 187

Eskimos, beliefs of, 7–8

Essence of Wine, 439

Essenes, longevity of, 57

Essential spirits, 439

Estrogen, hops and, 370

Ethiopian Tej, recipe for, 442–43

Euryphon, on St.-John's-wort, 315

Evelyn, John, 323; on elderflowers, 330; on hop beer, 365; on sycamore, 422

Evergreen trees, 152; beer and, 261–62

Excellent Metheglin, An: recipe for, 460–61

Eyebright (*Euphrasia officinalis*), 265; illustration for, 387; medicinal uses for, 388

Eyebright ale, 386–87; recipe for, 387

Family Receipt Book, Containing Eight Hundred Valuable Receipts in Various Branches of Domestic Economy, Selected From the Works of the Most Approved Writers, Ancient and Modern, The, 288

Fante, palm sap and, 130

Farb, Peter, 10, 11, 13; on Eskimo beliefs, 7–8; on magic/power, 9

FDA. *See* Food and Drug Administration

Fearful anxiety, 10–18

Felter, Harvey, 54, 346, 480; on alder, 244; on cowslip, 357; on ground pine, 363; on horehound, 327; on Irish moss, 414, 415–16; on *Ledum latifolium*, 181; on lesser burnet, 385; on marsh rosemary, 182; on spruce, 256; spruce beer by, 254–55; on wermuth beer, 189; on wormwood, 195

Felter and Lloyd's Spruce Beer (1895), recipe for, 254–55

Fennel seed and root (*Foeniculum vulgare*),

195; described, 472

Fermentation, 47, 81, 173; discovery of, 147, 148–52; distillation and, 142; evil influences on, 73; gift of, 425; humanness and, xvi–xvii; indigenous cultures and, 11, 425; origin legends of, 138, 139–40, 141; plants used in, 167; psychotropics and, 168; sacredness of, 72, 80–81, 160, 163, 167; traditional, 80; unsterile/unscientific, 429; wild, 66; yeast and, 62, 69

Fermented beverages: human consciousness/behavior and, xvi; nonindustrial cultures and, 10–11; relationship with, xv–xvi

Fermented Food Beverages in Nutrition (Gastanieu), 108

Fermenting jars, boiling in, 5

Fern, Catherine: nettle beer by, 267–68

Finnish sahti, 233

Fir, medicinal uses for, 261

Fir ale, recipe for, 260

Firemoss cassiope (Cassiope tetragona), 34

Flavonids, 46

Flavor, imparting, 436–38

Flora Medica, on Smilax, 284

Fogg, 31, 32, 33, 35, 152

Food and Drug Administration: mugwort and, 380; prohibition and, 168; on sassafras, 303; thujone and, 187–88

Foster, Stephen: on sassafras, 303

Frederick of Cologne, hopped beers and, 171

Freeman, Margaret: on clary, 199; on costmary, 410; on hyssop, 393; on rue, 395

Fructose, 37

Frutillada, 99

Fukuoka, Masanobu: quote of, 145

Fulder, Stephen: on ginger, 294, 295

Gaia, 74, 107

Gale Beer, 177

Galileo, 5

Garden, Peter: longevity of, 57

Garden chamomile (Anthemus nobile), 390

Garwe, garwela, 186

Gastanieu, Clifford: on corn beer, 108

Gayre, Robert, 19, 479; on honey, 35; on mead, 20, 35–36

Gentian (Gentiana lutea): illustration of, 382; medicinal uses for, 382–83

Gentian Ale (1829), recipe for, 381–82

Gerarde, John, 344; on borage, 324, 325; on cow parsnip, 376; on darnel, 215–16; on eyebright, 387; on ground ivy, 345; on hop beer, 365; on lemon balm, 397; on lesser burnet, 383; on meadowsweet, 322; on sage, 197, 202

German Commission E botanical monographs, 276

Germander, 170

Germination, 146

Geum, 401

"Gilgamesh and the Huluppu-Tree," 138–39

Gilmore, Melvin: on cedar, 240

Ginger (Zingiber officinale), 294–98, 416; illustration of, 294; medicinal uses for, 296–98

Ginger beer, 287–93

Ginger Beer (1819), recipe for, 288–89

Ginger Beer (1832), recipe for, 289

Ginger Beer (1846), recipe for, 289–90

Ginger Beer (1857), recipe for, 290

Ginger Beer (1898), recipe for, 291

Ginger Book, The (Fulder), 295

Ginseng, 213, 215

Gjedebrygger, 183

Glory bee products, 481

Glucose, 37, 62, 71

Godt ol (good ale), 231

Gonds: palm beer and, 129; rice beer and, 124

Gong, 64, 65

Goosegrass (*Galium aparine*), 268, 269

Gordon, Lesley: on elder, 330, 331; on St.-John's-wort, 315

Gotlandsdricka (modern, 1), recipe for, 236–37

Gotlandsdricka (modern, 2), recipe for, 237

Grabone, 189

Grain: domestication of, 146, 147; fermentation of, 147, 148–52; sacredness of, 158

Grain beer, Finnish, 152

Grains of paradise (*Amomum melegueta, Aframomum melegueta*), 413

Grains of paradise ale, 411–13

Great Mother Goddess, 20

Green, James, 480

Green gentian (*Swertia radiata*), 382

Green Pharmacy, The (Duke), 276

Grieve, Maude, 287, 322, 480; on avens, 400; on birch beer, 245; on bracken fern, 391; on broom, 203, 205; on burnet, 384; on cardamom, 375–76; on chamomile, 389, 390; on costmary, 411; dandelion beer by, 278–79; on dandelions, 278; on darnel, 216, 217; ebulon by, 333; on elderflowers, 331; on eyebright, 388; on gentian, 381; on

ground ivy, 345; on herbal healing, 439–40; on hops, 169–70; on juniper beer, 225; on licorice, 307–8; on meadowsweet, 321; meadowsweet ale by, 321; on mint, 405; on mugwort, 378–79; on *Myrica*, 177; nettle beer by, 268–69; on sage, 201; on wild carrot, 349–50; on wild rosemary, 180, 181–82; on yarrow, 183

Gromwell herb and seeds (*Lithospermum officinale*), described, 473

Ground ivy (*Glechoma hederacea, Nepta glechoma, Nepta hederacea*), medicinal uses for, 346–47

Ground ivy ale, 344–46; recipe for, 345–46

Ground pine (*Ajuga chamaepitys*), medicinal uses for, 364–65

Ground pine ale, 363–64

Ground Pine Ale (1694), recipe for, 364

Groundsel herb (*Senecio vulgaris*), described, 473

Gruit, 167, 172, 173, 174

Gruit ale, 169–75; assault on, 172, 173; properties of, 169; recipe for, 175

Guille, 345

Gundlad, 21, 22

Gunnerus, *Myrica* and, 177

Gwion Bach, 23, 157

Gyle, 345

Hainuwele, 154, 155

Handful, defined, 448

Hansenula, 70; chang and, 119

Hardbaus, 183

Harriot, Thomas: on sassafras, 302

Harrison, John: ebulon by, 334; gruit ale by, 175; mum recipe by, (*continued*) 418–19

Harrison, Kathleen: on plant song, 87

Hart's tongue (*Scolopendrium officinarium/Asplenium Scolopendrium*), described, 473

Hart, Jeffrey, 240

Hashani Mashad, 86

Hasheesh Eater, The (Ludlow), quote from, 166

Hatfield, Gabrielle, 268; on horehound, 325; on mustard, 362

Havel, Vaclav, 106; on ancient perspectives/scientific approach, 14–15

Healing Wise (Weed), 271

Healing Words (Dossey), 74

Health: hive products and, 56–59; temperance movements and, 71

Heath, 25

Heather (*Erica* spp.), 31; described, 28–35; mead and, 25, 33. *See also* Bell heather; Broom heather; Cornish heather; Cross-leaved heather; Ling heather; Scotch heather

Heather ale, 25–28, 34; recipe for, 27–28

Heather honey, 25, 32–33, 34, 58

Heather mead, 25–28; recipe for, 26–27

Helen of Troy, elecampane and, 386

Helicobacter bacterium, 39, 317

Henbane (*Hyoscyamus niger*), medicinal uses for, 208–10

Henbane ale, 206–7; recipe for, 207

Henry VIII, 345

Herbal Medicine Maker's Handbook, The (Green), 480

Herba militaris (soldier's grass), 185

Herbarium, 191

Herbs, 265, 266; medicinal, 4; used in Middle Ages, 469–77

Heron, Selena: borage and, 325

Herpes simplex, hyssop and, 395

HGH. *See* Human Growth Hormone Factor

Hildegard of Bingen, 172

Hippocrates, propolis and, 48

History of a Voyage to the Land of Brazil, Otherwise Called America (Lery), 110

HIV: hyssop and, 395; St.-John's-wort and, 316

Hive, illustration of, 56

Hnitbjorg, 21, 22

Hoffman, W. J.: on maple, 252

Hoffmann, David, 480; borage and, 325; on liver, 143

Home Brew (Remi), 292

Honey, 24–25, 35, 36–42, 148; ancient, 37; compound contents of, 38–39, 40; fermentation of, 20, 147; fireweed, 41; heather, 25, 32–33, 34, 58; longevity and, 57–58; medicinal uses for, 37, 39–41; nutritional value of, 41; orange, 41; poisonous, 38; propolis and, 52; royal jelly and, 54; wildflower, 40

Honey beers, 152

Honeymoon, 58

Honey water, 90

Hop beer, 365–68

Hops (*Humulus lupulus*), 227, 416, 431; adding, 229; ascendancy for, 172, 173; boiled, 231, 232; complaints about, 170–71, 174; illustration of, 370; introduction of, 170, 171; medicinal uses for, 70, 368–70

Horace, 23

Horehound (*Marrubium vulgare*), medicinal uses for, 327–28

Horehound ale, 325–27

Horehound Ale (1), recipe for, 326
Horehound Ale (2), recipe for, 326–27
Horizon Herbs, 480
Horizon Seeds, 215
Horseradish (*Cochlearia armoracia*), 344
Horton, Donald, 11, 13; anxiety theory
    and, 10
Hortus Sanitatis, or Gart Der Gesundheit, 393,
    395, 410
Household Companion (Salmon), 323
House of transformation of Mani, 116
Howell, John: on metheglin, 24
Human Growth Hormone Factor
    (HGH), 47; honey and, 43
Humbaba, 138
Humle, 183
Humlebramt, 231
Hupa, ginger and, 295
Hydromels, 441
Hypericum, 315, 317
Hyssop (*Hyssopus officinalis*), 195; illustra-
    tion of, 394; medicinal uses for,
    393–95
Hyssop ale, recipe for, 393

"I Draw the Rain," 85
Ifuagao, fermentation and, 76
I'itoi, Elder Brother, 84, 85, 89
Inau-korashkoro, 121
Indigenous cultures, 7–9; fearful anxiety
    and, 11; fermentation and, 11, 69,
    72–73, 74, 80, 81, 140–41; natural
    world and, 14; oral tradition and,
    140; plants and, 6
Indigenous Mind, 15, 16, 18; under-
    standing, 5
Indra, 23
Irish moss (*Chrondrus crispus*), medicinal
    uses for, 415–17

Irish moss ale, recipe for, 414–15
Irish Moss Ale (1890), recipe for, 415
Itpomu, Mother of Creation, 153

Jacobs, Alex: on corn, 102
James, William: quote of, xiv
Jefferson, Thomas, 141
Jimson weed (*Datura stramonium*), 208,
    209, 210
Jivaro, 113; manioc and, 110, 111, 114;
    sangucha shiki and, 115
John Harrison's Recipe for Ebulon
    (1976), 334
Johnson, Noel: honey/hive products
    and, 58
Johnston, J., on saffron, 217
Jora, 97, 98
Jordhumle, 183, 313
Josselyn, John, 307; licorice beer by,
    308–9
Joshi, D. P.: *Artemisia* and, 193; on
    banana, 127
Jujubes (*Ziziphus vulgaris*), described, 473
Jumping genes, 107
Juniper (*Juniperus* spp.), 172, 183, 195,
    239; illustration of, 239; medicinal
    uses for, 237–44
Juniper ale, 225–44, 233; brewing,
    227–28
Juniper beer, 114, 225–44
Juniper berries, 242, 243
Juniper branches, 226, 227, 233, 236;
    fermentation and, 65; use of, 152
Juniper extract, 225, 226, 227, 242;
    boiled, 228, 229, 230, 231, 232

Kaffir beers, 72, 120–22
Kai Chukalig Mashad, 86
Kalevala, 148–52, 253

Kalm, Peter: on dock, 353; on spruce beer, 261

Kamui Fuchi, 75, 121

Kanati, 103, 104

Katz, Solomon, 141; on grain malting, 147

Kautantouwits, 100

Kelbsiella pneumoniae, sage and, 202

Keller, Evelyn: on McClintock, 107

King's American Dispensatory (Lloyd and Felter), 54, 55, 290, 344, 480

Kirkaia, 212

Kitchen Guide, The (Fern), 267

Klebsiella, mugwort and, 380

Kneipp, Father: juniper berries and, 243

Koan, 158

Koit, 26

Koran, quote from, 35

Kronos, on mead, 24

Kung! Bushmen, diet of, 13

Kuurna, 226, 235

Kvaser, 21, 22, 64, 249; mead of, 24

Kvass, 249, 404

Kveik, 64, 66, 76

Kykeon, 159

Labrador tea (*Ledum glandulosum, Ledum latifolium*), 31, 179, 180, 181, 182, 495

LaChappelle, Delores: on *Artemisia*, 192

Lacnunga, 379–80

Lactobacillus, 70

Lactucarium, 221, 222

Lactuca serriola, 222

Lactuca virosa, 222

Ladies' Union Mission School Association, tiswin and, 89

Lambic, 3; fermentation of, 70

Lavender (*Lavandula* spp.), 322

Lavender herb (*Lavandula officinalis*), described, 473

Lawrence, D. H., 16

Leaves of Grass (Whitman), quote from, 16–17

LeClercq, Christien: on maple beer, 250

Ledol (*Ledum camphor*), 181, 182

Ledum groenlandicum, 179

Ledum palustre, 179, 181

Lee, Mrs. R.: on cardamom, 375

Lee, Richard: Kung! Bushmen and, 13

Lemon balm (*Melissa officinalis*), 195; medicinal uses for, 398

Lemon balm ale, recipe for, 398

Lemon Balm Ale (1827), recipe for, 397–98

Lepcha, 147, 153; chi and, 121

Lery, Jean de, 110, 120

Lesser burnet ale, 383–84; recipe for, 384

Letts, juniper and, 238

Leuconostoc, 70

Lewis, William: on bogbean, 372

Licorice (*Glycyrrhiza glabra*): Echinacea and, 312; illustration of, 311; medicinal uses for, 310–12

Licorice ale, 307–10

Licorice Ale (1), recipe for, 309–10

Licorice Ale (2), recipe for, 310

Lighibodt, F.: quote of, 429

Light Lager, A: recipe for, 367–68

Ling heather (*Erica vulgaris, Calluna vulgaris*), 25, 34; brewing with, 35

Linnaeus, 183; *Myrica* and, 177; on yarrow, 187

Little Ones, 240

Liver, alcohol and, 143

Liverwort herb (*Hepatica americana, Peltigera Canina*), described, 474

Lloyd, John Uri, 54, 346, 480; on alder,

244; on bee venom, 56; on cowslip, 357; on ground pine, 363; on horehound, 327; on Irish moss, 414, 415–16; on *Ledum latifolium*, 181; on lesser burnet, 385; on marsh rosemary, 182; on spruce, 256; spruce beer by, 254–55; on wermuth beer, 189; on wormwood, 195

London and County Brewer, cowslip ale and, 356

Lopez, Barry, 16

Lord of the Rings (Tolkien), 29

Ludlow, Fitzhugh: quote of, 166

Lumholtz, Carl, 87; on pine, 258

Lungwort lichen (*Lobaria pulmonaria*), described, 474

Luther, Martin, 172

McCaleb, Rob: on juniper, 239

McClintock, Barbara: on corn, 107, 108

Mabey, Richard: on coriander, 299; nettle beer by, 270–71

Mace (*Myristica fragrans*), described, 474

Mackenzie's 5000 Receipts, 412

Madhava, 23

Magic, 9; religion and, 8

Maidenhair fern herb (*Adiantum* spp.), described, 474

Maize, 156, 165

Majupuria, Trilock Chandra: *Artemisia* and, 193; on banana, 127

Malted grains, 160, 226; using, 434–35

Malt extract, 161–62, 163

Malting, 146, 161, 162, 226; grain, 147, 434–35

Mandrake (*Atropa mandragora, Mandragora officinarum, Podophyllum peltatum*), 208, 210, 211–15; illustration of, 211

Mandrake beer, 210–11; recipe for, 211

Manglesdorf, Paul: quote of, 145

Mani, 113; fermentation and, 116

Manioc (*Manihot esculenta*), 110, 112–18, 126; chewing, 111; cultivation of, 115, 117; fermentation of, 117; gift of, 112–14; medicinal properties of, 117

Mani oca, 113

Manioc ale, recipe for, 111–12

Manioc beer, 109–12; medicinal properties of, 116

Man's Rise to Civilization (As Shown by the Indians of North America from Primeval Times to the Coming of the Industrial State) (Farb), quote from, 7–8

Maple (*Acer saccharum*), medicinal uses for, 252

Maple beer, 250–51

Maple Beer (1846), recipe for, 251

Maple Beer (Modern), recipe for, 251

Maple Beer (New England), recipe for, 251

Marchant, W. T.: on darnel, 215; on heather beer, 28; on intoxication, 166; on lettuce, 219; on saffron, 218

Marigold (*Calendula officinalis*), medicinal uses for, 329–30

Marigold ale, 328–30

Marjoram (*Origanum vulgare*), 170, 195; described, 474

Maro, 154, 155

Marshmallow root (*Althea officinalis*), described, 475

Marsh rosemary (*Ledum palustre*), 31, 175, 182

Marsh tea, 180–81

Martha Washington's Recipe (ca. 1600), 445–46

Masato beer, 109–12

Mash, 226, 227; boiled, 228, 229, 230–31

Maude Grieve's Dandelion Beer (1931), recipe for, 278–79

Maude Grieve's Nettle Beer (1931), recipe for, 268–69

Maude Grieve's Version of Ebulon (1931), recipe for, 333

Mayahuel, Earth Mother: pulque and, 90

Mayel, 153

Mayer, Norbert: poem by, 16

Maytag, Fritz: on grain malting, 147

Mead, 20, 24–25, 148, 366; fermentation of, 41, 70; heather and, 25, 33; herbal, traditional recipes for, 444–47; longevity and, 57–58; medicinal uses for, 36; of Middle Ages, 441–68; recipes for, 448–68; royal jelly and, 54

Mead of Inspiration, 23, 25, 37, 58, 64, 155, 165, 167, 249

Meadowsweet (*Spiraea ulmaria*), medicinal uses for, 322–23

Meadowsweet ale, 320–22; recipe for, 321, 322

Medieval Household Beer (1512), recipe for, 368

Meiskeren, 231

Melezitose, 261

Melissaios, 24

Mellaceus, 419

Melomel, recipe for, 444

Mencken, H. L.: quote of, xiv

Menominees, pine and, 260

Merlin, 157

Mescalero Apaches, *tulpai* and, 96

Metheglin, 24, 366

Metheglin for the Colick and Stone of [Lady Stuart], A: recipe for, 463–65

Methyl salicylate, 249, 250, 306, 307

Metzner, Ralph, 15

Meyer, Joseph: on grains of paradise, 413

Middle Eastern evergreen (*Commiphora opobalsamum*), 47

Millet (*Panicum miliaceum, Eleusine coracana*), 120

Millet beers, 120–22

Millspaugh, Charles: on buckbean, 371; on honey, 37–38; on marsh tea, 180–81; spruce beer by, 253–54; on wormwood, 189

Mimir, 15

Mint (*Mentha piperita*), 195, 265; illustration of, 406; medicinal uses for, 405–6

Mint ale, 403–5

Mint kvass, recipe for, 405

Miss Beecher's Domestic Receipt-Book: Designed as a Supplement to her Traetise on Domestic Economy, 290

Mithra, 20

Mockingbird Speech, quote from, 77

Modern Elderflower Beer, A (1963), recipe for, 331

Modern Herbal, A (Grieve), 177, 225, 345, 480

Moerman, Daniel: juniper and, 239

Molasses ale, 419–21

Molasses Ale (modern), recipe for, 421

Montana—Native Plants and Early People (Hart), 240

Moore, Michael, 6, 222, 480; on cow parsnip, 378; on juniper, 238; on Ledol, 181; on St.-John's-wort, 316; on wild lettuce, 220; yarrow and, 186

Morda, 157

Morning glory seeds (*Ipomoea* sp., *Turbina corymbosa*), 165
Mosher, Randy: on grains of paradise, 412, 414
Mother Earth, 89; palm and, 129
Mount, John: longevity of, 57
Mountain ash, 422
Mountain heather (*Cassiope mertensiana*), 34
Mowrey, Daniel: on dandelion, 281
Mucor, chang and, 119
Mugwort (*Artemisia vulgaris*), 76; medicinal uses for, 379–81
Mugwort ale, 378–79; recipe for, 379
Muko, 95
Multiple sclerosis (MS): nettles and, 276; rosemary and, 409
Mum, 417–19
Mum (1991), recipe for, 419
Mustard (*Brassica nigra, Brassica alba*), medicinal uses for, 362–63
Mustard ale, 362
My Lady Morices Meath, recipe for, 451–52
Myrddhin, 157
Myrica (*Myrica gale*), 174–75, 207; medicinal uses for, 176–79
Myrica ale, recipe for, 175–76
Myrrh (*Commiphora absynnica*), 47

Navajo Indians, yarrow and, 184
Navapatrika, 124
Nawai, 82
Neanderthal Man, yarrow and, 185
Nectar, 37, 38, 42
Nettle beer, 267–68, 272
Nettles, 272–76; dietary function of, 267; illustration of, 273; medicinal uses for, 274–75, 276; products from, 273–74

New Age Herbalist, The (Mabey), 270
New Complete Joy of Home Brewing, The (Papazian), 430, 479
New England Rarities Discovered (Grieve), 308
New Holistic Herbal, The (Hoffmann), 480
New Orleans Mead, 285
Nietzsche, Frederick, 135, 141
Nihamanchi, 110, 114
Nordland, Odd, 225, 243, 313, 479; on caraway, 347; on henbane, 206; on hops, 173; on *Myrica*, 176; on pine ale, 257; on spruce beer, 252–53; on Tone Lund, 68–69; on wormwood, 189; on yarrow, 183
Norwegian Brewery Association, 225
Norwegian Research Council for Science and the Humanities, 225
Nsa, 131, 132
Nungui, Earth Mother: manioc and, 113–14
Nunusaku, 154
Nutmeg, 195

Oak (*Quercus* spp.), medicinal uses for, 263–64
Oak bark ale, recipe for, 262
Odin, 15–16, 21–22, 37, 155; mead and, 23, 24
Odomankoma, 132
Odyssey, 212
Okanagans, serviceberry and, 402–3
Oku'te, 11–12
Old English Beers and How to Make Them (Harrison), 334, 418
Olkong, 313
Ollas, 87
Onoruame, Great Father, 90; maize/corn beer and, 97

Onyame, 131, 132

Orris roots (*Iris germanica, Iris florentina, Iris pallida*), described, 475

Osage, cedar and, 239–40

Osiris, 159

Otomi: fermentation and, 74–75; pulque and, 72

Ott, Jonathan: *Artemisia* and, 194–95

Owen, Sir: longevity of, 57

Palm (*Cocus nucifera, Phoenix sylvestris*), medicinal uses for, 133–34

Palm beer, 128–29; recipe for, 132; sacredness of, 131–32

Palm sap: fermenting, 129–30; medicinal uses for, 134; tapping, 133

Palm wine, 128–29

Pan: elder plant and, 337; pipe of, 335–36

Pandora, tale of, xiii

Pantothenic acid, 52

Papago: ceremonial brewing and, 69; dancing/singing by, 87; fermentation and, 74, 76, 77, 87; saguaro and, 82–83, 85, 86; songs by, 81–82, 87–88; tiswin and, 67

Papazian, Charlie, 430, 479

Parkinson, on sage ale, 197

Parkinson's disease, rosemary and, 409

Parr, Thomas: longevity of, 57

Parsley herb and root and seed (*Petroselinum crispum*), 195; described, 475

Pasteur Institute, Saenz and, 52

Paticili, 97

Patoto'e, 124

Pechet, John, 473, 474; on avens, 399; on betony, 361; on birch, 249; on burdock, 276; on caraway, 348; on

elecampane, 386; on firs, 260; on hop beer, 365; on horehound, 327; on oak, 263; on pine, 257, 258; quote of, 335, 350, 352; on *Rumex* spp., 353; on scurvy grass, 339, 344; on wild carrot, 349; on wormwood, 191

Pedicularis family, 361

Pelletier, Kenneth, 492–93

Pellitory of the wall herb (*Parietaria diffusa*), described, 475

Pendell, Dale, 194, 479; on yeast, 61, 62–63

Penn, William: on sassafras, 300

Pennyroyal (*Mentha pulegium, Hedeoma pulegioides*), 265; illustration of, 359; medicinal uses for, 359–60

Pennyroyal ale, recipe for, 358–59

Penobscot, sweet flag and, 318–19

Peppermint, illustration of, 406

Peptide 401, 56

Peterson's Field Guide to Eastern/Central Medicinal Plants, 303

Pharmacopoeia of India, on rice water, 126

Pharmako/poeia (Pendell), 194, 479

Physica Sacra (Hildegard of Bingen), 172

Piast, King of Poland: longevity of, 57

Picts: heather ale and, 29–30, 31, 32, 33; mead and, 25; sacred beverages of, 28–29

Pilsen, 206, 207

Pilsenkrut, 206

Pilsner beer, 207

Pine (*Pinus* spp.), medicinal uses for, 243, 258–60

Pine Ale (1770), recipe for, 257–58

Pinene, 241, 242

Pink lady's slipper (*Cypripedium acaule*), 357

Pink mountain heather (*Phyllodoce empet-riformis*), 34

Plants: humanness and, xvi–xvii; medicinal use of, 4, 5; spirits of, 4

Plants of Love (Ratsch), yarrow and, 187

Plasmodia spp., 196

Plato, on mead, 24

Pliny the Elder, 445; *Artemisia* and, 193; propolis and, 48

Pliny's Mead (A.D. 77), recipe for, 445

Plutarch, pine ale and, 257

Pohjanmaan Sahti, recipe for, 234–35

Pollen: color of, 42; compounds/organics in, 43; medicinal uses for, 44, 46, 47; as nutritive food, 45; rutin/protein in, 44

Pombe, 126

Pomona (Evelyn), 365

Poria cocos, 283

Pors, 177

Post, 173

Propolis, 35, 47–50; color of, 48; compounds in, 48; honey and, 52; medicinal uses for, 49–50; problems with, 50; royal jelly and, 52

Pseudomonas, 70; mugwort and, 380

Psychotropics, 167, 168, 169

Ptyalin, 94

Pulque, 4, 72, 90–91, 93; medicinal uses for, 92; recipe for, 91

Purging Ale, A (Butler), 343

Purl, 417, 421–22

Pyment, recipe for, 443–44

Pythagoras, bee products and, 56

Quecha Indians, Chicha and, 94–95

Queen Anne's lace, 350, 351

Queen bees, egg laying by, 51

Radiotherapy, pollen and, 46

Rafinesque, C. S., 285; on birch beer, 245; on ginger, 294; on sassafras, 299; on wild rosemary, 181; on wintergreen, 306; on yarrow, 187

Rainforest, destruction of, 3, 4

Rain Song, 84

Rasmussen, Knud: Eskimo beliefs and, 8

Ratsch, Christian, 207; on henbane, 208; on inebriation, 165; on mandrake beer, 210; on saffron, 219; on wild rosemary, 181; on yarrow, 184, 187

Raudot, Antoine: nettles and, 273

Raynaud's disease, mustard and, 363

Receipt for Making of Meath, A, 449–50

Receipt for Meathe, A, 452–53

Receipt for Metheglin of My Lady Windebanke, A, 462–63

Recipe, sample, 433–34

Religion, magic and, 8

Religious and Useful Plants of Nepal and India (Majupuria and Joshi), 193

Remi, Bertrand: ginger beer by, 292; recipe by, 122, 125

Renfrow, Cindy, 288, 448

Rheumatoid Arthritis Foundation, nettles and, 276

Rhizopus, chang and, 119

Rhododendron ponticum, honey from, 38

Rice (*Oryza sativa*): medicinal uses for, 125–26; sacredness of, 124

Rice beer, 76, 123–25; recipe for, 125

Rice water, 126

Rice wine, 124, 125

Rich, Dark Mint Ale, A: recipe for, 404

Richard Mabey's Nettle Beer (1988), 270–71

Ridgely, Bill, 122; on chang, 118, 119; chicha and, 97, 98
Rig-Vedas, x, 23, 25
Robbins, M.: on banana beer, 126
Rocky Mountain juniper, 239
Rosemary (*Rosemarinus officinalis*), medicinal uses for, 409–10
Rosemary ale, 407–9; recipe for, 407
Rosemary Ale (1695), recipe for, 408–9
Royal jelly, 35, 36, 50–54; compounds of, 51; medicinal uses for, 52–54; propolis and, 52
Royal jelly wine, 54
Royal Society of Naturalists, pollen and, 45
Rue (*Ruta graveolens*): illustration of, 396; medicinal uses for, 396–97
Rue beer, recipe for, 395–96
Runahal, 23

Saccharomyces, 62, 70, 71, 118, 297
Sacred, 140; primitive man and, 7
Sacred Land, Sacred Sex, Rapture of the Deep (LaChappelle), 192
Sacred Plant Medicine (Buhner), 87, 480
Sacred plants/trees, listed, viii
SAD. *See* Seasonal affective disorder
Saenz, Albert: on royal jelly, 52
Saffron (*Crocus sativa*): medicinal uses for, 218–19; narcotic properties of, 219
Saffron ale, 217–18; recipe for, 218
Sage (*Salvia* spp.), 265; illustration of, 202; medicinal uses for, 201–2
Sage ale, 197–98
Sage Ale (18th cent.), recipe for, 199
Sage Ale (19th cent.), recipe for, 198
Sage Ale (modern), recipe for, 197–98
Saguaro (*Carnegia gigantea*), 81; alcohol

content of, 89; medicinal uses for, 86; Papago and, 82–83, 84–89
Saguaro beer ceremony, outlawing, 89
Saguaro wine ceremony, 89
Sahti, 233, 234–35
Sahti (1901), recipe for, 233–34
St.-John's-wort (*Hypericum perforatum*), 183; medicinal uses for, 314–17
St.-John's-wort ale, recipe for, 314
St.-John's-wort beer, 313–14
Sakambhari, 124
Salicylate, 323
Saliva, starch conversion with, 160
Salphi, 129
Salvia salvatrix, 201
Sambucus canadensis, 337
Sambucus Ebulis, 335
Sambucus nigra, 335
Sambucus racemosa, 337
Sanborn Brown's Ginger Beer (1978), recipe for, 293
Sangiang Serri, rice and, 124
Sangucha shiki, 110, 114, 115–16
Sarsaparilla (*Aralia nudacaulis*), 283, 284; curative effect of, 285; illustration of, 287
Sassafras (*Sassafras officinale, Sassafras albidum*): illustration of, 302; medicinal uses for, 302–4
Sassafras beer, 299–302
Sassafras Beer (1846), recipe for, 300–301
Sassafras Beer (1925), recipe for, 301–2
Scabiosa arvensis, 475–76
Scabious root (*Scabious succisa*), described, 475–76
Schenk, Gustav: on henbane, 209–10
Schizosaccharomyces, 70
Schmidt, H. W.: on royal jelly, 53

Scoparin, 205

Scotch broom, 205

Scotch heather (*Erica cinera*), 34

Scurvy grass (*Cochlearia officinalis*), medicinal uses for, 343–44

Scurvy grass ale, 339–43

Scurvy Grass Ale (1651), recipe for, 340–41

Scurvy Grass Ale (1692), recipe for, 341

Scurvy Grass Ale (1695), recipe for, 342

Seasonal affective disorder (SAD), St.-John's-wort and, 317

Secret Life of Plants, The, 74

Seed, John: on indigenous worldview, 17–18

Selu, 103–4; wisdom of, 106

Selu: Seeking the Corn Mother's Wisdom (Awiakta), 103

Serviceberry (*Amelanchier alnifolia*), medicinal uses for, 402–3

Serviceberry ale, 401–2; recipe for, 402

Sharp-pointed dock (*Rumex acetus*), 353

Shigella bacteria, yarrow and, 187

Shuya tree, 115

Simple Fermentation of Hops, A (1963), recipe for, 366–67

Sip Through Time, A (Renfrow), 288, 448

Sirakitehak, nettles and, 273

Sir Thomas Gower's Metheglin for Health, recipe for, 465–66

Sisselroot, 26

Sitting Man, Charles, 241

Skogshumle, 183

Smilax, 282, 283, 284–85, 286, 287

Solenander, 339

"Song of Eight Ales" (Taylor), 423

Songs, sacred, 88

Spanish fly (*Cantharis vesicatoria, Lytta vesicatoria*), 415, 416, 417

Sparteine, 205

Spassol, 231

Speck, Frank: quote of, 286

Speedwell (*Veronica officinalis*), described, 476

Spirit plates, 68

Sprakol, 233

Spruce (*Abies nigra*), medicinal uses for, 243, 256–57

Spruce beer, 226, 245, 252–56, 261

Spruce Beer (1796), recipe for, 255

Spruce Beer (Modern), recipe for, 255–56

Squash (*Curcurbita ficifolia*), 95

Stalks, sugar from, 100

Staphylococcus aureus, 39, 50; mugwort and, 380; sage and, 202; yarrow and, 187

Starry cassiope (*Cassiope sterreriana*), 34

Stevens, Chase: on *Artemisias*, 193; on calendule, 329

Stevenson, Robert Louis: on Picts/heather ale, 29–30

Storage, thoughts on, 439–40

Stories of Eva Luna, The (Allende), quote from, 1

Strandhumle, 313

Strawberry leaves (*Fragaria* spp.), described, 476

Strawberry tree (*Arbutus Unedo*), 31

Streptococcus faecalis, yarrow and, 187

Streptococcus mutans, mugwort and, 380

Strong ale, brewing, 230, 232

Sturtevant, Lewis: on sweet flag, 318

Sucrose, 37, 62

Sugar, 146; brown, 431; obtaining, 160; white/table, 431

Suriname Indians, corn beer of, 101–2

Surya, 193

Susun Weed's Dandelion Beer (1989), recipe for, 280
Susun Weed's Nettle Beer (1989), recipe for, 271–72
Suttung, 21, 22
Sweetbrier (wild rose) leaves and rose hips (*Rosa* spp.), described, 476
Sweet flag (*Acorus calamus*), 195; medicinal uses for, 318–20
Sweet flag ale, 317–18; recipe for, 318
Sweet gale (*Myrica gale*), 169
Sweet sap, 90, 93
Sweet wort, 227, 228
Sycamore, 422
Sysma-Style Sahti, recipe for, 235

Talbot, Rob: on ginger, 294; on mandrake, 211
Taliesin, 157
Tallur Muttai, Mother Earth, palm and, 129
Tannins, 436, 441
Tansy (*Tanacetum vulgare*), 196, 265; infusing, 437; medicinal uses for, 374
Tansy ale, recipe for, 373
Tape, 70
Tapioca, 111, 112
Tarahumara: agave and, 91; corn beer and, 99; fermentation and, 74, 75; maize and, 97; pulque and, 4, 90, 92; sugar extraction by, 100; Tesguino and, 96; wormwood and, 75
Taylor, John, 268; poetics of, 422–43; verse by, 423
Temperance movement, 137, 142; health and, 71
Tepary bean, 86

Tepehuane, agave and, 91
Terpenine, 241, 242
Tesguino, 96–98
Teton Dakota, yarrow and, 185
Therapeutics (Wood), on *Smilax*, 284–85
Thomas, Keith, 31; heather beer and, 32
Thonga tribe, palm and, 133
Thoreau, Henry David, 16
Thujone, 187–88, 195, 203, 241, 242
Tiswin, 65, 67, 68, 81–83, 88; making, 86; recipe for, 83
Tiswin ceremony, 86; quote from, 83, 84, 135–36
Tohono O'odham. *See* Papago
Tolkien, J. R. R., 29
To Make a Meath Good for the Liver and Lungs, recipe for, 466–68
To Make Another White Metheglin, recipe for, 461–62
To Make White Metheglin, recipe for, 458–60
Tone Lund, 68–69
Toward a Science of Consciousness (Pelletier), 493
Traditional African "Kaffir" Beer, recipe for, 122–23
Traditional Himalayan Chang, recipe for, 122
Traditional Norwegian St.-John's-Wort Ale, A: recipe for, 313–14
Trebisond, honey of, 37–38
Tree of Life, 129, 240
Trees, Plants, and Flowers (Lee), quote from, 375
Trinity Herbs, 480
Tryon, Thomas, 427, 431; on betony, 360; on flavor, 437–38; on herbs, 265–66; on hops, 368–69; on mint,

404; on pennyroyal ale, 358; on tansey, 373

Tungale rite, 76

Tunol, 231

Tupinamba, 120; manioc beverage of, 110

Turner, Nancy: on serviceberry, 403

Twi, 131

Two Mead Recipes (1695), 446–47

Tynning, 231

Umbelliferae family, 377

Underhill, Ruth: on songs/magic, 88

United States National Dispensatory, on wild rosemary, 181

United States Pharmacopoeia, 283; juniper berries and, 241; on sweet flag, 319

Universal Herbal, on sage, 197

Universe: knowledge of, 6–7; operation of, 5–6

Universe-as-machine perspective, 6, 15, 141

Urbock (Ratsch), 207

Urinary tract infections (UTI), 243; cardamom and, 376; sage and, 202; yarrow and, 187

Usefulness of Natural Philosophy (Boyle), 349

Uses of Plants by the Indians of the Missouri River Region, The (Gilmore), 240

Useuqbaugh, 141

Usnea spp., 238

Ustilago segetum, 109

UTI. *See* Urinary tract infections

Uva-ursi (*Arctostaphylos Uva-ursi*), 306

Vanir, 21

Varieties of Religious Experience, The (James), quote from, xiv

Veltehope, 313

Very Strong Meathe, A: recipe for, 453–54

Victory Celebration feast, 115

Violet leaves (*Viola odorata*), described, 476

Virginia snakeroot (*Aristolochia Serpentaria*), 294

Vishnu, 23, 193

Vogel, Virgil: on spruce, 256

Wachagga tribe, *pombe* and, 126

Warao, palm and, 129

Water, note on, 435

Watercress herb (*Nasturtium officinale*), described, 476

Weed, Susun: dandelion beer by, 280; nettle beer by, 271–72; on nettles, 267, 275

Weiss, Fritz: juniper berries and, 243

Well of Remembrance, 15–16, 18, 425

Wemale, 153, 154

Wergeland, Henrik, 189

Wermuth, 190

Whiskey, 141

Whiteman, Robin: on ginger, 294; on mandrake, 211

White Metheglin of My Lady Hungerford, recipe for, 456–57

Whitlaw's New Medical Discoveries, 412; on grains of paradise, 411

Whitman, Walt: quote of, 16–17

Whortleberries (*Vaccinium ulignosum*), 31

Whuea, 115

Wiccans, henbane and, 210

Wilber, Ken, 13; on ancient culture beliefs, 12

Wild carrot seed (*Daucus carota*): illustration of, 351; medicinal uses for, 350–51

Wild carrot seed ale, 349–50

Wild Carrot Seed Ale (1744), recipe for, 350

Wildflower honey, vitamins in, 40

Wild lettuce (*Lactuca* spp.), medicinal uses for, 220–21

Wild lettuce ale, 219–20; recipe for, 220

Wild rosemary (*Ledum palustre*), 169; medicinal uses for, 180–82

Wild rosemary ale, 179–80; recipe for, 180

Wild sarsaparilla (*Aralia nudacaulis*), 283; described, 286–87

Wild sarsaparilla ale, recipe for, 285–86

Wild yeast, 65, 70, 77, 87, 152, 444; sugars and, 63–64

Williams, Bruce, 31; heather ale by, 27–28

Williams, Roger: on corn, 99–100

Windsor Ale, recipe for, 412–13

Wine, fermentation of, 70

Winsloe, Thomas: longevity of, 57

Wintergreen (*Gaultheria procumbens*), 301; illustration of, 307; medicinal uses for, 306–7

Wintergreen ale, 304–6; recipe for, 305

Women: beer making and, 137, 429; fermentation and, 142

Wood, Matthew: on elder, 335, 338; yarrow and, 185, 187

Woodsage, 170

Wood sorrel herb and root (*Oxalis Acetosella*), described, 476–77

World Health Organization, *Artemisia* and, 196

Wormwood (*Artemisia absinthium*), 170, 172, 188, 265, 379, 432, 438; infusing, 437; medicinal uses for,

191–96; Tarahumara and, 75

Wormwood ale, 188–90; recipe for, 190

Wormwood Ale for Fevers, recipe for, 191

Wort, 430; boiled, 228–32, 236; heretical rules for, 431–32; infection, 432; sweet, 227, 228

Worth, W. P., 298; on bottling, 438–39; on flavor, 436; on heather, 25; on herbs, 469–70; on wormwood, 189, 190

Wright, Herbert, 192

Yarrow (*Achillea millefolium*), 26, 169, 170, 172–73, 174, 183, 196; bittering/preservative action of, 188; illustration of, 186; medicinal uses for, 184–88

Yarrow beer, 183–84; recipe for, 184

Yeast, 227; ancient culture and, 67; bread, 431; brewer's, 71; domesticated, 63, 76; fermentation and, 62, 69; nutritional qualities of, 71; relationship with, 63; reusing, 432; *Saccharomyces*, 62, 70, 71, 118, 297; temperature and, 66; waking up, 435; wild, 63–64, 65, 70, 77, 87, 152, 444; Windsor, 435

Yellow dock (*Rumex crispus*), 353

Yellow rosebay (*Rhododendron chrysanthemum*), 31

Young Housekeeper's Friend, or a Guide to Domestic Economy and Comfort, The, 289

Yucca, 110; toxicity of, 504

Zeus, mead and, 24

Zymurgy, 225, 233, 412